MW00558872

To my fellow student
of Jewish law and
tradition,

Neil Netanel

From Maimonides to Microsoft

From Maimonides to Microsoft

The Jewish Law of Copyright since the Birth of Print

Neil Weinstock Netanel

with contributions by

David Nimmer

OXFORD
UNIVERSITY PRESS

OXFORD
UNIVERSITY PRESS

Oxford University Press is a department of the University of Oxford. It furthers the University's objective of excellence in research, scholarship, and education by publishing worldwide.

Oxford New York
Auckland Cape Town Dar es Salaam Hong Kong Karachi Kuala Lumpur Madrid
Melbourne Mexico City Nairobi New Delhi Shanghai Taipei Toronto

With offices in
Argentina Austria Brazil Chile Czech Republic France Greece Guatemala Hungary
Italy Japan Poland Portugal Singapore South Korea Switzerland Thailand
Turkey Ukraine Vietnam

Published in the United States of America by
Oxford University Press
198 Madison Avenue, New York, NY 10016

Library of Congress Cataloging-in-Publication Data

Netanel, Neil, author.
From Maimonides to Microsoft : the Jewish law of copyright since the birth of print / Neil Weinstock Netanel with contributions by David Nimmer.
pages cm
Includes bibliographical references and index.
ISBN 978-0-19-537199-4 ((hardback) : alk. paper) 1. Copyright (Jewish law)—History. I. Nimmer, David, author. II. Title.
KBM1160.N48 2016
346.04'82—dc23
2015023573

1 3 5 7 9 8 6 4 2

Printed in Canada on acid-free paper

Note to Readers

This publication is designed to provide accurate and authoritative information in regard to the subject matter covered. It is based upon sources believed to be accurate and reliable and is intended to be current as of the time it was written. It is sold with the understanding that the publisher is not engaged in rendering legal, accounting, or other professional services. If legal advice or other expert assistance is required, the services of a competent professional person should be sought. Also, to confirm that the information has not been affected or changed by recent developments, traditional legal research techniques should be used, including checking primary sources where appropriate.

(Based on the Declaration of Principles jointly adopted by a Committee of the American Bar Association and a Committee of Publishers and Associations.)

CONTENTS

PREFACE

My friend and colleague, David Nimmer, and I planned to write a book together about the Jewish law of copyright for almost three decades. Our project was seeded, first, when we studied Talmud together as young lawyers in the early 1980s and, second, when Benyamin Bar-Zohar, the rabbi who officiated at my wedding, informed me about the existence of a Jewish law of copyright and lent me a manuscript by Jewish law scholar Naḥum Rakover about rabbinic reprinting bans. Hence my first debts are to Rabbi Bar-Zohar, without whom I might never have embarked on a study of Jewish copyright law, and to my collaborator David Nimmer. Before David had to drop off the project due to other pressing commitments, we studied sources together; discussed ideas for the book at length; traded drafts, editorial comments—and many jokes; presented our work at academic conferences; and wrote preliminary articles, both jointly and separately. Portions of Chapters 6, 7, and 8, and of the Glossary and Biographies, draw on David's early drafts, and the entire book bears his inspiration, guidance, and unending support. I cannot thank him enough.

As initially envisioned, our book was to be a basic introduction to the Jewish law of copyright for our fellow students and practitioners of secular copyright law, who are largely unaware that there even is such a thing as copyright in Jewish law. But as our study deepened, so did our project. The book now delves far more rigorously into questions of halakhic doctrine; the historical development of Jewish law and external, non-Jewish influences on that development; the historical context in which early modern rabbis enunciated a Jewish law of copyright; and parallels between the Jewish law of copyright and its secular and papal counterparts. I thus hope that our book will be of interest and use to students of Jewish history and the historical development of halakha as well as secular copyright law.

As might be expected of a project that has been decades in the making, I have numerous acknowledgments to those from whom I have learned so much along the way. Foremost among these, I am beholden to Rabbi Yitzhok Adlerstein, with whom David Nimmer and I studied the principal rabbinic rulings that are featured in the book. Rabbi Adlerstein shared his knowledge and insights with us with joy and rigor, ever supportive of our project even though we were relative novices in the study of Jewish law who couldn't distinguish between *grama* and *garmi* if our lives depended on it. I also owe a special debt of gratitude to Gil Graff, who generously read and commented on the entire manuscript, and to Ted Fram, who provided me with extremely helpful early guidance and who generously read and provided editing suggestions on the entire proofs. I extend particular thanks as well to Jane Ginsburg, who generously shared with me materials of relevance to my project that she uncovered at the Vatican in the course of her momentous study of sixteenth-century papal printing privileges.

I have benefited immensely from superb assistance on a broad spectrum of tasks in connection with this book, including research, translation, tracking down original sources, and editing. For this assistance, I thank, more or less in order of the extent of their involvement with my project, Naḥman Avraham, Aryeh Peter, Ariel Strauss, David Schultz, Nadav Molchadsky, Yuval Agmon, Todd Davidovits, David Kramer, Avi Pariser, Hanoch Hagar, Ran Madjar, Kelly Trimble, Elie Istrin, Lisa Kohn, Wyatt Sloan-Tribe, Yaron Ben Zvi, Nir Katz, Mik Larsen, Lynn McClelland, John Wilson, Scott Dewey, David G. Hirsch, and Tobias Stauss.

Many colleagues have graciously provided me their insightful comments, inspiration, assistance, and/or invitations to present portions of our book at workshops and conferences. In addition to those noted above, I particularly thank (in alphabetical order): Norm Abrams, Carol Bakhos, Michael Birnhack, Levi Cooper, Hanoch Dagan, Avihay Dorfman, Arye Edrei, Niva Elkin-Koren, Michael Factor, Noah Feldman, David Ginsburg, Ze'ev Gries, Boaz Huss, Assaf Jacob, Craig Joyce, Yehiel Kaplan, Samuel M. Krieger, Bobbi Kwall, Laurie Levinson, Assaf Likhovski, Steve Lowenstein, Peter Menell, Jennifer Mnookin, Fania Oz-Salzberger, Todd Presner, Amiḥai Radzyner, Naḥum Rakover, Steve Resnicoff, Moshe Rosman, Jennifer Rothman, Emile Schrijver, Marc Shapiro, Adam Shear, Yuval Sinai, Kim Treiger, Daniel Ungar, Melech Westreich, and Tal Zarksy.

I am grateful to the UCLA School of Law, UCLA Academic Senate, Memorial Foundation for Jewish Culture, and American Philosophical Society for their generous financial support for research on my book. Without that critical support, I could not have completed it. I also express my deep appreciation to the UCLA School of Law Deans whose terms coincided with my work on this book—Norm Abrams, Mike Schill, Rachel Moran, and Jennifer Mnookin—for their stalwart backing and encouragement. And I thank the UCLA School of Law library staff, particularly Linda O'Connor, Vicki Steiner, and Lynn McClellan, for their logistical support and supervision of student research assistants.

All illustrations in this book, save Illustration 16, appear by courtesy of the National Library of Israel. I owe special thanks to Noam Solan, Director of Copyrights at the Library, for his assistance in arranging for the images to appear in this book, and for his dedication to making National Library of Israel collections available to the public online.

Of course, my greatest debt is to my family: to my wife Niki and sons Shalev and Adam, for their love, patience, and willingness to hear more than they might have liked about the Jewish law of copyright, and to my mother, Barbara, for her abiding interest in my work and her repeated inquiries about when the book would finally be finished.

* * *

I dedicate this book to the memory of my father, Harold Weinstock ז"ל, who taught me more than I can possibly express about life, love, law, and writing books.

NOTE ON TRANSLITERATION, TRANSLATION, ACRONYMS, WORD CHOICE, AND DATES

Transliteration. This book includes numerous Hebrew language terms and sources. There are no standard rules for transcribing Hebrew into the Roman alphabet. I generally follow the simple version for signs and maps adopted by Israel's Academy of the Hebrew Language in 2006 (available at http://hebrew-academy.huji.ac.il/hahlatot/TheTranscription/Documents/taatiq2007.pdf). However, I use (1) ḥ rather than h̲ to connote the Hebrew letter ח , (2) tz rather than ts to connote the Hebrew letter צ, and (3) a regular apostrophe instead of a short straight line to transcribe the Hebrew letters א and ע when they are articulated in the middle of a word. In addition, when I cite a Hebrew publication that provides its own transliteration, I use that transliteration.

Translation. Translation is a challenge in any language. This is certainly the case for the language and subject matter of this book. In particular, English-language terminology often does not map precisely onto Hebrew terms used by rabbinic jurists or analogous concepts in Jewish law jurisprudence. Indeed, the very term "Jewish law" can connote the word *halakha,* which incorporates legal rules, moral norms, and ritual obligations, or the term *ha-mishpat ha-ivri,* which focuses solely on the rules and norms governing the subject areas of secular law, such as property, torts, contracts, and the like. Moreover, even in "legal" subject areas, rabbinic jurists and commentators often make no distinction between legal and moral obligation, and local custom is frequently regarded as a binding source of law. In any event, I include a glossary, which sets forth short, workable explanations of Hebrew terms and, in some instances, their English-language equivalents, that appear frequently in the book. Unless otherwise noted, I am the translator from the original Hebrew of all rabbinic rulings and reprinting bans that appear in English in the book.

Acronyms. In Jewish tradition, esteemed rabbis are often referred to by an acronym or by the title of their most famous work. I sometimes follow that convention in this book, or at least provide the acronym by which a rabbi is known, together with the rabbi's name. For example, I often refer to Moses Isserles as "the Rema." Some traditional acronyms for famous rabbis might not seem like acronyms to non-Hebrew speaking readers. That is, first, because of the way that Hebrew is written and pronounced, in particular that the first letter of each name might be combined with different vowels than those that follow the consonants in the full name. In addition, the acronyms for famous rabbis typically begin with the initial of an honorific for the rabbi, often "Rabbi" but sometimes "Moreinu Ha-Rav" meaning "Our Master (literally, Teacher), the Rabbi."

Word Choice: "Publisher" and "Secular Law." The choice of which English term to use for certain concepts also presents a challenge. For example, I generally use the modern term "publisher" interchangeably with "printer" to refer to the person who organized the printing of a book, even though early moderns typically used only the term "printer," which today has a more narrow meaning. The modern sense of a publisher as one who selects, organizes, and finances the manufacture and distribution of books did not come into use until the nineteenth century. In the early modern period it was the printer, with his unique access to the press and typeface, who fulfilled this role; but by the eighteenth century the printer had become merely the agent of the publisher.[1]

In addition, I generally use the term "secular law," and, in particular, "secular copyright law," to refer to the laws in force in sovereign entities, ranging from principalities to modern nations, other than the Holy See. I do so even though the term "secular" carries a modern connotation of being the opposite of religious, which was not the case of early modern European law. I decided not to use the obvious alternative, the term "civil law," because in copyright jurisprudence and other contexts "civil law" refers more narrowly to the legal systems of Continental Europe, in contrast to Anglo-American common law.

Dates. I cite many Jewish law sources, ranging from rabbinic rulings to journal articles, that give the year of issuance or publication according to the Hebrew calendar, but which I convert to the Gregorian calendar. The Hebrew year begins and ends in September or October on the Gregorian calendar, and thus overlaps with only three to four months of one Gregorian calendar year, but with eight to nine months of the succeeding Gregorian year. Accordingly, absent knowledge of a specific day or month of publication, the odds are greater that the ruling was issued or book or article was published during Gregorian calendar year in which the relevant Hebrew year ends. In those circumstances, I, therefore, use that later Gregorian calendar year to date the event. However, for volumes of journals identified by the Hebrew year of publication, I indicate both Gregorian years over which the Hebrew year spans.

1. Feather 1984: 409.

CHAPTER 1

Introduction

Microsoft in Bnei Brak

I. A RABBINIC COURT EDICT

In the 1990s, Israel earned the dubious reputation as a "one disk country." Software producers, record labels, and film studios complained that each CD or DVD they were able to sell in Israel immediately became the master for tens of thousands of illicit copies. Microsoft's Israeli subsidiary responded to the rampant piracy of its software with a campaign of consumer education—and litigation. Beginning in 1997, Microsoft brought dozens of lawsuits seeking to enforce its copyrights under Israel's then-applicable copyright law, an updated version of the British Mandate copyright statutes that had been in effect at Israel's independence.

Yet Microsoft was not content merely to seek redress under Israeli law in official Israeli courts. It also petitioned an esteemed rabbinic court in the ultra-Orthodox (or "ḥaredi") city of Bnei Brak to proclaim that anyone who pirates software violates Jewish law. On August 6, 1998, the court issued its ruling, a one-paragraph edict signed by seven rabbinic luminaries. Included among the signatories was Yosef Shalom Eliashiv, until his recent death at the age of 102 widely regarded as the paramount living rabbinic authority for Ashkenazi Jews; Ovadia Yosef, until his recent death, the foremost living authority for Israel's Mizraḥi Jews; and Nissim Karelitz, the court's presiding judge and a leader of Israel's Lithuanian ḥaredim. As is customary, the court's edict was promptly printed on wall posters, known as *pashkvilim*, and plastered on notice boards throughout the streets of Bnei Brak.

The rabbinic court's edict curtly states:

> We hereby emphatically announce in the matter regarding those who commit the act of copying computer disks and programs of various texts and selling them for a low price, and in so doing wrongfully encroach upon the business of those who invested years of labor and significant sums of money in developing those computer programs. Rabbinic authorities of the modern era have already expounded upon the prohibition of such wrongful competition at length, and every person who commits such act and copies any version is a trangressor. Moreover, each purchaser from such persons is an abettor of those who violate the law, and there is no excuse that such purchases are for the benefit of learning. The descendants of Israel shall not do wrong, and may all who obey the law find pleasantness.[1]

The edict raises myriad questions. Not the least of these is: Why was Microsoft, the multinational computer technology giant, seeking a ruling under Jewish law? For that matter, under what authority, and for what reason, would a rabbinic court of Israel's fervently Orthodox and militantly insular Ḥaredi community—a community whose rabbinic leaders prohibit all secular entertainment and condemn the Internet, computers, CD players, and films as "dangerous"—concern itself with software piracy?

Then there is the ruling itself. The rabbinic court forbids the combined act of copying computer programs and selling the copies for a "low price." But what about copying for oneself, giving copies away for free, or even selling pirated copies for the same price as that of the producer? What about loading free pirated software on personal computers that are offered for sale? Does the court mean to excuse those acts? Further, under U.S. and Israeli law alike, computer programs are protected by copyright and other intellectual property rights. Yet, the rabbinic court characterizes the violation of Jewish law as one of "wrongful competition," the illicit encroachment upon software producers' investment of labor and money, not infringing authors' copyright or property rights in their expressive creations per se. Does that doctrinal categorization suggest that the court in fact targets just those commercial pirates who wrongfully compete by undercutting the creator's price? Does it mean that the court, indeed, let off the hook individuals who are not commercial competitors, but merely engage in personal copying and file sharing? If so, why does the court cast a wide net—wider than would be the case under secular copyright law—when it comes to *consumers* of mass-marketed pirate copies, declaring that anyone who *purchases* a low-price pirated copy is an abettor, meaning that the purchaser violates Jewish law as well? Finally, who are those unnamed "rabbinic authorities of the modern era" who have already expounded upon the prohibition of such wrongful competition?

1. The rabbinic term for wrongful competition is "hasagat gvul." As used in the Pentateuch, that term originally referred to the prohibited act of moving one's neighbor's border markings, effectively seizing his land. Deuteronomy 19:14. But over the centuries it has come primarily to mean wrongfully encroaching upon another's livelihood or business opportunity, conduct that falls within the rubric of what is called unfair competition in secular law.

II. WHAT IS JEWISH COPYRIGHT LAW?

Our exploration of these questions will take us on a journey that begins with the dawn of print. Rabbinic authorities have, indeed, expounded upon the nature of authors' and publishers' rights under Jewish law, or "halakha," since the early sixteenth century, some 200 years before modern copyright law is typically said to have emerged full-grown from Parliament's brow with enactment in 1710 of the United Kingdom's Statute of Anne. Our exploration spans from 1518, when a Rome rabbinic court prohibited reprinting a trilogy of Hebrew grammar books without permission of their author or publisher, to the lively debates over private copying and Internet downloading among rabbinic jurists in Israel today. Along the way, we witness the proliferation of rabbinic reprinting bans and traverse several leading disputes, each featuring rulings on Jewish copyright law by preeminent rabbinic authorities of their age. Among those rulings, we encounter Moses Isserles's seminal dictum on Jewish copyright law, issued in Krakow, Poland, in 1550, in response to a bitter dispute over rival print editions of Moses Maimonides's iconic code of Jewish law, the *Mishneh Torah*. As we shall see, Isserles's reasoning reverberates in the ultra-Orthodox court's ruling on Microsoft's petition. All told, from the sixteenth century through the present, the rabbinic rulings and reprinting bans, supplemented by numerous additional rabbinic court decisions, responsa,[2] and, in our times, treatises, scholarly articles, and blog postings, present a rich, multifarious body of jurisprudence regarding the nature, scope, doctrinal specifics, and foundations for authors' and publishers' rights under Jewish law.

In fashioning a Jewish copyright law, the rabbis have grappled with many of the same issues that have long animated secular copyright jurisprudence: How long should copyrights last? Should copyright consist only of the exclusive right to print and reprint a book's original text, or should it include the exclusive right to make translations, abridgements, and new, modified editions as well? For that matter, should authors (or publishers) always have an exclusive right, or should they sometimes have only a right to receive reasonable compensation, perhaps just enough to cover their investment in creating the work, but no more? In that regard, is copyright a broad property right or, rather, a more limited form of protection grounded in trade regulation, unfair competition, unjust enrichment, state-awarded privilege, or a combination of those doctrines? Which law should be applied to a copyright dispute whose litigants reside in different countries? Should copyright extend to noncommercial copying, including Internet downloading for personal use and copying for classroom

2. "Responsa," or in Hebrew, "she'elot u-tshuvot" (literally "questions and answers"), are written answers by particularly learned rabbinic scholars to written questions posed to them, often by local rabbis seeking guidance from a greater rabbinic authority. Responsa have played a vital role in Jewish law for over 1,000 years. Their subject matter spans the entire spectrum of Jewish law, ranging from commercial disputes, to family matters, to questions of faith, ritual, and philosophy. For a detailed discussion, see Elon 1997: 1213–78.

instruction? If copyright law allows individuals to make copies for their own use, can authors prohibit copying anyway by distributing their work subject to a standard form, mass market contract that purports to obligate the recipient not to copy?

In addition to the shared doctrinal issues they face, Jewish and secular copyright law share common origins. Both grew from early efforts of jurists and ruling authorities to grapple with a central challenge posed by the technology of print: how to enable publishers of worthy books to undertake the significant investment required to bring a book to print without facing the risk of being undercut by a rival publisher who reprints the same book. Prior to the advent of print, Jewish law saw no need to recognize an exclusive right of authors or scribes in their manuscripts. Indeed, Jewish law in the pre-print era generally encouraged the copying, sharing, and dissemination of works of Jewish learning and liturgy. But with the invention of printing technology, rabbinic authorities, like their secular and papal counterparts, sought to forge a legal regime that would encourage both the printing and the widespread dissemination of valued books. As such, they endeavored to strike a balance. They would grant the first person who prints a particular book a period of market exclusivity, as needed for him to recover his investment in that printing. Yet they would also aim to foster the availability of books at a reasonable price, typically by allowing others to reprint and sell that book after the circumscribed period of exclusivity.

However, despite the commonalities between Jewish and secular law in regulating the book trade, when I refer to rabbinic rulings and pronouncements on questions of publishers' and authors' rights as "Jewish copyright law," I do so somewhat loosely. Rabbinic commentators have not actually used the term "copyright," or its modern Hebrew equivalent, "zkhut ha-yotzrim," until the last couple of decades. Further, the halakhic principles, methods of analysis, and doctrinal rules that govern the rights of authors and publishers—and thus make up what I denominate "Jewish copyright law"—often diverge sharply from those of Anglo-American and Continental European copyright law, the two principal systems of modern, secular copyright law, even if there are areas of convergence as well. (Of course, as comparative copyright scholars can attest, much the same can be said in contrasting Anglo-American copyright law with its Continental European counterpart.)[3]

The precursors of modern secular copyright law consisted of printing monopolies and exclusive book privileges that kings, princes, popes, and other authorities bestowed upon favored publishers and, in some cases, authors, a practice that began soon after the advent of print. Further, over time, printers' and booksellers' guilds came to establish legally sanctioned cartels in a number of countries. But in the eighteenth and nineteenth centuries, republican legislatures enacted modern copyright statutes that swept aside royal printing monopolies, book privileges, and guild cartels. The copyright statutes instead vested legal rights in individual authors. In so doing, lawmakers proclaimed the sanctity of literary property and celebrated authors' contributions to education, public liberty, and the progress of science.

3. See Netanel 1994 (detailing profound differences in ideology and doctrine between common law "copyright" and civil law "authors' rights").

To serve those ends, the copyright statutes provided that authors would, henceforth, have exclusive rights to publish, print, and, in some countries, publicly perform their newly authored books and plays. Authors could determine to which publishers, if any, to license or assign their rights. And a couple of decades following publication, the author's work would enter the public domain, meaning that anyone who wished to reprint and copy from the work would be free to do so.

In the ensuing centuries, judges and legislatures have greatly expanded the breadth and duration of copyrights. Copyrights have come to encompass new rights, new subject matter, new technologies, and new markets for creative expression. As a result, today's copyright law accords authors manifold exclusive rights to market, communicate, and reformulate creative expression in analog, hard copy, electronic, and digital media.

Microsoft, for example, enjoys the exclusive right under secular copyright law to reproduce and distribute its computer programs. Copyright law likewise accords novelists the exclusive right to translate, write sequels, and produce motion picture versions of their novels. It gives playwrights the exclusive right to authorize the public performance of their work on stage or on television; motion picture studios the exclusive right to exhibit their movies in theaters, to broadcast them on television, and to stream them over the Internet; photographers and visual artists the exclusive right to display their work on websites; and record labels and composers the legal (if not easily enforceable) right to prevent individuals from trading music recordings via peer-to-peer networks. In most countries, the law also recognizes authors' "moral rights," namely the rights to claim authorship credit and to prevent distortions in the author's work even after the author has transferred to a publisher or studio her exclusive rights of copying, distribution, adaptation, and public communication. Further, the rights that today's copyright statutes accord are as enduring as they are broad. Copyrights last a very long time: typically the life of the author plus 70 years; in some countries, the author's moral rights are perpetual.

For its part, Jewish copyright law took shape contemporaneously with the regime of printing monopolies and book privileges, as common responses to the challenge of print, well before the enactment of modern copyright statutes. Jewish copyright law emerged in the sixteenth century through a series of decrees of Jewish communal self-governing bodies, rabbinic rulings, and rabbinic reprinting bans. In that process, the communal councils and rabbis who formulated Jewish copyright law borrowed heavily from the basic template of early modern papal, royal, and municipal book privileges, even as they imbued that template with halakhic doctrine and adapted it to meet the particular needs of Jewish communities and the Hebrew book trade.

Modern copyright statutes and their embrace of the concept of literary property have also influenced rabbinic rulings on Jewish copyright going back to the nineteenth century and continuing today. But that influence has remained circumscribed and contested. Certainly, Jewish law has seen nothing like the fundamental paradigm shift from the book privilege model to modern copyright law. Nor has Jewish law articulated in a systematic fashion anything like modern copyright law's full pallet of exclusive rights.

III. THE NORMATIVE AND INSTITUTIONAL FRAMEWORK OF JEWISH LAW

Whatever the influences of secular copyright (of which I will have more to say shortly), the rabbis forged Jewish copyright law primarily from basic tenets of halakha. With ancient roots in the Bible and Talmud, Jewish law governed much of the commercial, social, and ritual life of Jewish communities for well over two millennia. Although Jews lacked political sovereignty for most of that period, the royal and feudal powers in the lands where Jews were permitted to live typically granted the Jewish community a considerable measure of self-governing, juridical authority. In accordance with their royal charters and feudal privileges, Jewish communities established governing councils that both represented the Jewish community before the sovereign power and enacted ordinances governing much of the community's internal life. Although the governing councils came to be headed by lay notables, they were heavily dependent on rabbinic leaders, who enforced and gave halakhic imprimatur to community ordinances, ruled on questions of halakha, issued decrees and regulations, and settled disputes.

The last vestiges of that semi-sovereign Jewish community status ended with political emancipation in the eighteenth and nineteenth centuries.[4] And although the State of Israel was established in 1948 as a "Jewish state," its laws are overwhelmingly secular in character, not a codification of halakha. Nonetheless, the halakha continues to be regarded as comprehensive and binding among religiously observant Jews, both in Israel and the Diaspora. Hence, although the ultra-Orthodox residents of Bnei Brak are no less subject to secular Israeli law and to the jurisdiction of Israeli courts than other Israeli citizens, they typically bring internal disputes before self-constituted ultra-Orthodox rabbinic courts, as do their ultra-Orthodox coreligionists in other countries. For the ultra-Orthodox petitioners and litigants, the rulings of those courts exert, very much, the force of law. Indeed, for many ultra-Orthodox Jews, the halakha is the system of law to which they owe their primary, if not sole, allegiance.[5]

In keeping with its millennia-old governance of day-to-day life, Jewish law contains extensive doctrine concerning property, tort, inheritance, unjust enrichment, contract, competition, sales, rabbinic and community regulation, tax, marriage, and judicial procedure, as well as matters of religious study and ritual. Thus, with the advent of print and the vibrant international trade in books of Jewish liturgy and learning that followed, rabbis had available a far-ranging, highly developed body of halakhic precedent to which they could turn to provide legal protection for authors'

4. Bartal 2005: 18–22, 30; Goldberg 1985: 1–8; Berkovitz 1995: 26, 41–42; Manekin 2008: 560, 561–63. In the Ottoman Empire, where modernization came largely at the behest of Western European powers, the legal autonomy of the Jewish community ended in 1856, after which criminal, civil, and commercial cases had to be tried according to new codes, based on French law, that applied to all subjects of the Empire. However, Jews could still turn to rabbinic courts to resolve disputes relating to personal status, including matters of divorce and inheritance. See Benbassa and Rodrigue 2000: 70.

5. Radzyner 2015: 171.

and publishers' investment in producing and printing books. Over the centuries, rabbinic decisors have produced a rich array of rulings and commentary, drawing upon a variety of halakhic doctrines, which collectively accord authors and publishers various rights to prevent others from copying and marketing their works. Those doctrinal underpinnings include the laws of wrongful competition, unjust enrichment, property, and conditional sales. Also relevant to Jewish copyright law are halakhic precepts regarding rabbinic authority to regulate commercial activity and those purporting to govern the conduct of non-Jews, including in their commercial dealings with Jews.

At the same time, printing and the book trade were commercial endeavors that were without precedent before the early modern era, and this fact has posed significant challenges for the rabbis. As expounded in the Talmud, for example, the Jewish law of wrongful competition regulated only the behavior of local artisans competing in the same local market. That centuries-old doctrine had uncertain applicability to international book markets, where a publisher might face ruinous competition from pirate editions produced in distant lands. International book markets also strain traditional limits on rabbinic courts' juridical authority to prohibit conduct outside their local jurisdiction. Further, in the view of many rabbinic scholars, the Jewish law of property recognizes property rights only in land and material objects, not in intangibles such as works of authorship. And for some rabbinic scholars that means that the Jewish law of unjust enrichment is likewise unavailable to protect authors and publishers from pirate editions; as in their view, Jewish law accords protection against unjust enrichment only when one person benefits from using another's *property*, as opposed to benefiting from another's labor or investment. As a result of these and other challenges, the nature, scope, and specific halakhic rationale for authors' and publishers' rights remain hotly contested right up to the present.

Given Jewish copyright law's halakhic foundations and constraints, it is no wonder that Jewish copyright law differs sharply from its secular counterpart in a number of respects. Yet the unique character of Jewish copyright cannot be entirely explained by differences in the doctrinal underpinnings of Jewish copyright law versus secular copyright law per se. Jewish copyright law also originated in very different institutional settings and has followed a distinct historical narrative from those of secular copyright law.

Most important, during the times that modern copyright statutes were enacted and then expanded to adapt to rapidly evolving communications technologies and markets, Jewish law has lacked the institutional mechanisms for such sweeping doctrinal changes. As noted above, that absence of broad-based regulatory authority has not always been the case. For nearly a millennium prior to the eighteenth century, Jewish communities enjoyed a considerable measure of juridical autonomy pursuant to royal and feudal privileges that carved out a realm of Jewish communal self-governance and defined Jews' legal and economic relationships with the sovereign and non-Jews. In line with that autonomy, Jewish communities established both local and regional legislative bodies. Foremost among them was the "Council of Four Lands," a transnational body that enjoyed far-reaching legislative and judicial authority over the Jews of Poland, Lithuania, and Galicia from the late sixteenth to the mid-eighteenth centuries.

However, early modern Jewish communities lost their powers of self-government more or less contemporaneously with the enactment of modern copyright law in the eighteenth and nineteenth centuries. Jews' communal privileges were abrogated by republican legislatures and reform-minded monarchies as part of the same broad movement of modernization that dismantled royal printing privileges and other royal dispensations.[6] The Council of Four Lands, for example, was abolished by order of the Polish Sejm in 1764, well before modern copyright law had reached Eastern Europe.

In theory, rabbinic leaders could subsequently have adopted something like modern copyright law through their power to interpret and apply the halakha, even absent a transnational communal legislative body. But rabbinic decisors of halakha lacked a national or transnational authority with the power to effect such a change. Not since the first millennium of the Common Era has there been a central rabbinic judicial body carrying authority to settle conflicting precedent throughout the Jewish world.[7] Since the demise of the Baghdad gaonate in the eleventh century, halakhic doctrine has evolved from a myriad of disparate, if often mutually referential, local rabbinic decisions, pronouncements, and ordinances. The temporal and geographic impact of any given halakhic ruling depends on the esteem, intellectual prowess, force of argument, position, and, at times, sectarian affiliation of its rabbinic author, not any formally established judicial hierarchy. Jewish copyright law emerged and evolved accordingly—through the discursive exchange of a dispersed community of rabbinic scholars, rather than an encyclical of a central authority.

In addition to these institutional barriers to sweeping legal change, rabbinic decisors would have been highly unlikely to embrace the Enlightenment underpinnings of modern copyright law. Although rabbinic thought greatly values the individual, it places the individual firmly within an inextricable matrix of communal and religious obligation. In that worldview, the Enlightenment ideology of individual self-expression, creative prowess, and even scientific progress—in the sense that human civilization steadily advances as a result of human discovery, education, and untrammeled critical inquiry—is largely foreign, if not anathema.[8] It is an often cited principle of rabbinic thought, indeed, that contemporary halakhic scholarship and spirituality are inferior to those of previous generations.[9] Further, the normative ethos of rabbinic jurisprudence leans heavily inward; it is tied fundamentally to maintaining the integrity and coherence of halakhic doctrine and the rabbinic tradition.[10] In that vein, it is often said that the Torah, which embodies the fundamental principles of the halakha, is timeless and immutable.

6. Bartal 2005: 18–22, 30; Goldberg 1985: 1–8; Berkovitz 1995: 26, 41–42; Manekin 2008: 560, 561–63.

7. The ancient Sanhredin dissolved in the fourth century; the Baghdad Geonim then exerted similar supreme judicial authority until the eleventh century. Elon 1997: 549–50.

8. For an illuminating account of the understanding of progress that underlies modern copyright, see Birnhack 2001.

9. The principle of contemporary inferiority is called "*yeridat ha-dorot*," meaning "the decline of the generations."

10. See generally Sacks 1992: 123.

Significantly, the inwardness of rabbinic jurisprudence also finds expression in an ideal in which the halakha is a perfectly self-contained system, one that is impervious—and superior—to non-Jewish law and morality. A Talmudic dictum admonishes: "Shall not our perfect Torah be as worthy as their idle chatter?"[11] In that vein, rabbinic decisors, exhibit great reluctance expressly to recognize a role for non-Jewish law or morality in interpreting and applying halakha. And, notably, that ideal of absolute normative self-sufficiency applies with equal force to issues presented by new technologies and circumstances on which rabbis of ancient days could not have directly opined. To give but one particularly forthright example, in a responsum on artificial insemination, Moshe Feinstein, a preeminent rabbinic decisor of the twentieth century, purported unequivocally to reject any place for non-Jewish views on the matter: "My entire worldview derives only from knowledge of Torah, without any mixture of external ideas, [and the Torah's] judgment is truth whether it is strict or lenient. Arguments derived from foreign perspectives or false opinions of the heart are nothing."[12]

IV. CREATIVE BORROWING, PRAGMATISM, AND COERCION

Given these formidable institutional and normative constraints, the rabbis have not adopted—and would not adopt—secular copyright wholesale. Quite strikingly, however, Jewish copyright law nonetheless reflects the influence of its secular counterpart at numerous junctures. In fashioning Jewish copyright law, the rabbis have not just drawn upon halakhic precedent. They have also creatively borrowed from contemporaneous non-Jewish law. In addition, often in interlocking step with that creative borrowing, rabbinic decisors have tailored their rulings to negotiate the ever tenuous and, over time, sharply diminished juridical autonomy of rabbinic and Jewish communal authorities vis-à-vis the Gentile world.

In that light, as noted above, the early sixteenth-century rabbis who crafted Jewish copyright law borrowed from the model of secular and papal book privileges in doing so. Likewise, subsequent rabbinic rulings and debate about the nature, scope, and doctrinal foundations of copyright under Jewish law have repeatedly taken cognizance, whether implicitly or explicitly, of ideas, perspectives, and developments external to the rabbis' "knowledge of Torah" narrowly defined. Among other matters, rabbinic decisors have grappled with the availability of secular and papal book privileges for books of Jewish law, learning, and liturgy; the establishment, throughout early modern Europe, of printers' guilds with certain state-backed powers of self-regulation; nations' enactment of copyright statutes beginning in the eighteenth century; the enforced subservience of Jewish law to that of post-Enlightenment states; debates in the secular world about the nature and scope of copyright; the ascendancy of

11. *Babylonian Talmud, Baba Batra* 116a. Rabbinic decisors have interpreted the dictum to stand for the superiority of halakha over non-Jewish law and morality. See Kleinman 2011: 19–21 and Broyde 2012.

12. Feinstein, *Responsa Igrot Moshe,* Even Ha-Ezer 2:11. I thank Aryeh Klapper for his comments on this point, cautioning that Feinstein's statement must be taken in its particular context.

international treaty regimes for the protection of intellectual property; prevailing commercial practices in the book trade—and more recently, in the motion picture, sound recording, music performance, and computer software trades. As such, the historical development of book trade regulation in the Gentile world and the precariousness of Jewish communal autonomy in early modern and post-Enlightenment Europe have left an unmistakable imprint on Jewish copyright law. And "foreign perspectives" continue to find expression in present-day rabbis' apparent concern that the halakha must comport with what they perceive to be universal legal and moral norms that recognize authors' exclusive rights in their creations.

In reflecting that external influence, Jewish copyright law has followed a similar path to that noted by scholars of the historical development of halakha in many other areas: over the centuries, despite the rabbinic ethos of insularity and conservatism, rabbis have, in fact, proven highly adept at shaping doctrine as required to meet changing social, economic, political, and technological circumstances.[13] That practice finds support in the halakhic dictum that the law is in accordance with the views of later rabbinic authorities, who, despite their inferiority to the giants of old, must be free to adapt the law to the prevailing circumstances of their time.[14] In so doing, moreover, despite the ideal of the normative self-sufficiency and superiority of the halakha, rabbinic authorities have not infrequently recognized, incorporated, and creatively adapted legal constructs from non-Jewish legal regimes.[15]

Rabbinic decisors have employed a variety of direct and indirect mechanism to marshal external legal constructs when helpful or necessary to resolve a dispute or fill a lacunae in Jewish law. These have included implicit borrowing, occasional explicit reference to foreign law, and giving legal imprimatur to Jewish merchants' adoption of commercial customs or Jewish lay leaders' communal enactments, which have not uncommonly reflected non-halakhic concepts prevailing in the surrounding society.[16] Rabbinic decisors have also created openings for bringing non-Jewish law to bear in adjudicating specific disputes, particularly under the halakhic rule that deference

13. See Fram 1997 (presenting in-depth studies of instances in which leading rabbinic jurists adapted Jewish law to pressing economic and communal issues of the day through legal fictions and reinterpretations of textual authority); Katz 2000: 52–62 (discussing rabbinic rulings regulating and partly accommodating previously forbidden activities, including charging interest and dealing in non-kosher wine and food, in response to prevailing economic pressures); Katz 1998b; Gamoran 2008; Westreich 2010: 435–36 (attributing adoption of negotiability to local economic conditions).

14. The rule that "the law is according to later halakhic scholars" was developed in the post-talmudic period and solidified in the fourteenth century. See Ta-Shma 1998. Ta-Shma conjectures that the rule came to be applied among Ashkenazic authorities centuries before Sephardic scholars because, as early as the twelfth century, Christian Europe came to accept that wisdom is cumulatively acquired and developing from generation to generation, whereas that view was not internalized in the Islamic world. Ta-Shma 2006: 163. If so, we see some rabbinic acceptance of the progression of knowledge, which might stand in tension with the rabbinic principle that previous generations were superior.

15. Broyde 2010: 363, 372–76; Jackson 1980 (presenting a critical survey of theories of foreign influence in Jewish law, including the difficulty of proving causation as opposed to parallel development); Goitein 1980: 61; Z. Kaplan 2007 (discussing rabbinic solution to the problem of marriages that were illegal under the French civil law).

16. See Katz 1998b: 179–83 (describing the rabbinic legitimization of community enactments, which sometimes reflected concepts found in the surrounding society that did not

must be accorded to the law of the sovereign state in commercial matters.[17] Hence, alongside the rabbis' immersion within and fidelity to the tradition of Jewish law and teaching, they—like Jewish culture, thought, and communal institutions generally—have both absorbed and creatively responded to the dominant cultures, societies, and markets in which semiautonomous Jewish communities have been embedded.[18]

Jewish copyright law has developed accordingly. Rabbis have drawn upon a wealth of halakhic precedents, extending back to the Talmud, in adjudicating copyright disputes, pronouncing reprinting bans, and debating the nature and scope of authors' rights. But they have done so against the backdrop of contemporaneous copyright-related developments in the surrounding non-Jewish world. In providing exclusive rights for authors and publishers, rabbis have creatively adapted non-Jewish legal constructs and made repeated reference to prevailing market customs and conditions. Yet, in doing so, they have framed their rulings and enactments in terms of halakhic doctrine, local custom, and the practical exigencies of the market for books of Jewish learning and ritual. Even as Jewish copyright law has borrowed from the framework of its counterparts in the Gentile world, it exhibits essentially no trace of the Enlightenment rhetoric and exaltation of authorial creativity that have driven secular copyright.

Jewish copyright law has been constituted by this dynamic dialectic process from its very beginnings, and that process continues to this day. The 10-year reprinting ban for three Hebrew grammar books that Rome's rabbinic leadership issued in 1518—the first such entitlement under Jewish law of which we have record—was most modeled, at least in part, on prevailing practice in the Gentile world, even as it cited halakhic precedent to justify rabbinic authority to issue such an exclusive right.[19] Jewish copyright law's perviousness to external influence was also evident in a decree of the Amsterdam rabbinic leadership, issued in 1716, that, henceforth, no rabbinic reprinting bans would be granted for prayer books, and that bans issued for prayer books by rabbis in other countries would not be enforced.[20] The decree followed the Amsterdam Booksellers and Printers Guild's earlier refusal to enforce an exclusive book privilege that had been issued by the States of Holland and West-Friesland for a Hebrew prayer book, on the grounds that the printing of prayer books had always been free in the Dutch Republic.[21] In that light, the

necessarily conform in substance to halakhic principles). See also Morell 1971 (discussing the rabbinic validation of communal enactments as having operative force under Jewish law).

17. The leading contemporary treatise on the rule of deference, termed, "dina de-malkhuta dina," or "the law of the sovereign is the law," is Shilo 1974. See also Graff 1985. Prevailing extra-halakhic norms might also influence rabbinic decisors' rulings when they exercise the discretion that rabbinic judges are said to enjoy to apply "reason and common sense" in adjudicating disputes, rather than being bound by precedent. See, generally, Lamm and Kirschenbaum 1979 (discussing rabbinic decisors' use of reason and the absence of binding precedent in adjudicating disputes).

18. For extensive discussion of historians' various theories of how surrounding cultures have impacted Jewish identity and culture, see Rosman 2007: 82–108.

19. Rakover 1991: 126–33.

20. Rakover 1991: 309–10.

21. Heller 2006: 221. In the Dutch Republic in the eighteenth century, publications by the church, as well as publications for school use and editions of the classics, were ineligible for a privilege. Hoftijzer 1997: 13n32. The guild's full name was the Amsterdam Guild of Booksellers, Bookprinters, and Bookbinders.

rabbinic edict explained, for the rabbis to grant their own monopolies in printing prayer books would harm both competing printers and the Jewish public at large, "particularly in this city in which there is [otherwise] considerable commerce [in such books] at an inexpensive price."[22] Similarly, when Joseph Saul Nathanson, rabbi of Lemberg, ruled in 1860 that, under Jewish law, authors have a property right in their creative works, he made reference to the Austrian Law for the Protection of Literary and Artistic Property, enacted 14 years earlier, and explained—turning the traditional Talmudic dictum on its head—that "common sense" rejects the possibility that the Gentiles' laws protect authors but "our perfect Torah" does not.[23] Present-day rabbinic commentators likewise measure Jewish copyright law against what they construe to be universal norms for copyright protection as embodied in international treaties. In partial counterpoint, a leading ultra-Orthodox authority, Asher Weiss, agrees that authors have property rights in their works, but posits that Jewish law should nevertheless take cognizance of what he has heard from music industry experts: that many artists and composers implicitly consent to having their music freely copied, as they would lose much of their audience if they were to insist on enforcing their copyrights in an age in which illicit music recordings are widely available for free.[24]

As such, Jewish copyright law bears much in common with what scholars of comparative law have identified as the ubiquitous phenomenon of *legal transplantation*, one legal system's incorporation of legal rules or even entire areas of doctrine from another.[25] As scholars have noted, legal transplantation is best understood as a process of legal translation, not rote duplication. Each legal system is firmly embedded in its own native society, culture, and ideology; legal rules acquire meaning only within that context. Further, any given legal rule within a legal system must interact with and be informed by the other rules and doctrines of that system. Hence, transplanting a set of laws from one legal system to another necessarily involves imbuing those laws with new meaning and, in many cases, new functions. Legal transplantation is a creative and dynamic process in which the outer textual form of a foreign legal doctrine is invested with a new normative framework, and sometimes interpreted to yield very different results.

Like many other instances of legal transplantation, particularly in colonial settings, rabbinic borrowing and adaptation have not been entirely voluntary. The coercive character of much rabbinic borrowing has been present in copyright law no less than in other areas. Jewish copyright law has developed under the shadow of the precariousness of Jewish community autonomy and rabbinic authority before the sovereign powers of kings, nobles, republics, and Church. Indeed, Jewish copyright has almost always served as a system of protection that is parallel—and subservient—to

22. Rakover 1991: 309.
23. Nathanson, *Shoel U-Meshiv*, pt. 1, no. 44.
24. See Y. Cohen 1999: Kuntras 560–62 (describing international copyright treaties as *takanat omanim* (guild regulation) within Jewish law, given authors' associations involvement in drafting them); Weiss 2009: 1.
25. For further discussion, see Bracha 2010: 1459–62; Langer 2004: 29–35.

those sovereigns' copyright laws, printing privileges, and licensing requirements. Numerous Jewish publishers, and numerous Christian publishers of books intended primarily for Jewish readers, have sought printing monopolies and privileges from secular or papal authorities in addition to or in lieu of rabbinic reprinting bans. In many times and locations, Hebrew and Jewish vernacular books, like all books, have also been subject to government or church censorship, including prepublication licensing requirements. Gentile authorities' printing privileges and book regulation have sometimes complemented rabbinic reprinting bans, but have often undermined their force. At the very least, a rabbinic ruling or ban issued in one country might not have been enforceable in another where the king had banned the import of Hebrew books or where a competing printer held a royal printing monopoly. On occasion, indeed, rabbinic judges have even favored a Jewish publisher holding a secular government book privilege over a competitor who had been granted a rabbinic ban for the same book, pursuant to the halakhic precept that deference must be accorded to the law of the sovereign in commercial matters.[26]

Rabbinic jurists have also sometimes run into direct conflict with papal and secular powers in adjudicating copyright disputes. When renowned rabbinic authority Moses Isserles ruled in 1550 that the Christian printer Marc Antonio Giustiniani had violated Jewish copyright law, Giustiniani complained to the papal authorities, leading, in combination with other factors, to a Papal Bull ordering that all copies of the Talmud be confiscated and burned. In the early nineteenth century, Chief Rabbi of Moravia Mordekhai Banet abruptly reversed his support for the enforceability of a rabbinic reprinting ban when Austrian authorities threatened to prosecute him for interfering with a Christian publisher's reprinting of the book in question. Some 50 years later, Joseph Saul Nathanson fashioned an alternative to rabbinic reprinting bans in part because the Russian government had forbidden rabbis from issuing them and the Austrian government had threatened to punish publishers who relied on rabbinic bans rather than on Austria's new copyright law.

Yet within those various confines and influences, rabbinic jurists have forged a body of copyright law that has remained fundamentally distinct from both early modern book privileges and present-day secular copyright law. Even as they have borrowed from those surrounding legal regimes, they have altered and sometimes subverted secular-law doctrines to meet particular needs of the Jewish book trade, semiautonomous Jewish communities, and the elite institution within the Jewish community of rabbinic study and teaching. Even as the rabbis have navigated the limits to their authority and retreated before hegemonic sovereign powers, they have formulated halakhic justifications for their rulings. In so doing, the rabbis have taken the secular-law constructs that they have implicitly or explicitly adopted and imbued them with halakhic norms, norms that differ substantially from the ideological underpinnings of secular copyright law.

26. Rakover 1991: 240–42 (discussing ruling of Rabbi Arieh Leibush ben Eliyahu Balḥuver in dispute between Zhitomir and Vilna printers of competing editions of the Jerusalem Talmud, eventually printed in 1866).

V. MAPPING OUR JOURNEY

Chapter 2 begins our exploration of this rabbinic innovation and adaptation by bringing to the forefront the context against which Jewish copyright law developed: the emergence of the early modern publishing industry and secular and papal authorities' regulation of the book trade. It also chronicles the dramatic move from book privileges to modern secular copyright law and explicates the principal theoretical foundations for modern copyright law. In so doing, it sets the framework for understanding what the rabbinic jurists might have borrowed from Gentile law and practice, and the ways in which, as the ultra-Orthodox rabbinic court's ruling on Microsoft's petition suggests, Jewish copyright law follows its own unique path.

In Chapter 3, we then turn to the first rabbinic reprinting ban, issued by the Rome rabbinical court in 1518. That chapter relates the story of that rabbinic ban, compares it with the Gentile book privileges of the time, and examines its halakhic rationale. The chapters that follow further measure the influence of rabbinic reprinting bans for publishers and authors of books marketed to Jewish readers. We also consider the relative roles of rabbis and lay-dominated Jewish communal government councils in regulating the Jewish book trade.

Finally, I recount a number of seminal disputes and rabbinic rulings that make up Jewish copyright jurisprudence. I present these disputes and rulings within their historical, sociological, and comparative law context. I elucidate in each case how the rabbis sought to protect the Jewish book trade and traditional Jewish teaching, while both selectively borrowing from secular law and grounding their rulings in traditional halakhic doctrine.

Our final chapter returns to the Microsoft ruling. Chapter 9 pieces together some of the puzzling aspects of the ruling and places it in the framework of the current rabbinic debate about the nature, significance, and perceived inadequacies of Jewish copyright law, that body of halakhic doctrine that aims to protect authors and publishers against ruinous copying.

CHAPTER 2

From Privileges and Printers' Guilds to Copyright

On September 18, 1469, the Collegio of Venice awarded the German printer Johann von Speyer a monopoly over the craft of printing in the Venetian Republic—this less than two decades after Johannes Gutenberg had successfully printed his landmark 42-line Bible. The Collegio's decree lauded Speyer's fortitude and the great labor and expense that he had incurred in printing classic texts with beautiful, large-type; it declared that the innovation of printing, "unique and particular to our age and entirely unknown to the ancients," must be supported and nourished, lest it be abandoned. The Collegio accordingly awarded Speyer a five-year exclusive privilege to print and sell books in the Republic. The decree provided that violators would be subject to fine and the loss of their equipment and printed books.[1]

Speyer died within a few months of receiving his monopoly. Although his business partner and brother Wendelin continued to print exquisite editions of Italian and Roman classics, the Collegio let the monopoly expire with the death of its original holder. The Venetian patricians likely realized that the craft of printing would be better supported by encouraging other printers to settle in the Republic, and that even Speyer's relatively short-term five-year monopoly would have the opposite effect.[2]

1. Johannes of Speyer's Printing Monopoly, Venice (1469), in *Primary Sources on Copyright (1450–1900)*. Printing monopolies were granted in other jurisdictions as well. In 1525, the Spanish Crown granted Jakob Cromberger an exclusive privilege to print in Mexico. Vera 2010: 408, 410. In 1505, the King Alexander of Poland granted Jan Haller a monopoly of printing in all the Polish territories, a monopoly that expired in 1517. Febvre and Martin 1984: 201–02.

2. Brown 1891: 6; Lowry 1979: 7; Kostylo 2010: 24. Unlike printing, most of the Republic crafts at that time were governed by guilds, and when the Venetian government granted

With its advanced mercantile system and proximity to the leading university of Padua, Venice soon emerged as the unrivaled printing capital of all of Europe. And the Republic would never again award a single publisher the exclusive right to print all books within its borders.[3] Yet it and other jurisdictions did grant exclusive privileges to print individual titles and, in some cases, entire classes of books. Indeed, the centuries prior to the enactment of modern copyright laws saw hundreds of thousands of such book privileges. The privileges covered a broad spectrum of titles, ranging from early print editions of classic manuscripts to new books of law, religion, history, philosophy, medicine, drama, and popular romance.[4] Like Speyer's short-term monopoly over printing, the privileges for individual books were typically limited to a fixed period—customarily between 2 and 25 years—even if over time, the powerful printers' guilds that came to dominate the book trade in many locations secured perpetual or indefinitely renewable privileges for their members.[5]

The first such individual book privilege that we know of was bestowed by the Prince-Bishop of Würzburg in 1479. Its beneficiaries were three printers commissioned to edit and print the breviary for the Würzburg Cathedral.[6] Yet, following Venice's lead in fostering a local publishing industry, it was in Italy that the practice of granting book privileges took root. In 1481, the Duke of Milan issued a six-year privilege to the celebrated publisher Antonio Zarotto for a book that glorified the Duke's accomplishments.[7] In 1486, the Collegio of Venice awarded the first known privilege to an author. It granted Marcantonio Cocci Sabellico, the historiographer to the Republic, permission to have his history of Venice, *Decades Rerum Venetarum*, printed by the printer of his choice, at the printer's "own expense," and prohibited anyone else from reprinting the book in Venetian territory on pain of a 500-ducat fine.[8] In 1489, King Ferdinand I of Naples granted an exclusive privilege for a collection of sermons of the renowned fifteenth-century Franciscan preacher Roberto

patents for inventions, typically to foreigners who were not members of the applicable guild, the monopoly lasted for up to 25 years. Shortly after the Speyer printing monopoly expired, the Venetian Senate enacted the Venetian Patent Act of 1474, which provided that patents would henceforth last for only 10 years, unless a longer period was approved by the Senate. Sichelman and O'Connor 2012: 1273–77.

3. As I explain on page xii, I use the modern term "publisher" interchangeably with the early modern term "printer" even though the term "publisher" did not come into use until the nineteenth century.

4. See Hirsch 1967: 84 n. 27; Armstrong 1990: 165–90.

5. See Feather 2006: 29–43 (describing the Stationers' Company); Hunt 1997 (discussing royal patents as an alternative privilege system to that of the Stationers' Company); Birn 1970–1971 (discussing the royal privilege system, establishment of the Paris Publishers' and Printers' Guild, and the royal order of August 30, 1777, that abrogated the printers' perpetual privileges); Hesse 1990: 112 (noting the Crown's practice of conferring extensive privileges on Paris publishers and then renewing those privileges automatically over generations).

6. Kostylo 2008e; Kawohl 2008l.

7. The Milan privilege was issued to Zarotto for Johannes Simonetta's book, *Rerum Gestarum Francisci Sfortiae*. See Witcombe 2004: 326, 328.

8. Marco Antonio Sabellico's Printing Privilege, Venice (1486), in *Primary Sources on Copyright (1450–1900)*; Armstrong 1990: 3–4.

Caracciolo, a privilege that remained in effect until the printer sold out his then-sizable print run of 2,000 copies.[9]

Venice also repeatedly granted privileges for entire classes of titles, particularly to reward investment in a specialized typeface. In 1496, the Collegio accorded the illustrious humanist and publisher Aldus Manutius a 20-year monopoly in whatever Greek texts he chose to publish. In 1498, Ottaviano Petrucci received a 20-year exclusive privilege for all printing of figured song, and Democrito Terracina was awarded a 25 year monopoly to print books in Arabic, Moorish, and Armenian, a privilege that was renewed in favor of Terracina's nephews for another 25 years in 1513 (even though Terracina, who died that same year, had not printed a single book in those languages).[10] In 1501, the Collegio granted Aldus another broad monopoly, this time a 10-year exclusive privilege for all books printed in his italic cursive typeface. Upon Aldus's petition, the pope granted his own privilege, extending Aldus's monopoly, initially, to all of Italy and, subsequently, to all of Christendom.[11] In 1515, the Venetian Senate bestowed upon the Christian humanist Daniel Bomberg a 10-year exclusive privilege to print Hebrew books, a matter to which we will return.

The practice of granting exclusive book privileges grew sporadically, but by 1520 it had spread throughout Europe. The earliest known book privileges in Spain, France, and the Papal States were issued in 1498, followed by Portugal and the first Imperial privilege in the Holy Roman Empire in 1501, and then Poland and Siena in 1505, Scotland in 1507, Sweden in 1510, the Low Countries in 1512, Florence in 1516, England in 1517, and Denmark in 1519.[12]

Venice began to grant book privileges regularly in 1492. By 1500, it was issuing some 30 per year.[13] Indeed, within two decades, the Republic was faced with a glut of privileges, dispensed by various Venetian authorities, for both individual titles and entire classes of books, many of which the privilege holder had no realistic prospect of actually printing. The surfeit of privileges locked up so many titles that it prompted an exodus of printers from the Republic. The resulting dearth of competition was also widely cited as a cause for books' high prices and shoddy quality. In 1517, the Venetian Senate responded by revoking all existing book privileges. The Senate's edict further provided that, henceforth, privileges would be granted only for books that "have never been printed before" and only upon approval by a two-thirds majority of the full Senate.[14]

9. The Naples privilege was granted to the printer Giovan Marco Cinico for an edition of Roberto Caracciolo's *Sermones de Laudibus Sanctorum*. See Witcombe 2004: 326, 328.

10. Brown 1891: 41 (Terracina), 55 (Aldus), 106 (Petrucci). See also Krek 1979: 209 (Terracina).

11. See Lowenstein 2002: 7–74; Kostylo 2008a. Elsewhere, royal patents were issued in all law books, all Latin schoolbooks, and other broad categories of titles. Johns 1998: 24–50.

12. Witcombe 2004: 32–38; Armstrong 1990: 2–20; Kawohl 2008d; Lowenstein 2002: 68–69 (first English book privilege).

13. Kilgour 1998: 93 (on Venice as printing capital); Hirsch 1967: 82–84 (proliferation of privileges); Brown 1891: 236 (data on numbers of privileges issued in Venice).

14. Venetian Decree on Press Affairs, Venice (1517), in *Primary Sources on Copyright (1450–1900)*; Witcombe 2004: 41–42. The Decree was not entirely effective in denying exclusive privileges for previously published books. In a number of cases, printers obtained

As book privileges proliferated and, in most European printing centers, intertwined with the establishment of powerful printers' guilds, they served as a key component by which early modern European monarchies, principalities, republics, city-states, colonial governments, and ecclesiastical authorities regulated the book trade. The regime of book privileges and printers' guilds continued in force for some 200 years. It served as a direct forerunner of the modern copyright statutes enacted in the eighteenth and nineteenth centuries, beginning with the Statute of Anne of 1710.

I. BOOK PRIVILEGES AND THE EARLY MODERN EUROPEAN BOOK TRADE

Book privileges did not proliferate merely because sovereign authorities viewed them as a useful tool for regulating the book trade. In its early decades, indeed, publishers could petition for a book privilege without any requirement that they also obtain a license from the sovereign or the Church granting them permission print a particular title. Nor were book publishers required to be a member of a guild. Rather, publishers—at least publishers of expensive, high quality books—sought book privileges for reasons that were entirely market-driven.

Early modern printing was a precarious enterprise—and of significance to our study, this was certainly no less true of printing books of Jewish learning and liturgy than for any other books. Printing entailed high fixed costs of labor, rent, printing equipment, and type; the considerable expense of paper; and extended delays before copies could be distributed and sold. At the same time, early modern publishers had to contend with the ever-present risk of pirated copies; loss of shipments to real pirates; loss of copies due to fire, warfare, or plague; and inability to collect from distant booksellers.[15]

To diversify and moderate risk, early modern publishers relied heavily on credit and barter. They typically established mutual accounts and traded their imprints for books of other publishers, which they would then sell at retail through catalogs or at their own book stores. Publishers also frequently exchanged printed books for paper, the cost of paper comprising about half the cost of a printed book.[16] Hence, book fairs, particularly the Frankfurt book fair, where booksellers and printers were able to store their books in warehouses between one fair and the next, came to be an important pillar of the complex financing and barter arrangements that constituted the European book trade—for Yiddish and Hebrew books as well as non-Jewish books.[17] Although the credit and barter economy, helped publishers to moderate risk, it also

privileges by issuing editions containing minor abridgments, additions, alterations, or corrections to previously printed books and successfully passing them off as a "newly printed" book. Kostylo 2008d.

15. See Richardson 1999: 25–38; Baruchson 1990: 24.

16. The cost of paper did not substantially decline until the invention and deployment of mechanized papermaking in the nineteenth century. Weedon 2010: 105, 108–09.

17. Baumgarten 2009: ¶¶ 1–2 (Jewish books). The Frankfurt Book Fair has medieval origins, when manuscripts were traded as part of the general Frankfurt fair. The first record

tended to tie up their capital in large quantities of illiquid stock.[18] In Chapter 6, we further explore those market risks and complex financing arrangements through the lens of two leading Jewish publishers in late seventeenth-century Amsterdam.

Book publishing remains a risky business today, albeit not for all the same reasons as during the early decades of print. In an attempt to achieve greater certainty, today's trade book publishers often focus on books that are relatively sure bets: those by celebrities and previously bestselling authors. Early modern publishers similarly sought to reduce their investment risk by publishing editions of preprint classics and liturgical texts.

Late fifteenth- and early sixteenth-century publishers could also achieve cost savings—and thus reduce their exposure to financial loss—by copying the page layout of a book that had already been printed. But that did not apply to the first printing of a classic manuscript. Unlike today's trade publishing industry, in which public domain classics are considerably cheaper to print than are new works by popular authors commanding six- or seven-figure advances, early modern publishers often had to make virtually the same substantial capital investment in a first printing of a classical manuscript as in publishing a newly authored book. Again, the same applied to books of Jewish learning and liturgy.

Classic preprint works frequently suffered from corruption and textual drift as scribes hand-copied one manuscript from another over the years.[19] Largely as a result, ambitious publishers came to view an investment in editing, including hiring a respected, celebrated editor—or "corrector"—as a primary key to success.[20] Editions of classic works, which made up a sizable portion of scholarly books through the first half of the sixteenth century, typically featured a publisher's dedication and editor's introduction trumpeting the editor's arduous work and expertise in producing an accurate and complete instantiation of the original manuscript and in correcting the many errors found in any earlier print editions.[21] For publishers, the costs of retaining a top-notch editor, skillful compositor, and able pressmen, together with the expenses of type and high quality paper, had to be incurred for printing classic manuscript era texts no less than newly authored works.

Moreover, the publisher's costs for editing, correction, and paper would typically far exceed any payment to an author for his newly authored manuscript. Indeed, few authors received cash payments even if their work was printed. At most, authors were given several copies of the book, which they could either sell or give to potential patrons. Other than that, authors of learned books generally wrote only for prestige

of printed books being traded at the fair is in 1462. Weidhass 2007: 24–26 (origins of the Frankfurt Book Fair), 33 (noting that early modern markets also spawned book fairs in the European publishing centers of Lyons, Strasbourg, Basel, and Leipzig), 34–36, 40–43 (growing importance of the Frankfurt Book Fair in the European book trade).

18. Pettegree 2010: 72, 80–81; Maclean 2012: 176–85.

19. See Eisenstein 1983: 78–79.

20. See Grafton 2011; Richardson 1994: 7. The earliest correctors were handsomely paid, but as time went on, they earned less than skilled compositors and pressmen. Grafton 2011: 70–71, 213.

21. Richardson 1994: 3; Grafton 2011: 23–26.

and career enhancement. Authors who wished to earn a share of sales proceeds had to invest their own funds in publishing the book.[22]

Adding to the precariousness of their trade, early modern publishers had to determine in advance how many copies they would print—and a mistake in calculation could spell financial ruin.[23] Given its high cost, publishers often acquired paper only as needed for a given print run. Moreover, the high cost of type and the nature of early modern printing technology required that, once an individual sheet had been printed, the body of type used for those pages would be broken up before being washed and rearranged for the next sheet. A second printing of the book would thus require the same laborious process of resetting the type for each sheet, and, accordingly, in proofing and correcting, as did the first printing, even if there presumably would be some savings in having already determined how the text would be arranged on each page.[24] Further the market for books was difficult to judge in advance. For large folio editions, which typically involved runs of between 1,000 and 3,000 copies, publishers had to be prepared to take several years to distribute and sell out the edition.[25] Hence unlike today's offset printing, which enables publishers to print additional books as the market demands, early modern printing involved a single, significant upfront investment in a print run of predetermined size that would be recovered or not, over a period of half a decade or more. Each successive print run involved a significant new capital investment—and risk.

In light of those market conditions, instability and ruinous competition were typical of the printing industry of that era. In 1480, there were 151 printing houses in Venice; by 1500 only 10 remained.[26] Printing in Venice soon recovered and thrived. But by 1588, the Venetian Senate complained that only 70 printing houses remained of the 120 that had been in operation earlier that century, and by 1596 their numbers had diminished to 40.[27] Data from the Frankfurt book fair for German and foreign publishers' declarations of Latin books, the life blood of the upscale early modern book market, reveal a similar instability. They show a steady increase, decade by decade, from 4,000 during the period 1580 to 1589, to almost 10,000 during the period 1610 to 1619, followed by a dramatic decline to only some 4,500 during the decade 1630 to 1639.[28] The causes seem to have been a combination of religious intolerance, censorship, the Thirty Years' War, hyperinflation, plague, overproduction, and cutthroat competition.[29]

Given these many potential hazards, book privileges provided no guarantee that the publisher would recover his investment, any more than copyright protection guarantees

22. Pettegree 2010: 162–64.
23. Dondi 2010: 53, 57–58.
24. Richardson 1999: 26; Mosley 2010: 89, 97. The need to reset type continued until the invention and deployment of reliable means of stereotyping in the late eighteenth century. Banham 2007: 273, 279.
25. Pettegree 2010: 71; Hirsch 1967: 66–67.
26. Baruchson 1993: 28.
27. Baruchson 1993: 28.
28. Maclean 2012: 221. Data for the Leipzig book fair shows a similar pattern. See also Pettegree 2010.
29. Maclean 2012: 225–34.

that a book will be a commercial success today. But even if book privileges could not eliminate commercial risk, one might think that obtaining a book privilege would be a prerequisite for making the extraordinary and risky investment required to publish high quality books. After all, even with substantial consumer demand and under the best of overall market conditions, publishing a book would be a losing proposition without protection against ruinous piratical competition.

Yet, the vast majority of books printed during the early modern era did not receive a book privilege. Even in Venice, the capital of European book printing in the first quarter of the sixteenth century, book privileges were bestowed on only about 5 percent of all books printed during that period.[30] For the same period, the proportion of privileged books in Paris, another early sixteenth-century center of printing, was likewise about 5 percent.[31] The percentage of books receiving privileges seems to have increased somewhat over time, especially where printing was dominated by guilds. But even then, in mid-eighteenth century Venice only about 20 percent of books received a privilege. Similarly, privileged editions amounted to only about 1 percent of the estimated 300,000 books produced in the Netherlands between 1584 (when the States General first issued a privilege valid throughout the territory of the Dutch Republic) and 1795, a period during which Amsterdam was a leading center of European printing.[32] And, although we do not have precise figures, we know that many books were not entered into the Stationers' Register in London during the century preceding enactment of the Statute of Anne of 1710, even though registration provided perpetual exclusivity for the registered title.[33]

Given the persistent, ubiquitous threat of book piracy, why would so few books be awarded a privilege? The primary reason was that petitioning for a book privilege often cost an exorbitant amount of money and effort, relative to the risk of piracy and the privilege's likely effectiveness in preventing it. Applying for a privilege was also a lengthy process that could potentially delay publication.[34] In 1516, it reportedly cost Michael Hummelberg six ducats (the equivalent of approximately 15 percent of average annual income and about 20 percent the cost of a horse) to secure a five-year privilege from Pope Leo X for Froben's multi-volume edition of the works of St. Jerome.[35] In the Holy Roman Empire, the fee for obtaining an imperial book privilege by the mid-sixteenth century was usually 10 guilders, more than the monthly salary of a veteran soldier.[36] In the Dutch Republic in the seventeenth century, a privilege could

30. Borghi 2003: 6.
31. Armstrong 1990: 78.
32. Hoftijzer 1997: 13.
33. Johns 1998: 58–186.
34. On the cost and lengthy procedure involved in obtaining papal privileges, see J. Ginsburg 2013: 352.
35. Armstrong 1990: 13.
36. Hirsch 1967: 87. In 1521 a foot soldier's pay was fixed at four florin per month. Holborn 1982: 44. A veteran soldier could be paid twice this amount or eight florin per month (*doppelsöldner*). A florin was worth approximately the same as a guilder. There was considerable price inflation in early sixteenth-century German so it is difficult to compare prices across decades with any precision Holborn 1982: 50–57, 180. The word "guilder" is English for the German (and Dutch) "gulden."

easily cost some 50 guilders, twice the average monthly wage for a skilled worker.[37] In sixteenth-century France, as likely elsewhere, obtaining a privilege required considerable payments in addition to the official fees for drawing up the document and for the use of the royal seal. Supplicants also needed to pay perquisites to secretaries and clerks as well as a customary "gift" to the official who granted the privilege.[38]

In many locations, the privilege holder was also required to deposit a specified number of copies of the book with the authority that granted the privilege.[39] In 1710, Joseph I granted to Michael Gottschalk a privilege to print the Talmud and, as in the case of non-Jewish books, required that five copies of the entire multi-volume set be given to the Imperial Court.[40] For a high quality folio edition with a print run of just a couple thousand copies, the cost of such a deposit requirement would have been not insignificant.

As result of the considerable expense of obtaining a book privilege, privileges were sought only for high quality books—typically folio editions featuring expensive paper, numerous pages, top-notch type and editing, and fine illustrations—which were expected to be sufficiently successful in the market that they would be a target for piracy. For publishers of elaborate folio editions for which there was high market demand in the territory that the book privilege would cover, the costs of obtaining a privilege might well be worthwhile, especially as the ruler's stamp of approval could add prestige for a book as well as provide protection against reprinting.[41] The most successful up-market publishers typically had access to considerable capital, as well as broad familial and social connections that could serve to build relatively efficient, secure, and geographically wide distribution networks.[42] For them, printing could be highly profitable. Even a print run of 300 to 400 copies could eventually yield returns as high as 100 percent, if production and sale proceeded without a hitch.[43] For example, Luca

37. Hoftijzer 1967: 13.
38. Armstrong 1990: 27–28.
39. Maclean: 2012 159 (France), 165 (Geneva and Venice).
40. Popper 1899: 111–12. Similarly, an Imperial privilege granted in 1784 provided that the privilege holder "is obliged—on pain of forfeiture of this Imperial privilege—to deliver the usual five copies of the whole work to Our Imperial Court Council." Imperial Privilege for Aloysius Blumauer's Travesty of Virgil's "Aeneid," Vienna (1785), in *Primary Sources on Copyright (1450–1900)*. The deposit requirement seems to have been imperfectly complied with, at best. See Order of Christian II, Elector of Saxony, Whereby Booksellers Are to Be Earnestly Admonished to Send Copies of Privileged Books to the Superior Consistory, 18 August 1609, in Electoral Saxon Printing and Censorship Acts from 1549 to 1717, Leipzig (1724), in *Primary Sources on Copyright (1450–1900)* (complaining that privilege holders have been failing to deposit the required copies, and requiring that each bookseller and printer deliver a list of the books he has printed and of which books he has duly deposited copies). In 1569, Venice also required that two copies of any publication be deposited. Witcombe 2004: 62.
41. See Hirsch 1967: 83. As Don Quixote quipped: "Books that are printed with a royal license and with the approval of those officials to whom they are submitted, and read to widespread delight . . . by all persons of every rank and station; can they possibly be a lie?" Quoted in Johns 2009: 10.
42. Baruchson 1990: 29.
43. Richardson 1999: 40–41.

Antonio Giunti (1457–1538), a Venetian printer and leading publisher and exporter of Catholic liturgical texts, reportedly sold books in Krakow to the value of 1,000 ducats—many times the cost of a privilege—every year.[44]

However, that was not the case for cheaper, low quality "small books." For such books a privilege would be of little practical value and would require exorbitant expense in light of their expected profit, even in the unlikely event that the sovereign would issue a privilege for a book that did not present a special benefit or require an extraordinary investment. And small books made up the lion's share of books sold in early modern Europe. Indeed, by the eighteenth century, ephemeral small books, such as almanacs and calendars, were the most frequently printed item in Europe, even far surpassing Bibles, given that people needed to purchase them every year.[45] Not surprisingly, such publications were typically printed with minimal printer investment in paper quality and illustrations, and were rarely the subject of a book privilege.[46]

II. BOOK PRIVILEGES AND COPYRIGHT COMPARED

Copyright law differs from book privileges in justification, legal foundation, and practical import, and, indeed, has become increasingly distinct from its forerunner as time has gone on. We survey those differences here, and return in succeeding chapters to compare and contrast rabbinic reprinting bans with both book privileges and secular copyright law.

First, copyright law vests rights initially in authors of newly created works, whereas book privileges were typically granted directly to publishers, not authors.[47] (Papal privileges might have been an exception; in the latter half of the sixteenth century, the Holy See granted many privileges to artists in their prints and to writers who were Jesuit clerics.)[48] Indeed, even when book privileges were granted to authors, their explicit focus, like the privilege that Venice granted to Sabellico, was on providing a means for a favored author to attract a suitable printer. The privilege was premised on the assumption that the author would transfer the privilege to the printer for a lump sum payment or, more often, in return for a specified number of copies of the book.[49]

44. Pettegree 2010: 259.

45. Carlebach 2011: 33–34.

46. One possible exception was the blanket 10-year privilege that Antwerp printer, Claes de Greve received from the Council of Brabant in 1512 for any work that he should be the first to print in the Duchy of Brabant following the piracy of his Almanac. Armstrong 1990: 16.

47. Pettegree 2010: 163–64. Of the 352 book privileges granted by the Holy Roman Emperor between 1511 and 1699, approximately one-fourth were awarded to authors, editors, compilers and translators, and the remainder were granted to printers, book sellers, publishers, religious orders, and bookbinders. Kawohl 2008d.

48. J. Ginsburg 2013: 353–55.

49. See Pfister 2010: 115, 122–23 Chartier 1994: 47–48; Birn 1971: 137 (royalty arrangements were apparently unknown in Ancien Regime France, and even if the author

Granted, the advent of modern copyright statutes in the eighteenth century did not herald a dramatic improvement in authors' market position. Authors still typically sold their rights to publishers for a lump sum. But from their inception, copyright statutes explicitly trumpeted the author as the primary juridical repository of the exclusive right to print books. For example, the U.K. Statute of Anne of 1710 provided that "the author of any book or books . . . that shall hereafter be composed, and his assignee, or assigns, shall have the sole liberty of printing and reprinting such book and books for the term of fourteen years" and "that after the expiration of the said term of fourteen years, the sole right of printing or disposing of copies shall return to the authors thereof, if they are then living, for another term of fourteen years."[50] Likewise, the French Literary and Artistic Property Act of 1793 provided that "[a]uthors of writings of any kind . . . shall throughout their entire life enjoy the exclusive right to sell, authorize for sale and distribute their works in the territory of the Republic, and to transfer that property in full or in part."[51] Even if these statutes' nominal elevation of authors over publishers initially had only limited practical import for authors, over time copyright law came to be understood increasingly as a regime for the protection of authors' economic and personal rights to control the public communication of their creative expression.

Second, copyright law vests rights in authors as a matter of blanket entitlement, applicable to all authors as a class. In contrast, book privileges were a special dispensation provided upon request to a favored subject on an ad hoc, case-by-case basis. Like publishers, authors enjoyed no statutory or other legal entitlement to obtain a book privilege. Authors and publishers did not apply, but rather supplicated, for a privilege.[52] And when an author was awarded a privilege, he could try to enforce his right only on the grounds that he was the privilege holder, not because he was the book's author per se.

Finally, by according exclusive rights to authors in newly composed works for only a limited period of time, the early copyright statutes established a public domain of books for which copyright protection had expired and which anyone was free to print. Book privileges, in contrast, were often awarded for printings of classic and even ancient manuscripts. Indeed, despite the Venice decree of 1517 purporting to allow privileges only for books that had never been printed before, book privileges were often bestowed upon reprintings of previously printed books or new editions with exceedingly minor alterations or abridgments. In addition, although book privileges were initially limited in duration to a term of years, they came to be perpetual or indefinitely renewable in many locations, particularly where a printers' guild held a legally sanctioned printing monopoly and divvied up titles among its members.

These doctrinal differences between book privileges and copyright law reflected fundamentally distinct jurisprudential foundations. Copyright law accentuated the

and publisher did agree to share profits, it is likely that the Paris printers' guild would have rendered the agreement void).

50. An Act for the Encouragement of Learning, by Vesting the Copies of Printed Books in the Authors or Purchasers of such Copies, During the Times therein Mentioned, 1710, 8 Anne, c.19.

51. French Literary and Artistic Property Act, Paris (1793), in *Primary Sources on Copyright (1450–1900)*.

52. See Biagoli 2006: 147 (discussing privileges for authors and inventors).

societal importance of authors and original expression, and came to be understood through the lens of eighteenth- and nineteenth-century theories of self-expressive individualism, republican liberty, private property as a linchpin of individual autonomy, progress through learning, and the Romantic conception of an author as a fount of creative imagination and personality. Book privileges, on the other hand, largely predated those post-Enlightenment understandings. They were, instead, akin to the patents and monopolies that early modern authorities issued for mechanical inventions, newly imported crafts, and other types of trade, such as selling salt, that promised to benefit the local commonwealth.[53] Book privileges were instruments for mercantilist protectionism, for kings to dispense favors, for awarding monopolies to printers' and booksellers' guilds, and for securing local printers' economic investment; they did not serve as a regime designed to promote individuals' self-expression, protect authors' personal and property rights in their intellectual creations, or enable writers to earn a living from their craft. Like other privileges, their origins lay in canon and Roman law, pursuant to which the Church or sovereign enjoyed the prerogative of granting an individual an advantage in derogation of the law generally applicable to the community, so long as others were not unfairly harmed. Within those parameters, privileges could be awarded for a variety of reasons, including as a gratuitous favor, in recognition of some extraordinary merit, in gratitude for the performance of some special service, or in consideration of a monetary payment.[54]

As we shall soon see, the privileges sometimes give reasons for why the author or publisher is deserving of the privilege, and sometimes underscore the social value of the book that is the subject of the privilege. But even so, they were understood to be a "special grace" bestowed by the king or other sovereign to reward someone for making a considerable investment and, in so doing, providing a particular utility to the common good. As such, book privileges were, not a form of legal recognition of any natural, moral, or subjective right.[55] During the eighteenth-century "Battle of the Booksellers," London publishers sought to reassert their hold on the British book trade against provincial upstarts by claiming that they held perpetual copyrights under English common law. Since time immemorial, the London publishers argued, authors have enjoyed a right of literary property grounded in universally recognized precepts of natural justice. In response, Lord Dreghorn, lead counsel for a Scottish publisher who had been sued for infringing such a common law copyright, scornfully—and accurately—observed: "[S]tood these Privileges all over Europe, it never having been once dreamed, that they were granted *ex justicia* [i.e., as an obligation of justice] in Virtue of a *perfect* Right [i.e., a right that must be honored under natural law], but [were rather] indulged from favour, and a View to public Expediency."[56]

53. Kostylo 2010: 21; Borghi 2003.

54. Mackeldey 1883: 164–65; McCormack 1997: 152. Canon lawyers have struggled with whether privileges constitute a form of "private law" or are rather extralegal favors. McCormack 1997: 69–80.

55. See Pfister 2005: 117; Borghi 2010: 137, 140–41.

56. John MacLaurin, Considerations on the Nature and Origin of Literary Property, quoted in Deazley 2004: 153. John Maclaurin, later Lord Dreghorn, was counsel for the

III. THE SCHLICK PRIVILEGE OF 1511

Arnolt Schlick (c. 1450–1460—after 1521) was a celebrated blind organist in the court of the Elector Palatine of the Rhine at Heidelberg, one of the larger and wealthier principalities in the Holy Roman Empire.[57] As such, he achieved acclaim throughout the Empire as a performer and expert in organ construction. Indeed, Schlick played the organ at the election of Maximilian I as King of the Romans in 1486. In the early sixteenth century, Schlick authored *The Mirror for Organ Builders*, the first German language treatise on building and playing organs. His book came to be a seminal work in that field.[58]

In 1511, Emperor Maximilian I awarded Schlick a 10-year privilege for his organ treatise, as well as for a book of organ music tablature. The privilege, which Schlick reprinted in full at the beginning of his treatise, was undersigned by Zyprian Northeim von Serntein, one of Maximilian's chancellors. It is likely that Schlick had petitioned von Serntein or another official whom Maximilian had authorized to grant book privileges on his behalf, although it is possible that Maximilian, who famously championed the arts and sciences, was personally acquainted with Schlick or knew of the organist by reputation.[59] It might also be that Ludwig V, who had recently succeeded his father, Philip the Upright, as Elector Palatine, interceded on behalf of his court musician.[60] In any event, the privilege conferred upon Schlick in the name of Emperor Maximilian I presents a vivid illustration of the style, form, and content of book privileges awarded in Central Europe through the eighteenth century:[61]

> We, Maximilian, by the Grace of God elected Roman Emperor, at all times Augmenter of the Empire in Germany, Hungary, Dalmatia, Croatia etc., King and Archduke of Austria, Duke of Burgundy, Brabant, Elector Palatine etc. send Our grace and best

Scottish bookseller Alexander Donaldson, whose defense against a lawsuit claiming that he was infringing copyrights under common law led to a ruling of the House of Lords that the Statute of Anne had preempted any such common law right. *Ex justicia*, an abbreviated form of *Ex debito justitiae*, literally means "as of right," in contrast to "as of grace."

57. Schlick served under the successive Counts, Philip "the Upright" (1448–1508) and Louis V (1478–1544). See generally Keyl 1989.

58. Kawohl 2008c; Elson 1912: 10.593.

59. Kawohl 2008c.

60. Following Philip the Upright's opposition to Maximilian in the War of the Bavarian Succession, Maximilian had revoked various privileges that had been previously granted to the Elector Palatine. In 1509, Maximilian refused to restore those privileges. But Ludvig V successfully worked to regain the Emperor's favor, so it is possible that by 1511, a petition by Ludvig V on Schlick's behalf might have assisted the organist in obtaining his book privilege. Keyl 1989: 17, 123 n. 44.

61. The unabridged English translation of the Schlick privilege, which is by Luis A. Sundkvist, can be found at Imperial Privilege for Arnolt Schlick, Speyer (1511), in *Primary Sources on Copyright (1450–1900)*. It is reproduced here, with some editing, by permission. On the Schlick privilege's similarity with book privileges issued by the Habsburg monarchy in the late eighteenth century, see Kawohl 2008a; Imperial Privilege for Aloysius Blumauer's Travesty of Virgil's "Aeneid," Vienna (1785), in *Primary Sources on Copyright (1450–1900)*.

wishes to all Electors, princes, spiritual and worldly prelates, counts, barons, lords, knights, knaves, captains, bailiffs, reeves, stewards, curators, administrators, officials, village and town mayors, magistrates, judges, councillors, townsmen, book printers, booksellers, municipalities, and all other of Our and the Empire's subjects and loyal followers—in whatever rank, estate or condition they may happen to be when they come across this letter or have it announced to them . . . .

Our and the Empire's beloved and faithful Master Arnolt Schlick, organist in Heidelberg, has brought to our knowledge how—on the frequently expressed request and wish of Philip, the late Elector Palatine, as well as of other spiritual and temporal princes—he has, with assiduous diligence, gathered together into a booklet various rules, principles, and instructions as to how to construct and mount a well-arranged mechanism of pipes etc. which is useful both for [accompanying] choral singing and for the organists [as such]. This booklet he is willing to put into print—first and foremost for the praise and glory of God—but also to promote the common good by revealing in this book how one can avoid the significant expenses which have hitherto been laid out on the works of an organ due to their instability.

And so as to find the more easily a skillful printer, who would agree to print his manuscript with a sharp and legible type, as well as to gain some reward for his labor and sorrow from the book's sale, he has humbly appealed to and requested Us to graciously provide him with Our Imperial privilege, to the effect that for the next ten years from the date of this Our letter, no one may reprint the aforementioned booklet—into which he has set his work—without his knowledge and consent; and the same applies to another work: "Tablature and such like: an aid for playing the organ and diverse stringed instruments," that he intends to write and publish in the near future.

This request We are willing to grant, in view of the aforesaid reasons, and for the sake, above all, of promoting the common good. And, thus, We advise you all, earnestly bid each one of you, and wish: that you firmly protect the said organist Arnolt Schlick in this grace and privilege which he has received from Us; and do not permit the first mentioned work and booklet—as well as the other work included above to be reprinted by anyone during the specified period without his knowledge, consent, or permission; or, if these works are [re]printed in French, Italian, or other lands outside of your realms and jurisdiction, that you do not allow these [copies] to be sold under any circumstances and that you yourself do not do anything of the sort. But, rather, that, on receiving any instruction or request [to this effect] from the said Master Arnolt Schlick—or the printer whom he has chosen to engage for this—you have these [copies] confiscated everywhere and forbid anyone from buying them; and that you act in such a way so as to avoid other measures having to be taken to ensure the application of this Our privilege. If you do all this, you will be fulfilling Our earnest intention.

Issued in Our and the Empire's City of Strasbourg, on the third day of the month April, 1511 AD; in the 26th year of Our Reign in the Roman Empire, and the 21st year of Our Reign in Hungary.

At the personal behest of the Emperor, at His court.

IV. GROUNDS FOR GRANTING PRIVILEGES

The character of book privileges as ad hoc, discretionary grants is apparent on the face of the Imperial decree, pronouncing a "grace and privilege" that the Emperor bestowed, at his "personal behest," as a special favor to a "beloved and faithful" subject. Indeed, as Elizabeth Armstrong discusses in her study of early modern book privileges in France, given that royal privileges were, in principle, a personal favor from the king, it was even uncertain whether a privilege granted by one monarch would remain in force under his successor.[62] Privileges issued by republican institutions, running from the Venetian Senate to eighteenth-century American colonial legislatures, were presumably the subject of collective deliberation.[63] But there, too, privileges were dispensed on a case-by-case basis at the sovereign's volition, not as a matter of universally applicable legal entitlement.

Yet, although sovereigns were under no legal obligation to award a book privilege to any particular supplicant, early modern jurisprudence dictated that when they did award a privilege, they could not do so entirely arbitrarily. Awarding a privilege required some implicit or explicit justification beyond mere personal whim or the bare receipt of payment in return for the privilege. In a provision that came to be a cornerstone of medieval and early modern jurisprudence in this area, the Theodosian and Justinian Codes forbade rulers from granting one person a privilege in derogation from generally applicable law when doing so would cause harm to another.[64] (As we shall see, rabbinic jurists debated whether rabbinic reprinting bans violated a similar injunction in Jewish law, which purports to invalidate rabbinic edicts that benefit one person while harming another.) At least on the surface, exclusive book privileges violated that prohibition against favoritism. Decrees that forbade everyone but the privilege holder from printing a given book were widely understood to constitute an exception from the default legal principle that individuals enjoy an unhindered right to engage in a given trade, and in particular to print books, so long as any licensing and guild requirements were met.[65] As such, book privileges required at least the implicit justification that the privilege was a reward for the supplicant's extraordinary personal sacrifice, investment, and/or authorial or editorial contribution, and

62. Armstrong 1990: 3; see also Imperial Privilege for Eucharius Rösslin, Strasbourg (1513), in *Primary Sources on Copyright (1450–1900)* (explicitly referring to the privilege as a "special favor"). Likewise, papal privileges generally recited that they were granted upon supplication and out of "apostolic benevolence." See, e.g., Bernardo Giunti's Privilege for Machiavelli's works, Vatican (1531), in *Primary Sources on Copyright (1450–1900)*.

63. On printing privileges issued in the American colonies, see Bracha 2008.

64. Pennington 2000: 255–74. See also Pütter: The Reprinting of Books, Gottinggen (1774), in *Primary Sources on Copyright (1450–1900)* (positing on that basis that all Imperial privileges tacitly presuppose the clause "without detriment to the right of a third party").

65. Pfister 2010: 117–18 (noting that in France, the privileges constituted an exception to the so-called *liberté publique de l'imprimerie*); Borghi 2003: 5 (stating that a "privilege is not just outside the law, it is an explicit *exception* to the law in favour of an individual or category of individuals").

that awarding the privilege benefitted the realm as a whole, not just the supplicant and the sovereign.[66]

It is unclear to what extent, if any, these jurisprudential strictures truly constrained sovereigns in awarding particular privileges, as opposed to being merely a formulaic recitation of justifications for the privilege. Yet, even if rulers could sometimes get away with simply dispensing personal favors, they nevertheless had to justify their grants of book privileges vis-à-vis rival, overlapping authorities that might assert their own, competing prerogative to grant privileges or regulate the book trade in that location. The fact that Maximilian I addressed the Schlick privilege to a lengthy list of officials and firmly requested that they protect Schlick in this grace and privilege was not merely a stylistic convention. The Holy Roman Emperor relied on principalities and Imperial Free Cities within his realm to enforce his privileges, and over time these authorities asserted their own, independent power to regulate the book trade.[67]

In France, similarly, privileges were issued by the Royal Chancery, Prevot of Paris, Parlement de Paris, provisional parlements, and the University of Paris.[68] In 1566, the Crown instituted an obligatory royal privilege, which combined commercial protection with a requirement that publishers obtain a royal license for each book they published. But France's provincial parlements often refused to ratify royal privileges and generally until the last quarter of the seventeenth century insisted upon maintaining their own prerogative to issue provincial privileges.[69] Likewise, as discussed below, secular sovereigns chafed at proclamations by the Holy See that papal book privileges were to be enforced throughout Christendom. Hence although popes and monarchs had inherent authority to issue book privileges within their realm, they not infrequently had to appeal to competing, nominally subordinate, or regional officials to recognize and enforce the privileges they issued—and such appeals met with varying degrees of success.

In sum, supplicants faced a dual obstacle in successfully petitioning for a book privilege. First, sovereign powers were under no legal obligation to accede to a supplicant's petition for a book privilege. Second, the sovereign faced jurisprudential constraints and practical limitations on enforcement if it did wish to grant a privilege.

Given those strictures, supplicants typically presented substantive arguments, beyond merely requesting a personal favor, for why they personally warranted a special privilege, and why it would be justified to deprive others of the right to print the book for the period of the privilege. In response, sovereigns often set out their policy justifications for granting the privilege in the text of the privilege itself. As recited

66. See J. Ginsburg 2013: 367–76 (describing the justifications set out in papal privileges).
67. In the Holy Roman Empire, the local authorities were initially understood to have an obligation to assist the Emperor in supervising the printing of books. But as time went on, the local authorities increasingly exercised this supervision as their own, independent right. Kawohl 2008a.
68. Armstrong 1990: 21–58.
69. Mellot 2007: 42, 47–48.

in Schlick's privilege, in his petition the organist had highlighted the usefulness of his book, in particular by advising the Church and monastery authorities how to arrange organ pipes, assess the quality of organ construction, and avoid expenditures on repairs of organs that are not well constructed or adequately maintained. Schlick had also underscored the skill, care, and labor he had expended in producing his book. He had asserted, in addition, that he produced the book upon the request of important people: "Philip, the late Count Palatine, as well as of other spiritual and temporal princes." Finally, Schlick apparently made the case that a privilege would enable him to find a printer capable and willing to print a high quality book, one with "a sharp and legible type," and thus "to gain some reward for his labor and sorrow [i.e., the time and effort he devoted to creating the book] from the book's sale." Maximilian, in turn, states that he is granting the requested privilege "in view of the aforesaid reasons, and for the sake, above all, of promoting the common good."

The grounds cited in the Schlick privilege are typical of book privileges across jurisdictions. The privileges and supplications made to obtain them contain repeated references to the book's merit, utility, and quality of print; the considerable time, labor, and money expended in production; the cost of obtaining the manuscript (when the supplicant is not its author); the interest or support of an important person; and the author's or editor's skill in composing or editing the work. Of course, they also commonly assert that the supplicant would face the loss of his investment and even financial ruin unless accorded an exclusive privilege to print and sell the book.[70] Indeed, a number of supplications in Venice deplored the ruinous cutthroat competition of unscrupulous publishers who reprint works that another has edited and sell the pirated edition at a low price, with the result, and sometimes the intention, of driving the supplicant to financial ruin.[71] (We encounter similar arguments in the Jewish copyright context in Chapter 4.) These grounds, I repeat, served only to justify granting a privilege in derogation of generally applicable law; they did not, until much later, undergird any claim that all authors or publishers are entitled to exclusive printing rights as a matter of natural justice.

V. SCOPE OF PROTECTION AND TERRITORIAL LIMITATIONS

The conduct prohibited by the Schlick privilege is illustrative of the extent of book privileges' scope. The privilege forbids the reprinting of Schlick's books without Schlick's permission, as well as the purchase of illicit reprints, during the 10-year period of the privilege. It also directs that no reprints produced in Italy, France, or elsewhere outside the Holy Roman Empire may be sold within the realm. That reference

70. See Witcombe 2004: 27–40 (Venice); Armstrong 1990: 78–91 (France). In addition, papal privileges often stated that they served to "reward the care the author or printer have taken to ensure the work's accuracy (and conformity to Church doctrine)." J. Ginsburg 2013: 367.

71. See Witcombe 2004: 35–37.

to foreign reprints might have also effectively placed translations of Schlick's books, not just German language reprints, within his exclusive privilege.[72] By the eighteenth century, privileges forbade printing extracts and enlarged or abridged editions as well.[73]

The practice of forbidding unauthorized imports as well as domestic reprinting began with the printing monopoly that Venice granted to Johann von Speyer in 1469 and became a standard feature of book privileges.[74] Although seemingly a far-reaching grant of exclusivity, the prohibition of unauthorized imports actually highlights a central weakness in the book privilege regime: the privilege was only effective within the territory of the sovereign authority that issued it. Emperor Maximilian could prohibit reprinting, importing, and selling Schlick's books without Schlick's permission *within Maximilian's realm*. The Emperor could also prohibit his own subjects from participating in the reprinting of Schlick's books in foreign countries. But if Schlick wanted a privilege that would also apply in France, Spain, Venice, Milan, Rome, and Naples, he would have had to petition separately in each of those jurisdictions, a time-consuming, uncertain, and costly proposition.[75]

Alternatively, or in addition, Schlick could have petitioned the Holy See for a papal privilege. From around 1515 on, papal privileges were regularly issued for books printed outside of Rome, and those privileges proclaimed their effectiveness throughout the Christian world, backed by the threat of excommunication as well as fines.[76] But following the Reformation, papal privileges were of no weight in Protestant lands. And even elsewhere, secular governments, notably that of Venice, staunchly resisted the Holy See's assumption of the right to grant privileges for territories outside the Papal States.[77] For that reason, sixteenth-century Italian printers who sought to print or sell their books in the Republic typically sought a Venetian privilege in addition to a privilege issued by the Holy See.[78]

72. But see Kawohl 2008e (stating that an Imperial privilege containing a very similar provision issued two years later was the first to prohibit translations).

73. See, e.g., Imperial Privilege for Aloysius Blumauer's Travesty of Virgil's "Aeneid," Vienna (1785), in *Primary Sources on Copyright (1450–1900)*.

74. See Putnam 1897: 347 (discussing Venetian book privileges).

75. Supplicants for privileges in Venice sometimes underscored that they lived and worked in the Republic and that the book would be printed in Venice. However, soon after 1517, the Venetian government began to grant privileges for books printed elsewhere as well, primarily so that foreign printers would not hesitate to have their books sold in the Republic. See Witcombe 2004: 39, 42–43. In addition, sixteenth-century Italian printers not uncommonly acquired privileges from the kings of France and Spain and the Holy Roman Emperor. Witcombe 2004: 329–30.

76. Witcombe 2004: 43, 49–50.

77. Indeed, after the Holy See granted Roman printers an exclusive privilege to print the new liturgical books brought in by the Council of Trent, Venice reacted by issuing on June 14, 1596, a decree declaring all papal privileges to be null and void in the Republic. Maclean 2012: 152. See also Putnam 1897: 355, 379 (discussing opposition of Venice).

78. Witcombe 2004: 43–44.

The territorial limitation of book privileges presented a sharp and troublesome contrast with the broad, international reach of much of the book trade. Commercially successful early modern publishers, typically centered in established trading cities, relied on a pan-European readership to purchase their titles, which remained largely in Latin well into the seventeenth century.[79] Yet, a Venetian privilege would only prohibit reprinting in the Republic of Venice and its overseas territories. It would not give the publisher exclusivity in other likely markets for the book, such as Spain, the German states, France, Poland, and the Low Countries. Indeed, the Venetian privilege would be of no help to the publisher in preventing a competitor from reprinting the book even in a neighboring Italian city-state and then selling the reprint in foreign countries and elsewhere on the Italian peninsula outside of Venice. The same was true for publishers who received privileges from any of the numerous small city-states, provinces, and principalities in the Netherlands or Germany (where the Holy Roman Emperor's authority to supervise books declined together with the disintegration of the Empire, beginning with the Peace of Augsburg in 1555). In those locations, a competitor's neighboring printing town could well fall within a separate jurisdiction.[80]

Nor was book piracy an isolated occurrence. The eighteenth and early nineteenth centuries saw flourishing reprint industries, in southern German states, Austria, Switzerland, Ireland, and the Low Countries.[81] In those territories, reprint publishers operated with the blessing and support of their local sovereign authorities. Typically, indeed, pirate editions would even be protected by a local privilege against imports of the original.[82]

Although leading authors complained bitterly about these practices, the reprinting of a book outside the jurisdiction of its initial publication was widely regarded as perfectly legitimate; and reprints often found their way through clandestine channels of trade back into the author's home country.[83] Early copyright laws, which typically accorded protection only to domestic authors, did nothing to alter this state of affairs. With a couple of exceptions, it was not until the advent of bilateral and multilateral copyright treaties in the mid- and late-nineteenth century that European countries accorded full protection within their borders to works of foreign origin.

79. Pettegree 2010: 33, 36, 52, 65. Out of the roughly 29,000 titles printed in the fifteenth century of which we have a record, 72 percent were in Latin, 10 percent in German, 8 percent in Italian, and 5 percent in French. The 154 Hebrew incunabula made up less than 1 percent of the total. See Dondi 2010: 53, 56. In 1650, 71 percent of the books in the catalogs of the Leipzig book fair, the leading international book fair of the day, were in Latin. Even as late as 1740, just over a quarter of the books in the Leipzig catalogs were in Latin. Flood 2010: 223–25.

80. Pettegree 2010: 74. Not infrequently, moreover, there was an absence of central book trade regulating authority even within a given territory, with various royal and municipal officials, universities, ecclesiastical authorities, and specific religious orders each issuing book privileges with uncertain force outside the issuing body's sphere of influence. Pettegree 2010: 74. On the decline of the Holy Roman Emperor's authority over books, see Kawohl 2008d.

81. Johns 2009: 13; Flood 2010: 230–31.

82. See Vliet 2007: 254.

83. See Johns 1998: 168–71; Feather 1984: 410–11.

VI. DURATION AND NOVELTY

The Schlick privilege covered two newly authored books and remained in effect for 10 years. That 10-year period was common for privileges issued in Venice and the Holy See during the first quarter of the sixteenth century; yet, it did not become the standard term in the Holy Roman Empire until the second half of the sixteenth century. Most Imperial book privileges during the early sixteenth century were from three to five years, although we see a steady trend toward longer terms as the century progressed.[84] French book privileges issued during the first half of the sixteenth century were typically for an even shorter period: most commonly two or three years and only occasionally as long as 10 years.[85]

The reasons for the variations in duration, both within and across jurisdictions, are unclear.[86] However, it appears that the book privileges were typically designed to enable the privilege holder to recover his investment only in the first printing of the book, not any subsequent edition. Although a print run of high quality books could take several years to sell, publishers' business models typically required that they dispose of a significant share of the run at the first book fair following publication.[87] Hence, early modern authorities apparently estimated that a privilege lasting a few years would provide adequate time for the privilege holder to earn a sufficient profit by selling most, if not all, of the initial print run. Any subsequent print run would have required a substantially new capital investment, and would not have been regarded as part of the original enterprise for which the supplicant sought a privilege.

In addition, a number of jurisdictions followed Venice's example of issuing privileges only for books that had not previously been printed.[88] At least through the early sixteenth century, moreover, book privileges were renewed only if war or other external circumstances had made it impossible to sell the initial print run.[89] In that era, therefore, a title could be subject to an exclusive privilege for only a few years, following which anyone would be free to reprint the book.

Over time, however, book privileges came to be issued increasingly for books that had already been printed and came to last for steadily longer time periods. In some countries, indeed, privileges became effectively perpetual. In 1625, the

84. Kawohl 2008k.

85. See Armstrong 1990: 118–24.

86. See Witcombe 2004: 29 ("As far as can be determined, there was no obvious correlation between the duration of the *privilegio* and the item for which it was granted."); but see Borghi 2010: 145 (asserting that Venetian authorities usually issued a longer privilege to books requiring an exceptional investment, such as dictionaries, illustrated books, and editions of classics).

87. Pettegree 2010: 80.

88. In France, for example, privileges were rarely granted for books that had already been printed, the exceptions being those that had been printed abroad and were not readily available in France. Armstrong 1990: 92–95.

89. Witcombe 2004: 33.

Elector of Saxony deemed it necessary to proclaim that a privilege for a book should *not* be understood to last in perpetuity.[90] But he did so to retain the prerogative to grant multiple, succeeding privileges for editions of the Bible to competing supplicants; throughout the German states, it was common practice for local rulers to grant—and renew—privileges for classic works and other already printed titles. In France as well, by the 1630s, royal book privileges for favored Parisian printers were regularly renewed as a matter of course, and were often awarded anew for works in the public domain.[91] France's system of de facto perpetual privileges was not terminated until 1777, when a series of royal decrees sought to break the monopoly control of the Paris printers' guild, which had come to view perpetual privileges as their right. The decrees provided that printers would henceforth enjoy royal book privileges that lasted only for 10 years or until the death of the author, whichever was later. Further, privileges could be renewed only for a new edition containing at least one-fourth new material.[92]

Venice followed a similar, if more complex, trajectory. By its decree of May 11, 1603, the Senate codified a three-tier privilege regime easing the strictures of its 1517 decree that only newly printed books would receive a privilege. Under that new regime, privileges could be granted for a period of 20 years for books never printed before anywhere; 10 years for books lacking such absolute novelty but which were never printed before in Venice and other books of great value that had been out of print for at least 20 years; and 5 years for books of great value that had been out of print for at least 10 years. This meant that, in practice, only books that were not of "great value" and had previously been printed in Venice were permanently ineligible for any privilege.[93] Moreover, just as they had under the 1517 regime, publishers were often able to evade this restraint by issuing a "new edition" containing only minor changes from a previous one. It was not until 1753 that Venice put into place an examination procedure to assess "the worth of supplements and additions" to previously printed titles.[94] In 1767, the Senate further lengthened the term of book privileges, providing Venetian publishers with a standard 30-year term for newly printed books.[95] Then, in 1780, citing a crisis in the Venetian publishing industry due to a purported excess of cheap reprints that "fatten the bookstalls of colporteurs, unlicensed, and unregistered sellers," the Venetian Guild of Printers and Booksellers successfully lobbied for a law that effectively established perpetual book privileges by enabling the original privilege holder to renew his privilege

90. Electoral Saxon Printing and Censorship Acts from 1549 to 1717, Leipzig (1724), in *Primary Sources on Copyright (1450–1900)*.

91. Armstrong 1990: 207; Birn 1970–1971: 137; Hesse 1990: 112; Mellot 2007: 48–55, 62–65.

92. Birn 1970–1971: 131–32; Pfister 2010: 134. Authors were given perpetual privileges so long as the work remained unpublished.

93. Borghi 2010: 147–48.

94. Borghi 2010: 147.

95. By comparison, the standard term of privilege issued by States of Holland in the eighteenth century was 15 years, with the option of an extension. Hoftijzer 1997: 13.

indefinitely.[96] Finally, in 1789, the Venetian authorities issued a report concluding that perpetual privileges cause more harm than good for the publishing industry. The Senate re-established the previous three-tier system soon thereafter. That regime, too, was short-lived; in 1797 Venice fell to the army of Napoleon and the Greater Council declared the end of the Republic.

VII. AUTHORS

In one important respect, the Schlick privilege is something of an anomaly. Unlike the vast majority of book privileges (with the possible exception of papal privileges), it was awarded to an author, not a publisher. As such, what, if anything, might be gleaned from the Schlick privilege about the place of authors in the early modern book trade?

Most important, the privilege entitled Schlick, the author, to prevent publishers from printing his manuscript without permission. That entitlement was by no means a certainty in early modern Europe. Ancient precedent stemming back to the manuscript era posited that a person's possession of a manuscript carried with it the right to make copies of the manuscript ad libitum, at the possessor's pleasure, without any legal requirement of asking the author's permission.[97] That legal precept reigned throughout Europe through much of the first half of the sixteenth century. Accordingly, publishers were in the habit of printing any manuscript they were able to obtain, even when in direct opposition to the wishes of the author.

Hence, like Schlick, an author who wished to prevent unauthorized printing by a publisher in possession of the author's manuscript would have to obtain a book privilege from the sovereign. The legal right of authors to control the printing of their work did not receive recognition until the Venetian Council of Ten issued a decree in 1545 that forbade printing or selling a book without the consent of its author.[98] The Venice decree did not aim primarily to recognize authors' rights to print their manuscripts. Its purpose, rather, was to limit publishers' abuse of the book privilege regime by preventing them from competing for a privilege for the same title, especially when only one of the publishers had paid the author to obtain the manuscript. Nonetheless, as an incidental by-product, the Venice decree did fashion an embryonic right of authors to their work.

96. Borghi 2010: 151–53. For an English translation of the Guild petition and resulting law, as well as of the unsuccessful lawsuit challenging the law, see "Pezzana e Consorti" Case: Supporting Documents, Venice (1780), in *Primary Sources on Copyright (1450–1900)*.
97. Putnam 1897: 408.
98. Venetian Decree on Author-Printer Relations, Venice (1545), in *Primary Sources on Copyright (1450–1900)*. See also Kostylo 2008c. Similarly in France, by 1554, privileges issued by royal chancery typically stated that a wrong was committed against the author by unauthorized and erroneous printings of his work, and that the author was naturally the best person to oversee the printing. Armstrong 1990: 83–84.

Schlick's privilege provides a good indication of why the author sought to control the printing of his manuscripts. The celebrated organist, it states, petitioned for a privilege in order "to find the more easily a skillful printer, who would agree to print his manuscript with a sharp and legible type, as well as to gain some reward for his labour and sorrow from the book's sale." First and foremost, then, Schlick apparently sought to have his manuscript printed and distributed by a reputable, high quality publisher. Schlick would likely have shared a concern common among early modern authors: that the publisher would produce a shoddy book made of poor quality paper, marred by illegible print, and full of printing errors. Correctors were also notorious for altering manuscripts to reflect their own judgment about style and content without consulting the author. Thus in 1526, the Venetian physician Alvise Cinzio de' Fabrizi requested a privilege so that his book on the origin of proverbs should not be "perverted, corrupted and torn to pieces" by derelict publishers, "because no literate person can look at, let alone read, any of the works they bring out."[99] Around the same time, Martin Luther complained of publishers, "[t]here are many now busying themselves with the spoiling of books through misprinting them."[100] It was not until the second half of the sixteenth century that correctors came generally to desist from radically rewriting authors' texts and inserting their own materials into them.[101] But it remained a vital interest for authors of scholarly books—and far from a certain proposition—to find a publisher who would invest in a high quality publication.

Schlick's privilege identifies, as an additional motivation for the author's petition, his desire "to gain some reward for his labor and sorrow from the book's sale." As previously noted, early authors typically received no payment for their manuscript. If Schlick actually expected to receive a lump-sum payment or royalties from the book's sale, he would have been an exception to that general rule. It is more likely, therefore, that, in addition to authoring his organ manual, Schlick contributed substantially to the cost of its printing. Early modern authors would generally receive a share of the proceeds from a book's sales only if they had financed or had some financial stake in its publication, not by virtue of their status as authors per se.[102]

Although we have no specific information regarding Schlick's financial stake, Schlick apparently had the means to finance his organ manual's publication. When he petitioned for his book privilege, he was the highest-paid musician at the court of Elector Palatine, with a salary almost twice that of the next-highest-paid musician, and comparable to the salary of the court treasurer.[103] He was also retained, and paid handsomely, for giving advice about the purchase, construction, and maintenance of organs.[104]

99. Quoted in Kostylo 2008c.
100. Putnam 1897: 408.
101. Grafton 2011: 213.
102. See Armstrong 1990: 81 (France).
103. Keyl 1989: 135–36. Schlick's annual salary in 1509 was 75 guilders, 10 measures of grain (equivalent to 5 guilders), and an additional payment in wood. Keyl 1989: 135–36.
104. Keyl 1989: 127–30, 138.

The example of Ludovico Ariosto, another well-heeled author of that era, is similarly illustrative of the primary focus on protection of investment. The papal privilege granted to Ariosto on March 27, 1516, for his monumental Italian epic poem, *Orlando Furioso*, famously specified that the book should be corrected by the author's own care and diligence, and that any profit from its sale should be enjoyed by Ariosto rather than by others.[105] But far from recognizing the author's proprietary right in his work, that privilege reflected the fact that Ariosto acted as the book's publisher as well as author. Ariosto, a Ferraran noble, personally arranged for the importation of the 200 reams of paper needed for its printing. He also took a direct, active role in selling copies to booksellers and raised a personal loan to finance a second edition. In addition to the papal privilege, Ariosto also incurred the time and expense of seeking privileges to protect the book from unauthorized publication from the Holy Roman Empire, France, Venice, and Milan.[106]

VIII. CONDITIONS FOR ENJOYING PRIVILEGE

Early modern authorities granted book privileges subject to various conditions. In Venice, for example, privilege holders were required to print the book within a year from the date of supplication, and to print using good quality paper.[107] As discussed above, in the German states and elsewhere the privilege holder was often required to deposit a specified number of copies of the book with the authority that granted the privilege.[108]

Yet the most common condition was some form of price regulation. Sometimes authorities determined the actual price at which the book could be sold in the local market. Venetian authorities often took that step in the wake of the 1517 decree seeking to curb the abuse of the privilege system. But more often, the privilege included a clause admonishing the holder to sell the book at its "just price," a concept with roots in Roman law.[109] Although that general admonition was difficult to enforce, publishers' alleged practice of consistently charging more than the just price was often touted as a justification for piracy and, conversely, for greater state regulation of the book trade.[110]

105. Kostylo 2008c.

106. Pettegree 2010: 162; Ariosto's Printing Privilege, Venice (1515), in *Primary Sources on Copyright (1450 -1900)*.

107. These requirements were imposed sporadically in individual privileges until the Venetian Senate imposed them on all books receiving a privilege, by its decrees of January 3, 1533/1534 and June 4, 1537. See Witcombe 2004: 31–32; Brown 1891: 57, 75–76.

108. The deposit requirement was a feature of several early copyright statutes as well, including those of the United States, the United Kingdom, France, Holland, and several German states, including Bavaria, Hamburg, Holstein, and Lübeck. Gompel 2010: 157, 161–63.

109. Witcombe 2004: 32 (Venice); Baldwin 1959; Ehrman 1980.

110. Whittman 2004 (piracy); Elector of Saxony, Mandate against Offensive Works, Lampoons, Copper Engravings and Pamphlets, as well as Concerning the Censorship of Books, the Reprinting of Privileged Ones, and the Sending in of Copies in Due Course of

IX. PENALTIES AND ENFORCEMENT

Book privileges often set forth the penalties to be imposed on anyone who reprinted the book in violation of the privilege. The nature of those penalties and the manner in which book privileges were meant to be enforced further demonstrate that book privileges stood for the sovereign's prerogative to favor worthy subjects, not a property right of the privilege holder as we might understand such a right today.

As with the Schlick privilege, book privileges typically provided for the confiscation of counterfeited copies, and sometimes of printing plates and equipment as well. In addition to confiscation, the most common penalty was the imposition of a heavy fine. The first Imperial privilege providing for a specified fine was issued in 1513, two years after the Schlick privilege. It provided for a fine of "ten marks of full-weight gold," an amount roughly equivalent to Schlick's annual salary, to be levied upon each instance in which a transgressor printed, offered for sale, or sold the subject books "in defiance of this Our privilege."[111]

Given their significant size, the fines seem to have been set for their *ad terrorem* effect, or were perhaps a maximum amount that could be levied by the magistrate. In the event of a violation of the privilege, the fines' primary purpose seems to have been to serve as a stick that could be used to threaten the transgressor should he fail to deliver all illicit copies of the book.[112] Whatever the size and import of the monetary fines, for devout Catholics the risk of incurring a monetary penalty might well have paled in comparison to the threat of excommunication set out in papal privileges. Papal privileges typically threatened transgressors with automatic excommunication (*excommunicationis latae sententiae*), a threat that was also commonly used against debtors to the Apostolic Camera (the central board of finance in the papal administrative system) until it was limited in 1570.[113]

Early modern European law did not recognize a sharp distinction between what we would today define as civil wrongs versus criminal offenses. Conduct that we might regard as merely a civil wrong, including verbal insults, were often viewed as affronts to the public order, enforceable as a criminal offense. Moreover, individuals

Time, 27 February 1686, in Electoral Saxon Printing and Censorship Acts from 1549 to 1717, Leipzig (1724), in *Primary Sources on Copyright (1450–1900)* (criticizing printers for "overcharging buyers in their greed for excessive profit" and providing for greater control over the book trade).

111. Imperial Privilege for Eucharius Rösslin, Strasbourg (1513), in *Primary Sources on Copyright (1450–1900)*; Kawohl 2008e. In early sixteenth-century Venice, the typical fine set out in a privilege was 25 ducats for each counterfeited book printed or sold. In France, the typical fine was 100 silver marks (more than 25 times the annual wage of an unskilled building laborer), or an amount set by the court.

112. See Kostylo 2008a (describing the prosecution of one Zuan Battista Rizzo for printing a book without a license—likely a more serious offense than violating a printing privilege—in 1590).

113. Witcombe 2004: 50.

wronged by what we would regard as criminal offenses, including theft and assault, often had the right to bring or initiate a criminal prosecution, which, either through pretrial settlement or judicial order, might result in some payment of compensation from the offender to the injured party.[114]

Reprinting a book in violation of a privilege was likewise something of a hybrid between a civil wrong and a criminal offense. On one hand, as we see in the Schlick privilege, the privilege holder typically bore the burden of bringing his "instruction or request" to the authorities for them initiate enforcement proceedings against violators.[115] This suggests that privileges were enforced to vindicate the privilege holder. On the other hand, enforcement actions were typically under the jurisdiction of judicial bodies responsible for criminal offenses or violations of sovereign decrees. In Venice, for example, book privileges universally provided that violators would be prosecuted by the Avogardori di Comun, who where state attorneys responsible for prosecuting crimes against the public order, or the Signori di Notte, a magistracy charged with investigating, judging, and sentencing criminal offenses—not by the Giustizia Vecchia, the magistracy responsible for enforcing the laws of the marketplace.[116] As such, reprinting seems to have been seen primarily as an affront to the sovereign by violation of the sovereign's decree.

The allocation of any fines imposed for violation of a book privilege similarly reflected general practice in other sorts of cases. Early modern European law often provided that any sum paid to a complainant had to be split with the sovereign, primarily on the justification that the wrongdoer had offended the sovereign and the public peace as well as harming the complainant.[117] Likewise, the book privilege holder typically received only between a third and a half of the sums collected from transgressors.[118] In Venice, money collected was divided in thirds: one to the privilege holder, one to the person who denounced the counterfeiter, and one to the magistrate or office to which the case was brought, with portions sometimes allocated to the prosecutor and various public institutions as well.[119] Papal privileges usually

114. On the criminal enforcement of insults, see Horodowich 2008: 97–98. On the private prosecution of criminal offenses, see Langbein 1974: 177–78, 225–26; N. Landau 1999 (British common law).

115. See Armstrong 1990: 195–96 (describing enforcement of royal privileges in France); Kostylo 2008a.

116. Avogadori di Commun acted as public accusers in a wide variety of cases ranging from homicide and physical fights to theft, rape, and physical and verbal injury. They also served to oversee the regular and systematic application of laws passed by the Council. The Signori di Notte was divided into the Signori di Notte al Criminal and the Signori di Notte al Civil at some point during the sixteenth century. But both magistracies had responsibility over a wide spectrum of crimes, including crimes of blood, illegal arms, crimes against property and honor, improper behavior, fraud, and generally violent or improper practices. See Horodowich 2008: 97–98. The Giustizia Vecchia is discussed in depth in Shaw 2006.

117. See Woodbine 1924: 803–06 (common law); Calisse 1928, vol. 8: 231–32, 295–96 (civil law).

118. Witcombe 2004: 30 (Venice), 49–50 (papal); Leuschner 1998: 366; Imperial Privilege for Eucharius Rösslin, Strasbourg (1513), in *Primary Sources on Copyright (1450–1900)*.

119. The need to make a formal or informal payment to the presiding judge or magistrate was standard in early modern Europe. See Sawyer 1988: 97.

provided that any fine collected from transgressors was to be paid half to the privilege holder and half to the Apostolic Camera, although sometimes the division was into thirds, with a payment made to the magistrate or to the person who identified the counterfeiter as well. Imperial privileges commonly provided that money collected would be paid half to the aggrieved privilege holder and half to the Imperial Treasury.[120]

We have scant information about how book privileges were actually enforced and whether they served as an effective deterrent against piracy. In the absence of systematic judicial record-keeping, we have descriptions of only a handful of early cases. In 1503, the editor-publisher Amedeo Scotti successful petitioned the Signori di Notte in Venice to order one Bernardino Benalio to cease printing the book *Continens Rasis* in violation of the privilege that Scotti had obtained in 1500. The same year, the same court found one Andrea Torresani guilty of violating a 12-year privilege held by the merchant-publisher Gironimo Durante and fined Torresani 500 hundred ducats, the amount stipulated in the privilege.[121] On the other hand, Aldus Manutius helplessly railed against those who brazenly counterfeited his best-selling editions of Greek and Latin classics in Lyons, Florence, Brescia, and Breslau. In so doing, the reprinters evaded Manutius's Venetian privileges and ignored his papal privilege (apparently on the grounds that, despite purporting to apply to all of Christendom, the papal privilege was in fact limited to Rome).[122] In 1507, Aldus did succeed in convincing the Signori di Notte to issue a sentence of banishment against Filippo Giunti, a leading Florentine printer who had counterfeited Aldus's editions and violated Aldus's exclusive privilege to print in italics. Yet in 1514, Pope Leo X apparently granted Giunti permission to print in an italic font that was only marginally different from that of Aldus.[123]

120. See, e.g., Imperial Privilege for Eucharius Rösslin, Strasbourg (1513), in *Primary Sources on Copyright (1450–1900)*; Imperial Privilege for Aloysius Blumauer's Travesty of Virgil's 'Aeneid,' Vienna (1785), in *Primary Sources on Copyright (1450–1900)*. Likewise, in England, according to the Decrees of the Court of Star Chamber, "[p]rinting or importing books contrary to letters patent or the ordinances of the Company of Stationers could lead to . . . a penalty of twenty shillings for every offending copy (with half to the Crown and half to the person who reported the offense)." Gómez-Arostegui 2008: 1217.

121. Witcombe 2004: 85.

122. Loewenstein 2002: 72–74; Kostylo 2008a.

123. Lowry 1979: 155–59. Much later, in his treatise, *Short Account of the Useful and Laudable Book Trade and Its Privileges*, published in 1690, Adrian Beier (1634–1698), a law professor at the University of Jena in Saxony, argued that publishers have a natural right to prevent reprinting, but that privileges provide a distinct procedural advantage in enforcement: "The lawsuit will indeed be faster where one is suing for violated privileges (since in such a case there is no need for the tedious and irksome demonstration of interests, cf. §.7, Inst. de verb. oblig.), the redress will be more emphatic, and the punishment more painful." Adrian Beier, Kurtzer Bericht von der Nützlichen und Fürtrefflichen Buch-Handlung und Deroselben Privilegien (§ 70, p. 52) (1690), quoted in Encyclopaedia Article on "The Reprinting of Books," Leipzig and Halle (1740), in *Primary Sources on Copyright (1450–1900)*.

X. PRINTERS' GUILDS

Book privileges were initially granted at the supplication of an individual publisher or author. But as decades passed, local printers and booksellers organized guilds in most major printing centers, and those guilds typically operated as cartels. In most printing centers, no one was permitted to print a book unless he was a member of the guild—and the guilds often capped local competition by limiting the number of accredited printers. Further, guilds allocated printing rights among their members pursuant to internal guild regulations and registration procedures. In other respects as well, the guilds served as vehicles of trade protectionism, giving local printers and booksellers advantages over foreign imports. The printers' and booksellers' guilds thus supplemented and, at times, supplanted book privileges issued by sovereign authorities for individual titles.

In many locations, the printers and booksellers guilds were established at the instance or with the cooperation of the sovereign authorities, as was generally the case with medieval and early modern crafts guilds. Sovereigns saw printers' guilds as a tool for bringing greater order to the book trade. The guilds, they hoped, would guarantee quality of print, ameliorate ruinous competition, and regulate relations among the trades involved in printing, including by limiting competition among guild members for skilled pressmen, compositors, and correctors. Sovereign powers also saw guilds as a vehicle for enhancing their censorial control over the content of printed material, control that European sovereigns had begun to institute through formal prepublication licensing procedures in the 1520s and that became further entrenched with the Counter-Reformation.[124] Even where there were no exclusive and officially chartered printers' guilds, sovereigns regulated the printing industry, along both economic and censorial lines, largely by codifying industry-wide agreements among leading local printers.

On January 18, 1549, by the Decree of the Council of Ten Establishing the Venetian Guild of Printers and Booksellers, Venice became the first jurisdiction to charter the establishment of a printers guild.[125] The Decree called upon all Venetian printers and booksellers to join the Guild, citing the need to put an end to the "extreme disorder and confusion" in Venice's printing industry, which had led to the publication of "scandalous and heretical books." As such, the Decree to establish

124. In most locations, prepublication censorship was not systematically instituted until the 1520s and did not firmly take hold until the papal authorities issued Indices of Forbidden Books as part of the Counter-Reformation, beginning in 1544. Pettegree 2010: 204–06. In the Holy Roman Empire, it was not until 1760 that the censor's approval became a formal precondition to obtaining an Imperial book privilege, and by this time Imperial privileges were irrelevant outside of Austria. Kawohl 2008e. In the relatively tolerant Dutch Republic, book privileges appear to have remained entirely a market prerogative, unconnected to censorship. Hoftijzer 2010: 215; Orenstein 1995: 242.

125. Decree Establishing the Venetian Guild of Printers and Booksellers, Venice (1549), in *Primary Sources on Copyright (1450–1900)*; Kostylo 2008b; Brown 1891: 83.

the Guild went hand in hand with the Council's introduction of censorial control spurred by the Counter-Reformation.

There appears to have been considerable resistance to the establishment of the Guild among Venice's printers. Many saw the Guild—with reason—as a tool for more effective censorship of the book trade at the behest of the Catholic Church and, indeed, for prosecutions of the Inquisition, which had already conducted its first trial for a press offense in Venice in 1547.[126] Although the Council established the Guild in 1549, it was not formally incorporated until 1567, following the Council's decree of 1566 directing, once more, that the Provveditori di Comun (a magistrate body that oversaw trade and industry) approve a set of Guild bylaws.

Supplementing its censorial role, the Guild also sought to arrest the decline in quality of Venetian imprints by raising workmanship standards and to provide economic protection to its members. To those ends, the Guild regulated entry into the printing and bookselling professions and restricted book imports, even if those guild regulations were imperfectly enforced. It also came to assume some of the responsibility for issuing book licenses and privileges, which it exercised with the backing of the Council of Ten, the Provveditori di Comun, and other government bodies.

The Venetian Printers and Booksellers Guild was not given exclusive authority to issue book privileges until the Venetian Senate issued its Decree of May 11, 1603, the same decree that relaxed the restriction of awarding privileges only to newly printed books and set a three-tier term of protection.[127] By the 1603 Decree, the Venetian Senate reiterated that no book could be printed without the imprimatur of the Inquisitor and a license from the Ducal Secretary, undersigned by two Reformatori of the University of Padua. It further provided that printers who had obtained the necessary licenses could apply to the Guild for a book privilege, which would then be awarded in accordance with the three-tier term specified in the Decree.[128] The Senate decree also regulated printing quality in some detail, including by specifying that publishers must employ master-printers certified by the Guild, that the copy from which a new edition of a book is to be made must be carefully reviewed before the printer begins his work, and that each book must contain an errata page identifying the proofreader responsible for correction of the proofs. It also provided that a privilege would become void if printing did not commence within a month of the privilege's issuance and continue at the rate of at least a half-folio per day, if the publisher printed the book abroad, or if the book was badly printed or full of errors.

Other printing centers followed a similar pattern in which local printers were given the legal mechanism and organizational apparatus to protect themselves against ruinous competition in return for their acquiescence and assistance in government

126. Brown 1891: 110.
127. Brown 1891: 175–77.
128. Venetian Decree on Privileges for New Books and Reprints, Venice (1603), in *Primary Sources on Copyright (1450–1900)*.

supervision of content and regulation of printing quality.[129] The tangled relationships between printers' guilds based in Paris and London and the censorship apparatus of their respective monarchs were a prime target of modern copyright legislation, and thus central to the story of modern copyright law.[130] But most directly relevant to Jewish copyright law were the printers' guilds established in or adjacent to centers of Jewish printing, including, in addition to Venice, in central Europe and Amsterdam.

In Prague, which saw the printing of Hebrew books of Jewish learning and liturgy beginning in 1514 and continuing well into the nineteenth century, the printers, binders, and booksellers formed a guild in 1597. The guild's aim was to regulate an overcrowded marketplace, increasingly populated by newly arrived booksellers and merchants from other locations.[131]

In the Holy Roman Empire, printers' guilds arose in numerous Imperial Free Cities. During the late fifteenth and early sixteenth centuries, book printing was typically classified among the free arts, meaning that printers were not required to join a guild.[132] Yet most printers joined a guild voluntarily in any event. Initially, printers joined the merchants' guild or the goldsmiths' and metalworkers' guild, but over time they typically established their own guilds. In some cities, printers' guilds were organized at the explicit request of local authorities or by local ordinance. These included Leipzig, where the Buchhandlungsgesellschaft was founded in 1595, and Nuremberg and Augsburg, which enacted printers' ordinances in 1673 and 1713, respectively, setting out detailed provisions on the organization of printers' guilds. Some 25 printers' ordinances were enacted in Imperial Free Cities. The ordinances typically codified agreements among local printers, and like guild regulations, accorded local printers perpetual reprinting rights, limited the number of printers who could set up shop in the city, and regulated labor relations and competition among local printers.[133] They also contained provisions on censorship. The Strasburg ordinance of 1706 proclaimed that, although the invention of printing is unquestionably one of the most valuable inventions of human ingenuity, in order to preserve it unsullied the authorities must "take stringent measures against those who would misuse book printing to desecrate religion, subvert public morals, and provoke sedition."[134]

The Amsterdam Booksellers and Printers Guild, which was established in stages in 1661 and 1662, was exceptional for being the only printers guild to accept Jews as members. Further it operated in the Dutch Republic, which was relatively free from heavy-handed government censorship. Its predominant focus was trade regulation. The Amsterdam printers organized a guild and petitioned for its juridical recognition in order to thwart competition from outsiders, prevent ruinous competition

129. The pattern was likely followed in provincial printing centers as well. See, e.g., Gehl 1995: 215–53.

130. On the Paris printers guild, see Mellot 2007: 49–52; Birn 1971: 132–34. On the London guild, the "Stationers Company," see Deazley 2008; Feather 2006: 29–45.

131. See Wischnitzer 1954: 345 (on the establishment of the first Hebrew press in Prague); Edwards 2012: 19 (discussing establishment of guild).

132. Landau and Parshall 1996: 10–11.

133. Kawohl 2008h.

134. Quoted in Kawohl 2008h.

from illegal auctions by small booksellers, and to sharpen the occupational divisions among the various craftsmen engaged in book production.[135]

XI. COPYRIGHT AND LITERARY PROPERTY

The first copyright statutes—the U.K. Statute of Anne of 1710, the French Revolutionary Decrees of 1791 and 1793, and the U.S. Copyright Act of 1790—were enacted against the backdrop of the previous regime in which monarchs had doled out privileges as a mechanism to curry favor and elicit the assistance of loyal printers and booksellers in prepublication censorship of potentially subversive content.[136] Under that regime, printers' guilds had come to enjoy broad monopolies over classic and new titles alike. Copyright law did not end censorship. But, in most places, it conclusively decoupled the exclusive right to print a book from legal mechanisms for prepublication censorship and criminal punishment of subversive content. Moreover, copyright statutes vested exclusive, short-term rights in authors of new works, ensuring that newly authored works could be freely reprinted after a relatively short period of exclusivity—in the United Kingdom and United States, a maximum of 28 years following the work's publication; in France, 10 years after the death of the author. As such, copyright law brought an irrevocable end to printers' guilds' perpetual monopolies.

At copyright's origins, the idea that authors have an inherent right in their expressive creations played only a partial and uncertain role.[137] Authors were made the initial repository of the copyright primarily as a device to deny exclusive printing rights in old titles, not to exalt the role of the author per se. At copyright law's origins, just as under the book privilege regime, authors typically transferred copyrights to a publisher for a lump sum.

Nevertheless, by making authors, rather than publishers, the initial repository of its legal entitlement, copyright law accentuated the role of the author in creating original expression. Hence, contemporaneously with the enactment of the first copyright statutes, theories of what it means to be an author, why authors merit a proprietary right in original expression, and what is the role of original expression in contributing to the advancement of knowledge came to occupy center stage in debates over the nature and justification for copyright law. Indeed, not just authors, but also publishers eager to acquire exclusive rights that were not limited to the short terms set out in the early copyright statutes, argued that authors have a natural right of property in their creations—akin to property in chattels or land—that the law should recognize and secure.[138]

135. Rasterhoff 2014: 183–85.

136. Statute of Anne, 1710, 8 Anne, ch. 19; Act of May 31, 1790, 1 Stat. 124; Decree of the National Convention of 19 July 1793.

137. See generally J. Ginsburg 1990. See also Feather 2006: 55–56; Rose 1993: 47–48.

138. See Chartier 1994: 32–43 (describing the rise and ideology of the author-function); see also Rose 1993.

The ensuing debates over the nature of authorship and copyright were joined by some of the leading philosophers, jurists, and writers of the eighteenth and nineteenth centuries. Through their influential writings, copyright law came to reflect a disparate amalgam of conceptual foundations, including the Lockean idea that authors are entitled to property rights in the products of their intellectual labor, the German idealist theory that authors' intellectual creations are extensions of their personality, and the Enlightenment's exaltation of creative self-expression and scientific progress. For example, the iconic British jurist William Blackstone invoked Locke's labor-desert theory of property when he successfully argued in court in 1769 that authors have a perpetual copyright under common law:

> [T]he labours of the mind and productions of the brain are as justly intitled to the benefit and emoluments that may arise from them, as the labours of the body are: and the literary compositions being the produce of the author's own labour and abilities, he has a moral and equitable right to the profits they produce; and is fairly intitled to the profits forever.[139]

Victor Hugo, like other authors' rights proponents of the nineteenth century, declared, indeed, that as authors' works are the unique, newly created products of mental labor, ingenuity, and personality, they are the "first and most sacred of all properties."[140]

Immanuel Kant laid the foundation for the prevalent Continental European view that copyright is, at least in part, a right of personality. Kant characterized literary works, not as a physical commodity, but rather as the author's exercise of his communicative powers. The author's communicative act, Kant posited, is integral to the author's self. It is thus entitled to protection against a publisher who prints or modifies the author's words without the author's permission, thereby effectively forcing the author to speak against his will.[141]

Copyright law followed a different narrative in the United States, where copyright has long been viewed primarily as a kind of statutory privilege accorded to authors to provide them with fair compensation and an incentive for their contributions to the storehouse of knowledge. In that vein, the United States Supreme Court has repeatedly referred to copyright as a set of "monopoly privileges" that, "while 'intended to

139. Blackstone presented his argument as counsel in the case of *Millar v. Taylor*. His argument was paraphrased in the minority opinion of Justice Yates. Millar v. Taylor, 4 Burr. 2303, 2359, 98 ER 201 (1769).

140. Victor Hugo, Speech to the Council d'Etat (September 30, 1849), quoted in Boyle 2008: 31.

141. Immanuel Kant, *Von der Unrechtmassigkeit des Buchernachdruckes, in* Kant 1913: 213. According to some commentators, the paradigm shift in German legal theory to viewing authors' rights as a right of personality (rather than attempting to fit the rights within the constraints of property) came not from Kant directly, but rather from Leopold Josef Neustetel's landmark treatise, *The Reprinting of Books from the Perspective of Roman Law*, published in Heidelberg in 1824. Kawohl 2008i.

motivate the creative activity of authors . . . by the provision of a special reward,' are limited in nature and must ultimately serve the public good."[142]

But it was Continental, not American (or British), copyright that formed the backdrop for the historical development of Jewish copyright law. Naturally, the seminal rulings, decrees, and regulations that constituted Jewish copyright law were issued in the locations where the vast bulk of Jewish books were produced, distributed, and purchased. And from the advent of print through the nineteenth century, the major centers for printing—and distributing—books of Jewish learning and liturgy, were all on the European Continent (and, to a lesser extent, Constantinople). More specifically, during the eighteenth and nineteenth centuries, the printing of books of interest to the rabbinic elite was concentrated in central and eastern Europe. In that regard—of importance, as we shall see, for the development of Jewish copyright law—as the states of central and eastern Europe enacted copyright statutes in the first half of the nineteenth century, they endorsed the view that authors hold a property right in their creative works, even if that right is limited in duration, fully transferable to publishers, and accorded only to domestic nationals, not foreigners (unless the foreign state had reciprocal copyright relations).

Russia was the first country with a sizable Jewish population to enact a modern copyright statute. Russia did not initially sever copyright from censorship. Indeed, the Russian copyright statute was enacted as a part of the Statute on Censorship in 1828.[143] Nonetheless, Russia's copyright law granted authors (and their heirs) exclusive rights to print their works for a term lasting for 25 years after the author's death. The law also provided that the author's copyright arose automatically upon creation of the work, with no requirement of registration. Further, although the Russian statute did not initially refer to the author's copyright as a property right, by a decree issued in 1830 the Tsar's Council of State provided that the author's rights were proprietary in nature and could be assigned, devised, or otherwise transferred. Unlike other copyright statutes, however, Russia's 1828 law decreed that an author's copyright would be extinguished if the work did not meet censorship regulations. Copyright law was not separated from the censorship statute in Russia until 1887.

In central Europe, Prince Metternich, the famously conservative and powerful Foreign Minister and Chancellor of the Austrian Empire, called for similarly linking copyright protection with censorship. But the first modern copyright statutes in central Europe rejected Metternich's call. They also emphasized, more so than did the Russian statute, that authors have property rights in their creations.[144] Following the nomenclature in the French Revolutionary Decrees, which had referred to the "property rights of authors," the Prussian statute, enacted in 1837, was entitled the "Law for the Protection of Property in Works of Scholarship and

142. Fogerty v. Fantasy, Inc., 510 U.S. 517, 526–27 (1994) (quoting Sony Corp. of America v. Universal City Studios, Inc., 464 U.S. 417, 429 (1984)).
143. Newcity 1978: 6–7.
144. On the German states' early nineteenth-century rejection of Austrian chancellor Metternich's proposal for a German Confederation authority that would bestow copyrights only on works that had passed an internal censorship body, see Kawohl 2008b.

the Arts against Reprinting and Reproduction." To safeguard that "property," it provided authors with the exclusive right to print and, with certain limitations, to translate their works, an assignable and descendible right that lasted for the life of the author plus 30 years.[145] The Saxon copyright act of 1844 provided similarly that the author's right to reproduce his literary products and works of art by mechanical means is a "property right which can be transferred to other persons."[146] That right also lasted for the life of the author plus 30 years, at least when the work was published during the author's lifetime. Likewise, in 1846, Austria enacted its first modern copyright statute, the "Law for the Protection of Literary and Artistic Property against Unauthorized Publication, Reprinting, and Reproduction."[147] The Austrian law declared in its first article: "Literary products and works of art constitute a property of their originator (author), i.e., of the person who originally wrote or composed them."

Those nineteenth-century copyright statutes in central and eastern Europe recognized that authors have "property" in their creative works more as a vehicle for providing for the transferability of copyrights from authors to publishers than to endorse the authors' rights theories of Kant, Hugo, and others. Nonetheless, the ideologies of authors' rights came to be a powerful force in copyright jurisprudence. In any event, as we shall see, Jewish copyright law came to bear the imprint of the nineteenth-century statutory recognition of literary property, just as it still carries the influence of the book privilege regime that preceded modern copyright statutes. We now examine the beginning of that external influence on Jewish copyright law: with the very first rabbinic reprinting ban.

145. Prussian Copyright Act, Berlin (1837), in *Primary Sources on Copyright (1450–1900)*.
146. Saxon Copyright Act, Dresden (1844), in *Primary Sources on Copyright (1450–1900)*.
147. Austrian Copyright Act (1846), in *Primary Sources on Copyright (1450–1900)*.

CHAPTER 3

Rabbinic Reprinting Bans

Between Ktav Dat *and Privilege*

I. THE FIRST RABBINIC REPRINTING BAN

The illustrious rabbinic scholar and Hebrew grammarian Eliyahu Ha-Levi Bakhur (1469–1549) personified the eclectic intellectual crosscurrents of his time. Bakhur gained fame—and, in some Jewish circles, notoriety—for tutoring prominent Christians in the ways of Jewish mysticism and serving as lead editor in prominent Christian Hebraicist printing establishments.[1] He was also the author of a foundational work of Yiddish romance. Bakhur's *Bove Bukh*, an adaptation in Yiddish verse of the English chilvaric tale *Sir Bevis of Hampton*, was the first nonreligious book in Yiddish ever printed. It became an enduring classic, reissued in at least 40 editions following its initial publication in 1541.[2]

In 1518, Bakhur was granted a papal "gratia e privilegio"—printing license and privilege—for his three books of Hebrew grammar, *Sefer Ha-Bakhur, Sefer Ha-Harkhava*, and *Luah Be-Dikduk Ha-Poalim Ve-Ha-Binyanim*, on the condition that

1. A number of Bakhur's contemporaries warned against teaching the secrets of Kabbalah to Christians. See, e.g., Yoḥanan Treves, Responsum on Jews Teaching Hebrew to Christians (1534); Elijah Menaḥem Halfan, Epistle on the Transmission of Kabbalist Knowledge (Venice c. 1540). On Bakhur's defense of teaching Christians, see Aranoff 2009: 21–22.

2. Bakhur wrote *Bove Bukh* in 1506–1507, but it did not appear in print until 1541. Frakes 2009: 120–21; Baumgarten 2005: 175; Smith 2003: ix–xx; Turniansky and Timm 2003: 102. Some sources assert that *Bove Bukh* was published in Pizarro in 1515. That assertion traces back to a single source, Ephraim Deinard (1846–1930), *Atikot Yehuda*, Maḥlaka Shnia 14 (A. M. Luntz 1915), and is apparently incorrect.

he have them printed at the shop of a Christian printer in Rome.[3] As was typical of sixteenth-century papal book privileges, the papal decree purported to forbid reprinting the books not just in Rome, but throughout all of Christendom.[4] Yet, Bakhur was not content to rely on the papal privilege's capacious reach. He also petitioned a rabbinic court in Rome for a decree, directed at Jews, forbidding reprinting of his books without his or his publishers' permission.

Bakhur had good reason to seek rabbinic protection in addition to a papal privilege. Ten years earlier, during the chaos following a plague in Bakhur's home city of Padua, a scrivener had absconded with the manuscript of Bakhur's first major scholarly work, his commentaries on Moshe Kimḥi's classic twelfth-century exposition of Hebrew grammar, *Journey on the Paths of Knowledge*. The scrivener brought the manuscript to the Pizarro printing house of Gershom Soncino, the leading Jewish publisher of the day. Perhaps unwittingly, Soncino printed Bakhur's commentaries, together with Kimḥi's text and an introduction by Benjamin ben Judah of Rome, without identifying Bakhur as their author.[5] As Bakhur later prepared to print his three grammar books in Rome, his bitter experience of being deprived of authorship credit and financial remuneration undoubtedly loomed large.

In response to Bakhur's petition, the Rome rabbinic court issued a decree jointly in favor of Bakhur and his Jewish publishers, three brothers who had fled Padua with Bakhur when the city was plundered by the soldiers of Emperor Maximilian I in 1509 and who were now financing the printing of his grammar trilogy.[6] The decree forbade reprinting the books anywhere in the world, for a period of 10 years, without written permission from Bakhur or his publishers. Lest the books be reprinted in violation of the decree, or by a non-Jew, the decree also prohibited knowingly purchasing such a reprinted copy. Bakhur made certain that potential reprinters would be aware of the

3. The title, "Sefer Ha-Bakhur," means "Book of the Young Man," but is, at the same time, a play on the author's chosen last name, Bakhur. The companion books were *Sefer Ha-Harkhava* ("Book of Compilation"), and *Luah Be-Dikduk Ha-Poalim Ve-Ha-Binyanim* ("Grammatical Table of Verbs and Conjugations"). As Bakhur indicated in his introduction to *Sefer Ha-Bakhur*, the books were intended for Gentile as well as Jewish readers. There was considerable demand among early modern Christian Hebraicists for books of Hebrew grammar, which many viewed as a gateway to greater understanding of the Scripture and to uncovering the secrets of Kabbalah. In his printer's introduction to a contemporaneous book of Hebrew grammar, Abraham ben Meir de Balmes' *Mikneh Avram*, published in 1523, the Christian Hebraicist printer Daniel Bomberg expressed sympathy for Kabbalistic learning, and stated that he wished "to publish kabbalistic books which are important to every Christian." See Burnett 2012: 106 n. 48.

4. The privilege was, no doubt, specifically intended to tie the hands of Daniel Bomberg, a Christian printer and scion of one of the leading merchant families in Europe, who held a monopoly over printing Hebrew books in the Republic of Venice. Indeed, Bomberg published a competing book of Hebrew grammar in 1523, the aforementioned *Mikneh Avram*. Nonetheless, the Bomberg and Bakhur reconciled two decades later, when Bomberg published two of Bakhur's later works and hired Bakhur as his main proofreader. Brisman 2000: 51.

5. C. Ginsburg 1867: 13; Amram 1988: 109 (noting that the work was published by Gershom Soncino in Pesaro); Brisman 2000: 286 n. 16.

6. The three brothers financed the printing. The actual printing was undertaken by a Christian printer. Baruchson 1990: 35 n. 21; Amram 1988: 238. According to one source, the brothers were Bakhur's relatives. Brisman 2000: 286 n. 17.

rabbinic prohibition. He included the entire text of the rabbinic court's decree near the beginning of *Sefer Ha-Bakhur*, under the heading *ktav dat*, meaning a pronouncement of Jewish law.[7] The original decree, as printed in *Sefer Ha-Bakhur*, appears in Illustration 1; my English translation follows below it.

Hebrew-language books of Jewish learning had begun to appear in print as early as 1470. By 1518, over 250 such Hebrew titles had been published.[8] Nonetheless, the decree that the Rome rabbis issued in favor of Elihayu Bakhur and his publishers was the first rabbinic reprinting ban of which we are aware. Even following that decree, it took several decades for the practice of issuing reprinting bans to take hold in the Jewish world. Yet in the ensuing centuries, rabbinic authorities came to issue thousands of such bans, typically as part of a "haskama," a rabbinic approbation consisting of a statement of imprimatur and praise for a particular book.[9] To this day, leading rabbis in Israel and the Diaspora continue to issue *haskamot* and reprinting bans providing for exclusive rights to copy and distribute books, sound recordings, databases, and videos that present rabbinic commentary, foundational texts of Jewish law, ethical lessons, homilies, and liturgy.[10]

In some respects, rabbinic reprinting bans appear to be cut from the same cloth as the book privileges issued by early modern secular and ecclesiastic authorities. As I discuss presently, a number of similarities suggest that early modern rabbinic authorities actively looked to the book privileges as a model for framing their own reprinting bans. Other homologous elements reflect the confluence of shared understandings among early modern Jews and Gentiles regarding the nature of authorship. Still others, including prohibitions on buying as well as producing reprinted books and enforcement by the threat of excommunication (which we see in both papal privileges and rabbinic bans) apparently derive from the fact that similar juridical tools were available for making exclusive printing rights effective and enforceable in the early modern era. They also reflect an understanding that a violation of the privilege or ban was at least as much an affront to the public order and the papal or rabbinic authority that issued it, as it was an infringement of any private right of its beneficiary.

Yet the rabbinic reprinting bans strikingly differ from the book privileges on a number of axes as well. Most fundamentally, as we have seen, the privileges were in essence extralegal favors, an exercise of the sovereign's personal prerogative to grant certain subjects special rights in derogation of generally applicable law. Granted, the sovereign's prerogative was cabined to some extent by the venerable legal precept, with roots in Roman law, that the sovereign could not grant one person a privilege

7. The rabbinic decree appears on page 6 of *Sefer Ha-Bakhur*, immediately following the listing of the book's contents.

8. Raz-Krakotzkin 1999: 344 (stating that some 200 Hebrew books had been printed by 1500).

9. The first *haskama* consisting only of a rabbinic approbation was issued for the book, *Agur*, by Yaakov bar Yehuda Landau, printed in Naples in 1490. Rakover 1991: 125.

10. Ultra-Orthodox rabbis also sometimes issue bans against writings that they deem heretical and yet have the potential to infiltrate the Ultra-Orthodox world; the meaning of such bans, which are not the topic of our study, is that it is forbidden to read the targeted work. Shapiro 2003: 1.

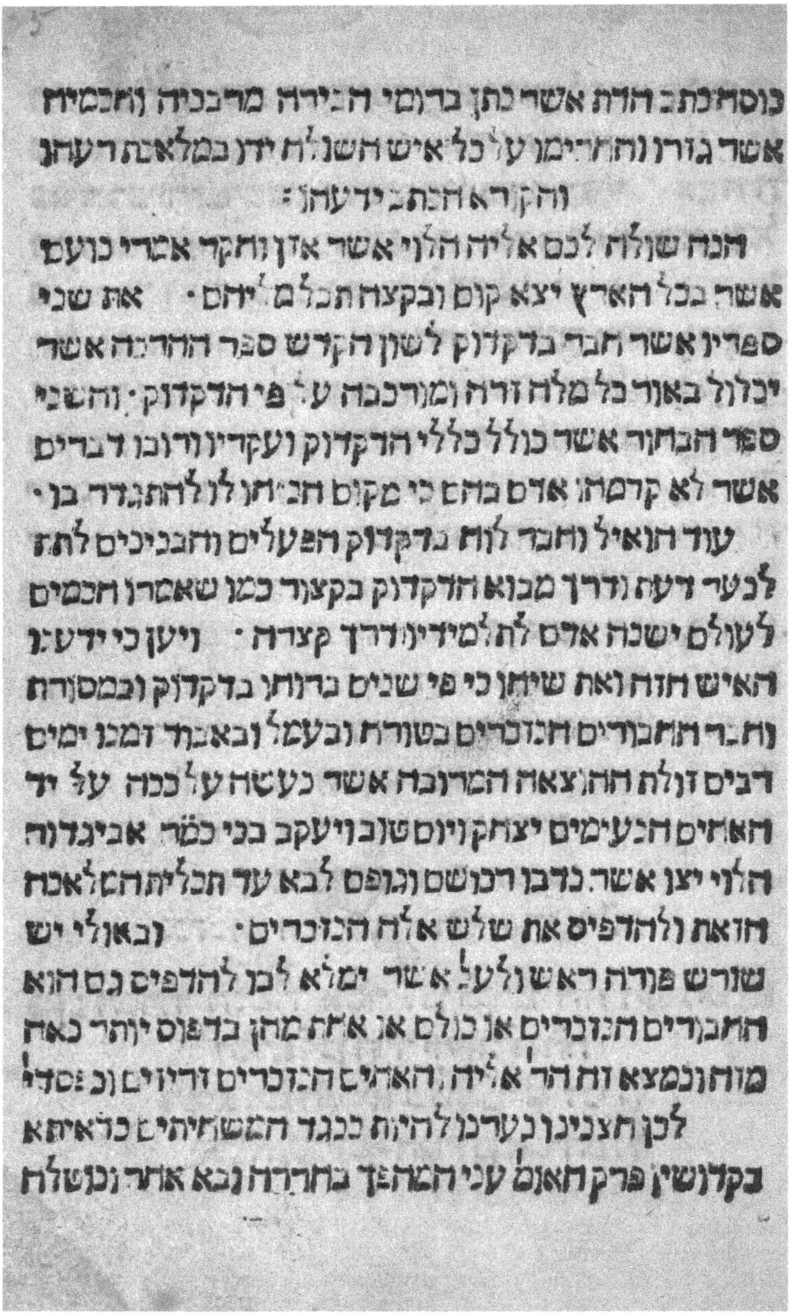
נוסח כתב הדת אשר נתן ברומי הבירה מרבניה וחכמיה
אשר גזרו והחרימו על כל איש השולח ידו במלאכת רעהו
והקורא הכתב ידעהו:
הנה שולח לכם אליה הלוי אשר אזן וחקר אמרי נועם
אשר בכל הארץ יצא קום ובקצה תבל מליהם · את שני
ספריו אשר חבר בדקדוק לשון הקדש ספר ההרכבה אשר
יכלול באור כל מלה זרה ומורכבה על פי הדקדוק · והשני
ספר הבחור אשר כולל כללי הדקדוק ועקריו ורובו דברים
אשר לא קדמוהו אדם בהם כי מקום הניחו לו להתגדר בו ·
עוד הואיל וחבר לוח בדקדוק הפעלים והבנינים לתת
לבער דעת ודרך מבוא הדקדוק בקצור כמו שאמרו חכמים
לעולם ישנה אדם לתלמידיו דרך קצרה · ויען כי ידענו
האיש הזה ואת שיחו כי פי שנים ברוחו בדקדוק ובמסורת
ונ·ר התחבורים הנזכרים בשורת ובעמל ובאבוד זמנו ימים
רבים זולת ההוצאה המרובה אשר נעשה על ככה על יד
האחים הנעימים יצחק ויום טוב ויעקב בני כמ״ר אביגדור
הלוי יצו אשר נדבו רכושם וגופם לבא עד תכלית המלאכה
הזאת ולהדפיס את שלש אלה הנזכרים · ובאולי יש
שורש פורה ראש ולענה אשר ימלא לבו להדפיס גם הוא
החבורים הנזכרים או כולם או אחת מהן בדפוס יותר כאת
מזה ונמצא זה הר׳ אליה והאחים הנזכרים דחוקים ונפסדי׳
לכן הצבינו נערכנו להיות כנגד המשחיתים כדאיתא
בקדושין פרק האומר עני המהפך בחררה ובא אחר ונטלה

Illustration 1
Rome Rabbinic Court *Ktav Dat* for Eliyahu Bakhur 1518, page 1.
(courtesy National Library of Israel).

הימנו כקרא רשות ואמרי פרק לא יתפור מרחיקין מן הדג
כמלא ריצת הדג משום דיורד לאומנות חברו ואפילו לרבי
מאיר דמיירי בדג מת והדגים מתאספים וכולי אם היה
היה חברו פורש היה כאלו גוזל אם כן זה שטרח ועמל
מי שיורד לאומנתו הרי זה גוזל ממש · ואיתא בסנהדרין
ואל אשת רעהו לא קרב זה שירד לאומנות חברו ובהיות
שספרי דפוס כעים מים אל ים לא שמנו גבול אלא גזרנו
בסתם כל מי שיודעתו שראה או שמע גזרותינו שלא יד
ידפס הספרים האלו וכל המדפיס אותם או הוא או שלוחו
יהא בכלל פורץ גדר וישכנו נח״ש והקונה ממנו בידיעה
והכרה אחרי שמעו גזרותינו יהא באל״ה ובשמתא וכל
ישראל יהיו נזופים וזה יהיה עד זמן עשר שנים דהיינו
עד שנת רפ״ט אם לא שיקבל רשות מכמר אליה הנזכר או
האחים הנזכרים ויהיה הרשות בכתוב והשומע לדברינו
יתברך באלהים אמן והקונה מאלו אשר נדפסו פה רומי
על יד הר׳ אליה הנזכר והאחים הנזכרים יגל וישמח
ויזכה במקחו ושלום תבא ברכת טוב: אמן
נכתב ונחתם יום ו׳ ח׳ תשרי רע״ט

נאם הטרוד הנשלל אשר לבו בקרבו חלל זעיר חבריא
ישראל בן הר״ר יחיאל זלה״ה
זעירא דמן חבריא שבתי בר מרדכי ז״ל
נאם הקטן יוסף הגרי בן אברהם ז״ל

Illustration 1 (*cont'd, Ktav Dat,* page 2.)

that would harm another. It seems to have been implicitly understood, however, that if the sovereign wished to reward a publisher or author who had made a substantial investment of money and/or labor in producing a useful book, that was a permissible exercise of sovereign authority, even if the book privilege prevented another from exercising his liberty to reprint the book.

In contrast, as the *ktav dat* that the Rome rabbinic court issued in favor of Eliyahu Bakhur exemplifies, rabbinic reprinting bans often purport to pronounce, affirm, and enforce generally applicable Jewish law. To be certain, halakhic decisors have disagreed about the specific halakhic basis and character of rabbinic reprinting bans. Moreover, rabbis have exercised considerable discretion regarding the length and scope of bans protecting particular books. They have also selectively determined which books merit a reprinting ban at all, heavily favoring rabbinic literature and books of Jewish liturgy for both approbations and protection against reprinting. But rabbinic authority to issue reprinting bans flows from the rabbis' juridical role as decisors of Jewish law and, during the era of Jewish communal self-governance, from the rabbis' circumscribed powers to enforce and lend halakhic imprimatur to community ordinances. Hence, rabbinic reprinting bans are far from an exercise of personal prerogative. Rather, they require halakhic justification beyond the rabbis' desire to reward a worthy publisher or author. Accordingly, the issuing rabbis have not uncommonly propounded legal rationales for granting, as well as delimiting, the reprinting ban.

That interweaving of the book privilege model with the normative foundations of rabbinic jurisprudence is strikingly evident in the groundbreaking rabbinic decree regarding Bakhur's three books of Hebrew grammar. On one hand, the Rome rabbis' decree stands in palpable contrast to the language, tone, and content of Arnolt Schlick's Imperial privilege and other book privileges issued by non-Jewish authorities of the early modern era. Most obviously, the reprinting ban draws heavily on Biblical, rabbinic, and halakhic sources. Indeed, in line with the stylistic conventions of rabbinic literature of the early modern era, virtually every sentence invokes, quotes, or plays upon traditional Jewish texts. Yet on the other hand, as I discuss below, the ban simultaneously bears the unmistakable imprint of early modern book privileges and shared understandings of authorship.

Here is the English translation of the *ktav dat* that the Rome rabbinic court issued for Eliyahu Bakhur. To convey the decree's richly referential character, I indicate the traditional sources in footnotes and place each in quotation marks (although they bear no such identifying demarcation in the original).

> "Lo, I send to you" Eliyahu Ha-Levi,[11] who has "listened to and tested"[12] [i.e., carefully weighed and formulated] pleasant words that "are carried throughout the

11. A rhyming play on words and reference to: "Lo, I will send to you Eliyahu Ha-Navi [i.e., the prophet Elijah] before the coming of the awesome, fearful day of the Lord." Malakhi [Malachai] 3:23.

12. Likening the author to the sage, Kohelet: "Because Kohelet was a sage, he continued to instruct the people. He weighed and tested the soundness of many maxims." Kohelet [Ecclesiastes] 12:9.

earth to the end of the world."[13] We refer to the two books that he authored about the grammar of the holy tongue: first, a compilation that includes an explanation of every foreign and complicated word in accordance with the grammar and, second, the book for the "young man,"[14] which includes the rules and principles of grammar, most of which are matters that no one has previously set out, since "[previous scholars] left the matter open for him to come and delineate it."[15] He has also been so kind to compose a table of the grammar of verbs and conjugations to "endow the young with knowledge"[16] and an abridged "path of learning through grammar",[17] as the Sages said: "An [effective] teacher will always teach his students in an abridged [i.e., precise and direct] manner."[18] And since we know this man and his words and know that he "has a double portion of his spirit"[19] [i.e., he is doubly wise] regarding grammar and *masorah* [the rules of spelling, lettering, and notation that precisely define the traditional text of the Bible], and that he authored the writings referred to above with effort and labor and the devotion of many days of his time, which is in addition to the considerable sums expended by the fine brothers, Yitzhak, Yom Tov, and Yaakov, sons of our rabbi and teacher, Avigdor Ha-Levi, may God protect him, who contributed their assets and selves to this project until its fruition and printed the three works mentioned above.

"Perchance there is a stock sprouting poison weed and wormwood"[20] [i.e., an evil actor] who, in his heart, is planning that he, too, will print one or all of the aforementioned works in a more attractive printing,[21] and as a result Rabbi Eliyahu and the aforementioned brothers will find themselves in the situation of having acted nimbly, and yet having lost. Therefore, we take the initiative to stand against such vandals. There is in *Kiddushin* [a tractate of the Talmud that principally concerns matters of marriage and betrothal] a passage that states: "If a poor man is reaching for a crust of bread and another comes and seizes it, that person is called a wicked

13. "The heavens declare the glory of God . . . . Their voice carries throughout the earth, their words to the end of the world." Tehilim [Psalms] 19:2,5.

14. "Bakhur" means young man in Hebrew, and was also the surname that the author had previously adopted for himself.

15. *Babylonian Talmud, Ḥolin* 6:72.

16. "For endowing the simple with shrewdness, the young with knowledge and foresight, the wise man, hearing them, will gain more wisdom." Mishlei [Proverbs] 1:4–5.

17. The phrase *derekh mavo ha-dikduk*, appears to be a play on *derekh mavo-ha-shemesh*, the "path of the sunrise," or the west road at the entry point of the Israelites into the land of the Canaanites, described in Dvarim [Deuteronomy] 11:30.

18. *Babylonian Talmud, Psakhim* 3:2, quoted in *Mishneh Torah*, Hilakhot De-ot 3:9.

19. "Elijah said to Elisha, 'Tell me, what can I do for you before I am taken from you?' Elisha answered, 'Let a double portion of your spirit pass on to me." 2 Melakhim [Kings] 2:9–10.

20. "Perchance there is among you some man or woman . . . whose heart is even now turning away from the Lord our God to go and worship the gods of those nations—perchance there is among you a stock sprouting poison weed and wormwood." Devarim [Deuteronomy] 29:17.

21. The initial edition of Bakhur's grammar books was of decidedly low quality, with much eroded, unclear lettering. Benayahu 1971: 20.

person."[22] And it is said in tractate *Baba Batra* [a tractate of the Talmud that principally concerns civil wrongs]: "One [who wants to spread a fish net] must distance himself from a fish [that another fisherman has staked out with his net] by the full distance that a fish swims, since [to do otherwise] is encroachment upon another's livelihood."[23] And even according to Rabbi Meir [c. 1060- after 1135], who posited that this rule applies only when the first fisherman is using a dead fish [as bait] to attract other fish [i.e., is taking concrete steps that cause the fish to gather around his net], to spread one's net in such circumstances is akin to misappropriation.[24] It is certainly the case, therefore, that when one has taken pains and labored, and another encroaches upon his livelihood, that person is an actual misappropriator [*gozel mamash*]. And we find in *Sanhedrin* [a tractate of the Talmud that largely concerns courts and judicial procedure]: "[The righteous man] refrains from drawing near to him his neighbor's wife; this is a matter that relates to [the rule against] encroaching upon another's livelihood."[25]

And since printed books travel from sea to sea, we have not limited our ruling to acts occurring within a territorial border, but rather simply decree: Anyone who knows of, saw, or heard this our decree prohibiting the printing of those books, and who proceeds to print them nevertheless, whether by himself or through his agent, is a violator of the law and will be "bitten by the snake" [of ostracism, excommunication, and anathema].[26] Further any person who knowingly purchases from such a transgressor after hearing of our decree will suffer anathema, while all of Israel who obey our decree will be blessed. Our decree will remain in force for the period of ten years, that is until the year 5289 [the Hebrew year spanning 1528–1529]. It applies to all who have not received permission from the honorable aforementioned Eliyahu or the aforementioned brothers, and said permission must be in writing.

Those who hear and abide by our words will be blessed, Amen. And he who purchases the books printed here in Rome by Rabbi Eliyahu and the aforementioned

22. *Babylonian Talmud, Kiddushin* 59a:71. The interloper is generally regarded as having engaged in immoral, but not illegal conduct. As such a rabbinic court would not require the interloper to deliver the item to the poor person. See generally Jachter 2010.

23. *Babylonian Talmud, Baba Batra* 21b.

24. Tosefot to *Kiddushin* 59a:71. Rabbi Meir ben Samuel was a founder of a school of medieval commentators on the Talmud from northern France and Germany, known as *tosafists* (or "those who made additions"), and the father of the most prominent *tosafist*, Jacob ben Meir (Rabbeinu Tam). In the same passage of Tosefot, Rabbi Meir's interpretation of the rule is applied to mean that a tutor who offers his services to one who has already hired another tutor engages in wrongful conduct that is tantamount to misappropriation.

25. *Babylonian Talmud, Sanhedrin* 81a.

26. *Naḥash*, the Hebrew word for "snake" is also an acronym for *niddui* (ostracism), *ḥerem* (ban or excommunication), and *shamta* (anathema), which are different aspects and stages of punishments in which a transgressor is denied a part of community life and religious ritual, with *ḥerem* being the most severe. They were, collectively, the most effective device for enforcing communal ordinances and rulings in medieval and early modern Jewish communities. See Cohn 2007: 14–15; Y. Kaplan 2000: 108–35 (presenting a detailed discussion of the social functions of the *ḥerem* in the Sephardi community of Amsterdam during the seventeenth century); Katz 2000: 84–86.

brothers will "exult and rejoice"[27] with his purchase and there will be good tidings upon him, Amen.

Written and signed this Friday, the fifth day of Tishrei, 5778 [September 10, 1518].

The speaker who is troubled and dejected, "whose heart is empty within him,"[28] the most insignificant, Yisrael, the son of the rabbi Yeḥiel, may his memory have a place in the world to come[29]

The most insignificant, Shabbatai, the son of Mordecai, may his memory be blessed

The small speaker, Yosef Hagri, the son of Avraham, may his memory be blessed.

II. BORROWING FROM BOOK PRIVILEGES

As noted above, the Bakhur decree stands far apart from papal and secular book privileges of its era in fundamental respects. The rabbinic decree purports to be a specific application of generally applicable halakhic precepts that forbid encroaching on another's livelihood; in contrast, the book privileges rest on the sovereign's prerogative to reward deserving subjects. Similarly, the decree's copious references to traditional Jewish texts find no parallels in papal or secular book privileges. Nor, for that matter, do the characteristically self-effacing signatures ("most insignificant," "small") of the esteemed members of Rome's rabbinic court. That verbal display of humility is meant to signify that the rabbis are merely diffident faithful servants in the transmission of venerable halakhic precepts already laid down by the greats of earlier generations; they are not legislating new law or exercising a prerogative of high office to grant special rights.

Nonetheless, the Rome rabbis evidently borrowed from the book privilege model, even as they translated its fundamental features into halakhic and rabbinic terms. To begin with, the Rome rabbis were undoubtedly familiar with papal and secular book privileges. By 1518, book privileges had already played a prominent role in the early modern book trade, centered in Italy, for some three decades. Indeed, just three years earlier, the Christian Hebraicist Daniel Bomberg, a leading publisher of Hebrew books of the day, had been awarded a 10-year papal privilege for his monumental four-volume edition of the *Mikraot Gedolot*, the Hebrew Bible with Rabbinic Commentaries, and had then successfully petitioned the Venetian Senate for an exclusive 10-year privilege to print any book in the Hebrew language.

27. "When the Lord restores the fortunes of his people, Jacob will exult and Israel will rejoice." Tehilim [Psalms] 14:7.

28. "Now You, Oh God, my Lord . . . save me. For I am poor and needy, and my heart is empty within me." Tehilim [Psalms] 109: 21–22.

29. Yisrael ben Yeḥiel Ashkenazi was a leading rabbinic authority in Italy. He was highly regarded for his knowledge of Talmud and served as the corrector of the Soncino edition of the Talmud printed in Pesaro from 1511 to 1513. See David 1973: 170–73; Rakover 1991: 131 n. 15.

For that matter, of course, prior to petitioning for a rabbinic ban, Eliyahu Bakhur had himself received a papal printing license and privilege for his grammar books. Bakhur obtained that papal "gratia e privilegio" with the assistance of his student and patron, the Catholic Kabbalist Cardinal Petrus Egidius of Viterbo, to whom Bakhur's three Hebrew grammar books were dedicated.[30] Hence, papal and secular book privileges, no less than Christian Hebraicist involvement in Hebrew printing, were salient features of the landscape in which the Rome rabbinical court issued its reprinting ban to Bakhur.

It is thus not all that surprising that, despite its rabbinic tenor, the Bakhur ban contains central features of the book privileges regularly issued by non-Jewish authorities. Indeed, a careful reading of the Bakhur ban strongly suggests that in crafting their decree the Rome rabbis drew specifically upon the book privileges with which they were familiar. The most obvious example is the rabbinic ban's 10-year term. Despite some variation, the 10-year term was standard for those issued by the Venetian Republic and the Holy See in the early sixteenth century. In contrast, recall that in other locations, notably France and the Holy Roman Empire, shorter terms were more common (even if, like Arnolt Schlick's privilege, Imperial authorities in the first quarter of the sixteenth century occasionally issued book privileges for 10-year terms as well). It is possible that the Rome rabbis independently determined that 10 years was the most appropriate period of time for Bakhur and his publishers to enjoy an exclusive window to print their books. But it appears more likely that the rabbis adopted the standard term for privileges with which they would have been most familiar: that of the Venetian Republic and the Holy See.

The fact that the Bakhur ban equally protects the author and his publishers also parallels the book privileges of the era. As we have seen, the book privileges served primarily to protect the publisher's economic investment, and were typically granted only to the publisher. The same was true of rabbinic reprinting bans, which only occasionally were awarded to an author of a new work in the author's own name. Indeed, like book privileges, rabbinic reprinting bans were often issued for print editions of centuries' old manuscripts, as well as for successive editions of previously printed books. Although the Bakhur books were newly authored, the Rome rabbis awarded their ban not just to Bakhur but also to his publishers, and made clear that either party could give written permission to another person to reprint the books.

Further, in extending their ban beyond any territorial borders, the Rome rabbis likely looked to the example of papal privileges, which typically asserted that they were enforceable throughout the Christian world. The worldwide reach of the rabbinic decree lacked a firm, native foundation in halakhic doctrine. Under long-established halakhic precepts, extending back to the demise of the Badhgdad Geonim in the tenth century, no rabbi had the authority to issue rulings binding upon all the Jewish people.[31] Even rabbinic decisors of great stature had no power to rule outside

30. Benayahu 1971: 19–20; Simonsohn 1988: vol. 3, 1602.

31. See Elon 1997: 548–55; Fram 1996: 361–62. As discussed in later chapters, the preeminent nineteenth century halakhic authority Moses Sofer (1762–1839) opined that

their local community, but rather had to garner wider acceptance for their rulings through the power of their reasoning and the respect accorded to them.

This territorial limitation applied with particular force to supplemental rabbinic edicts (referred as "de-rabbanan"), as opposed to rabbinic rulings that purport to interpret and apply a foundational rule expressly stated in the Torah or otherwise deemed to have been given to Moses at Mount Sinai (a rule that is "de-oraita"). In declaring that one who reprints a book without the author's or publisher's permission is an "actual misappropriator" (in Hebrew, "gozel mamash"), the Rome rabbis evidently posited that the juridical basis for their decree, the prohibition against encroaching on the livelihood of one who has invested money and labor in a commercial enterprise, amounts to a *de-oraita* legal rule. In so formulating their decree, the Rome rabbis stood contrary to the weight of rabbinic authority at the time, which understood the prohibition against encroaching on another's livelihood only as *de-rabbanan*, or even just as an ethical obligation.[32] In line with that prevailing understanding, a rabbinic edict prohibiting an act of wrongful encroachment would be limited to the city and environs in which the rabbi presided.

Even beyond this territorial constraint on rabbinic authority, the substantive rule protecting an individual against another's encroachment upon his livelihood was itself limited to that individual's territory. Prior to the Rome rabbis' decree, rabbinic jurists had never recognized, or even considered, a craftsman's right to prevent competition outside his local market. Certainly, the paradigm cases upon which the Jewish law of wrongful encroachment rested all involved the physical proximity of competitors engaged in premodern commercial enterprises that were tied to a particular geographic location. As introduced in the Talmud and subsequently debated, elucidated, and reformulated in later generations, the putatively wrongful competitor is one who sets up a mill in the same alleyway as the incumbent, spreads his net to seize fish that another fisherman was poised to capture, or grabs a crust of bread just as a poor man extends his hand to take possession of it.[33] In certain circumstances, a resident of another city who comes to compete in the incumbent's neighborhood also commits wrongful encroachment. But in no instance does a person commit a wrongful act by selling the same type of good or engaging in some other commercial activity in a different city—just as a fisherman does not wrongfully encroach by spreading his net the requisite short distance away from the first fisherman, even if both are then competing for the same school of fish.

Finally, the Rome rabbis' issuance of a general decree of excommunication (in Hebrew a "stam ḥerem") against any Jew who knowingly violates the Bakhur

cross-border enforcement of rabbinic reprinting bans is proper given that the market for books transcends local borders, but his was a minority view.

32. See Joseph Karo (1488–1575), *Beit Yosef*, Ḥoshen Mishpat 156; Meir ben Barukh (1215–1293), *Responsa of Ha-Maharam Me-Rotenberg*, No. 677.

33. *Babylonian Talmud, Baba Batra* 21b (the alleyway and the fish); *Kiddushin* 59a:71 (poor man and the bread). In Jewish tradition, the fish case is referred to as "sayara" (meaning that the fish have "set their sight" on the bait), and the poor man reaching for the bread as "ani mehapekh harara."

reprinting ban anywhere in the world would have been controversial in and of itself. According to the prevailing halakhic precept, if rabbinic decisors lacked the authority to issue substantive rulings that were binding on those outside their own community, all the more so were they lacking in authority to excommunicate a resident of another community.[34] Indeed, in 1511, the rabbis and lay leaders of Bologna had issued an edict prohibiting decrees of excommunication issued by non-local Jewish courts against any member of the Bolognese community. According to the edict, anyone seeking to enforce the *ḥerem* in Bologna would himself be cursed and excommunicated, as well as fined 100 florin, regardless of why or against whom the *ḥerem* was sought.[35]

In short, halakhic precepts and tradition imposed significant limits on the rabbinic court's authority to prohibit commercial activity in another country or to issue a *ḥerem* against residents of another country. The Rome rabbis sought to overcome these territorial constraints with the practical argument that, unlike traditional sources of livelihood, "printed books travel from sea to sea." But the rabbis also had before them the example of papal book privileges, which purported to apply throughout Christendom. While we cannot know for certain, the rabbis might have taken inspiration from that model.[36]

In contrast, the Rome rabbis' use of the threat of excommunication (alongside ostracism and anathema) to enforce their decree is probably not indicative of any borrowing from papal book privileges, even though the Holy See's privileges also typically declared that violators would suffer excommunication.[37] The rabbinic prerogative to order that a recalcitrant transgressor be shunned by the community and denied participation in religious ritual has roots in Talmudic times. Excommunication, or *ḥerem*, was typically the final stage, consisting of near absolute isolation for an indefinite period of time, following the lesser, temporary punishments of ostracism (*niddui*) and anathema (*shamta*).

34. See Isaac bar Sheshet (1326–1408) (known in Jewish tradition as "Rivash"), *Responsa Ha-Rivash*, No. 271. As we see in Chapter 6, Chief Rabbi of Moravia Mordekhai Banet (1753–1829) expressly applied Rivash's ruling to rabbinic reprinting bans. That precept appears to have been honored in the breach in early sixteenth century Italy, where rabbinic judges came to be embroiled in a series of bitter disputes between powerful Jewish groups, and issued decrees of excommunication and counter-excommunication against residents of neighboring Italian communities as well as their own. Unlike the Rome rabbis' reprinting ban, they did so in an effort to enforce their rulings elsewhere in Italy, not across the seas. Yet even within Italy, there was no guarantee that a general decree of excommunication would be enforced outside the community where it was issued. Cooperman 2004: 378.

35. Cooperman 2004: 367. As Cooperman describes, the Bologna edict itself gave rise to considerable controversy.

36. As we see in subsequent chapters, the Rome rabbis' halakhic innovation came to be a central feature of rabbinic reprinting bans. But the initial acceptance of rabbis' authority to ban reprinting anywhere in the world floundered in the late eighteenth century; rabbinic decisors of that era, adapting to external political developments and the waning juridical autonomy of Jewish communities, ruled that rabbinic reprinting bans were indeed limited to the territory where they were issued.

37. Maclean 2012: 153 (describing papal privileges).

Although semiautonomous medieval and early modern Jewish communities were sometimes able to imprison and fine those who violated community norms, excommunication was the ultimate tool by which rabbis could punish violators and bring about compliance with rabbinic decrees. By the early modern era, lay Jewish communal councils often limited rabbinic power to issue a decree of *ḥerem*. But with communal council support, the Rome rabbis' order that their decree banning the reprinting of Eliyahu Bakhur's books would be enforceable by *ḥerem* came to be a universal feature of rabbinic reprinting bans. In the traditionally observant Jewish world, indeed, a rabbinic reprinting ban is commonly referred to as "a ḥerem."

The threat of excommunication distinguishes both rabbinic reprinting bans and papal book privileges from secular privileges, inasmuch as secular sovereigns enjoyed no power to excommunicate. At the same time, the presence of the threat of excommunication in both rabbinic reprinting bans and papal book privileges likely reflects only that it was a venerable and highly effective tool of enforcement for rabbis and the Holy See alike. Given that rabbinic authorities had already employed the threat and sanction of *ḥerem* for centuries prior to the advent of print, the Rome rabbis would not have needed to look to the example of papal book privileges to resort to that means of enforcement in their rabbinic ban.

Finally, beyond their commonalities in legal framework, the Bakhur ban and the Schlick privilege, like other book privileges of their era, express prevailing early modern understandings regarding the nature of authorship (even if they do so in stylized terms designed to provide justification for granting the author an exclusive entitlement to print the book in question). The early sixteenth century preceded the Western world's recognition and embrace of individuals' capacity for self-expression and imagination. The view of authors as originators of creative expression, as opposed to reformulators of classic knowledge, began to take hold much later, during the Enlightenment; indeed, the exaltation of the author as creator reached its peak only with early nineteenth-century Romanticism.[38] It is no accident that neither the Bakhur ban nor the Schlick privilege were for works of fiction—nor that Bakhur applied for a privilege for his grammar books and not his Yiddish romance, *Bove Bukh*. In the early modern period, virtually no rabbinic reprinting bans, and only a small percentage of book privileges, were awarded for works featuring the author's creativity and imagination.[39]

Granted, the rabbinic reprinting ban notes that Bakhur's books present rules and principles of grammar that no one had previously elucidated. But it does so only to highlight the books' important contribution to understanding Hebrew grammar, not to recognize the author's capacity for creating original expression. Like the Schlick privilege, the ban lauds the author's initiative, expertise, diligence, and generosity in producing a useful book. In contrast to post-Enlightenment thought and modern copyright jurisprudence, it does not depict the author as one who possesses distinct

38. See Taylor 1989: 167–75; Sherman and Bently 1999: 35–38.

39. As discussed below, relatively few rabbinic bans were issued for books in Yiddish either, and when Bakhur wrote *Bove Bukh*, the rabbinic leadership generally opposed printing texts in Yiddish. See Smith 2003: xxi.

personality, a gift of creativity, or the power of bringing something new into the world. Indeed, in referring to Bakhur's act of authoring the grammar books, the rabbinic ban uses the Hebrew word, *ḥiber*, which connotes joining together or composing from pre-existing materials, not *yotzer*, which means "to create," and is the modern Hebrew term used to refer to original authorship.[40] Similarly, the Schlick privilege describes how the organist, diligently "gathered together" various rules, principles, and instructions to compose his organ manual.

To be certain, both the ban and privilege also tout the preeminence of the author as a renowned expert. The Rome rabbis emphasize that they "know this man" and can attest that he is doubly wise in matters of Hebrew grammar. Emperor Maximilian notes that the Elector Palatine and other princes had repeatedly asked Schlick to share his knowledge of organ construction by authoring a manual. That emphasis on the author's expertise lends credence to the assertion that the protected works are especially useful. It also suggests, perhaps, that it is not just the book as a product of the author's expertise and labor but the author himself who is especially deserving of protection. Even so, the author is especially worthy because he is a fount of useful knowledge, not because he is a self-expressive creator.

The Bakhur ban and Schlick privilege are also indicative of early modern understandings of authorship in the way they depict the author's efforts in producing useful books. The ban and privilege do not merely underscore the considerable labor that the author has devoted to creating the book. They further characterize that labor in terms of self-sacrifice—an act of abnegation as opposed to a self-expressive, creative project that the author would likely find fulfilling. The rabbinic ban refers to the Bakhur's "effort," "labor," and "pains." Maximilian's privilege invokes Schlick's "labor and sorrow." Granted, both the ban and privilege are postured to justify granting an exclusive printing privilege to the respective authors rather than to explicate a broad understanding of what is the true nature of authorship. But it is telling, nonetheless, that both justify awarding such a privilege by reference to the pain and sorrow that the authors purportedly suffered in the process of writing the books. That trope of self-sacrifice contrasts with the modern notion, which, indeed, is the dominant premise of the Continental European copyright tradition, that copyright law serves to enable authors to fulfill their creative impulse and to protect the stamp of the author's personality embodied in his work.

In sum, the Rome rabbis who awarded Bakhur a 10-year reprinting ban seem to have knowingly adopted as a norm of Jewish law the practice, regnant among the Gentile sovereigns of early sixteenth-century Europe, of granting books privileges to protect authors' and publishers' investment in producing books. In support of according Bakhur and his publishers an exclusive entitlement to print Bakhur's three grammar books, they lauded Bakhur as a purveyor of useful knowledge

40. *Yotzer* is the term used in the State of Israel's current copyright (or "authors' rights") statute, the Copyright Act of 2007. The English terms originally had similar connotations. In Late Middle English, to "create" meant "to form out of nothing," while to "compose" meant "to put something together." In medieval English, the word "author" referred to a person who originated, invented, or caused something, and God was sometimes described as "the Author of all." Cresswell 2009: 28, 96, 107.

who devoted considerable labor and self-sacrifice to make a generous, valuable contribution to the public good. The rabbis thus expressed a view of authorship that was common to secular and papal privileges of the early modern era as well.

Yet the Rome rabbis did not—and, indeed, could not—simply transplant the privilege regime into halakhic doctrine. Rather they borrowed central features from papal and secular book privileges and combined them with rabbinic sensibilities, halakhic principles, and rules designed to meet the needs of far-flung Jewish communities. In the process, the rabbis produced a blueprint for reprinting bans that reflected the particularities of Jewish law and experience even as it borrowed from and evinced some of the same cultural understandings as the book privileges issued by secular and papal authorities.

III. DELAYED ADOPTION OF RABBINIC REPRINTING BANS

The Rome rabbinic court's issuance of a reprinting ban to Bakhur and his publishers did not rapidly lead to widespread adoption of the practice in the Hebrew book trade. With the notable exception of Meir Katzenellenbogen's petition to Moses Isserles in 1550 (the subject of our next chapter) and a couple of rabbinic reprinting bans issued in Salonika and Constantinople, printers and authors who sought exclusive entitlements to print Hebrew books continued to rely primarily on secular and papal privileges until the final quarter of the sixteenth century.[41] Indeed, when Eliyahu Bakhur published the *Book of Psalms with Commentary of Rabbi David Kimḥi* in Isny im Allgäu, Germany, in 1542, he included a prominent Hebrew notice of the exclusive 10-year privilege that he had received from the Emperor, but made no mention of any rabbinic ban.[42] It was not until 1578 that the first rabbinic reprinting ban was issued in the major Hebrew printing center of Venice—although from that point forward, rabbinic bans largely supplanted Venetian privileges for Hebrew books printed in the Republic.[43]

Given the ubiquity of secular and papal book privileges in the early sixteenth century, why did the Rome rabbinic court's decree in favor of Eliyahu Bakhur remain for several decades a near lone example of a rabbinic reprinting ban? The Rome rabbinic court itself would have had no immediate occasion to issue additional reprinting

41. In 1551 a reprinting ban was issued for Yitzhak Yosef Ha-Cohen's, *Perush Megilat Rut Megale Sod Ha-Geula* in Salonika. In 1554, Moshe bar Yosef Pigo issued a decree forbidding the reprinting of his own book, *Zikharon Torat Moshe*, printed in Constantinople. In 1566, a ban was issued for a Constantinople edition of *Sefer Yuḥasin*, by Avraham ben Shmuel Zecuto (1452–1514).

42. Benayahu 1971: 21

43. Benayahu 1971: 30. The first complete edition of the Babylonian Talmud protected by a rabbinic reprinting ban was printed in Frankfurt an der Ode, in 1699; it followed eight complete editions of the Babylonian Talmud that had been printed since 1519 without a rabbinic ban, those printed in Venice by Daniel Bomberg (1519–1523; 1526–1539; and 1543–1549) and Marc Antonio Giustiniani (1546–1551), and later editions published in Basel (1578–1581), Constantinople (1583–1585), Krakow (1612–1615), and Lublin (1617–1639).

bans inasmuch as, following the printing of Bakhur's grammar trilogy in 1518, no other Hebrew book was printed in Rome until 1540.[44] But what of their contemporary rabbinic authorities in printing centers elsewhere in Italy and the wider Jewish world? Why did they not emulate the example of their Roman colleagues by promulgating their own reprinting bans?

There are a number of plausible explanations. The first concerns the fundamentally conservative character of rabbinic jurisprudence. Despite the Rome rabbis' effort to cast themselves as mere faithful amanuenses of long-standing halakhic precepts, their decree necessarily constituted a bold halakhic innovation. To protect Bakhur's books against reprinting, the rabbis took venerable Talmudic injunctions against encroaching on another's livelihood and applied them to the new business of printing and selling books, a business that the technology of the printing press made at once possible and vulnerable to ruinous competition. In so doing, the Rome rabbis stretched beyond traditional halakhic precepts to rule that one who reprints a book anywhere in the world, not just one who wrongfully competes in his fellow craftman's local market, violates those injunctions. Granted, the rabbis cited proof texts and reasoned from traditional sources in support of their innovative ruling. But they did so in a relatively cursory fashion. It was not until well after 1550, when Moses Isserles—the young rabbi of Krakow who would soon become the leading rabbinic authority of Ashkenazic Jewry of his generation—adduced more extensive argumentation why a reprinter might violate the injunction against encroaching on another's livelihood, that other rabbis began to issue reprinting bans.[45]

In addition, rabbinic reprinting bans spread relatively slowly because there would have been little demand for them among the printers of Hebrew books until the mid-sixteenth century. In the decades immediately preceding and following the Rome rabbis' decree, three successive well-heeled printers, Gershom Soncino, Daniel Bomberg, and Marc Antonio Giustiniani, overwhelmingly dominated the lucrative market for high quality Hebrew books of Jewish law, learning, commentary, and liturgy—the very books for which the subject matter and considerable printing expense would most lend themselves to petitioning for a rabbinic reprinting ban. During their respective periods of dominance—for Soncino roughly from 1488 to 1516; Bomberg, from 1516 until his death in 1549; and Giustiniani, initially competing with Bomberg, from 1545 to 1552—each publisher repeatedly issued large print runs of superior quality editions of major classics of Jewish learning for international distribution. Many of these titles were in multi-volume folio sets and involved the costly purchase and expert editing of aged manuscripts. None of the

44. That book was also a book of Hebrew grammar: *Sefer Dikduk*, printed by Shmuel Tzarfati and authored by the rabbi, grammarian, and philosopher, David ben Yosef ibn Yahya (1465–1543), who fled with his family from Lisbon to Italy in 1496.

45. It is also possible that the Rome rabbis lacked sufficient prestige in other countries to convince other rabbis to follow their lead. But that is not likely. The Rome rabbinic court's presiding rabbinic judge, Yisrael ben Yeḥiel Ashkenazi, was a leading rabbinic authority in Italy and, later, Jerusalem. David 1973: 170–73.

three leading printers faced serious competition in their lucrative markets—except from one another during the periods in which they overlapped. Other Hebrew book publishers of that era could not have hoped to match the leading printers' resources, workmanship, and widespread distribution networks. They survived instead by printing shorter and smaller books of lower quality type and paper for local markets. Those books rarely warranted the time and expense required to petition for a rabbinic reprinting ban.[46]

That overwhelming market dominance helps to explain why none of the three printers would have bothered to seek rabbinic reprinting bans. But what about rivalry between them? Why did Soncino not seek rabbinic bans to prevent Bomberg from reprinting titles that Soncino had printed? And why did Bomberg not do the same vis-à-vis Giustiniani? After all, there were periods of intense competition between them, as Bomberg supplanted Soncino and Giustiniani supplanted Bomberg. Further, each successor did, in fact, copy from his predecessor's titles. Soncino complained, vociferously and accurately, that Bomberg's first complete edition of the Babylonian Talmud, which Bomberg published between 1519 and 1523, plagiarized portions of Soncino's previously printed tractates.[47] And decades later, Giustiniani quickly followed a number of Bomberg printings with a competing edition of the same or similar title.

Further, despite their market dominance, Soncino and Bomberg were far from uninterested in seeking privileges from Gentile authorities. Before Bomberg arrived on the scene, Soncino had petitioned the Venetian Senate for a license to print Hebrew books in Venice, and, possibly, for a monopoly over Hebrew printing as well. Soncino was unsuccessful in his quest. In addition to the Senate's likely unwillingness to grant such a privilege to a Jew, Soncino faced the staunch opposition of the leading Venetian printer of that time, Aldus Manutius, who had his own ambitions to print Hebrew books.[48] Spurned in Venice, Soncino then proceeded to set up shop in a series of Italian towns whose leaders were eager to attract printers, including

46. Benayahu 1971: 20; Heller 2006; Amram 1988; Baruchson 1990: 27–34; Baruchson 1986: 55–57 (noting that early sixteenth century Hebrew printers in the Ottoman Empire lacked the knowledge and financial resources to compete with Venetian Hebrew printers); Teter and Fram 2006: 32–37 (comparing books printed by the first Hebrew printers of Krakow in 1530s and those of their contemporary, Daniel Bomberg). For example, Gershon ben Shmuel Ha-Cohen, who established a Hebrew press in Prague in 1512 and who, in 1527, was granted a monopoly by King Ferdinand I for the printing of Hebrew books in Bohemia, printed almost entirely prayer books and other short liturgical works. See Wischnitzer 1954: 345 (referring to Ha-Cohen's press and royal monopoly). In addition to those differences in quality, the Soncino family members were virtually the only Hebrew printers in the world from 1494 to 1504, a decade shortly following the expulsion of Jews from Spain, while Bomberg, as we have noted, obtained a legal monopoly in 1515 over all Hebrew printing in Venice, the capital of the Hebrew book trade, a monopoly he was able to extend until 1536.

47. Heller 2006: 61, 74. Among other sources, Bomberg copied medieval Ashkenazi commentary on the Talmud known as the Tosafot, which Soncino had painstakingly selected and printed alongside the pertinent Talmudic text in his tractates. Heller 2006: 70–71.

48. See Stern 2011: 76, 79.

Fano, Pizarro, Brescia, Ortona, and Rimini. In each location, Soncino held at least a de facto, if not de jure, printing monopoly as well as other concessions.[49]

For his part, the well-heeled Bomberg petitioned the Venetian Senate for his 10-year monopoly to print Hebrew books after he had already received a papal license and privilege for his edition of the *Mikraot Gedolot*. Bomberg then paid the Venetian treasury the sizable sum of 500 ducats to renew his monopoly for another 10 years in 1526.[50] Bomberg and his early collaborator, the Jewish apostate turned Augustinian friar Felix Pratensis, also obtained papal privileges for three substantial book projects. These included, in addition to the *Mikraot Gedolot*, a Latin translation of Psalms and Bomberg's first edition of the Talmud. Later, Bomberg also sought, without success, to obtain a new 10-year papal privilege for his second edition of the Talmud. Further, after his monopoly in Venice expired, Bomberg continued to petition for privileges for particular books.[51]

So why, in each instance, did the incumbent printer, namely Soncino and Bomberg, seek privileges from Gentile authorities, but not rabbinic protection against reprinting? Here, too, there are a number of plausible explanations, primarily stemming from the complexities of Jewish-Christian relations in early sixteenth-century Europe. First and foremost, Bomberg and Giustiniani, like all leading Venetian printers of Hebrew books until the eighteenth century, were Christians. In Venice, as in the leading printing centers of Germany, Jews were forbidden from engaging in printing, whether by trade guild regulations or municipal ordinance.[52] Likewise, as previously noted, Pope Leo X required Eliyahu Bakhur and his Jewish publishers to retain a Christian printer to print Bakhur's three Hebrew grammar books in Rome.

The fact that the two printers who dominated the high-end Hebrew book trade from 1516 to 1552 were Christians presented an obvious obstacle to any rabbinic decree purporting to grant either Soncino an enforceable privilege against Bomberg or Bomberg

49. See M. Marx 1935: 437, 457–58, 470–71. While in Fano, Soncino took his revenge against Aldus: he lured away Aldus's type founder, Francesco da Bologna, and, with Bologna's help, proceeded to reproduce Aldus's new italic typeface. Loewenstein 2002: 73–74.

50. Heller 1999: 73; Baruchson 1993: 131–33; Bloch 1976: 70–72. In 1489, the Collegio of Venice granted Democrito Terracina a 25-year monopoly to print books in esoteric languages, including Arabic, Moorish, Syriac, Armenian, and Abyssinian. It renewed the monopoly for another 25 years in 1513 in favor of Terracina's nephews even though Terracina, who died in 1513, had not printed a single book in those languages. See Krek 1979: 208–09.

51. The papal brief of July 16, 1532, issued in response to Bomberg's petition, is reproduced in Simonsohn 1988, Doc. 1559, 1837–38. See also Benayahu 1971: 23 (noting that Bomberg received Venetian privileges for newly printed books).

52. As in Venice, Jewish publishers regularly circumvented those restrictions by partnering with Christian printers, who served as a cover for their Jewish partner by publishing Hebrew and Yiddish books in their own name. Baumgarten 2009: ¶ 3. In addition, Christian printers of Hebrew books heavily depended on knowledgeable Jews, or Jewish apostates, to act as editors and correctors. When Daniel Bomberg applied to the Council of Ten for a monopoly of Hebrew printing in 1515, he thus made a special request to allow Jews to work in his printing house. Benayahu 1971: 17. Similarly, the prominent Christian Humanist printers Johan and Ambrosius Froben received permission from the Basel city council to print Hebrew books in that city, but had to apply for special residency permits for their Jewish compositors, typesetters, and master printer. Heller 2008: 133–35. Jews did print Hebrew books under royal license in sixteenth-century Prague, Krakow, Lublin, and Constantinople. Gries 2008.

an enforceable privilege against Giustiniani. Christians had no obligation and, typically, little reason to abide by rabbinic decrees. Rabbis might have circumvented that enforcement barrier, at least in part, by forbidding Jews from aiding in or financing a Christian's reprinting of a book protected by a rabbinic ban. Additionally, Jews could arguably be prohibited from buying such a book, as in the Rome rabbinic court decree in favor of Eliyahu Bakhur. But as a matter of Jewish law, such strategies stood on uncertain ground unless the Christian printer could be said to be violating Noaḥide law, the body of Jewish law that purports to govern the conduct of non-Jews. And that complex issue was not authoritatively addressed until 1550, with the halakhic ruling that is the subject of our next chapter—the ruling issued by Moses Isserles of Krakow in response to Meir Katzenellenbogen's complaint against none other than Marc Antonio Giustiniani.

Of course, problems surrounding the enforceability and applicability of rabbinic reprinting bans against non-Jews might have been confronted before 1550 had Soncino or one of Bomberg's Jewish editors sought a rabbinic ruling on that point. But given the surrounding political circumstances and market conditions, it is highly doubtful that either Soncino or Bomberg would have seriously considered seeking rabbinic protection against the successor who eventually supplanted him.

Soncino correctly viewed Bomberg's plan to publish the Talmud as a major competitive threat. And there is evidence that Soncino hoped to undercut Bomberg by reissuing his own edition of the Talmud's first tractate, *Berakhot*, before Bomberg could print his.[53] Yet, as Soncino must have been palpably aware, it would have been futile to petition rabbinic authorities to favor him over Bomberg by ruling that Soncino had an exclusive right to print the Talmud and that Jewish law forbade Jews from assisting Bomberg by editing or buying Bomberg's tractates. At that juncture, a rabbinic reprinting ban in favor of Soncino—and against Bomberg—would have posed a direct affront to the Holy See and its nascent, yet fragile support for Hebrew printing. It would also have flown in the face of Bomberg's steadfast resistance to papal pressure that he include Christian apologetics in his books of Jewish law and learning.

In 1520, Pope Leo X granted an imprimatur and 10-year privilege for Bomberg's first edition of the Talmud, akin to that which the Pope had issued in 1515 for Bomberg's printing of the *Mikraot Gedolot*.[54] Pope Leo's imprimatur for the Talmud reversed long-standing papal policy, formally in effect since the early thirteenth century, if sporadically enforced in practice, that the Talmud was heretical and thus to be suppressed or censored.[55] It also effectively put to rest a campaign to confiscate and burn all copies of the Talmud in the Holy Roman Empire, which had been instigated pursuant to a mandate issued by Emperor Maximilian I in 1509.[56]

53. See Rosenthal 1987: 384.

54. The text of Bomberg's privilege for the Talmud has not survived. However, it is described in a papal brief, dated July 26, 1532, absolving Bomberg for printing the Talmud without the responses of the Augustine friar, Felix Pratensis.

55. See, generally, Shamir 2011. The Church's position on the Talmud stood in tension with ecclesiastical doctrine that called for preserving the Jews and their books. For that reason and others, the Church's active interference with Jews' hand-copying and study of the Talmud was local and sporadic. J. Cohen 1999: 331–36.

56. Shamir 2011: 7.

Pope Leo's motives were hardly philo-Semitic. His imprimatur and privilege for Bomberg's Talmud required that Bomberg include a written "response" from the apostate, Felix Pratensis, pointing out fatal weaknesses and contradictions in passages that challenged the Christian faith. For that reason and others, the rabbinic leadership initially had considerable reservations about an edition of the Talmud published by a Christian. Ultimately, however, Bomberg chose to risk incurring papal wrath rather than alienating potential Jewish buyers: his lavish multi-volume edition of the Talmud was devoid of any such Christian rebuttal. (At least that was the case regarding the Talmud tractates that Bomberg printed for the Jewish market; it is possible that he printed a different version for Christians, as he had for several other books, including the *Mikraot Gedolot*.)[57] Under those circumstances, it was well-nigh inconceivable that rabbinic leaders in Italy or elsewhere would issue a reprinting ban in favor of Soncino's Talmud in direct conflict with Bomberg and his papal privilege.

In any event, Soncino was no match for Bomberg, the wealthy scion of one of the leading trading families in Europe and the holder of the highly profitable monopoly over all Hebrew printing in Venice, the world capital of the book trade.[58] The itinerant Soncino struggled to issue 13 individual tractates of the 37 comprising the Babylonian Talmud between the years 1493 and 1519, including some that had previously been printed by his uncle, Joshua Solomon Soncino. In contrast, Bomberg had the financial wherewithal, as well as a team of esteemed rabbinically trained scholars serving as editors and correctors, to publish 10 tractates the first year and the full Talmud in three years. And although Bomberg did copy from some of Soncino's tractates, he also added new commentaries and worked with manuscripts that were unavailable to Soncino.[59]

For his part, the Venetian patrician Marc Antonio Giustiniani began to print Hebrew books in fierce competition with Bomberg in 1545. By that time, although Bomberg's Venetian press remained active, Bomberg, a Calvinist, had returned to his home city of Antwerp, reportedly to escape the repressive Counter-Reformation

57. See Nielsen 2011: 71–72 (enumerating a number of occasions in which Bomberg printed and marketed a different version of a title for Christians than for Jews). In addition to issuing two versions of his 1517 edition of the *Mikraot Gedolot*, Bomberg reissued the *Mikraot Gedolot* in 1525 under the direction of a Jewish editor and without Pratensis's condemnation and Christian typologies. Bomberg eventually incurred a sentence of excommunication from the Catholic Church for flouting the requirements of his papal imprimaturs that he include Christian apologetics in the publications. In 1532 he appealed to Pope Clement VII for exoneration and for a new 10-year privilege for his second edition of the Talmud. Pope Clement issued the exoneration (but not a new privilege) on the condition that Bomberg refrain from printing or selling the Talmud without Pratensis's responses. Indeed, Pope Clement insisted that Bomberg desist from printing any additional books at all. See Simonsohn 1988: Doc. 1559, 1837–38 (reproducing the papal brief of July 16, 1532). Bomberg ignored that papal order as well. He continued to print the second edition of the Talmud (1526–1539) and subsequently printed a third edition (1543–1549) without Pratensis's responses.

58. As a result of his monopoly, Bomberg's printing house was one of the most profitable enterprises in the Venetian print industry. Baruchson 1990: 27.

59. Heller 1999: 74–75.

atmosphere in Venice.[60] The Bomberg press continued to issue some titles that had not previously been printed; as these were eligible for Venetian book privileges, they were generally protected against Giustiniani.[61] However, Bomberg also printed classic, previously printed titles that Giustiniani then reprinted, albeit sometimes with some added commentary and further editing.[62]

Perhaps Bomberg or his Jewish editor could have sought a rabbinic decree to protect those titles against reprinting—or, more precisely, to forbid Jews from buying competing reprints. It later came to be common practice in Venice for the Jewish editor or financer of a Christian printer's edition of a book of Jewish liturgy or learning to seek a rabbinic decree banning reprinting of the book. But, as we shall presently see, the rabbinic leadership in Venice would likely have been no more willing than the Venetian Senate to award bans for previously printed titles. In any event, by the time Giustiniani emerged onto the scene, Bomberg—whose familial status and multifaceted international trading enterprise had gained him entry to royal courts all over Europe, and who marketed his high-end Hebrew-language books to Christian Hebraicists as well as to Jews—would hardly have stooped to seek rabbinic protection rather than simply continuing to compete on the basis of his sterling reputation, seamless distribution network, and the quality of his books.[63] Bomberg would also have had a lot to lose by petitioning for a rabbinic reprinting ban. As it was, some Christian authorities suspected him of Judaising, and it would have hardly been beneficial for his publishing or broader trading enterprise to lend credence to that charge.[64] When it suited him, moreover, Bomberg also appropriated some of Giustiniani's editing and improvements, including in Bomberg's third and final edition of the Babylonian Talmud, completed in 1549.[65]

It was not until the following year that the fierce competition among Christian Venetian publishers for dominance of the Hebrew book trade finally came before a rabbinic decisor. In 1550, the Jewish partner of Giustiniani's new rival, Alvise Bragadini, petitioned Moses Isserles of Krakow, Poland, for a ruling recognizing exclusive printing rights against Giustiniani. Isserles's judgment in that matter still stands as a cornerstone of Jewish copyright law. We now turn to that seminal dispute, the Maharam of Padua versus Giustiniani.

60. Heller 1999: 76.

61. Benayahu 1971: 23. As noted in Chapter 2, the Venetian Senate decree of 1515 permitted book privileges only for works that had not previously been printed.

62. Bomberg printed an edition of *Midrash Rabba* in 1545 and Giustiniani printed his edition of the same work in 1546. Bomberg also issued a new edition of the holiday prayer book, Roman rite, in 1545; Giustiniani issued the same book that year and again in 1547. Bomberg published *Seder Maamadot* in 1545; Giustiniani in 1547. Bomberg published *Halakhot Gedolot* in 1545; Giustiniani in 1548.

63. For an illuminating account of Bomberg's international trade enterprise and familial status, see Nielsen 2011. Bomberg's books sold well to Christians throughout Europe, even if the centers of Christian printing of Hebrew books were generally concentrated in Germany, France, and the Netherlands. See Ruderman 2010: 117.

64. Maclean 2012: 125 (noting that Bomberg had been suspected of Judaising).

65. Heller 1999: 76.

CHAPTER 4

Maharam of Padua versus Giustiniani

Rival Editions of Maimonides's Mishneh Torah

In 1550, Rabbi Meir ben Isaac Katzenellenbogen of Padua (known in Jewish tradition as the "Maharam of Padua") completed a new edition of Moses Maimonides's seminal code of Jewish law, the *Mishneh Torah*. Katzenellenbogen invested significant time, effort, and money in producing the edition. When the rabbi from Padua embarked on his project, Maimonides's classic code had already been printed several times—the first in Rome before 1480 and the latest by Daniel Bomberg in 1524.[1] Katzenellenbogen worked from these editions, primarily Bomberg's, but added commentaries by Maimonides and other medieval authorities that had not previously appeared with the *Mishneh Torah* in print. He and his son also appended sparse annotations of their own (numbering only roughly a dozen) to Maimonides's text.

Katzenellenbogen initially approached Marc Antonio Giustiniani to print the work. By that time, Daniel Bomberg had died and his printing house had ceased to operate. Giustiniani had stepped into the breach left by his formal rival; he now enjoyed a near monopoly over Hebrew printing in Venice. For whatever reason, the rabbi from Padua and the Christian printer did not come to terms. Katzenellenbogen instead joined forces with the Venetian patrician Alvise Bragadini to establish a new Hebrew press in Venice in Bragadini's name.[2] Bragadini's first publication was

1. Posner and Ta-Shema 1975: 211.

2. Amram 1998: 255–56; Breger 1995: 940. The dispute over the *Mishneh Torah* was the beginning of a bitter rivalry between the two presses, with Bragadini ultimately gaining the upper hand. Giustiniani ceased publication in 1552, while the House of Bragadini emerged to dominate Hebrew printing in Venice until well into the eighteenth century. Bloch 1976: 86.

Katzenellenbogen's edition of the *Mishneh Torah*, printed in Venice in 1550 and apparently financed by the rabbi.

Giustiniani was not to be outdone. He countered by issuing his own edition of the Maimonides's seminal code, one that both copied Katzenellenbogen's annotations and included an introduction criticizing them as worthless. Giustiniani further proclaimed that he would sell his edition for one gold coin less than his competitor's, ostensibly to enable more Jewish readers to have access to the foundational text. Katzenellenbogen then petitioned Rabbi Moses Isserles to forbid Jews from buying the Giustiniani edition. Isserles's resulting responsum and decree presented an extensive explication of a right to prevent reprinting under Jewish law.

I. THE MAHARAM, MOSES ISSERLES, AND THE *MISHNEH TORAH*

The Maharam of Padua was a leading rabbinical authority of his day. He was born in Katzenellenbogen, Germany, in 1473. After studying in Prague, he moved to the Venetian town of Padua, a seat of secular and Jewish learning that drew students from all over Europe.[3] Katzenellenbogen succeeded his father-in-law, Abraham Minz, as chief rabbi of Padua in 1525. Katzenellenbogen held the title, *Moreinu Ha-Rav* (meaning "Our Master, the Rabbi"), which connoted great academic distinction and gave him authority to exercise the highest functions of rabbinical office.[4] As such, Katzenellenbogen served the semiautonomous Jewish community of the Venetian Republic in a multifaceted role of spiritual leader, judge, legislator, professor, and dean, presiding over the Jewish community court of the Venice Republic, the Venetian regional council of rabbis, and the renowned *yeshiva* of Padua until his death in 1565. Although Katzenellenbogen was especially prominent in Italy, rabbis from throughout the Ashkenazic world praised and followed his rulings.[5]

For his part, Moses Isserles (known in Jewish tradition as the "Rema") came to be one of the preeminent Ashkenazic rabbinical authorities of the modern era, a place cemented by the publication of his glosses on the *Shulḥan Arukh*. But in 1550, Isserles was still a relative youngster—between 20 and 30 years old, depending on differing estimates of his year of birth—and had just been appointed Rabbi of Krakow.[6] In fact, his ruling on Katzenellenbogen's petition was his very first responsum.[7] The Rema

3. Tal 2007: 19–20; Ziv 1968: 160. Padua's university was the second oldest in Italy, its medical school generally regarded as the best in Europe. Ruderman 1995: 105–06.

4. See Bonfil 1994: 137–43 (discussing the power, prerogatives, and role of rabbis in Renaissance Italy). "Maharam" is an acronym of "Moreinu Ha-Rav Meir," meaning "Our Master, the Rabbi Meir."

5. Elbaum 1990: 35.

6. Ben-Sasson 1984: 5 (noting the disagreement among scholars regarding Isserles's year of birth).

7. Elbaum 1990: 34 n. 5.

later remarked that he had felt exceedingly unprepared to undertake the responsibility of serving as a rabbinic judge at such a young age.[8]

Thus, in 1550, the Maharam of Padua was very much Isserles's senior, both chronologically and in terms of rabbinic authority. The young Isserles would have been far more likely to seek Katzenellenbogen's authoritative ruling on matters of halakha than the other way around. Indeed, Isserles actively sought and cited Katzenellenbogen's opinion in a number of instances following his proto-copyright ruling in 1550.[9]

So why, in this instance, did Katzenellenbogen seek assistance from the young rabbi in Poland rather than turning to a senior colleague in Italy? We consider several possible reasons.

A. The Market

The centers of Jewish learning in Poland constituted the largest market for both Katzenellenbogen's and Giustiniani's editions of the *Mishneh Torah*. Katzenellenbogen published his edition of the *Mishneh Torah* in the midst of over a century of persecution and turmoil for European Jewry. The Spanish Inquisition, formally instituted in 1481, and the expulsion of Jews from Spain in 1492 were part of a tide of violence, pillage, forced conversion, and expulsion that swept through the monarchies and principalities of France, Germany, Portugal, the Low Countries, Switzerland, Austria, and Naples and that was soon followed by the further virulent anti-Semitic ferment of the Protestant Reformation.[10] The result was a mass exodus of Jews from western and central Europe. By 1550, the central and northern Italian peninsula had become home to thousands of Jewish refugees, and was virtually the only part of western Europe where Jews remained. However, most Ashkenazic Jews had migrated not south to Italy, but east to Poland, whereas most Jews from Spain and Portugal had migrated to the Ottoman Empire. By the middle of the sixteenth century, between a half to two-thirds of the world's Jewish population lived in Poland, and about a half of the remainder lived in the Ottoman Empire, principally in Salonika and Constantinople.[11] Hence, aside from Italy, which, in the first half of the sixteenth

8. Moses Isserles (d. 1572), *Darkhei Moshe*, Introduction. *Darkhei Moshe* is a commentary on the *Arba'a Turim* (known in Jewish tradition as the "Tur"), a seminal halakhic code composed by Jacob ben Asher (c. 1269–1343).

9. Ziv 1968: 178–79, 181.

10. See Israel 1998: 4–14. Jews had been expelled from England in 1294, and were readmitted by Oliver Cromwell in 1656. Fram 1996: 362.

11. Population numbers are loose estimates. Jonathan Israel puts the Jewish population of Poland in 1500 at 30,000 (less than the Jewish population of Italy at that time), but at between 100,000 and 150,000 by 1575. He estimates that the Jewish populations of Constantinople and Salonika each exceeded 20,000 in 1550. The Jewish population of Safed in 1560 was approximately 5,000. Israel 1998: 22–24. Another source estimates the Jewish population of Venice and Padua in the middle of the sixteenth century at less than 1,000 each and the Jewish population for all of Italy in 1630 at 30,000. Shulvass 1951: 10, 15. Another survey puts the Jewish population of the Ottoman Empire at between 50,000

century, still housed the leading Ashkenazic *yeshivot*, potential Jewish purchasers of the *Mishneh Torah* were concentrated primarily in Poland and secondarily in the Ottoman Empire.[12]

B. Communal Ties

In that era, moreover, relations among Ashkenazic Jews of Italy and Poland were especially close. Indeed, given their common origin, customs, outlook, and Yiddish language, Ashkenazic Jews of Italy had greater kinship with their coreligionists in Poland than with Sephardic and native Italian Jews in Italy.[13] During the first half of the sixteenth century, Polish students frequently came to study in Italy, and Ashkenazic scholars traveled regularly between the two Ashkenazic centers, sometimes migrating from one to the other. In addition, rabbinic decisors from one center often turned to rabbis from the other for rulings or support on various matters.

The flow of print both manifested and strengthened those close ties between Italy and Poland. Most of the printed books of halakha upon which Ashkenazic rabbinic decisors relied in the mid-sixteenth century were printed in Venice. That phenomenon was all the more pronounced for the books of philosophy, commentary, and ethics that came to populate Askhenazic centers of learning. Of note, Giustiniani, in particular, seemed to target his edition of the *Mishneh Torah* at that Ashkenazic market. His edition presented, side by side with the relevant sections of Maimonides's twelfth-century code (a classic work of the Sephardic orbit), the corresponding precepts and commentary found in two medieval restatements of Ashkenazic halakhic rulings and customs, namely the *Arba'a Turim* and the *Sefer Mitzvot Gadol*, which were standard textbooks in Polish *yeshivot* at the time.[14]

C. Intellectual Kinship

The relationship between Katzenellenbogen and Isserles personified the kinship between the Ashkenazic communities of Italy and Poland. In fact, the two rabbis were literally kinsmen: second cousins once removed.[15] On at least one occasion,

and 150,000 at the end of the first quarter of the sixteenth century. Benbassa and Rodrigue 2000: 10.

12. There is evidence that Katzenellenbogen's edition of the *Mishneh Torah* was sold in the Ottoman Empire as well as Poland. See Ziv 1968: 190 (noting that the edition was cited by Joseph Karo (1488–1575) (Safed) and David ben Shlomo ibn Abi Zimra (1479–1573) (Egypt)).

13. Elbaum 1990: 31–48. On the tensions between Ashkenazim and other Jewish groups in early sixteenth-century Italy, see Bonfil 1990: 108–09.

14. On the curriculum of Polish *yeshivot*, see Rosman 2002: 534. The *Sefer Mitzvot Gadol*, a leading supplement to the *Mishneh Torah* containing Talmudic and post-Talmudic sources for Maimonides's precepts, was authored by the great thirteenth-century French rabbinic scholar, Moses ben Jacob of Coucy. See Ta-Shma 2007: 549–50.

15. Ziv 1968: 195. See also Elbaum 1990: 34 (noting family connection).

some five years after Isserles's ruling, they were also partners in a potential bookselling venture. They planned to sell 50 copies of an edition of *Halakhot Rav Alfasi* Isaac Alfasi's glosses on the Talmud, which was printed in Sabbioneta in 1554 and 1555.[16]

No less important, the two rabbis shared a common intellectual outlook. Far more than many of their Ashkenazic rabbinic colleagues, Katzenellenbogen and Isserles were intellectual heirs to Moses Maimonides, the twelfth-century rabbinic authority, jurist, philosopher, and royal physician, whose magnum opus, the *Mishneh Torah*, was the subject matter of the dispute.[17] Maimonides, known in Jewish tradition as "Rambam," is a central, if historically controversial figure in Jewish thought, law, and religious practice. In particular, although sixteenth-century Ashkenazic traditionalists recognized Maimonides's works as integral to the rabbinic canon, they regarded the great medieval Sephardic scholar with suspicion. Accordingly, they staunchly resisted his growing influence, and the influence of other Sephardic scholars, as the Hebrew printing houses of Italy flooded Ashkenazic *yeshivot* with books of Sephardic works of philosophy, biblical interpretation, medieval science, halakha, and Kabbalah.[18] In the midst of those stormy cross-currents, Katzenellenbogen and Isserles aligned themselves with Maimonides in several respects.

1. Maimonidean Rationalism

Maimonides was a supreme rationalist. His principal philosophical work, *Guide for the Perplexed*, presents a far-ranging synthesis of Jewish faith, Greek-Arabic Aristotelian philosophy, and natural science. In his introduction, Maimonides argued that Judaism must be grounded in reason and that metaphysics ("divine science") can only be successfully undertaken after studying physics ("natural science"). Elsewhere in the work, he contended that the contemporary knowledge of scientists, astronomers, and mathematicians, whether Jewish or Gentile, supersedes that of the rabbinical sages of old and should be accepted even when it contradicts the views of the rabbis.[19] Maimonides's emphasis on science and human reason and his express incorporation of Aristotelian thought brought a virulent reaction from those who espoused a traditionalist, theistic, and mystical approach to Jewish faith and practice. Ashkenazic traditionalists were Maimonides's most virulent opponents. Throughout the Middle Ages and well into the early modern era, the Maimonidean project of attempting to reconcile revealed religion with philosophy and reason was thus far more a feature of the Sephardic than of the Ashkenazic world.[20]

16. Bonfil 1990: 191.

17. "Rambam" is an acronym for Maimonides's Hebrew name, "Rabbi Moses ben Maimon." For a penetrating, comprehensive study of Maimonides's life and work, see Davidson 2005.

18. Rosman 2002: 146–48; Ruderman 2010: 101–02. Print also altered Sephardic study. The Talmud, as printed with Ashkenazic commentaries by Bomberg and Giustiniani in Venice, came to be standard in the Sephardic world of the Ottoman Empire as well. Baruchson 1986: 62.

19. Maimonides, *Guide for the Perplexed* 2:8, 3:14; Ruderman 1995: 30–32.

20. Polonsky 2010: 116; D. Berger 2004: 72–124. Some Sephardic scholars, notably Abraham Abulafia and Moses ben Joshua Narboni (d. 1362), also sought to

The Maimonidean controversy continued to reverberate in the sixteenth century, with Katzenellenbogen and Isserles serving as leading proponents of the view that a conservative understanding of Maimonidean rationalism was fully compatible with traditional rabbinic thought. Isserles most obviously falls within that category.[21] When the traditionalist Solomon Luria reproached him for referring to Aristotle's teaching in his rulings, Isserles famously defended the study of Aristotelian philosophy and science, at least as filtered through Maimonides and other rabbinic sources.[22] As Isserles put it: "There is certainly no fear of any error in the works of the great Rambam. His books have already been disseminated among all the wise scholars of recent generations, and they laud and rely on his teachings like the halakha given to Moses at Sinai. And this great rabbi and teacher has written that all that Aristotle understood is the truth and that Aristotle's teachings are the same as those of our rabbinic sages except for a few matters of faith."[23] Isserles also quoted from Maimonides's philosophical treatise, *Guide for the Perplexed*, at the beginning of his glosses on the *Shulḥan Arukh* and in the introduction to his work *Darkhei Moshe*, Isserles's glosses on the *Arba'a Turim*. Indeed, due to his intellectual prowess and rationalist outlook, Isserles came to be known as the "Maimonides of Polish Jewry."[24]

Asher Ziv, a biographer of Isserles and of Katzenellenbogen, has posited that the Rema received much of his appreciation for philosophy and science from the Maharam of Padua.[25] Yet, even though the Maharam's direct influence is certainly possible, the Rema would have had ample opportunity to gain that appreciation from other sources as well. I already noted the influx of Jewish philosophical writings into the Ashkenazic community of Poland during the first half of the sixteenth century. Additionally and more generally, Aristotelian philosophy, science, and scholasticism were dominant intellectual forces in the University of Krakow and other centers of learning in Poland when the Rema assumed his rabbinic post.

Whatever the extent of the Maharam's contribution to the Rema's rationalist outlook, the Maharam hailed from a similar intellectual milieu. Along with its neighboring Venice, Katzenellenbogen's Padua was home to a vibrant stew of traditional Ashkenazic rabbinic culture, Italianate philosophical trends, and secular science.[26] The University of Padua, which, like the University of Krakow, was a center of scholastic rationalism, attracted students from all over Europe. As in Poland, this rationalist outlook must have seeped into rabbinic thought as well, particularly as the University of Padua's celebrated medical faculty began to matriculate Jewish students in 1520.[27] Although the Padua *yeshiva* adopted the traditional Ashkenazic

reconcile Maimonides and Aristotle with mystical and Kabbalistic thought. See Tirosh-Samuelson: 232–36, 238–39.

21. See D. Berger 2004: 123.

22. Elbaum 1990: 156–59; Ruderman 1995: 69–76. Solomon Luria (1510–1573) is known in Jewish tradition by the Hebrew acronym Maharshal.

23. Isserles, *Responsa Rema*, No. 7.

24. Fishman 1997: 571.

25. Ziv 1957: 28. See Elbaum 1990: 34 n. 3 (questioning Ziv's hypothesis).

26. Bonfil 2001: 176–78.

27. Ruderman 1995: 105.

curriculum of German and Polish *yeshivot*, eschewing secular studies and philosophy, its eclectic mix of students, including both medical students and non-Ashkenazic Italian Jews, likely contributed to a more scientific, philosophical outlook.[28] Indeed, the renowned, prolific defender of Maimonides, philosophy, logic, and scientific study, David ben Judah Messer Leon (c. 1470–c. 1526), was Katzenellenbogen's fellow student at the Ashkenazic Paduan *yeshiva* of Judah Minz. Given those multiple influences, by the second quarter of the sixteenth century, the Paduan rabbinic establishment generally identified with a more rationalist, Maimonidean outlook—at least within the parameters of Ashkenazic thought.

Katzenellenbogen himself was not known as a philosopher, and left no philosophical writings. He gained esteem, rather, for his judicious resolution of disputes and decidedly succinct rulings on questions of halakha.[29] Katzenellenbogen's commitment to Maimonidean rationalism can be gleaned in part from his selection of the *Mishneh Torah* as the rabbinic text he labored to edit and publish. In that code, Maimonides famously sought to reflect and systematize what he discerned were the rational bases for Jewish law. Although Maimonides ruled that when science directly conflicts with rabbinic rulings and ritual, science must defer, his introductions and explanations, particularly in the Book of Knowledge, the first of the 14 books of the *Mishneh Torah*, bear the heavy, if unidentified, influence of Aristotelian metaphysics, science, and ethics. Further, the *Mishneh Torah* informs us that the Talmudic sages studied philosophy, insists upon the abstract incorporeality of God, and omits various Talmudic directives that are based on beliefs in ministering angels, evil spirits, and magical incantations.[30] Maimonides also presents an extended description of Ptolemaiac cosmology, which he terms the "science of mathematical astronomy, on which the Greeks composed many treatises."[31]

In addition, in the tradition of Maimonides's disdain for the supernatural and occult, Katzenellenbogen resolutely opposed the study of the mystical, ecstastic teachings of the Kabbalah, and, indeed, signed two bans forbidding the publication or purchase of Kabbalistic works, including *The Zohar*.[32] In his ban on the printing of the medieval Kabbalistic work *Ma'arekhet Ha-Elohut*, Katzenellenbogen objected specifically to the appending of a commentary authored by the fourteenth-century Italian kabbalist Reuven Tzarfati. Tzarfati propounded an esoteric interpretation

28. Shulvass 1952: 126. It is likely that a number of Jewish medical students attended Katzenellenbogen's lectures at the Padua *yeshiva*. For example, Avtalyon Modena (1529–1611), an eminent physician and Talmudic scholar, studied with the Maharam while a medical student at the University of Padua. Judah Saltaro Fano, *Mikveh Yisrael* (Venice, 1607), pp. 35a, 36b. Berger hypothesizes that the influx of Padua-trained physicians to Poland may have contributed to the rationalism there as well. D. Berger 2004: 123.

29. Ziv 1968: 181–82.

30. Davidson 2005: 222–29, 232–47.

31. *Mishneh Torah*, Ha-Madda, Yesodei Ha-Torah 37a. See discussion in Rudavsky 2010: 76–78 (noting that, subsequently, in the *Guide for the Perplexed*, Maimonides criticized Ptolemaiac astronomy as contrary to Aristotelian physics).

32. See Tishby 1967–1968: 163–65 (quoting and discussing Katzenellenbogen's ban); Tal 2007: 20 (noting that Katzenellenbogen signed two bans against the study of Kabbalah). On Maimonides's opposition to mysticism, see generally Kellner 2006.

of Aristotelian precepts, particularly the notion of intellectual union with God, and the mystical power of combining certain letters, which he had drawn from Abraham Abulafia's mystical rendering of Maimonides's metaphysics and psychology in *Guide to the Perplexed*.[33] Katzenellenbogen singled out for particular condemnation Tsarfati's enlistment of Aristotle in support of those ecstatic speculations.

Like Katzenellenbogen, Isserles opposed metaphysical speculation, whether Kabbalist or philosophical, and expressed particular concern about the popular substitution of Kabbalah for studying traditional sources of halakha. However, as was characteristic of a number of early modern Jewish rationalists, Isserles incorporated certain Kabbalistic teachings into his understandings of natural science: in the Rema's case, astronomy.[34] He also evinced an appreciation for the spiritual vitality that Kabbalah brings to the rabbinic tradition. Indeed, in his philosophical work *Torat Ha-Olah*, printed in 1570, Isserles famously stated that "the wisdom of the kabbalah is the wisdom of philosophy, only they speak in two languages."[35] Isserles referred, however, to what he called the "true kabbalah," a teaching, he argued, that had been irrevocably lost by his generation.[36] Further, Isserles largely subordinated Kabbalah to rationalist philosophy and analysis; he aggressively interpreted Kabbalistic works so as to render them consistent with mainstream Maimonidean philosophical premises and condemned elements of Kabbalist theosophy that ran counter to Maimonides.[37]

33. Katzenellenbogen's ban is quoted in Tishby 1967–1968: 163. Following Katzenellenbogen's ban, the book was reprinted without Tzarfati's most "pernicious" passages. Tishby 1967–1968: 170; Idel: 1992: 44. On Reuven Tzarfati and his commentary, see Idel 2011: 148–50, 251. On Abraham Abulafia (1240–c. 1292), the founder of the ecstatic school of Kabbalah, and his combination of Ashkenazic mysticism with Maimonides, see Idel 2011: 30–33. See also Tirosh-Samuelson 2003: 232–36 (contending that Abulafia's "prophetic kabbalah" was largely faithful to Maimonides's ideal of the power of intellectual perfection); Idel 1990: 39–40 (discussing Kabbalists' adoption of Aristotelian notion of intellectual union with God). Some 80 years later, Leon Modena, in *Ari Nohem*, also "fought strenuously against the kabbalistic appropriation of Maimonides and sought to restore the study of the *Guide of the Perplexed* to the pursuit of philosophical wisdom." Dweck 2011: 11.

34. Kabbalah was not universally viewed as incompatible with science or philosophy. A number of leading early modern Jewish thinkers merged Kabbalah with one or both disciplines, to varying degrees. See Ruderman 1995: 118–52; Twersky 1983: 431–43. It is possible that Katzenellenbogen did so as well. Horowitz contends that the Maharam "composed a work of practical kabbalah that included many medical remedies." E. Horowitz 2002: 585; E. Horowitz 1992: 139–41. However, Tishby concludes, in contrast, that the book's true Kabbalist author falsely ascribed the book to Katzenellenbogen in order to attain greater credibility. Tishby 1967–1968: 165. On Isserles's opposition to irrational Kabbalist speculation, see Ziv 1957: 120. On his opposition to philosophical metaphysical speculation, see Ruderman 1995: 74. See also Reiner 1997: 95–96 (noting that Isserles's work on astronomy, *Torat Ha-Olah*, both draws heavily upon the tradition of Jewish Aristotelianism and reveals his affinity with Kabbalistic philosophy as it was then emerging from north Italian *yeshivot*).

35. Part III, Chapter 4, 75 Isserles quotes Moses Botarel.

36. Part III, Chapter 4, 73, quoted and discussed in Ben-Sasson 1984: 37–38.

37. Levin 2008: 31, 34–36; Ben-Sasson 1984: 32–40.

2. The Codification Project

In addition to their philosophical rationalism, Katzenellenbogen and Isserles jointly embraced Maimonides's central project, that of codifying Jewish law. Here, too, they did so in the face of considerable resistance from Ashkenazic traditionalists.

Upon its completion in 1180, Maimonides's 14-volume *Mishneh Torah* was no less controversial than *Guide for the Perplexed*. The *Mishneh Torah* was the first systematic codification of the entire corpus of Jewish law ever undertaken. Jewish law derives from express injunctions and subtle references in the Pentateuch as interpreted and supplemented by a dizzying array of majority and minority opinions, rabbinic judgments, and opposing arguments found in the Talmud and post-Talmudic commentary, regulations, custom, and rulings. Prior to Maimonides's work, a handful of scholars had crafted redactions of those laws relevant to their contemporary practice. But those redactions largely followed the structure of the classic sources, thus lacking the logical arrangement that would enable most users to find what they need with relative ease.[38] In contrast, Maimonides systematically classified the entire existing legal literature by subject matter, ranging from matters of religious practice and faith to marriage and sexual relations to criminal, property, and tort law. He then restated the legal doctrine in plain language. Maimonides's restatement covered the entire spectrum of rabbinic law, including not only laws of practical application in his time, but also those relating to life in ancient Israel, when the Temple still stood in Jerusalem.[39]

Maimonides's grand purpose, stated in the introduction, was that "the entire Oral Law might become systematically known to all, without citing difficulties and solutions of different views . . . but consisting of statements, clear and convincing . . . that have appeared from the time of Moses to the present, so that all rules shall be accessible to young and old." According to some critics, Maimonides meant that Jews could henceforth rely on his code alone to determine Jewish law.[40] That view finds some support in Maimonides's wholesale omission of citations to the rabbinic authorities from which he drew in extracting legal norms.[41] Indeed, even though the *Mishneh Torah* recommends that students devote substantial time grappling with Talmudic disputation, Maimonides's letters suggest that, in his view, studying the Talmud is merely a means—a tortuously difficult means—to discerning the law, not an end in and of itself.[42] At the very least, Maimonides seems to have intended that his opus would obviate the need to study post-Talmudic rulings and disputation.

38. Davidson 2005: 193–95.

39. Maimonides also canvassed more classic rabbinic sources in extracting legal norms than had earlier codifiers. Davidson 2005: 197.

40. Davidson 2005: 208–10.

41. Maimonides does list his sources in the introduction, but he does not cite the authority for his enunciation of specific laws in the text.

42. Davidson 2005: 197–202, 208.

Maimonides's *Mishneh Torah* aroused a storm of opposition not only to its rationalist outlook, but to the essence of Maimonides's codification project. Opponents feared that, whether Maimonides intended it or not, his code would turn students away from studying the Talmud, which the traditionalists viewed as the wellspring of Jewish creativity and thought. They also feared that the *Mishneh Torah* would blind judges to the contrasting opinions required to understand the law and reach a just result.[43] For them, the need for careful study of the cases, parsing rabbinic argument, and wrestling with contrasting arguments was the very essence of Jewish jurisprudence, hardly an obstacle to be avoided. In that vein, they also castigated Maimonides for failing to cite authority for his conclusions. As one opponent put it: "As he does not adduce proofs from the sayings of the Talmudic sages for his decisions, who is going to follow his opinion? It is far better to study Talmud."[44]

By the sixteenth century, the *Mishneh Torah* had earned a central place in the Jewish canon, but Maimonides had failed in his goal of providing a single authoritative code that would resolve all disputes. Maimonides's work had spawned several competing codes, each reflecting a different organization and interpretation of the law. The *Mishneh Torah* had also inspired numerous commentaries: some seeking to explicate and find Talmudic authority for Maimonides's conclusory statements of law, others aiming to refute his conclusions, and still others appending the rulings and glosses of later scholars.[45]

In addition, several leading sixteenth-century Ashkenazic rabbinic authorities remained fiercely opposed to the very idea of codifying Jewish law. They included Jacob Pollak (c. 1460–1541), who was Katzenellenbogen's teacher in Prague, and Shalom Shakhna (c. 1495–1558), who studied with Katzenellenbogen under Jacob Pollak and then went on to become Isserles's teacher in Krakow. Pollak and Shakhna posited that a rabbinic decisor must decide each case on its own merits, in line with his individual study of legal sources and understanding of the equities—"according to what he sees with his own eyes" and "the dictates of his own heart."[46] In that view, the decisor's authority rests in his own erudition, scholarly acumen, and integrity, not a facile reduction of halakhic precepts into a set of generally applicable rules. The scholar must wrestle with each case before him, fully weighing it on its own merits in light of Talmudic law, authoritative interpretation, and local custom. The law's redaction in a code, they argued, would necessarily deprive halakhic scholars of their individual authority and would rob the halakhic tradition of its responsiveness and vitality.

43. Elon 2007a: 772–73.

44. Ben-Sasson 2007: 374, quoting from Sheshet ben Isaac Saroggosa, a Maimonides defender writing about 1200, the opinion of a rabbinic judge who refused to rule according to Maimonides. See also Davidson 2005: 266–67 (discussing Maimonides's contemporaries and Maimonides's response).

45. Elon 1997: 1019–22.

46. See the statements of Israel, son of Shalom Shakhna, quoted in Isserles, *Responsa Rema*, no. 25. See also Rosman 2002: 544–45; Reiner 1997: 87–88.

Katzenellenbogen and Isserles rejected their mentors' uncompromising opposition to codification.[47] They believed that, so long as codes are accompanied by commentary succinctly presenting alternative views, such restatements can make the law accessible while still encouraging rabbinic decisors and students to grapple with competing positions and interpretations. Their own projects manifest that measured view. In his edition of the *Mishneh Torah*, Katzenellenbogen added some early sources that Maimonides had expressly rejected, together with subsequent commentary that took issue with Maimonides's position.[48] He also expressed sensitivity to the concern that the *Mishneh Torah* could dissuade readers from grappling with rabbinic sources. In his introduction, Kaztenellenbogen stated that although he provides Talmudic references for Maimonides's most obscure statements, he resisted the temptation to provide citations for all Maimonides's conclusions out of fear that some readers would then rely on his citations as a shortcut rather than searching for authority in the Talmud themselves.

For his part, Isserles drafted his own codes and added critical glosses to both the *Arba'a Turim* and the *Shulḥan Arukh*. Like the *Mishneh Torah*, Joseph Karo's *Shulḥan Arukh*, which was completed in 1563 and first printed in 1565, presented a comprehensive code, setting out the bare law, without sources, commentary, or alternative opinions. It also largely reflected Sephardic customs and interpretations. Isserles's *Mappa*, his glosses on the *Shulḥan Arukh*, added Ashkenazic practices to Karo's text, section by section.[49] In those glosses, however, the Rema quite deliberately discarded the bulk of Ashkenazic customs remaining from the Middle Ages, primarily favoring Polish over German customs.[50] As such, he built on the *Shulḥan Arukh* to create a new Ashkenazic restatement of the law, one in which the Ashkenazic halakha was narrowed, systematized, and, to some extent, rationalized. Like Karo, Isserles aimed to make the law widely accessible, presenting "the proper order of all the laws . . . in a manner easily comprehensible to every man be he small or great."[51] It is largely because of Isserles's commentary and counterpoint that the *Shulḥan Arukh*

47. Katzenellenbogen might not have felt much loyalty to his teacher. Two decades previously, Jacob Pollak had issued an order excommunicating Katzenellenbogen's father-in-law, Abraham Minz. Tal 2007b: 355.

48. In *Sefer Ha-Mitzvot* [Book of Commandments], which he wrote as a freestanding prolegomenon to the *Mishneh Torah*, Maimonides enumerated 613 commandments that Jews are obligated to follow and set out 14 principles that guided him in identifying those commandments in Biblical narrative and Talmudic disputation. In so doing, Maimonides expressly rejected an earlier attempt to identify such commandments. Naḥmanides (known in Jewish tradition as "Ramban"), the foremost Jewish law scholar in the generation following Maimonides, published a critique of the *Sefer Ha-Mitzvot*, called the *Hasagot* [the Criticisms], in which he defended the earlier authors against Maimonides's criticism. Katzenellenbogen included in his edition the earlier writings, Maimonides's *Sefer Ha-Mitzvot*, and Naḥmanides' *Hasagot*.

49. Rosman 2002: 545–47. "Shulḥan Arukh" means "the set table." Isserles labeled his commentary, "Mappa," or "table cloth."

50. Zimmels 1958: 54–56; Reiner 1997: 97.

51. Moses Isserles, *Torat Ha-Ḥatat*, introduction, quoted in English translation in Reiner 1997: 94.

remains the principle authoritative redaction of Jewish law—for both Ashkenazim and Sephardim—to this day.

3. Broad Tent

Katzenellenbogen's publication of the *Mishneh Torah* also reflected his engagement with the traditions of Italy's native and Sephardic Jews. Given the mass migrations of Jews from western and central Europe, mid-sixteenth century Italy contained a complex mix of Jews of various geographic origins and distinct sociolegal traditions. These included a group whose presence in Italy dated back to ancient times; Ashkenazic Jews, who began arriving in northern Italy from Germany and France in the late thirteenth century; Sephardic Jews, who came from Spain and Portugal after the Inquisition and expulsion in the late fifteenth century; and Jews who lived in regions conquered by Italian states in the Balkans and Greek Islands.[52] In various matters of law and ritual, Ashkenazic Jews followed different rules and customs than Jews from the Iberian Peninsula, southern Europe, and the Levant. In that vein, Ashkenazic jurists generally ruled in accordance with the *Arba'a Turim*, a code of laws compiled in the early fourteenth century by Jacob ben Asher (who fled from Ashkenaz to Spain at the age of 33), while Sephardic, Italian, and Oriental Jews gave considerable weight to the *Mishneh Torah* of Maimonides (who lived in Spain and Egypt).[53] Indeed, after having become generally accepted in Italy in the late fourteenth century, the *Mishneh Torah* was largely pushed to the side under the dominance of rabbinic scholars from France and Germany who brought with them their own, deeply entrenched Ashkenazic tradition.[54]

In keeping with his training and roots, Katzenellenbogen primarily followed Ashkenazic precedent.[55] But his rulings drew upon Sephardic authorities as well, and he broke with Ashkenazic tradition in his Sephardic-influenced rulings in some cases. Further, unlike his more sectarian Ashkenazic counterparts, Katzenellenbogen frequently cited Maimonides in his rulings, even if he regularly cited the *Turim* as well and did not always follow Maimonides's position.[56] Katzenellenbogen's edition of the

52. Westreich 2002: 199; Shulvass 1952: 116–18.

53. Elon 2007a: 775; Davidson 2005: 284–85 (noting Joseph Karo's observation, made in the sixteenth century, that the *Mishneh Torah* served as the standard law code for Jewish communities in all the Arab lands). A study of book ownership among Jews in Mantua in 1595 found, accordingly, that a considerably higher percentage of Sephardic and Italian households than Ashkenazic households owned a copy of the *Mishneh Torah*, while the opposite was the case regarding ownership of the *Turim*. Baruchson 1993: 134. See also Bonfil 1990: 255–65.

54. Bonfil 1990: 255–64; Ta-Shma 2006: 175–83.

55. See, e.g., Bonfil 1990: 150–55 (describing Katzenellenbogen's decidedly Ashkenazic understanding of the office of the rabbi).

56. See, e.g., *Responsa Maharam of Padua,* No. 78 (citing Maimonides in support of a ruling that portions of the Bible may be read in vernacular translation on Yom Kippur). Notably, the Maharam cited Sephardic legal sources in relaxing the ban on polygamy (which had been instituted in Ashkenaz in the eleventh century and subsequently accepted in northern Italy). See *Responsa Maharam of Padua*, Nos. 13 and 19. For discussion, see Weistreich 2002: 208–10.

Mishneh Torah, which his publisher Alvise Bragadini touted as the work of the great Maimonides "the Sephardi," exemplified the Maharam's inclusive approach, and might have been seen as such by his contemporaries.

Isserles, likewise, was simultaneously protective of Ashkenazic traditions and open to Sephardic learning. Isserles's Ashkenazic glosses on the *Shulḥan Arukh* were meant to supplement and improve upon the original, not to attack it. He referred to Karo as the "Light of Israel," and in some places his glosses quote Sephardic scholars and accept their views.[57] Further, as noted above, Isserles began both his *Darkhei Moshe* and *Mappa* with a quotation from Maimonides's *Guide for the Perplexed*, an affirmation of the essentially Sephardic philosophical tradition.

Finally, from the *Mishneh Torah* to the *Shulḥan Arukh*, the codification project writ large, like the attempt to reconcile revealed religion with philosophy, was essentially a Sephardic enterprise. The Ashkenazic tradition placed great normative significance on varied local custom. The Ashkenazic canon thus consisted of multiple versions of classic texts that had been emended anew in each generation and in each location. The notion that there could be a single, standard code for all Jews, or even all Ashkenazic Jews, was anathema to that tradition.[58] Yet Katzenellenbogen and Isserles embraced the codification project and, indeed, brought printed editions of Sephardic codes, supplemented with those scholars' glosses, to the heart of the Ashkenazic world.

II. THE COMPETING EDITIONS

As discussed in Chapter 2, sixteenth-century publishers—like their counterparts today—sought to minimize their risk by printing books that were assured of considerable consumer demand. During the first century of print, that meant printing classics and liturgical works written before the age of print. The first half of the sixteenth century thus saw numerous Italian editions of the works of Dante, Petrarch, and Boccaccio, just as Hebrew printers invested primarily in issuing successive editions of the Bible, Talmud, and other central texts of Jewish law, liturgy, and literature.[59] Largely as a result, ambitious printers and publishers came to view an investment in editing, including hiring a respected, celebrated editor (or "corrector"), as a primary key to success. Editions of classic works typically featured printer's dedications and editor's introductions trumpeting the editor's arduous work and expertise in producing an accurate and complete instantiation of the original manuscript and correcting the many errors found in earlier editions. Printers and editors also sought to distinguish their editions by supplementing the text with the editor's commentary, annotations, and explanatory notes.[60]

57. Zimmels 1958: 54–55.
58. See Reiner 1997: 85–89, 96–97.
59. See, generally, Richardson 1994; Baruchson 1993: 83 (Hebrew presses).
60. Richardson 1994: 7, 99–103; Baruchson 1993: 43.

The Katzenellenbogen-Bragadini edition of the *Mishneh Torah* (the title page of which is reproduced in Illustration 2) falls squarely within that framework. Like most works that had been repeatedly hand-copied in manuscript prior to the invention of print, the manuscripts of Maimonides's *Mishneh Torah* suffered from numerous discrepancies, partly because Maimonides himself had made emendations and corrections to some early manuscripts.[61] Moreover, in producing his edition, Katzenellenbogen had before him previous print editions, principally the Daniel Bomberg edition of 1524, as well as an uncertain number of handwritten manuscripts.

As typical of his high quality work, Bomberg had invested heavily in his edition. He employed as editor the noted Italian Talmudist and physician, David ben Eliezer Ha-Levi Pizzighettone, and gathered a large number of manuscripts and marginal glosses for use in the edition's preparation.[62] The Bomberg edition also included leading medieval scholars' glosses and commentaries on Maimonides's work.[63]

In the introduction to his edition, Katzenellenbogen lavishes praise on Pizzighettone and states that he initially saw little value in "gleaning the last crumbs remaining" from the great work of his predecessor.[64] But the Maharam emphasizes that, through his own arduous study of the text and handwritten manuscripts and his understanding of Talmudic and post-Talmudic commentary—together with the help of his son—he has nevertheless made a number of corrections vis-à-vis the earlier edition, both in Maimonides's text and that of the medieval commentators. Katzenellenbogen also indicates that he has annotated the text with references to Talmudic sources and added some brief commentary of his own. Finally, both Katzenellenbogen's introduction and Bragadini's preface announce that the Maharam has, for the first time, incorporated with the *Mishneh Torah* not only the commentaries included in the earlier edition, but also Maimonides's *Sefer Ha-Mitzvot*, a free-standing prolegomenon to the *Mishneh Torah* and in which Maimonides criticized certain earlier authorities; Naḥmanides's *Hasagot*, in which that medieval scholar defended the authorities that Maimonides had criticized; and the writings of the early authorities at issue in the dispute.

61. See Davidson 2005: 269–70. Printed editions of the *Mishneh Torah* are said to still contain many mistakes. A. Marx 1935. On the phenomenon of textual drift in manuscripts that were copied and recopied many times by hand, see Eisenstein 1983: 78–80.

62. Posner and Ta-Shema 1975: 211; Amram 1998: 172.

63. These included the *Migdal Oz* and *Maagid Mishneh*, which were authored by two fourteenth-century Spanish scholars, and *Haggahot Maimoniot*, which was authored by a thirteenth-century French scholar with the purpose of supplementing the *Mishneh Torah* with Franco-German precepts. In the sixteenth century, *Haggahot Maimoniot* was a standard text in Italian Ashkenazic *yeshivot*. Bonfil 1990: 262 n. 195.

64. Katzenellenbogen was known for his modesty and benign disposition. In addition, Pizzighettone had sided with Katzenellenbogen's father-in-law, Abraham Minz, in a vituperative early sixteenth-century disagreement among Italian rabbis regarding the proper venue for deciding a major commercial dispute. It was over this disagreement that Jacob Pollak, Katzenellenbogen's teacher in Prague, excommunicated Minz. Rothkoff 2007: 40–41.

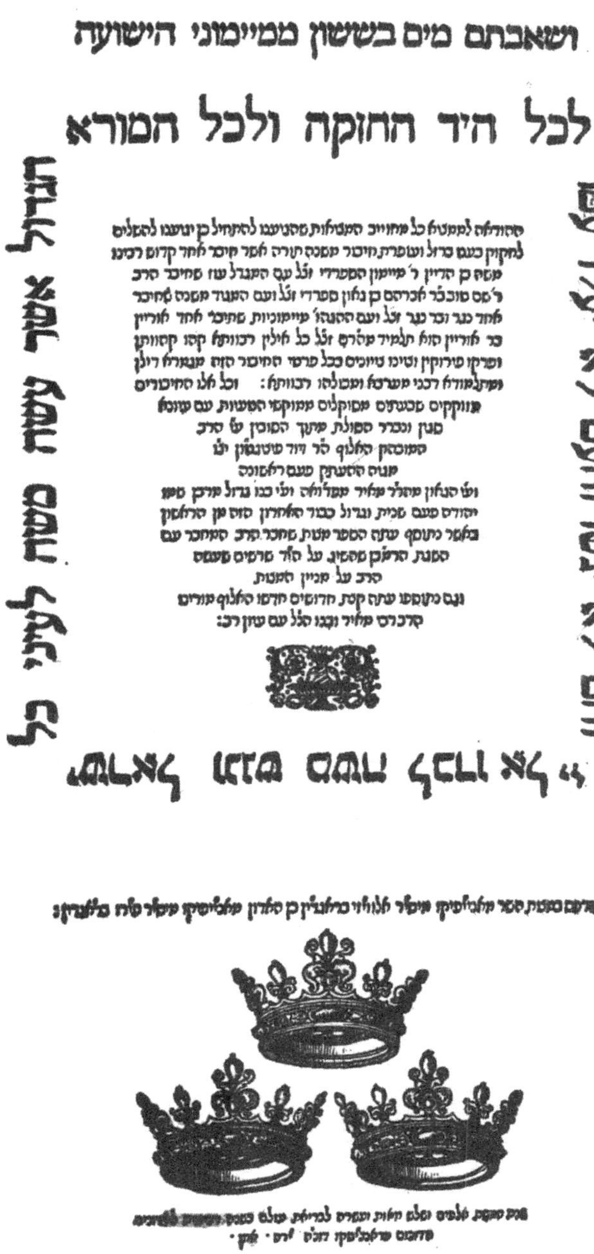

ושאבתם מים בששון ממיימוני הישועה
לכל היד החזקה ולכל המורא
הגדול אשר עשה משה לעיני כל
בויניציאה

Illustration 2
Mishneh Torah Title Page, Bragadini-Katzenellenbogen Edition, 1550.
(courtesy National Library of Israel).

Giustiniani published his edition of the *Mishneh Torah* (the title page of which is reproduced in Illustration 3) closely on the heels of Bragadini's. Giustiniani included Katzenellenbogen's source references as well as the dozen or so annotations authored by the Maharam and his son. In a show of denigration, however, he moved the Maharam's annotations to an appendix and, in his preface, Giustiniani criticized them as worthless—"having been written for nothing." With bravado typical of fiercely competitive printers of that era, Giustiniani claimed that leading scholars from "Yemen to the West" had told him that Katzenellenbogen's annotations should be removed from the text because in each annotation the Maharam had either "erred" or "sought to explain things understood even by one who is one day old."[65] He decided to append Maharam's annotations after all, Giustiniani continued, only to give the learned reader the opportunity to judge their worth independently.

In like vein, Giustiniani announced that leading scholars (whom Giustiniani left unnamed) had pleaded with him to rush out an alternative to the shoddy edition of "one rabbi from Padua who longed to stand among the greats." Those scholars, Giustiniani touted, had also given his own edition added value by providing him with additional material not found in Bragadini's publication. These included the precepts corresponding to Maimonides's provisions from two seminal Ashkenazic codes, the *Arba'a Turim* and the *Sefer Mitzvot Gadol*, as well as page references to recent print editions of two leading medieval commentaries on the *Mishneh Torah*, the *Migdal Oz* and *Ma'agid Mishneh* (which, Giustiniani noted, had no numbered pagination prior coming out in print).[66]

To add injury to insult, Giustiniani sold his edition at a significantly lower price than the Katzenellenbogen-Bragadini *Mishneh Torah*. Indeed, although Giustiniani had apparently spared no expense in producing a woodcut-illustrated, perfectly justified hand-set edition of stunningly high quality, he promised in his preface to sell the edition for a price of at least a gold coin less than that of his competitor. His intention, he proclaimed, was to enable the Jewish community to purchase books as cheaply as possible. In response, Bragadini charged in a postscript to his edition that his rival acted only to maintain a monopoly on Hebrew printing by driving Bragadini out of business, as he done previously to Daniel Bomberg.

65. Giustiniani's anonymous editor further charged that Katzenellenbogen had apparently failed to read Maimonides's letter to Pinḥas of Alexandria in which Maimonides had stated, in essence, that his readings of the law were straightforward and needed no annotative explanation—and thus that Katzenellenbogen should have stuck to providing Talmudic sources rather than presumptuously adding his own glosses.

66. These claims were set forth in a separate preface by an unnamed person (presumably Giustiniani's editor). In fact, Giustiniani's promised page references were not entirely carried out. His edition contains ample page references for *Migdal Oz*, but very few for *Maagid Mishneh*. Spiegel 1996: 550 n. 47. The Maharam states in his preface that he first thought to add page references to the corresponding passages in the Talmud, but decided that it was not worth the effort given that few readers would have the Talmud in front of them. Giustiniani retorted that, in contrast to Giustiniani's editors, the Maharam merely did not want to undertake the effort to add page references. Spiegel 1996: 551.

Illustration 3
Mishneh Torah Title Page, Giustiniani Edition, 1550.
(courtesy National Library of Israel).

Bragadini, whose printing house later came to dominate Hebrew printing in Venice, financed most of his books from his own capital. However, he sometimes acted as a contractor for Jewish backers who sought the publication of a particular book.[67] In this case—the Venice patrician's first publication, Bragadini acted largely or entirely as a contractor. Indeed, Katzenellenbogen reportedly invested much of his own savings in the edition, in addition to contributing his labor and expertise.[68]

Giustiniani financed his printing by subscription, a common practice in the early modern print industry. He pre-sold half of his planned print run prior to commencing printing.[69] Katzenellenbogen and Bragadini most certainly followed this practice as well. Indeed, it seems that pre-sold orders for their edition remained outstanding in Poland well after they had shipped copies to the Ottoman Empire. In his introduction, Giustiniani belittled his rivals' edition as being of inferior quality and proclaimed that "those who purchased from them have already regretted and worried after hearing how the edition was [dimly] received in the communities of the East."

It was Katzenellenbogen who took the initiative to produce a new edition of the *Mishneh Torah* in 1550. And, as several statements in the respective prefaces to the rival editions make clear, the Katzenellenbogen-Bragadini *Mishneh Torah* came out in print prior to Giustiniani's. Nonetheless, there is considerable question regarding who copied more from the other. On one hand, Giustiniani brazenly copied the Maharam's brief annotations. Aside from that, however, as Yaakov Spiegel—a leading scholar of the Hebrew book—has demonstrated, a close inspection of the two editions reveals that Bragadini and Katzenellenbogen most probably copied far more from Giustiniani's manuscript than the other way around.[70]

As Spiegel explains, Bragadini announced in his preface that he would deviate from the text of the Bomberg edition of 1524 only if he found evidence of errors in that text from reading other printings or manuscripts that were before him. If he lacked such specific evidence, but nevertheless believed the Bomberg text to be in error, Bragadini added, he would advise the reader of the possible error, but leave the original text as is. However, there are numerous instances in which the Bragadini text in fact differs from Bomberg's and for which Bragadini provides no explanation. And in many of these instances, Giustiniani's edition contains the very same alteration, but does present an explanation, based on authoritative rabbinical sources, for why the text was changed. In those instances, it is far more likely that Bragadini and his principal editor, the Maharam of Padua, copied the alteration from Giustiniani wholesale, without incorporating their rival's explanation, than that Giustiniani (and his editor) would have copied Bragadini's unexplained alterations and then taken the trouble to search for a justification for each one. It thus appears that Bragadini was able either to lay his hands on Giustiniani's manuscript or to obtain information about Giustiniani's corrections from one of Giustiniani's editors or typesetters before the Bragadini edition went to press.

67. Baruchson 1990: 33.
68. Breger 1995: 940.
69. Baruchson 1990: 32.
70. Spiegel 1996: 551–58.

Perhaps that is why Bragadini did not seek to obtain a book privilege from the Venetian Senate. It is also possible that neither edition contained enough original material to qualify for a Venetian book privilege, given the Senate decree of 1517, still in force in 1550, that only new books not previously printed were eligible for a privilege. (On the other hand, many other publishers did evade that restriction by making minor changes in a previously printed edition.) In any event, Bragadini had no recourse against his rival under Venetian law. It was in that context that Katzenellenbogen appealed to Rabbi Moses Isserles of Krakow to rule that the Giustiniani edition violated Jewish law.

III. THE REMA'S RULING

Although Katzenellenbogen petitioned Isserles to issue a halakhic ruling, he did not initiate a civil lawsuit against the Christian printer in rabbinic court per se. The semi-autonomous Jewish courts of that era followed intricate rules guaranteeing each litigant a fair opportunity to present evidence and argue his case.[71] But as a Gentile Venetian patrician, Giustiniani would hardly have deigned to appear before a Jewish court—in Poland no less. Further, Isserles himself acknowledged on another occasion that, although Jews are generally prohibited from bringing a claim against other Jews in a non-Jewish court, the sole jurisdiction in commercial disputes between Jews and non-Jews does indeed lie in the appropriate civil court.[72] Nor would Isserles or Katzenellenbogen have had any way of enforcing a hypothetical rabbinic ruling against Giustiniani.

Rather Katzenellenbogen sought—and received—from Isserles a rabbinic decree in the form of a responsum. Based on the Rema's halakhic reasoning, given in response to the version of the dispute that Katzenellenbogen had presented to him, the rabbi of Krakow forbade Jews from purchasing the Giustiniani edition—or any other competing edition of the *Mishneh Torah* —until Katzenellenbogen had sold his print run. In effect, then, Isserles issued a reprinting ban in favor of the Maharam of Padua.

The young Isserles faced a complex case. It required him to grapple with several fundamental questions—issues that the Rome rabbis largely skirted when they issued their *ktav dat* in favor of Eliyahu Bakhur: How could halakhic doctrine regarding wrongful competition among neighboring craftsmen be applied to book publishers competing in distant lands? Even if halakhic proscriptions against usurping another's livelihood apply, how could a non-Jew violate those proscriptions? Further, on what halakhic basis can Jews be prohibited from purchasing books from a non-Jewish printer who is not himself subject to Jewish law? And finally, may a rabbi forbid such reprinting and purchasing outside of his local jurisdiction?

71. See Sinai 2010: 21–222; Cohn and Sinai 2007: 434–46.
72. *Shulḥan Arukh,* Ḥoshen Mishpat, 369: 11, Isserles commentaries.

Isserles issued his ruling on August 16, 1550. He began with an extensive discussion of an issue to which the Rome rabbis had not even referred: the applicability of Jewish law to a non-Jewish printer.

A. Noaḥide Law

Jewish law contains intricate rules governing commercial, familial, and communal relations among Jews as well as conduct of Jews towards non-Jews. According to Jewish tradition, these rules were first given to Moses at Mount Sinai and then became the subject of further delineation and supplement by subsequent rabbinic interpretation and enactment. In principle, neither these rules nor those pertaining to matters of faith and religious ritual obligate non-Jews.

That does not mean Jewish law is silent regarding the conduct of non-Jews, however. In what is perhaps the closest that it comes to embracing a concept of natural law, Jewish law sets forth seven "Noaḥide laws" (or laws governing the offspring of Noah") that do purport to apply to non-Jews.[73] As Maimonides wrote in the *Mishneh Torah*, six of these laws are said to have been given by God to Adam and Eve. These are the prohibitions against idolatry, blasphemy, sexual immorality, murder, and robbery, as well as the obligation to establish a system of courts and law. The seventh was given to Noah and his offspring, the first generation to eat meat. It forbids eating a limb torn from a live animal.[74]

According to tradition, the Noaḥide laws governed Jews and non-Jews alike until Jews were given the more extensive set of commandments at Mount Sinai.[75] Since then, the Noaḥide laws apply primarily to non-Jews,[76] who are neither required nor expected to comply with (other) Jewish law or, for that matter, to convert to Judaism. A non-Jew who formally accepts the Noaḥide laws is entitled to the respect and material support of the Jewish community.[77] The Noaḥide obligations also provide the framework for the Talmudic dictum that the "righteous men of all nations have a share in the world to come."[78] Hugo Grotius, the great Dutch philosopher of international law, analogized Noaḥide law to the *ius gentium* of Roman law—those laws, putatively discernible by the exercise of reason, that the Romans understood to

73. On Maimonides's understanding of Noaḥide law as natural law, a set of rules that is both revealed by God and known by all rational persons, see Novak 1983: 294–300; Bleich 1991: 852–57.

74. *Mishneh Torah*, Sefer Shoftim, Hilkhot Melakhim 9:1.

75. Novak 1983: 53. The first explicit enumeration of the Noaḥide laws is in the *Tosefta*, a work commonly believed to have been edited late in the second century. Novak 1983: 3.

76. There is a strand of rabbinic thought that views the Noaḥide law as providing a residual source of law for Jews, supplementing Sinaitic law. See Stone 1991: 1202–12.

77. Schwarzschild 2007: 284–87.

78. See Stone 1991: 1165. According to Maimonides, a non-Jew who abides by the Noaḥide laws out of a belief that they were Divinely revealed, as opposed to out of rational imperative, is entitled to a place in "the world to come" (the rough equivalent of "heaven"), like a Jew who abides by and accepts the Divine revelation of Jewish law. *Mishneh Torah*, Sefer Shoftim, Hilkhot Melakhim 8:11; Novak 1983: 276–78.

be common to all nations and that applied to foreigners living under Roman authority in lieu of Roman civil law and state religion.[79]

There is considerable disagreement among rabbinic authorities regarding the content of each Noaḥide law and the role of Jewish courts in interpreting and applying them. Most basically, given that one of the Noaḥide commandments is the creation of a system of courts and laws, do Jews have any role in enforcing Noaḥide law? Or is enforcement an entirely non-Jewish responsibility, something that Jews believe is obligatory, but not a rule that Jews are themselves obliged to enforce?[80] The *Mishneh Torah* instructs that any non-Jew living under Jewish political control who violates Noaḥide law is to be executed.[81] But when Maimonides wrote, no non-Jew had lived under Jewish political control for over a millennium, and no such Jewish dominion was expected until the coming of the Messiah. Rabbinic commentators thus almost universally understood Maimonides to refer to an entirely theoretical possibility. Concomitantly, they posited that, until the coming of the Messiah, neither Jewish courts nor Jews as individuals have any obligation to enforce Noaḥide law and, indeed, should not attempt to punish non-Jews for failing to abide by Noaḥide law.[82]

Rabbinic jurists have also differed over the precise substance of the Noaḥide laws. Maimonides held, for example, that the Noaḥide law of *dinim*, the obligation that non-Jews establish a legal system, is essentially a procedural requirement. It means that non-Jews must adjudicate and enforce the other six Noaḥide laws.[83] In contrast, the great thirteenth-century rabbinic scholar Naḥmanides maintained that the *dinim* obligation has a substantive element as well: it requires non-Jews to enact laws governing interpersonal and monetary matters that do not otherwise fall within the other six laws.[84] Although Naḥmanides did not prescribe the detailed content of those laws, he did indicate that they should include prohibitions of fraud, deceit, overcharging, and withholding wages.[85] Other scholars insisted that the *dinim* obligation means no more than that non-Jews must obey the reasonably just laws of their own society.[86]

Isserles sided with the weight of authority holding that Jews should not attempt to sanction non-Jews for violating Noaḥide law.[87] In that vein, his decree did not

79. Grotius 1964. For discussion, see Stone 1991: 1163–64. Grotius viewed Noaḥide law as an early universal law, the foundation for international law. Rothstein 2004: 548. For discussion of *ius gentium* and its relationship to natural law, see Waldron 2005: 133–35.

80. Novak 1983: 53. For an illuminating, in-depth discussion of this issue, see Broyde 1998.

81. *Mishneh Torah*, Sefer Shoftim, Hilkhot Melakhim 9:10, 9:14.

82. See Broyde 1998: 98–103.

83. *Mishneh Torah*, Sefer Shoftim, Hilkhot Melakhim 9:14.

84. See Broyde 1998: 93; Novak 1983: 55.

85. Commentary to the Torah, Genesis 34.13. See also Bleich 1991: 853 (stating that "Nahmanides defines 'dinin' as commanding the establishment of an ordered system of jurisprudence for the governance of financial, commercial and interpersonal relationships").

86. See Novak 1983: 55. See also Bleich 1991: 853 (describing the positions taken by Naftali Tzvi Yehuda Berlin and I. Meltzer).

87. See Broyde 1998: 101–02.

explicitly call for or even consider the theoretical possibility of imposing a fine or other sanction on Giustiniani per se. Its focus, rather, was on enabling the Maharam to recover his investment; the Rema ordered the Jews of Poland to buy only the Maharam's *Mishneh Torah* and not any other edition, including Giustiniani's, until the Maharam had sold his entire print run. But in formulating his ruling, Isserles nevertheless devoted substantial attention to the question of whether the Christian Giustiniani acted in violation of Noaḥide law by issuing his edition of the *Mishneh Torah* in competition with the Maharam of Padua.

Given that Isserles eschewed imposing a sanction, it is not entirely obvious why he needed to rule on the issue of whether Giustiniani violated Noaḥide law. Seemingly, he could have simply issued a reprinting ban forbidding Jews from purchasing editions of the *Mishneh Torah* that competed with that of the Maharam of Padua. We return to this point later.

In any event, Isserles's consideration of whether Giustiniani violated Noaḥide law in issuing his competing edition of the *Mishneh Torah* required Isserles to determine the substantive content of the Noaḥide laws that might apply to Giustiniani's conduct. Which Noaḥide law might Giustiniani have violated? And most interesting from our perspective: Which of the seven Noaḥide laws, if any, might serve as a foundation for a law of copyright?

Isserles begins by propounding a far-reaching proposition regarding the content of Noaḥide law. He holds that the laws non-Jews must follow are, in essence, the very same laws that govern the conduct of Jews. Isserles derives this proposition from contested authority holding, on the basis of Scriptural exegesis, that Noaḥide obligation of *dinim* means that "Noaḥide laws are the same as the Jews were commanded at Sinai, . . . except where there is direct evidence of a difference."[88] Isserles cites the *Mishneh Torah* for further support; according to Isserles's reading, Maimonides concluded that although, in principle, non-Jews need follow only the seven Noaḥide laws, the actual content of those Noaḥide laws are derived from Jewish law applicable to Jews.[89]

For Isserles, then, "Noaḥide laws" are informed not simply by basic universal principles of justice and equity that lie outside the framework of Jewish law, but rather by the entire set of intricate rules governing Jews, unless Talmudic authority explicitly indicates a dissimilarity. In so holding, Isserles pushes even further than what he takes to be Maimonides's conclusion that each Noaḥide law is informed by the Jewish law in that area. Isserles posits that, at least in regards to civil law, including commercial and monetary matters, Noaḥide law is generally no different from

88. See Isserles, *Reponsa Rema*, No. 10, in which Isserles concludes that the law is in accordance with the view of Rabbi Isaac, not Rabbi Yochanan.

89. Isserles, *Reponsa Rema*, No. 10. But see Moses Sofer (1762–1839), *Responsa Ḥatam Sofer*, Likkutim, No. 14 (opining that, in contrast to Isserles's understanding, neither Maimonides nor, for that matter, Naḥmanides posited that the content of Noaḥide law in monetary matters is equivalent to Jewish law).

Jewish law even when Jewish law does not fit within one of the remaining six categories of Noaḥide law.

Isserles's interpretation of Noaḥide law is expansive in another sense as well. As noted in Chapter 3, Jewish law is traditionally divided into two fundamental categories, typically labeled by the Aramaic terms *de-oraita* ("of the Torah") and *de-rabbanan* ("of the scholars").[90] Even those rabbinic authorities who hold that Noaḥide law is to some degree informed by Jewish law typically limit that holding to the foundational precepts of *de-oraita* law. But in defining and applying Jewish law in the remainder of his ruling, Isserles subjects Giustiniani to the scrutiny not only of *de-oraita*, but also of *de-rabbanan* law. In sum, although he does not say so explicitly, Isserles evidently posits that the requirement of *dinim* means that non-Jews must abide by Jewish law in monetary and commercial matters, including rabbinical edicts that go beyond the fundamental precepts given to Moses at Mount Sinai.

Isserles's broad interpretation of Noaḥide law—and in particular his evident application of commercial *de-rabbanan* law to non-Jews—was unprecedented at the time and has not been generally followed since.[91] As we shall see, the eminent early nineteenth-century rabbinic decisor Mordekhai Banet held explicitly that non-Jewish publishers are not subject to the Jewish law of copyright because the Jewish law of copyright originates in rabbinic edict, not *de-oraita* law.[92] Be that as it may, Isserles concludes his discussion of Noaḥide law: "We have clarified and proven that we judge non-Jews according to the laws of Israel and a dispute between a non-Jew and a Jew just like a dispute between two circumcised people."

B. *Gezel*

Isserles then proceeds to consider how Giustiniani might have violated the Jewish law that applies to him through Noaḥide law. But before doing so, and almost as an aside to his discussion of Noaḥide law, Isserles frames the dispute in terms that go to the heart of a long-standing—and ongoing—debate about copyright's doctrinal foundation, both in Jewish and secular law. After citing Maimonides for the proposition that the content of each Noaḥide law is determined by reference to Jewish law in that area, Isserles notes that "the matter before us is *gezel*, which is one of the seven Noaḥide commandments." *Gezel* is typically translated as "robbery" or, more loosely, "theft." So if Giustiniani engaged in "*gezel*," does that mean that the Maharam as an author, editor, and/or publisher has a property right that Guistiniani has taken? For

90. See Elon 1997: 185–98.

91. See Broyde 1998: 94. For an effort to find plausible interpretations of Isserles's ruling that would not require an application of *de-rabbanan* law to non-Jews, see Bleich 1995/1996.

92. Mordekhai Banet, *Responsa Parshat Mordekhai*, Ḥoshen Mishpat, No. 8.

that matter, in its decree in favor of Eliyahu Bakhur, the Rome rabbinic court similarly labelled one who would reprint Bakhur's books without permission as a "*gozel mamash*," an actual misappropriator. Did that court likewise mean to recognize an author's right in literary property?

Common law jurists have long struggled with whether an author's original expression constitutes "property" that can be "stolen." Following enactment of the Statute of Anne, which granted only a short-term copyright in new works, London publishers petitioned the courts to recognize a perpetual common-law property right in authors' literary compositions. Opponents of the common-law right insisted, among other things, that intangible creations cannot be the subject of property. As Justice Joseph Yates opined in his dissent in the 1769 case of *Millar v. Taylor*: "Their whole existence is in the mind alone; incapable of any other modes of acquisition or enjoyment, than by mental possession or apprehension; safe and invulnerable, from their own immateriality: no trespass can reach them; no tort affect them; no fraud or violence diminish or damage them. Yet these are the phantoms which the author would grasp and confine to himself . . . ."[93] Proponents of a common law copyright responded by characterizing literary compositions in metaphorically physicalist terms. Blackstone, for example, grounded the author's composition firmly in the actual language of the manuscript, portraying the author's words as markers for the bounds of the author's literary property: "Now the identity of a literary composition consists entirely in the *sentiment* and the *language*; the same conceptions, clothed in the same words, must necessarily be the same composition."[94] We see the theoretical and doctrinal imprint of this reification as late as the 1853 case of *Stowe v. Thomas*,[95] in which the court ruled that Harriet Beecher Stowe's copyright in *Uncle Tom's Cabin* did not extend to a translation of her novel. After citing and paraphrasing Blackstone's definition of a literary composition as "the same conceptions, clothed in the same words, the court held: "A 'copy' of a book must, therefore be a transcript of the language in which the conceptions of the author are clothed; *of something printed and embodied in a tangible shape*. The same conceptions clothed in another language cannot constitute the same composition, nor can it be called a transcript or 'copy' of the same 'book'."[96]

Jewish law similarly reflects a distinction and tension between rights in tangible things and rights in intangibles, but the dividing lines and issues raised differ from those of the common law. Most important for our purposes, although the word *gezel* is typically translated as robbery, and at its core connotes the open, coercive taking of property, rabbinic authorities often use the term *gezel* to encompasses a broader set of wrongs, including fraud, withholding payment from laborers, and other monetary and commercial matters. In that vein, rabbinic scholars have debated at least since the time of the Talmud whether *oshek*—meaning "oppressing your neighbor," specifically by

93. Millar v. Taylor, 98 Eng. Rep. 201, 233 (K.B. 1769) (Yates, J., dissenting).
94. Blackstone 1825: 405–06.
95. 23 F. Cas. 201 (1853).
96. 23 F. Cas. at 207.

enriching oneself or deriving material benefit from violating your neighbor's rights—falls within the category of *gezel* or stands as a distinct offense.[97]

Moreover, the Noaḥide law of *gezel*, although typically translated as robbery or theft, is understood to have an even broader meaning than the term *gezel* as applied in law governing Jews. The seven Noaḥide laws have been interpreted more as category headings than specific provisions. They refer to seven broad areas of legislation, connoted by their respective titles.[98] Accordingly, the Noaḥide law of *gezel* is commonly seen to prohibit kidnapping, coveting another's property, cheating, overcharging, using false weights and measures, repudiating debts, and forbidding one's farm laborers to eat from the fruits of the harvest, as well as conventional stealing and robbery.[99]

Isserles's labeling of the matter before him as *gezel* under Noaḥide law must be understood within that broad umbrella. It means only that Isserles saw the matter as falling within the category of monetary and commercial wrongs—not that he necessarily viewed Giustiniani's conduct as a taking of property. In fact, it is clear that Isserles did not view Giustiniani's conduct as conventional robbery or theft, and did not hold that Katzenellenbogen held a property interest in the product of his intellectual labor. Elsewhere, Isserles suggests that for something to constitute property, it must be tangible.[100] That proposition is fully in accord with the *Mishneh Torah*, *Shulḥan Arukh*, and other authority—even if, as we shall see, some rabbinic authorities today contend that copyright is, indeed, a property right. Nor does Isserles's ruling give any indication that a right of literary property is at stake.

Isserles, rather, analyzes Giustiniani's conduct under the Jewish law of wrongful competition, not as theft of literary property. To the extent that Isserles does mean "*gezel*" to refer to some kind of misappropriation, it is a misappropriation of the Maharam's business opportunity or source of livelihood, not the taking of an author's literary property in the sense that came to be recognized much later in modern copyright jurisprudence. The same applies to the Rome rabbis' use of the term "*gozel mamash*." An unauthorized reprinter of Bakhur's books would be an "actual misappropriator" of Bakhur's and his publishers' expected return on investment and means of livelihood, akin to the fishermen who divert a fish from one who has already spread his net in anticipation of catching it. Neither Isserles nor the Rome rabbis imagine that an author's intellectual creation is the author's property and that it is stolen when another reprints it without his permission.

97. See Albeck 2007: 452–53.

98. See Lichtenstein 1995: 90–93.

99. Lichtenstein 1995: 18–26. Naḥmanides might be an exception. See Moses Sofer, *Responsa Hatam Sofer*, Likkutim, No. 14 (opining that the disagreement between Maimonides and Naḥmanides was fundamentally over whether laws regarding monetary matters are covered within the Noaḥide law of *gezel*, as Maimonides contended, or *dinim*, which Naḥmanides argued.)

100. In his glosses on the *Shulḥan Arukh*, for example, Isserles writes: "If in a contract someone only wrote 'and he acquires from him in order to allow him to live in his house' this is not effective for the essence of the acquisition is on the right to dwell, which is not something tangible ...." *Shulḥan Arukh*, Ḥoshen Mishpat, Hilkhot Mekakh U-Memkhar [Laws of Commercial Transactions] 212: 1.

C. Wrongful Competition: Encroaching on Another's Livelihood

In their *ktav dat* in favor of Eliyahu Bakhur, the Rome rabbis briefly referred to three Talmudic cases that propound the rule that, in certain circumstances, it is wrongful to encroach on—or "misappropriate"—another's source of livelihood: the poor man reaching for a crust of bread, the fisherman who has staked out a fish, and the righteous man who refrains from taking what another dearly values. In his ruling, Isserles delves into the Jewish law of wrongful competition in far greater depth. In particular, he underscores that the prohibition on encroaching on another's livelihood is an exception to the general rule permitting competition. That restriction on competition thus requires special justification.

The rabbinic literature discusses at length whether competition should be restricted to protect existing suppliers.[101] This question presents a difficult quandary for the rabbinic authorities. On one hand, competition benefits consumers by providing goods at lower prices. On the other, untrammeled competition can deprive suppliers of their livelihood. For the rabbis, it is by no means a foregone conclusion that the former justifies the latter. Nonetheless, Jewish law ultimately comes down heavily on the side of allowing free competition, and rabbinic authorities generally decline to regulate prices or restrict entry to existing markets in order to protect incumbent suppliers. There are exceptions, however, particularly when incumbent suppliers are harmed without a clear benefit for consumers.[102]

The paradigm case occurs in a Mishnah, a discussion of law from the second century.[103] The Mishnah in question appears in a chapter concerning commercial relations and consumer protection:

> Rabbi Judah said: "A shopkeeper must not distribute corn or nuts to children, because he thereby accustoms them to come to him. But the Sages permit it. [Rabbi Judah also held:] "Nor may he reduce the price." But the Sages say that he is to be remembered for good.[104]

As is generally the case, the Sages' view (which was the majority view) became the rule of Jewish law. It favors free competition, including through reductions in price. As Maimonides summarized, "A storekeeper . . . may sell below the market price in order to increase the number of his customers, and the merchants of the market cannot prevent him."[105]

101. For an illuminating survey and analysis, see Deutch 1993/1994; Lieberman 1989; S. Warhaftig 1990.

102. Lieberman 1989: 34.

103. The Mishnah is a collection of rabbinic rulings, disputation, and teachings from the first and second centuries. See the Glossary for further explication.

104. *Baba Metzia*, 60a. See Deutch 1993/1994: 15–16. Rabbi Judah Ha-Nasi lived during the latter half of the second and beginning of the third century. He was the patriarch of Judea and redactor of the Mishnah.

105. *Mishneh Torah*, Sefer Kinyan, Hilkhot Mekhira 17:4.

The favorable view of competition through price reduction applies to market entry as well. As the *Mishneh Torah* states:

> If there is among the residents of an alley [what would be a neighborhood today] . . . a bathhouse or a shop or a mill, and someone comes and makes another bathhouse opposite to the first, or another mill, the owner of the first cannot prevent him and claim that the second cuts off his livelihood. Even if the owner of the second is from another alley, they cannot prevent him.[106]

The law makes an exception to this general rule of free entry when the newcomer is from another land and does not pay the taxes imposed on local residents. In that case, the newcomer has an unfair advantage over local suppliers. But even in that case, Joseph ibn Migash (1077–1141), whom Maimonides revered as his father's teacher, ruled that a non-taxpaying out-of-town merchant must be allowed to enter if he sells merchandise of better quality or at a lower price than local suppliers.[107] Ibn Migash reasoned that when competition brings a direct benefit to consumers, the consumer's interest prevails over that of the local merchants. Ibn Migash's ruling was subject to strong criticism by Naḥmanides. Naḥmanides insisted that the law's embrace of price competition applies only when competition can lead to a *substantial*, wholesale reduction in price. Absent this material benefit to consumers, competition by outside competitors should not be allowed.

Ibn Migash's position became the majority view. It favors free competition, at least when competition affords some benefit to consumers. The consumer's interest prevails over the incumbent sellers', even when the new entrant enjoys advantages, including having greater resources or smaller expenses, such as by not having to pay local taxes.

In his commentary on the *Shulḥan Arukh*, Isserles followed that majority view. He opined that competition is permitted when outside competitors offer a lower price, even absent an indication that this will lead to a substantial market-wide price reduction.[108] Isserles also cited ibn Migash's position in ruling on a petition by foreign merchants to invalidate a town's regulation restricting their entry. But there, Isserles qualified his support for unlimited competition along the lines of Naḥmanides's dissent: he suggested that competition from foreign merchants, and the resulting harm to local incumbents, may be permitted only if it brings a substantial price reduction.[109]

At least at first glance, Isserles's ruling on the Maharam's petition represents a far more radical departure from his general embrace of the majority rule favoring competition than did his suggestion that foreign merchants may compete only if that would bring a substantial price reduction. Giustiniani had expressly offered a significant price reduction, promising to sell his edition for one gold coin less than Bragadini's so that more Jewish readers would have access to Maimonides's

106. *Mishneh Torah*, Sefer Kinyan, Hilkhot Shkhenim 6:8.

107. See Deutch 1993/1994: 25–26. On Maimonides reverence for ibn Migash, see Davidson 2005: 76–78, 194.

108. *Shulḥan Arukh*, Ḥoshen Mishpat, 156: 5–7, Rema commentary, cited and discussed in Lieberman 1989: 32, 38, and Rakover 1991: 247.

109. Isserles, *Responsa Rema*, No. 73, discussed in Lieberman 1989: 32.

foundational restatement of the law. Nonetheless, Isserles ruled Giustiniani's competitive conduct to be a violation of the Jewish law of wrongful competition as incorporated into Noaḥide law.

Isserles begins his discussion of wrongful competition by reference to a Mishnah in which the third-century Babylonian sage Rav Huna held that a resident who establishes a mill for commercial purposes may prevent a competitor—even a fellow resident—from setting up an adjacent mill, on the grounds that the competitor is cutting off the first mill owner's livelihood.[110] Rav Huna's position was in the minority and, as indicated in Maimonides's restatement quoted above, did not gain acceptance as the operative rule of Jewish law.[111]

Isserles recognizes that Rav Huna's holding does not generally apply. But he finds an exception to the majority pro-competition rule in a teaching of *Avi'asaf*, a work of commentary on the Talmud addressing civil wrongs and other matters, written by the German rabbinic scholar Eliezer ben Joel Ha-Levi (1140–1225): "When an alleyway is closed on three sides and is open for entry on only one side and where Reuven lives [and operates a mill] on the closed end and Shimon comes to live [and erect a mill] on the open end, so that potential customers cannot enter the alleyway without passing Shimon's door, the law is that Reuven may prevent Shimon [from entering the market]."[112] In the case of the closed alleyway, therefore, the new entrant is *certain* to damage the first comer's business, because many potential customers will buy from the new entrant (at the open end of the alleyway) without even seeing the first comer's goods (at the closed end). In such circumstances, the rule follows Rav Huna's minority stance: the first merchant may prevent entry by the competitor.[113] Isserles finds this exception directly on point: "Therefore, in our case there is also certain damage. The second printer has announced that he will sell all of his books for a gold coin cheaper than those of the *Gaon* [i.e., the Maharam].[114] Who will see this and not come to buy from him [the second printer]? And he is able to sell cheaply because he is one of the wealthiest men in the country."

110. *Babylonian Talmud, Baba Batra* 21b. Rav Huna was one of the leaders of the second generation of Babylonian "amoraim," the scholars of the third to sixth centuries whose disputes and teachings make up the Gemara.

111. As reflected in the Mishnah, Huna bar Joshua held at the end of the fourth century that one craftsman could not restrain a fellow craftsman and resident of the same alley from setting up business in the same alley. For discussion, see Elon 2007b: 448–53.

112. Eliezer ben Joel Ha-Levi is known by the Hebrew acronym, Ravyah. His works were considered a basic source of Jewish law until the publication of the *Shulḥan Arukh*. See Y. Horowitz 2007a: 326–27. The passage in his work, *Avi'asaf*, was cited by the Mordekhai, *Baba Batra* 516, and *Hagahot Maimoniot*, Hilkhot Shkhenim 6:8.

113. Isserles insisted elsewhere as well that *Avi'asaf* correctly opines that even opponents of Rav Huna's position agreed that a new business opened at the entrance to a dead-end alleyway would surely cripple the competing business farther inside the alley and thus may be prevented. Isserles, *Darkhei Moshe* 156:4.

114. Throughout his ruling, Isserles refers to Katzenellenbogen as the *Gaon*. The title, *Gaon*, was accorded to the heads of the two great rabbinic academies of Babylonia where the Talmud was produced. It remained an honorific in Jewish tradition.

Isserles's somewhat cryptic reasoning on this point has puzzled subsequent rabbinic authorities. A new competitor's entry is often fairly certain to cause at least some loss to the incumbent. Why should the fact that the competitor has certain advantages, whether owing to location (erecting a mill at the open end of the alley) or great financial resources (Giustiniani), make a difference in the legal rule? Moreover, the rule in *Avi'asaf* would seem to entitle the first comer to an exclusive entitlement to operate his business in the alleyway for so long as he continues in business. But Isserles ruled that the Maharam has only an exclusive right to sell out the existing edition and thus to recoup only his initial investment. If the law is in fact according to *Avi'asaf*, why should the Maharam not have a continuing right to unobstructed sales, even after selling out his first printing?

Explanations center on the nature, degree, and certainty of the incumbent's harm, as well as on the conduct of the competitor. Two late eighteenth-early nineteenth-century rabbinic jurists, Ephraim Zalman Margoliot (1760–1828) and Moses Sofer (1762–1839), each read Isserles to mean that the incumbent merchant may prevent competition that is certain to cause severe harm to his business.[115] Sofer goes on to say that Isserles ruled as he did because book publishers cannot profit without making a substantial investment in printing a new edition, and will not make that investment if a competitor can effectively eliminate the original publisher's ability to earn a livelihood by thwarting any expectation of profit.[116] That interpretation finds support in Isserles's assessment of what was at stake in the dispute: "It is obvious that if the *Gaon* will not be successful in selling the books, his load will be overbearing [i.e., he will be financially ruined]."

Focusing on Isserles's reference to Giustiniani's ability to sell cheaply, Margoliot also suggests that the incumbent merchant may prevent a competitor from selling below the reasonable market price.[117] Isserles intimates that Giustiniani has the resources and motive to sell at a loss and that doing so constitutes wrongful competition where the result is to cause severe harm to the incumbent. In that vein, Isserles emphasizes elsewhere in his ruling that Giustiniani produced his competing edition "for spite and in order to exhaust the Gaon's money."

Couched in these terms, Isserles's ruling seems to be more a narrow proscription of predatory pricing than a right of authors and publishers generally to prevent pirated or otherwise competing editions.[118] Like any merchant, a publisher may not sell at a below-market price with the intent of driving a competitor out of business. And Katzenellenbogen is entitled to protection against the harm of predatory pricing, not an ongoing proprietary right that would insulate him from normal competition.[119]

115. Ephraim Zalman Margoliot (1762–1828), *Responsa Beit Ephraim*, Ḥoshen Mishpat, No. 27; Sofer, *Responsa Ḥatam Sofer*, Ḥoshen Mishpat, No. 41.

116. Sofer, *Responsa Ḥatam Sofer*, Ḥoshen Mishpat, No. 41. We will return to Sofer's argument in Chapter 6.

117. See discussion in Lieberman 1989: 38.

118. See Deutch 1993/1994: 27–28.

119. The present day rabbinic scholar Judah David Bleich suggests another possible interpretation of Isserles's ruling on this point. Like the common law prior to the emergence of modern tort law in the late nineteenth century, Jewish law distinguishes between direct

In sum, as understood by later commentators, Isserles held that Giustiniani violated the Jewish law of wrongful competition, as applied to the Christian publisher through Noaḥide law, because Giustiniani intended to cause the Maharam significant harm by selling at a loss, and because that harm was certain to occur as an immediate consequence of his conduct. Of importance to current understandings of copyright law and to subsequent rabbinic debate, Isserles did not ascribe any harm or wrongful conduct to Giustiniani's copying of the Maharam's annotations per se. Indeed, Isserles does not even mention Giustiniani's copying. His ruling, therefore, most definitely does not sound in "copyright," as that term would be understood in present-day secular law. For Isserles, rather, Giustiniani engaged in wrongful conduct solely because of the economic damage that he intended to inflict and was certain to inflict upon Katzenellenbogen, given Katzenellenbogen's substantial monetary investment in publishing his edition of the *Mishneh Torah*.

D. Abetting in a Transgression

There remains the question why Isserles devoted so much attention to the issue of whether Giustiniani violated Noaḥide law. After all, Isserles did not hold that Giustiniani was liable to the Maharam for the loss he caused. Nor was there any realistic possibility of imposing a fine on Giustiniani, even if Isserles had held that such a sanction was warranted.

Isserles might have wished to dazzle his peers with his ability to flesh out the intricacies of halakha on a complex issue. But he probably also intended that his holding that Giustiniani violated Noaḥide law would provide support for his order prohibiting Jews from buying Giustiniani's less expensive edition rather than the Maharam's. The halakha prohibits Jews from assisting non-Jews, not just other Jews, to commit a transgression.[120] For example, the Talmud forbids a Jew from feeding a limb torn from the body of a living animal to a non-Jew, as it would violate Noaḥide law for the non-Jew to eat it. Isserles might thus have underscored that Giustiniani's conduct violated Noaḥide law in order to lay a strong halakhic foundation for prohibiting Jews from buying Guistiniani's edition and thus abetting in the Christian publisher's transgression.

and indirect harm. Unlike the common law, however, Jewish law holds that causing harm indirectly (the Hebrew term is *grama*) gives rise to no legal liability, but only a moral obligation. Not surprisingly, rabbinic jurists have developed exceptions to that rule. One is the rule of *garmi*. Under that rule, legal liability does arise when certain conditions are met. Commentators differ on what those conditions are, but according to some early authority, legal liability arises when indirect harm is accompanied by an intent to cause damage, an immediacy of harm (roughly akin to proximate cause), and a certainty of harm. Under this doctrine, Giustiniani would be liable for any real loss, but not frustration of profits, that he intentionally caused the Maharam, as that harm is a certain and immediate consequence of Giustiniani's competing edition. Although Isserles does not mention *garmi*, Bleich speculates that it might have been the basis of Isserles's ruling nonetheless and that Isserles invoked *Avi'asaf* only as an example of certain harm caused by competition. Bleich 1995/1996: 43–45.

120. *Babylonian Talmud, Avodah Zarah* 6b.

On the other hand, unlike the Microsoft ruling's labeling of purchasers of illicit copies as "abettors," Isserles nowhere states explicitly that Jews are forbidden from buying Giustiniani's edition because that would constitute unlawful abetting in the commission of a transgression. Moreover, it is unclear whether the rule against assisting transgressors would apply in Giustiniani's case. Rabbinic authorities have long disputed whether a Jew is prohibited from assisting a non-Jew to transgress when the non-Jew would be able to transgress even without the Jew's assistance.[121] Indeed, Isserles elsewhere ruled that assisting a non-Jew to transgress in those circumstances is halakhically permitted, although a pious person should nonetheless refrain from doing so.[122]

That stance poses a possible problem regarding Giustiniani. Although Giustiniani's transgression depended on having a market for his edition, arguably it did not depend on any given sale of a copy of his *Mishneh Torah* to a particular purchaser. Moreover, Giustiniani might have marketed his edition to Christian Hebraicists as well as Jews. In that regard, rabbinic authorities differ on whether a particular Jew's obligation to refrain from abetting in a transgression applies when the transgressor could transgress regardless, with the assistance of other people, whether they be Jews or non-Jews.[123]

We cannot know how Isserles might have viewed this issue as it pertained to Giustiniani because he makes no mention of it in his ruling. Nonetheless, it is doubtful that Isserles would have intended his extensive analysis of Giustiniani's violation of Noaḥide law to be entirely theoretical. He must have meant it in some way to lend support to his order forbidding Jews in Poland from buying Giustiniani's edition. His order might have been tacitly grounded in the premise—which Isserles might have assumed all would understand without explanation—that such purchases would be halakhically prohibited as abetting in a transgression. Alternatively, he might have meant to convey that lending Giustiniani assistance was an act that pious persons should refrain from doing. Finally, even absent a direct connection to the rule against assisting transgressors, he might have wished simply to color Giustiniani as a transgressor in order to inspire greater willingness among Polish Jews to buy the Maharam's more expensive edition instead of Giustiniani's.

E. Anxiety over Print

Early modern Ashkenazic rabbinic traditionalists were at best deeply ambivalent about the technology of print. Isserles shared that ambivalence, even if he ultimately embraced print as a vital tool for countering erroneous teachings of halakha. The

121. Rashi maintains that assisting a non-Jew to transgress is prohibited even if the non-Jew could transgress without such assistance. Shlomo Yitzḥaki (1040–1105), *Commentary to Talmud*, Avodah Zarah 55a. In contrast, Magen Avraham maintains that such assistance is permitted. Abraham Abele Gombiner (1633–1683), *Magen Avraham*.

122. *Darkhei Moshe*, Oraḥ Ḥayim 343:4.

123. See David ben Solomon ibn Abi Zimra (1479–1573), *Commentary to Mishneh Torah*, Hilkhot Nezirut, 5:20 (holding that abetting in non-Jew's transgression is permitted when the transgressor could anyway transgress with the assistance of non-Jews); Yosef Babad (1800–1874), *Minḥat Ḥinukh* (positing that a Jew may not assist in transgression even when the transgressor may transgress with the assistance of other Jews).

Rema's ruling highlights two particular facets of the rabbinic anxiety over print: concern over the perpetuation of scribal error and deep suspicion that Christian printers would introduce Christian apologetics into rabbinic works. I consider each of these shortly. But, first, we examine the context of rabbinic anxiety over print more generally.

Ashkenazic tradition relied largely on oral teaching and the personal authority of local rabbinic scholars in each generation.[124] Two of Isserles's leading predecessors, Jacob Pollak and Shalom Shakhna, deliberately left behind no written—let alone printed—commentaries or rulings. They feared that their students and future generations would rely on those writings too heavily, rather than grappling with and applying Talmudic precepts on a case-by-case basis, accounting for evolving local conditions and customs. When Ashkenazic authorities and their students did commit commentaries, rulings, and teachings to writing, they typically followed the tradition of the open book. Writings were meant to be works in progress rather than completed, immutable texts. Authors and their students would frequently revise and update them to reflect further study and discussion.[125] In contrast to printed books, handwritten manuscripts also had limited circulation. Indeed, they were often intended merely as an aide-memoire to their author—or, at most, to serve as study tools for a highly select readership of the author's students and perhaps other halakhic scholars. Further, as manuscripts were studied, each succeeding generation of scholars and each leading *yeshiva* community appended their own glosses. Hence, multiple versions of foundational texts came into being, each containing emendations and glosses reflecting local customs and scholarly interpretation. In that world, the authority of any particular text resided largely in the prestige of its most recent rabbinic interpreter.

Print posed a fundamental challenge to that tradition. With print, texts were standardized, distributed over a broad geographical area, and rendered immutable, at least in the form in which they appeared in any particular print edition. As such, the proliferation of printed texts arrested the creative process of the open book and undermined the Ashkenazic tradition of modifying legal precepts in accordance with local custom and teaching. With print, indeed, the standardized text, not each rabbinic teacher, became the authoritative final word.

Print weakened local rabbinic authority in other ways as well. It brought forth a welter of books presenting different perspectives on a broad range of topics, some produced primarily for rabbinic scholars and some for a broader readership than just the intellectual elite of rabbinic academies. Thus, in addition to challenging the Ashkenazic method of transmission, print also brought changes to the canon of study and empowered a new class of readers: semi-learned ones who were not part of the intellectual elite, but who could learn directly from books, as well as write their own. The rabbis resisted these developments. But they proved incapable of preventing the outpouring of small books produced for the lay public. As a result, new readers gained access to aspects of the tradition that had previously been the exclusive prerogative of the rabbinic elite.

124. On the challenge that print posed to Ashkenazic tradition, see Elbaum 1990: 24–32; Reiner 1997: 85–92; Rosman 2002: 532–42; Ruderman 2010: 101–02.

125. Ta-Shma 2006: 194, 198–99.

Isserles shared the rabbinic elite's grave misgivings about the power of print to lend false authority to the ignorant and to perpetuate and disseminate error. In his introduction to *Torat Ḥatat*, Isserles's codification of ritual law, he cites the pressing need to correct the many errors that had arisen from the proliferation of printed editions of the *Sharei Dura*, an abbreviated work that was written to serve as a handbook for Ashkenazic scholars.[126] As Isserles puts it: "[I]n this last generation . . . [*Sharei Dura*] was copied and printed several times since every person desires it because of its shortness and wishes to study all ritual law while standing on one foot [i.e., quickly and cursorily]. And through print those books have fallen into the hands of many small and great, and they added many interpretations to them. Time perishes, and their words do not perish . . . and afterward these books [the interpretations of *Sharei Dura*] themselves are printed and the one who reads them then claims that they are given at Sinai and rules according to them mistakenly." In contrast to some Ashkenazic traditionalists, however, Isserles nevertheless embraced the printing of comprehensive and accurate codes as a necessary response to the duplication of error wrought by other printed texts. Isserles cited that need to harness the power of print as his primary motivation for authoring *Torat Ḥatat* and releasing it for publication.[127]

F. Scribal Error

The rabbinic anxiety over the subsersive power of print helps to illuminate a seemingly more narrow, immediate focus of Isserles's ruling on the matter of the *Mishneh Torah*: that of scribal error.

Rabbinic tradition places a high value the study and teaching of "Torah," meaning not only the Pentateuch but more generally Jewish thought and law. Of course, Isserles shared that value. In principle, therefore, he would not have lightly dismissed Giustiniani's claim that providing the *Mishneh Torah* at a low price would vastly increase access to that foundational text in the Jewish community. Elsewhere, in fact, Isserles held that in a place where Torah study suffers because books are unavailable, a rabbinic tribunal may require a book owner to lend his books for study, so long as he is compensated for any wear and tear that might be caused to the books in the process.[128] Isserles also held that although a bailee may not normally open and read books in his care, when the bailee is a rabbinic scholar who lacks the volume himself, he may read and copy from such books.[129]

126. Halbertal 1997: 164 n. 57.

127. Isserles also saw how Joseph Karo's code, *Beit Yosef*, had been widely disseminated in light of the invention of the press, and evidently realized that unless he printed his own codification highlighting Ashkenazic practices, the Sephardic interpretations, rulings, and customs reflected in *Beit Yosef* would gain force within the Ashkenazic world. Spiegel 1996: 275–76.

128. *Shulḥan Arukh*, Ḥoshen Mishpat, Hilkhot Pikadon 292:20, Rema commentary.

129. *Shulḥan Arukh*, Ḥoshen Mishpat, Hilkhot Pikadon 292:20, Rema commentary.

But books of Jewish law are valuable only if they accurately set out the law, and Isserles expresses grave doubts about the accuracy of Giustiniani's text. In that vein, in addition to his analysis of wrongful competition, Isserles grounds his ruling on the halakhic injunction that foundational texts of Jewish law bearing textual errors must be destroyed. That injunction stems from the Talmudic prohibition against keeping a Torah scroll containing scribal errors for more than 30 days. Isserles cites that early rule and subsequent authorities who extended the intolerance of scribal error to other legal texts. As Isserles puts it (echoing the medieval Ashkenazi sage, Asher ben Yeḥiel (c. 1250–1327)): "If a book contains even minor textual errors, one is liable to make erroneous legal rulings: to prohibit that which is permitted, to permit that which is prohibited, to hold as ritually pure that which is impure, etc." Indeed, Isserles continues, citing Talmudic dictum, it is best to teach in great quantity and with accuracy; but if that is not possible, it is far better to teach in lesser quantity but accurately, than to teach in greater quantity but with less accuracy, hoping that students will eventually realize that some of the teachings were mistaken. Accordingly, Isserles broadly concludes, a book of Jewish law should not be disseminated—or purchased—unless it has been thoroughly and competently proofread.

The advent of print greatly magnified rabbinic anxiety over scribal error. On one hand, print obviated the need for serial handwritten copying and thus carried the potential for eliminating a source of textual error. More than that, a skilled, learned scholar and corrector might draw upon his expertise and careful reading of a number of written manuscripts to produce a printed text that eliminates previous scribal errors once and for all. But on the other hand, print posed the grave danger of perpetuating and multiplying error many times over in a standardized text. Print also brought a new source for error: that introduced in the process of typesetting. As Daniel Bomberg's corrector, Jacob ben Ḥaim ibn Adonijah (c. 1470–1538), noted in his colophon to Bomberg's 1524 edition of the *Mishneh Torah*: "We all know that in the printing process it is impossible that no mistakes appear in the first version. Therefore, I made as certain as possible that I caught all printing mistakes. I beg the reader not to blame me if he finds a mistake. Please understand that I did my very best and that such is what happens in printing."

Accordingly, in the universe of halakhic texts, no less than in that of the non-Jewish book trade, the printing of previously handwritten manuscripts placed a premium on the expertise of the scholar corrector. In that vein, for rabbinic authorities the role of the proofreader and corrector was even more crucial, given that textual error could lead to erroneous interpretations of law.[130] We see a vivid expression of the central importance that the rabbis placed on textual correction even in the very first printed book to contain rabbinic approbations, Yaakov bar Yehuda Landau's *Agur*, published by Azriel Gunzenhauser in Naples in approximately 1490.[131] Gunzenhauser retained Judah Messer Leon, a leading rabbinic scholar of his generation, to proofread the

130. Spiegel 1996: 276–77. Papal book privileges also placed a premium on textual accuracy—and on fidelity to Catholic doctrine. J. Ginsburg 2013: 367–68.

131. See Hurvitz 1978: 16–25.

work. Leon supplied an approbation for the book as well. In his statement of praise for the work, Leon noted: "[I]t is in the manner of the craft of printing for many errors to fall in books on account of the laziness of the workers, who do not correct errors in accordance with what has been marked for correction in the manuscript . . . . And sometimes these errors are blamed on the author or commentator. And I, therefore, decided to purify [this book], to purify the purified, until I would leave virtually no error that is not corrected on this page, together with what is already corrected in the previous pages."[132] Isserles's ruling in favor of the Maharam of Padua echoes that emphasis on the vital importance of expert, scholarly correction.

Isserles evidently gave no credence to Giustiniani's charge that Katzenellenbogen and Bragadini had produced a shoddy product. As Isserles describes it, the Maharam diligently proofread his edition of the *Mishneh Torah*, removing errors "with his pure wisdom until there was 'no straw remaining in the field' and 'no stone left in the path.'" To the contrary, Isserles suggests that Giustiniani might have produced in great quantity, but, unlike the Maharam, could not be depended upon for accuracy. We are thus to prefer the Maharam's edition over Giustiniani's even if Giustiniani's cheaper edition would reach more readers.

Isserles also took greater comfort in the Maharam's stated method for contending with and correcting possible errors in preprint manuscripts and earlier printed editions. As is apparent from the rabbinic sources that Isserles cited requiring the destruction of texts bearing scribal errors, rabbinic concerns over errors in copying one manuscript from another long predated the advent of print. Such errors were far from uncommon, especially because scribes in medieval Jewish Europe were generally recruited from the lower, relatively less educated rungs of literate society.[133] Further, scribal errors tended to proliferate as hand-copied manuscripts served as sources for successive copies. As a result, rabbinic texts that had been copied and recopied by hand for many years often degenerated into multiple variants, each reflecting different scribal errors introduced at some stage in the transmission.

Yet, rabbinic anxiety extended as much to *correcting* suspected errors as to the presence of scribal errors to begin with. Rabbis feared that efforts to correct suspected errors could introduce new errors. In addition, if readers felt free to edit texts that they claimed to be in error, people who have difficulty understanding some passage of the Talmud or another work might be inclined simply to edit the text rather than grappling with apparent contradictions. Such a practice, if widespread, would undermine the traditional approach to Talmud study and, indeed, the textual integrity—and sanctity—of the Talmud and other foundational texts.[134]

Rabbis and scribes of each generation then faced a quandary. When a manuscript appeared to have a textual error, should the rabbi or scribe correct it? How is the reader to know that the text contains an error? And on what basis should any correction be made?

132. Leon c. 1490: 184–85 (folio).
133. Ta-Shma 2006: 194.
134. Spiegel 1996: 233.

Because of their anxieties over correction, most early modern rabbinic decisors flat-out prohibited making any corrections, required that the original uncorrected text appear together with any corrected text, or allowed corrections only if there was general agreement among scholars regarding the error.[135] Isserles shared in his contemporaries' concern about undue corrections to foundational texts. But he took a relatively liberal approach to allowing corrections. In his annotations to the *Shulḥan Arukh*, Isserles held: "It is forbidden to correct (edit) any book according to *s'vara* (reason) unless there is clear evidence that there is a mistake in it."[136] In other words, even if reason tells one that the text must be in error, one may not correct the book absent clear evidence of the mistake, such as an older version of the text that supports the correction. Although that rule requires an abundance of caution in making corrections, Isserles did not prohibit making any corrections at all. He was thus somewhat more permissive in that regard than most of his contemporaries.[137]

In addition to his scholarly expertise, Katzenellenbogen's stated correction practice gave Isserles further comfort that the Maharam-Bragadini *Mishneh Torah* faithfully rendered Maimonides's original text and the associated commentaries. In his introduction, Katzenellenbogen states: "I used three texts in proofreading. I never corrected using only my reasoning. If I did not find a basis for correction in the books in front of me, I did not change the text. Rather, I just added a note in the margin." That correction practice fit well within Isserles's injunction that one may not correct a book according to one's reason alone, but must rely on clear evidence of error. Isserles could rest assured that Katzenellenbogen did not alter the text, possibly mistakenly, merely because he believed it was in error.

* * *

Aside from the Maharam's stated correction practice, Isserles's great faith in the Maharam's correction of errors seems to have been based more on Isserles's esteem for his senior colleague than on an actual comparison of the competing editions. As Yaakov Spiegel points out, a close reading of the Bragadini and Giustiniani editions does not support the Rema's suggestion that the Bragadini edition was diligently and expertly proofread, while the Giustiniani edition remained riddled with textual errors. In fact, one finds little difference between the two editions in the quality of their editing. Each contains variations from the 1524 Bomberg edition, sometimes for the better, sometimes for the worse. And in each, there is virtually no discussion of editing issues regarding particular wording and text. If anything, Giustiniani's

135. Spiegel 1996: 229–33.

136. *Shulḥan Arukh,* Yoreh De'ah 279: 61, Rema commentary.

137. In line with the majority rule, Isserles also forbade corrections when the same alleged error in a particular passage appeared in two different books (i.e., manuscripts of two different works), unless one was copied from the other. Isserles, *Responsa Rema*, No. 38. It would be uncommon, Isserles and other rabbinic decisors posited, that the same error would be repeated in two distinct works. Hence, if same textual variant appeared in two different books, the variant was adjudged to arise from something other than scribal error, unless one book was copied from the other. Spiegel 1996: 248–49.

edition might be an improvement over the Bomberg and Bragadini editions as it provides copious notations and cross-references that the others do not.

Nor, for that matter, did the Maharam's annotations meet with universal acclaim, even if Giustiniani's sweeping mockery of them can be dismissed as the bellicose gamesmanship so typical of rival printers of the era. A leading rabbinic authority of the mid-sixteenth century, David ben Solomon ibn Abi Zimra (c. 1479–1573), more dispassionately assessed the Maharam's annotations in one of his responsa. Zimra concurred with some of the Maharam's annotations, but expressed disagreement with most of them.

G. Suspicion of Christian Printers

Isserles's holding that Giustiniani had committed wrongful competition by issuing his edition out of spite, to deprive the Maharam of his livelihood, reads like an even-handed exposition of Jewish commercial law, applicable to Gentiles (in their dealings with Jews) and Jews alike. But elsewhere his ruling is brazenly sectarian. Most broadly, he rules that Jews are obligated to buy from a fellow Jew rather than from a Gentile competitor even when the Gentile—like Giustiniani—offers to sell for a lower price. More specifically, Isserles bespeaks a certain suspicion of Christian printers who are motivated fundamentally by a desire for profit—and who might be perfectly willing, if not eager, to insert Christian apologetics into rabbinic texts at the behest of papal authorities.

Isserles presents Christian printers in marked contrast to Katzenellenbogen. The "Gaon Rabbi Meir of Padua," Isserles relates, has applied his "direction, thoughts, and ideas" to producing his edition, "drawn water from a deep well" (of his extensive knowledge of Torah), and proofread with his "pure wisdom" in single-minded devotion to removing all error so that the law may be correctly taught. Giustiniani and his editors, Isserles intimates, are instead devoted only to achieving financial advantage. Towards the end of his ruling, Isserles considers and summarily rejects the notion that non-Jewish printers might cease printing Jewish books in the wake of his ruling (and, one presumes, other rulings like it). In so doing, he paints Christian printers in crass, self-interested, commercial terms: "As a matter of common sense, those who publish do so for their own benefit, in order to profit, like those who deal in other types of commerce. Thus even if they lose on one occasion, they will not refrain from printing. On the contrary they will be even more eager to replenish their loss."

Isserles well understood that, ever since Daniel Bomberg had received his monopoly from the Venetian Senate to print Hebrew books, Jews depended heavily on Venetian Christian printers for print editions of foundational rabbinic texts. Indeed, Giustiniani's edition of the Talmud, which the Venetian patrician had begun to print, tractate by tracate, in 1546, was designed to meet the needs of Polish *yeshivot*—and became the standard for all subsequent editions.[138] Isserles recognizes in his ruling that one might well claim that, "these [Christian] printers have taught Torah and

138. Raz-Krakotzkin 2014: 100–101.

without them, Heaven forbid, the Torah would have already been forgotten from Israel, and thus it is appropriate to assist this mission so that there will be no ruin." Nonetheless, Isserles may have had particular reason to question the continued trustworthiness of Venetian Christian printers and to hope that Jewish financiers and publishers might be poised to supplant Christians' heretofore central role in Hebrew publishing.

Daniel Bomberg had overcome initial rabbinic suspicion about his trustworthiness. He gained rabbinic acceptance through his consistently lavish, high quality publications of foundational Jewish texts and through his willingness to incur the wrath of papal authorities rather than alter those texts to expurgate allegedly anti-Christian passages or to add Christian apologetics. Bomberg also insisted that Jews be allowed to work in his printing house and repeatedly hired expert rabbinic scholars (including Eliyahu Bakhur), not just Jewish apostates.

However, at the twilight of Bomberg's printing enterprise, both the papacy and the Venetian Senate took steps that cast a cloud over the continued viability of uncensored Christian publications of Jewish texts. In November 1548—just two years before Isserles's ruling, papal authorities tasked the Papal Nuncio Giovanni Della Casa with obtaining the expurgation of allegedly anti-Christian passages in Hebrew manuscripts set for publication in Venice.[139] Bomberg strenuously objected, arguing that no changes could be made in ancient manuscripts. By contrast, Della Casa readily obtained the consent of Marc Antonio Giustiniani.

Given the dearth of Christian experts in Hebrew who could identify such anti-Christian passages, Della Casa ultimately took no action. But it is not unreasonable to assume that word would have spread—and have been brought to Isserles's attention by Katzenellenbogen—of Giustiniani's willingness to comply with the censorial dictates of papal authorities. Hence, Isserles might have come to suspect Giustiniani's future trustworthiness even as he most likely continued to use Giustiniani's edition of the Talmud in his Krakow *yeshiva*.

Further, as we have seen, in the same year that Della Casa enlisted Giustiniani, the Venetian Senate instituted a sharp new measure, forbidding Jews not only from printing books, but also from even working in presses, whether as typesetters or correctors.[140] The measure also forbade Jews from employing a Christian printer as a front by publishing under the Christian's name. The new prohibition was put forth in the charter setting out the conditions for permitting continued Jewish residency in the Republic. Anyone disobeying it would incur loss of the books in question and a fine of a 100 ducats.

The prohibition of any Jewish involvement in printing followed two prior measures, no doubt influenced by the fervor of the Counter-Reformation. The first, in 1543, ordered the punishment of all those publishing, selling, or possessing books that were offensive to the honor of God and Christianity. The second, in 1547,

139. Grendler 1978: 105 (citing correspondence between Della Casa and Rome from November 24, 1548 through February 23, 1549).

140. Ravid 1979: 137.

ordered the seizure and public burning of any religiously offensive books that had been imported into Venice.[141] Further, 1547 saw the establishment of a tribunal of the Inquisition in Venice, an institution charged with ensuring the supremacy of the Catholic religion in the Republic.[142] These measures laid the groundwork for the 1548 prohibition of Jewish involvement in the print trade.

As Benjamin Ravid has pointed out the 1548 prohibition was likely also instituted in direct anticipation of establishing the Venetian printers' guild.[143] The Venetian Council of Ten enacted legislation for the establishment of a guild of printers and booksellers in Venice on January 18, 1549. That legislation contemplated that all printers and booksellers in Venice would be members of the guild. Given the religious nature of guilds, it was unthinkable that Jews would be admitted to the guild, and it was thus necessary to ensure that Jews would not be employed in the printing or selling of books.

The prohibition against Jews working in presses or publishing in the name of Christians was not rigorously enforced. Witness Katzenellenbogen's collaboration with Bragadini to print the *Mishneh Torah*. For that matter, the Venetian printers' guild was not actually established until 1567. Nevertheless, in 1550, the measures would have given Isserles cause for serious concern that Venetian Christian printers of Hebrew books could no longer be depended on to produce texts that were untainted by Christian apologetics. Isserles might have worried as well that, absent a Jewish presence in Venetian print shops, inadvertent printing errors would multiply at the hands of Christian typesetters and correctors who lacked the expertise of rabbinic scholars such as the Maharam of Padua. Such errors were not uncommon. Indeed, sixteenth-century Jewish correctors employed by Christian printers sometimes pleaded in their colophons that they could not be held responsible for mistakes in pages that were printed by Christian workers on the Jewish Sabbath, a day that Jews would not be at work.[144]

Isserles's suspicions about Giustiniani and other Christian printers would likely have been informed by the experience and attitudes of the Jewish community of Krakow and its environs as well. The first Jewish printers in Poland were three brothers, Samuel, Asher, and Elyakim Helicz, of Krakow.[145] In 1537, however, after about three years of printing a few modest editions of relatively short Hebrew and Yiddish books, the brothers converted to Christianity. They were apparently enticed by the promise of financial reward.[146] Upon their conversion, King Sigismund I granted them a monopoly on importing and selling Hebrew books in Poland, and ordered that all their debts were to be forgiven. They were also given a plot of land in Krakow and the opportunity to acquire better quality paper, including stock, imprinted with a double cross, which had been used by the Cathedral Chapter in Krakow. Following

141. Ravid 1979: 137–38.
142. Pullan 1983: 3–7.
143. Ravid 1979: 138–39.
144. Heller 2008: 266–69.
145. Teter and Fram 2006: 31.
146. Teter and Fram 2006: 39–41.

their conversion, the brothers began to publish far more substantial volumes of classic Hebrew works, intended primarily for use in *yeshivot* and houses of prayer. However, the Jewish community refused to buy their books, presumably to avoid supporting apostates. Once again strapped for cash, the brothers petitioned King Sigismund who responded by issuing a decree forcing the Jewish communities of Krakow, Pozen, and Lvov to purchase all of the remaining inventory of Hebrew books held by the Helicz brothers.[147] The Jews of Poland apparently destroyed most of the books they were forced to purchase, and the Helicz brothers turned to printing books for Christian readers, including anti-Jewish polemics.[148]

The communal memory of the bitter experience regarding the Helicz brothers would still have been very much alive when Isserles issued his 1550 ruling. Moreover, Isserles might have hoped that, with support of a new, more supportive Polish king, Jewish printers in Poland would soon be able to produce foundational Jewish texts for the Polish market and beyond. In 1547, Ḥayyim ben David Shaḥor, a well-known itinerant Bohemian printer, had established a printing house in Lublin, attracted by the possibility of printing and selling directly to the Polish Jewish market. In 1550, following Shaḥor's death, King Sigismund II Augustus granted a privilege to Shaḥor's son-in-law, Joseph ben Yakar, and son, Isaac Shaḥor, awarding royal authorization to establish a press for Hebrew books in Lublin (even though the printing house had issued at least two titles even prior to that date).[149] The royal privilege to print Hebrew books was the first issued in Poland to Jewish printers and the first such privilege issued since the monopoly that King Sigismund I had granted to the apostate Helicz brothers.[150] Isserles thus had reason to think that the establishment of the Lublin printing house, with its royal backing, might herald a new era in which a Jewish printer, untrammeled by the restrictions imposed by the Inquisition and Venetian Senate, could meet the needs of Polish *yeshivot* and houses of prayer. Indeed, although the Lublin press got off to a slow start, it successfully printed the Hebrew Bible in 1557 and a complete edition of the Talmud between 1559 and 1576.[151]

Isserles's responsum hints at his hope—expectation—that the newly established Jewish printers in Poland could— and would—supplant the Christian printers of Venice in publishing seminal books of Jewish learning, to ensure that Torah would not be forgotten among the people of Israel. His ruling against Giustiniani will not foment anti-Semitic strife, he insists, because if Christian printers complain of being targeted by a sectarian rabbinic edict, we Jews can say that we refrain from buying from their books solely as a commercial matter. We can say, after all, that "we do not need the books they print."

147. Teter and Fram 2006: 47, 53. The Polish name for Pozen is Poznan. Following the Polish partition in the late eighteenth century, Lvov fell within the orbit of the Austrian Empire. It then came to be known by its German name, "Lemberg."

148. Heller 2004: vol. I, xxxix.

149. Friedberg 1950: 45; Heller 2004: vol. I, xxxv–xxxvi, xli–xlii. Of note, Yakar had worked previously as a corrector for Marc Antonio Giustiniani.

150. Teter and Fram 2006: 39.

151. Heller 2004: vol. I, xlii.

H. Decree

Although much of Isserles's ruling focuses on Giustiniani's wrongful conduct, his decree reads more like a rabbinic reprinting ban in favor of the Maharam than a finding of liability against Giustiniani. Isserles ordered that because "the *Gaon* has prevailed on his claim that he should be granted the right to sell his books first, no person shall buy a book [of Maimonides's *Mishneh Torah*] that has been recently printed unless it has been published under the auspices of the *Gaon* or his agents."[152] And to enforce that injunction, Isserles further ordered that Jews are obliged to excommunicate anyone "in our country" who buys or possesses such a rival book. Hence, although Isserles's decree was clearly meant to direct that Polish Jews buy the Bragadini, rather than Giustiniani, edition of the *Mishneh Torah*, it is couched, like a rabbinic reprinting ban, in more general terms: it gives the Maharam an exclusive privilege to sell his edition, until he has sold out his first printing.

Notably, unlike the Rome rabbis' reprinting ban in favor of Eliyahu Bakhur, Isserles limited the geographical scope of enforcement of his order. His order of excommunication applied only to those who buy or possess an illicit edition of Maimonides's classic work "in our country," namely Poland. That left Katzenellenbogen with the burden of petitioning rabbinic authorities in other lands, including Venice and the rest of Italy, to adopt Isserles's ruling and enforce it by threat of excommunication in their respective locations.[153]

Isserles does not discuss why he limited his order of excommunication to Poland. It is possible that he followed a venerable ruling of the Spanish Talmudic authority, Isaac ben Sheshet (1326–1408) (known in Jewish tradition by the acronym "Rivash"). Ben Sheshet ruled that a rabbinic court has no authority to impose excommunication outside of the territory of its jurisdiction.[154] The young Isserles might have also been reluctant to presume that rabbinic scholars outside of Poland would have seen themselves as bound to accept the halakhic basis and result of his ruling. Long-standing rabbinic precedent—also extending back to medieval Spain—strongly favored following local rabbinic authority over halakhic rulings issued by rabbis outside of one's territory.[155] Or perhaps Poland constituted the lion's share of the market for Katzenellenbogen's remaining print run and thus there was no need to reach beyond that country.

Regardless of the possible explanation, in a later ruling on Jewish copyright law, Moses Sofer criticized Isserles for imposing excommunication only in Isserles's own land. Sofer held that cross-border rulings are proper in Jewish copyright matters given that the market for books transcends local borders. We return to Sofer's ruling in Chapter 6.

152. *Responsa Rema*, No. 10.

153. Benayahu speculates that Kaztenellenbogen must have planned to do just that. Benayahu 1971.

154. Isaac ben Sheshet, *Responsa Ha-Rivash*, No. 271.

155. Shlomo ben Aderet (1235–1310) (known as the "Rashba") ruled that one may follow one's local rabbi even in instances in which his halakhic ruling contradicts the majority opinion elsewhere. Shlomo ben Aderet, *Responsa Ha-Rashba*, Part 1, No. 253. A leading authority of the next generation went further. Nissim ben Reuven Gerondi (1320–1376) (known as "Ran") ruled that one is *obligated* to follow one's local rabbi in such circumstances. *Responsa Ran*, No. 48.

IV. POSTSCRIPT

By the mid-sixteenth century, Poland was a haven for Jews. At the same time, Isserles was undoubtedly well aware of the precarious existence of Jewish communities elsewhere and that even in Poland, Jewish autonomy and well-being lay at the pleasure of the "king and his nobles."[156] Nonetheless, in assessing the Maharam's claim, Isserles twice dismisses concern about the risk of untoward consequences that might result from ruling against a Christian patrician. At one point in his ruling, Isserles considers a halakhic precept that forbids taking money from non-Jews and requires judicial leniency where necessary to preserve peace and avoid hatred. He holds, however, that the precept does not apply to commercial matters. Accordingly, Isserles insists, the precept favoring leniency provides no reason to "forego this line of justice."[157] Likewise, as noted above, Isserles summarily rejects the notion that non-Jewish printers might cease printing Jewish books and thus forgo a profitable market if subjected to the strictures of Jewish law.

Isserles (and Katzenellenbogen) grossly underestimated Giustiniani's fury and ferocity. The Venice printer responded to Isserles's ruling by hiring an apostate Jew to scrutinize Katzenellenbogen's commentary on the *Mishneh Torah* for statements that could be interpreted as being objectionable to the Church, and to then bring a complaint before the papal authorities.[158] Bragadini defended against the charges, but as the case dragged through the pontifical courts, it became a lightning rod for those who claimed that all Jewish texts and Hebrew printing were inimical to Christianity.

We do not know for certain whether the Bragadini case directly impacted papal policy. But it seems likely to have reverberated in the highest echelons of the Church, which by the mid-sixteenth century bore the considerable influence of the Counter-Reformation and Roman Inquisition. The virulent suspicion of Hebrew books, epitomized and further fueled by the Bragadini case, thus found fertile ground. The result was disastrous for Hebrew printing in Venice and the Jewish community generally. By decree of the Roman Inquisition, on September 9, 1553—corresponding to the Jewish holy day of Rosh Hashanah—all copies of the Talmud found in Rome were gathered and set on fire in the Campo dei Fiori.[159] Three days later, Pope Julius III issued a Bull directing the confiscation and burning of all copies of the Talmud throughout the Catholic world. Jews were ordered to deliver their copies to papal authorities, and Christians were forbidden to read or possess them or to assist Jews in writing or printing them, upon pain of excommunication from the Church. The decree spread rapidly throughout Italy. Hebrew books and manuscripts

156. See Fram 1997: 33–34 (discussing Isserles's awareness of Jews' vulnerability); Weinryb 1973: 165–66 (discussing Isserles's awareness that Jews were more secure in Poland than elsewhere, but potentially vulnerable nonetheless).
157. *Reponsa Rema*, No. 10.
158. Amram 1988: 261–66.
159. See Bloch 1976: 18–19; Amnon Raz-Krakotzkin 2004: 125.

were burned in public squares in Bologna, Ferrara, Mantua, Ravenna, and Romagna. In Venice, the Council of Ten issued a decree, on October 21, 1553, ordering the confiscation and burning within 10 days of all copies of the Talmud, as well as "all compendia, summaries, or other books depending on said Talmud." Among the books confiscated and burned were numerous copies of Maimonides's *Mishneh Torah*.[160]

The pope modified the severity of his decree on May 29, 1554.[161] He issued a new Bull allowing Hebrew books to be printed, but requiring that they first be submitted to a papal censor, and permitting their possession only after offending passages had been blotted out.

However, the Talmud itself remained completely off limits. In one of his later rulings, Katzenellenbogen warned that he referred to the Talmud by memory without being able to consult a printed copy. As late as 1638, the distinguished Venetian rabbi Leon of Modena wrote that the Talmud "remains prohibited; and in Italy particularly it is neither seen nor read."[162] By that time, the printing of the Talmud—and the locus of further disputes of Jewish copyright law—had moved from Venice to printing houses beyond the reach of the Roman Inquisition.[163]

160. Baruchson 1993: 134 (noting inventory of books seized from the Jews of Manua).
161. See Bloch 1976: 18.
162. Quoted in Bloch 1976: 18 n. 66.
163. Centers for printing the Talmud in the late sixteenth and early seventeenth centuries included Krakow, Lublin, Basel, and the Ottoman Empire. Pilarczyk 2002: 60–62.

CHAPTER 5

Rabbinic Reprinting Bans Take Hold

Moses Isserles's seminal ruling was instrumental in spurring the widespread practice of issuing rabbinic reprinting bans. However, its immediate influence came less from the force of Isserles's argument than from the unintended role that his ruling played in radically altering the Hebrew book trade. Publishers of high quality Hebrew books did not begin to petition regularly for rabbinic reprinting bans until the Hebrew book trade became more competitive and diversified, both within Venice and between Venice and other cities. Isserles might have hoped that the Lublin printing house of Joseph ben Yakar and Isaac Shaḥor would be able to compete with Venetian Christian publishers in producing books of Jewish learning and liturgy for the burgeoning Jewish communities of Poland. But he did not anticipate the way in which his ruling would indirectly contribute to that development by providing a spark for papal suppression of Hebrew printing in Italy.

Venetian publishers' domination of the Hebrew book trade came to an abrupt end with the events described in Chapter 4, beginning with the Papal Bull issued in September 1553 ordering the confiscation and burning of all copies of the Talmud. The Bull unleashed a wave of destruction of Hebrew books throughout Italy. The destruction of Hebrew books and imposition of rigorous papal censorship led to a precipitous decline in Hebrew book production in Venice, including, indeed, to the demise of Giustiniani's printing house. During the five-year period, 1555 to 1559, no Hebrew books were printed in Venice.

In July 1559, however, the Venetian Council of Ten, acting through the Esecutori (its subcommission charged with suppressing sin and blasphemy), ruled that Hebrew books, with the exception of the Talmud and its commentaries, could be published so long as any offending passages were expurgated.[1] Hebrew book production in the Republic recommenced in 1560 with the modest printing of a Jewish calendar and a heavily censored reprinting of the *Aram Tzuba Maḥzor*, a prayer book following the rite of Jews in the Land of Israel, Persia, Syria, and Kurdistan, which had been initially published by Daniel Bomberg in 1527.[2] Alvise Bragadini resurfaced in 1563 with an edition of *Oraḥ Ḥaim*, part of the *Arba'a Turim*, with commentary by Joseph Karo, followed by the first printing of Karo's *Shulḥan Arukh*, in 1565. But Venetian production of Hebrew books amounted to only some 58 titles during the decade following the Esecutori's 1559 decree, less than half the production during the 10 years preceding the Papal Bull of 1553. Many rabbinic scholars who had previously sent their works to Venice now declined to do so, unwilling to engage in the self-censorship that would be required for their book to receive the required papal imprimatur, or to face the risk that their writings would be distorted at the censor's hand.

Moreover, in 1568, amid charges that the Jews were disloyal to the Venetian Republic in its armed conflict against the Ottoman Empire, the Esecutori descended upon the Hebrew press once again.[3] It declared that certain Jews had published Hebrew books without the censor's approval, in violation of the decree of July 1559, and ordered thousands of copies of recently printed books destroyed or corrected. Three years later, the Venetian Senate voted to expel all Jews from Venice, but then renewed the Jewish community's condotta in 1573, after the Turks agreed to peace. It was only then that Hebrew printing in Venice began to revive—only to suffer yet another disastrous setback when the Great Plague of 1575 to 1577 brought printing and most other economic activity in the Republic to a standstill.[4]

As Hebrew printing slowly became re-established in Venice, several Christian publishers, most of whom printed books on contract for Jewish sponsors, entered the market in competition with one another. For the first time, leading Venetian publishers of Hebrew books also faced stiff competition from publishers in emerging centers of Hebrew printing in Constantinople, Prague, Lublin, Krakow, and Amsterdam. The emerging competition in the Hebrew book trade helped to ignite the practice of issuing rabbinic reprinting bans.

I. RABBINIC REPRINTING BANS IN VENICE

The rabbinic leadership of Venice issued its first reprinting ban in 1578. The ban was for Isaac Abravanel's (1437–1508) work of Biblical commentary, *Perush Ha-Torah*, printed by the houses of Bragadini and di Gara. The rabbinic decree (which is reproduced, together with Abravanel's papal license in Illustration 4) forbade anyone other than those publishers from reprinting or selling the book for a period of 15 years, under pain of *ḥerem*.

1. See Grendler 1978: 108.
2. Benayahu 1971: 175–76.
3. The remainder of this paragraph draws upon Grendler 1978: 111–17.
4. The epidemic of the bubonic plague is estimated to have killed almost one-third of Venice's population. Pullan 1964: 408.

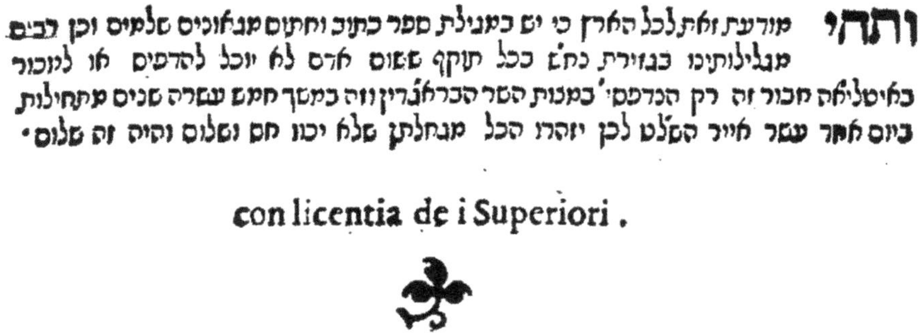
ותהי מודעת זאת לכל הארץ כי יש במגילת ספר כתוב וחתום מגאונים שלמים וכן רבים
מגלילותינו בגזירת נח"ש בכל תוקף שבשום אדם לא יוכל להדפיס או למכור
באיטליאה חבור זה רק המדפסי' במצות השר הגראנדין וזה במשך חמש עשרה שנים מתחילות
ביום אחד עשר אייר השל"ט לכן יזהרו הכל מגחלתן שלא יכוו חס ושלום והיה זה שלום·

con licentia de i Superiori.

Illustration 4
Haskama and Papal License for Abravanel's *Perush Ha-Torah*, 1578.
(courtesy National Library of Israel).

The Abravanel reprinting ban was the first of numerous such bans issued in Venice over the next 100 years.[5] Yet it was atypical of those that followed in two respects. For one, the Abravanel ban was issued directly in favor of a Christian printing house rather than the book's Jewish editor, financial backer, or author. In addition, most of the reprinting bans issued in Venice were for shorter periods—generally 10-year periods, although they varied from 5 to 20 years.

In other respects, however, the Abravanel ban is illustrative of virtually all of those issued by the Venetian rabbis for at least the next century. First, the Abravanel ban was for a book that had not previously been printed as a stand-alone title. All but one of the early Venetian rabbinic reprinting bans were for first printings, although, like Abravanel's work, not all the books were newly authored; some, indeed, were centuries'-old manuscripts that had not previously been brought to print.[6] The Venetian rabbis' general practice of awarding reprinting bans only to newly printed books mirrored the rule, which the Venetian Senate had promulgated in 1517 and only somewhat relaxed in 1603, that the Venetian Republic would grant book privileges only to books that had not yet been printed. Indeed, given that rabbis in other times and places often granted reprinting bans to reissued editions of previously printed titles, it appears that the Venetian rabbis' practice was either designed to minimize the possibility of conflict with the Council of Ten or simply was modeled on the secular book privilege regime with which the rabbis were most familiar.[7] (On the other hand, the

5. My discussion of Venetian rabbinic reprinting bans is based on the *haskamot* collected and reproduced in Benayahu 1971, together with bibliographic information provided in the Bibliography of the Hebrew Book, available on the website of the National Library of Israel.

6. The sole exception was *Lavush Ha-Botz Ve-Argeman* by Mordecai ben Avraham Yoffe (1530–1612), one of the rabbinic leaders of the Council of Four Lands. The Venetian edition of that book, which had previously been printed in Krakow in 1599, received a reprinting ban in 1621. In addition, a number of books that received Venetian rabbinic reprinting bans had previously been printed as part of a larger work or had been printed only in part.

7. In the sharpest contrast to the Venetian rabbis, the preeminent rabbinic decisor Yeḥezkel Segal Landau (1713–1793) (known in Jewish tradition as Noda Be-Yehuda) avowedly declined to grant *haskamot* to new books not previously published. Landau made

Venetian Senate Decree of 1603 provided for a term of 20 years for a newly printed book, while the rabbinic bans were typically for only 10-year periods.)

Second, like the Abravanel reprinting ban, all but one of the bans issued by the Venetian rabbinate were for books authored or printings commissioned by Jews from Italy or the Ottoman Empire.[8] By this time, authors and publishers from central and eastern Europe apparently sought rabbinic bans only from Ashkenazic authorities or—as I discuss shortly, relied for protection on the Council of Four Lands, a bicameral body consisting of rabbis and lay leaders that served as the supreme, overarching Jewish communal authority for Poland, Lithuania, and parts of what are now Ukraine, Belarus, and western Russia. Central and eastern European publishers also preferred to print books in Lublin, Krakow, Prague, or, Amsterdam. By the end of the sixteenth century, the Lublin and Krakow printing houses, each Jewish-owned and operating under a royal privilege, came to dominate the Polish market for Hebrew books.[9] And by the mid-seventeenth century, Amsterdam had supplanted Venice as the center of the Hebrew, as well as Yiddish, book trade. For books published in those locations, Venice was typically a marginal market, not worth the time and expense of petitioning the Venetian rabbinic court for a reprinting ban, even assuming that the Venetian rabbis would have been willing to grant a ban for a book printed outside the Republic.[10]

Third, all of the Venetian bans were for Hebrew language books of Jewish liturgy, law, or learning.[11] The singular devotion to rabbinic subject matter is not surprising; it characterized rabbinic reprinting bans in other times and locations as well, even if we do see occasional *haskamot* for books of science, medicine, and Jewish Enlightenment. Less to be expected, perhaps, is the exclusion of Jewish books in languages other than Hebrew. In the late sixteenth and early seventeenth centuries, Venice was the primary source for Jewish prayer books and other specifically Jewish books in Spanish, Portuguese, and other European languages.[12] It was also a major center for printing books in Yiddish and, to a lesser extent, other Jewish vernacular languages, including Ladino, and Judeo-Italian.[13] Indeed, Giovanni

an exception the year before he died, granting a *haskama*, which included a 10-year reprinting ban, for Aryeh Leib Zuenz's work, *Yael Ḥen*, published in Prague in 1793.

8. The sole exception, as with the sole exception for the rule against bans for previously printed books, was the reprinting ban issued in 1621 for *Lavush Ha-Botz Ve-Argeman* by Mordecai ben Avraham Yoffe, a rabbinic leader of the Council of Four Lands.

9. Polonsky 2010: 128.

10. At the beginning of the seventeenth century, there was little importation of Hebrew books to Italy from elsewhere. Most of the books that were in the possession of Italian Jews at that time were printed in Italy. Baruchson-Arbib and Prebor 2007: 14.

11. Depending on how one defines Jewish liturgy, a possible exception was the reprinting ban issued in 1623 for Solomon Rossi's *Canto Ha-Shirim Asher Le-Shlomo*, a Hebrew-language collection of Jewish liturgical music, written in the polyphonic Baroque tradition and largely unconnected to traditional Jewish cantorial music. Virtually all Hebrew books printed for Jewish readers in the late sixteenth and early seventeenth century were books of Jewish liturgy, law, or learning. See generally Baruchson 1993 and Burnett 2006: 521.

12. Israel 1987: 95, 96–97.

13. See Baumgarten 2010: 44 (Yiddish, Ladino, and Judeo-Italian); Schrijver 2007: 159 (Ladino). Yiddish printing underwent a sharp decline in Venice in the first quarter of the

di Gara—who, together with the house of Bragadini, printed and obtained the *haskama* for Abravanel's *Perush Ha-Torah*—was a central figure in Yiddish publishing in Venice during that period.[14]

Yet, reflecting rabbinic disdain for books of Jewish ritual and learning in the vernacular, none of those non-Hebrew books received a reprinting ban from the rabbinic leadership of Venice.[15] Like the devotion to rabbinic subject matter, that focus on Hebrew language books is also typical of *haskamot* throughout history. Of particular note, Yiddish and Ladino books represent only a small minority of the books that have received *haskamot*. As in early modern Venice, the rabbinic elite have generally scorned such books as tracts for women and the uneducated masses.

Authors, publishers, and editors also viewed Yiddish books as less important than those written in Hebrew, and thus often treated them with a certain frivolity, such as by including witty, rhyming verses on the title page.[16] Typical of that widely held view of Yiddish books is the introduction of the celebrated editor, Cornelio Adelkind, to Eliyahu Bakhur's Yiddish translation of Psalms, printed by Guistiniani in 1545. Adelkind explains that although he had devoted his youth to editing "grand and precious holy books" in the house of Daniel Bomberg, he has now turned to producing a book for "pious young women" and for "certain masters of the house who did not have the time to study when they were young" for them to peruse during "their idle time on Shabbat and holidays."[17] Further, part and parcel with Yiddish books' secondary status, those books tended to be smaller editions of cheaper, mediocre quality that did not warrant the time and expense of petitioning for a rabbinic approbation and ban.[18]

Despite these factors, rabbis have occasionally granted *haskamot* to Yiddish books. As discussed in the next chapter, in its *haskamot*, issued in 1677 and 1678 for a Yiddish translation of the Bible, the Council of Four Lands congratulated the publisher for enabling women and children to learn the Torah in the only language they would understand. Likewise, in his *haskama* for *Shtern Shus*, a Yiddish book of popular ethics, printed in Amsterdam in 1695, Moshe Yehuda, the chief rabbi of Amsterdam's Ashkenazic community, explained that the book would helpfully introduce Jewish law and customs to "the masses of men and women who do not understand the language of learning, the holy tongue."[19]

seventeenth century, with the last Yiddish book, a reprinting in 1629 of the Passover Haggadah, originally printed in 1609. Bonfil 2003: 222; Baumgarten 2010: 252. By then, the local market for vernacular Jewish texts strongly favored books in Italian.

14. Di Gara printed 14 Yiddish books, of which 11 were newly printed, between 1588 and 1609. Baumgarten: 2010: 242–43.

15. On the long-standing objection to printing in Ladino among Sephardic leaders in the Ottoman Empire, see Schrijver 2007: 159.

16. S. Berger 2004: 31–61.

17. The quoted passage is my English translation from the French translation of the original Hebrew in Baumgarten 2010: 238. Adelkind worked as a master editor of Hebrew, Aramaic, and Yiddish texts in a number of printing houses in Italy, primarily for Daniel Bomberg. Raz-Krakotzkin 2007: 250 n. 57.

18. Baumgarten 2009: 4 ¶ 6.

19. Quoted and discussed in S. Berger 2004: 43–44.

But, again, these *haskamot* are exceptions: for the most part approbations and bans have generally been awarded only to Hebrew (and Aramaic) texts that the rabbis deemed worthy of serious study and use within the academies of rabbinic learning. Indicative of the persistence of this rabbinic practice over the centuries is the example of Joseph Saul Nathanson, the illustrious rabbi of Lemberg in the mid-nineteenth century. Nathanson, who gained a reputation as a particularly prolific and thoughtful author of *haskamot* for a wide range of titles, issued some 240 *haskamot* between 1840 and 1875, of which only two were for Yiddish books—and neither of those included a reprinting ban.

Finally, the Abravanel reprinting ban was typical of the bans that followed in asserting a geographic reach beyond the Venetian Republic. The Abravanel ban prohibited reprinting anywhere in Italy. Perhaps because of growing competition in Constantinople, eastern Europe, and Amsterdam, subsequent bans went even further: they prohibited reprinting anywhere in the world. The worldwide reach of the reprinting bans issued by the Venetian rabbinic leadership seems generally to have been respected among the far-flung communities of the Jewish Diaspora.[20] Indeed, that worldwide reach was the principal reason that, beginning in the late sixteenth century, Christian printers of Hebrew books in Venice, in conjunction with their Jewish editors and financers, turned to rabbinic bans rather than book privileges issued by the Venetian Republic.[21]

II. JEWISH COUNCIL REGULATION OF THE BOOK TRADE

Beginning in the late sixteenth century, the practice of seeking rabbinic reprinting bans gained further impetus from repeated efforts by Jewish communities' self-governing bodies to regulate the Hebrew book trade. In early modern Europe, Jewish communities enjoyed considerable autonomy to govern their own affairs.[22] Jewish communal autonomy saw countless local variations and qualifications, but as a general rule it meant that taxes and laws imposed by the communal leadership were mandatory for all Jews, and that rabbinic courts could enforce their rulings by imposing sanctions backed, if need be, by the non-Jewish sovereign authority.[23] The internal dynamics of Jewish communal structures were likewise subject to considerable variation, but were typically characterized by a mutually dependent yet competitive relationship between lay and rabbinic authority.[24] The lay council, dominated by wealthy merchants and other notables, held sole power to regulate commercial activity, levy taxes, provide for the needy, and appoint and pay the local rabbi.[25] But the council depended on the rabbi for its legitimacy. In most locations, the rabbi was asked to authorize council

20. There were some exceptions in which a reprinting began during the period of the Venetian rabbinic ban. But it is possible that in such cases the recipient of the reprinting ban had already sold out his first printing. See Benayahu 1971: 53.

21. Benayahu 1971: 57.

22. Ruderman 2010: 58–59; Rosman 2007: 71. See generally Finkelstein 1964.

23. On state backing for the rabbinic courts in mid-sixteenth century Poland, see Polonsky 2010: 45.

24. Katz 2000: 71–75.

25. Israel 1998: 156

ordinances, even if he had no role in formulating them. The lay leadership also relied on the rabbi to provide religious sanction for its decisions, warn against infractions of communal ordinances, authorize especially severe punishments (including excommunication and ostracism), and defend community members against judgments issued against them by rabbis from other locations.[26] Esteemed rabbinic scholars who lacked any formal position in communal governance might also exert considerable influence on the council and community by force of their halakhic rulings and moral authority.[27] Much the same division of power and mutual dependence between lay and rabbinic leaders applied to regional councils, including the Council of Four Lands.[28]

Over time, lay authorities steadily gained in power over the rabbis, especially in western Europe. In particular, beginning in the first half of the seventeenth century, lay councils in Amsterdam, Italy, and Germany limited the rabbis' authority unilaterally to impose the sanction of *ḥerem*.[29] The decline of rabbinic power was also pronounced in the Council of Four Lands, where the lay council regularly issued regulations and even orders of *ḥerem* without any rabbinic sanction.[30]

Unlike other matters, however, lay and rabbinic authorities alike generally viewed the book trade as the special province of the rabbinate. The vast majority of Hebrew books published in early modern Europe involved Jewish learning, law, and liturgy: matters that fell within the domain of the rabbis.[31] Further, *yeshivot*—academies of rabbinic learning—were primary markets for many such books. Thus, even when the lay councils enacted ordinances to regulate the book trade, they typically required publishers to obtain rabbinic approval to print Hebrew books, and the councils backed that requirement with the threat of a rabbinic decree of *ḥerem*.

Venice provides a good example of this intricate sharing of power. In 1608, the Venetian Jewish community's governing lay body, the Small Assembly, issued a regulation explicitly prohibiting the publication of any work, or its reprinting, without rabbinic permission. Hence, all *haskamot* issued in the Republic contained rabbis' signatures, even if some were also signed by lay members of the Small Assembly. Further, only rabbis could excommunicate offenders, but the rabbis were expected to issue orders of excommunication only with the consent of the lay authorities.[32]

Jewish communal authorities regulated books for three reasons. In broad brushstrokes, each rationale shows unmistakable parallels to early modern non-Jewish

26. Katz 2000: 74–75.
27. Katz 2000: 142.
28. Katz 2000: 106; Fram 1997: 40–46.
29. Ruderman 2010: 65–81.
30. See Teller 2004. See also Rosman 2010 (noting that the leaders of the Council were mostly laymen and that the rabbis who sat on the Council did so as representatives of their local communities, not by virtue of their rabbinic office or authority).
31. Baruchson's seminal study of Jewish book ownership in Mantua, based on Mantuan censors' lists compiled in 1595 demonstrates the overwhelming preference for owning Hebrew books of a religious nature. Baruchson categorizes the books as follows: Liturgy (34.6 percent), Bible 22.2 percent, halakha 10.7 percent, ethics 6.2 percent, grammar 4.2 percent, philosophy 3.8 percent, mysticism 2.7 percent, and belles-lettres (nonreligious) only 1.4 percent. Baruchson 1993.
32. Malkiel 2001: 117, 137.

authorities' regulation of the book trade.[33] But the Jewish communal bodies' book regulations also reflected the particularities of Jewish communal life, the rabbinic tradition, and the Hebrew book trade.

First, Jewish communal bodies regulated books for the purpose of subject-matter censorship. Above all, Jewish communal authorities sought to regulate Jewish books for much the same reason as they forbade Jews from engaging in provocative behaviors, spending extravagantly, and picking quarrels with Christians: to avoid conflicts with non-Jews.[34] In particular, they sought to suppress books containing passages that could be interpreted as an affront to Christianity. Ever cognizant of the precariousness of Jewish communal autonomy and well-being, they sought to prevent the publication of books that might incur the wrath of Christian authorities and thus lead to the widespread destruction of books of Jewish learning or violence against the Jewish community.

The communal leaders mandated such self-censorship with good reason. The mid-sixteenth century papal and Venetian directives against Hebrew books were part of a virulent wave of sectarian Christian censorship, headlined by the first Roman Inquisition's Index of Forbidden Books, which swept through Europe during the Counter-Reformation.[35] Jewish communal bodies began to regulate Hebrew books in the wake of attacks, from both the Counter-Reformation and Protestant clergy, on Hebrew and other literature deemed slanderous to the Christian faith.

Yet, although the primary initial impulse for Jewish council censorship was to preempt outside intervention and violent reaction, the lay and rabbinic leadership also aimed to suppress books that they deemed internally subversive to the Jewish community.[36] Notable among these were Sabbatean tracts and a medieval compilation of erotic Hebrew poetry by Immanuel of Rome.[37] Books that presented heretical beliefs, advanced mystical or antinomian themes, questioned the veracity of the Talmudic sages, or otherwise challenged rabbinic authority were also subject to censorship.[38] As we have seen, a number of sixteenth-century Italian rabbis,

33. For an illuminating discussion of secular and ecclesiastical authorities' book trade regulation in early modern Europe, see Maclean 2012: 134–70.

34. See Israel 1998: 162–63 (Jewish community sumptuary laws); Wierzbieniec et al. 2000: 225 (prohibitions on drinking liquor in Christian taverns and picking quarrels with non-Jews).

35. Maclean 2012: 153–54, 162. On the precariousness of Hebrew printing in early modern Germany, see Burnett 1998.

36. Hacker 2011. At the same time, there are numerous instances of rabbis granting approbations for books across the *mitnagdim*-hasidic sectarian divide, books of secular science, and even literature written by proponents of the Jewish Enlightenment. See Gries 2007: 163; Hundert 2006: 151; Feiner 2004: 38 (describing Tzvi Hirsch Levin's approbation for a two-volume book on astronomy and anatomy, published in 1777).

37. Sabbatean literature was seen to pose an external threat as well. Jewish expression of messianic expectations seems to have provoked anti-Jewish violence in Poland-Lithuania and led to a royal decree that all Sabbatean printed pictures, pamphlets, and broadsheets be destroyed. Polonsky 2010: 139–40.

38. Hacker 2011: 114–19 (describing instances in Italy); Carmilly-Weinberger 1977: 211–13 (describing Venetian rabbis' ban, in 1573, of Azariah di Rossi's *Me'or Enayim*, a book that used critical methods to challenge the traditional chronology of Jewish

including Meir Katzenellenbogen, also prohibited the printing of the *Zohar* and other Kabbalistic literature.[39]

Second, of signal importance to the rabbinic tradition, book regulation was understood to serve as a safeguard for textual integrity and accuracy.[40] Books of Jewish law, learning, ritual, and commentary were the linchpin of halakhic rulings and liturgical practice. In the rabbinic tradition, every word and letter of these sources carried potential significance. Recall Moses Isserles's admonition: "If a book contains even minor printing errors, one is liable to make erroneous legal rulings: to prohibit that which is permitted, to permit that which is prohibited, to hold as ritually pure that which is impure, etc."[41] Hence rabbinic decisors often refused to give their imprimatur to books that contained errors, be they printing errors or what the rabbis perceived to be flatly erroneous statements and interpretations.[42]

Finally, Jewish communal authorities regulated books for economic reasons. Councils acted repeatedly to prevent ruinous competition in the Hebrew book trade and to protect local printers against foreign competitors. These regulations, the most closely analogous to copyright law, form the primary focus of our study.

The book trade regulations were far from effectively enforced. In particular, countless short, inexpensive tracts in Yiddish, sold primarily to the uneducated masses, flew under the radar screen of Jewish communal regulation.[43] Nor were rabbinic leaders able to stem the flow of books containing Sabbatean themes and other subversive content.[44] Nevertheless, the Jewish council regulations requiring rabbinic permission to publish were a significant factor in fueling the practice of granting rabbinic reprinting bans. As prominent printers of significant books of Jewish learning sought to obtain rabbinic permission to print particular books, they began more frequently to request an exclusive privilege to print the book as well.

history); Ruderman 2010: 150–52 (describing rabbinic leaders' inability to suppress such subversive literature).

39. Carmilly-Weinberger 1977: 54. For a discussion of the suppression of heretical books among contemporary ultra-Orthodox rabbis, see Shapiro 2003.

40. Although textual integrity was of particular importance within the rabbinic tradition, the sixteenth century saw a gradual movement toward greater attention to textual integrity and accuracy in printing practice and book regulation generally. See Grafton 2001. Nonetheless, printed books commonly contained errors and variations from one copy of the same book to the next until well into the eighteenth century. McKitterick 2003.

41. Moses Isserles, *Responsa Rema*, No. 10.

42. In the late eighteenth century, for example, the rabbinic court of Volozhin, in what is now Belarus, forbade the printing of an edition of the Vilna Gaon's commentary on a tractate of the Mishnah because it contained many errors. See Stampfer 2012: 19. At the same time, however, by the eighteenth century, rabbis not infrequently issued approbations based on the reputation of the author or printer, without having examined the book. Gries 2007: 146; Gries 2008: 1454–58.

43. Ruderman 2010: 103; Rosman 2007: 147. The outpouring of books in Yiddish and other vernacular languages challenged the privileged place of Hebrew books and, indeed, of learning controlled by the rabbinic elite. Ruderman 2010: 105.

44. Ruderman 2010: 105, 150.

One of the first such book trade regulations was the edict issued by a general synod of Italian rabbis, on behalf of a congress of lay and rabbinic leaders, in 1554 in Ferrara. The synod—in which Meir Katzenellenbogen played a prominent role—was convened in the immediate wake of the papal bulls ordering the burning of all copies of the Talmud and allowing Hebrew books to be printed only if first submitted to a papal censor, such that any passages determined to be offensive to Christianity would be blotted out. In an apparent act of protective self-censorship, the synod decreed:

> Printers shall not be permitted to print any hitherto unpublished book except with permission of three duly ordained Rabbis, and the consent of the heads of one of the communities nearest the place of printing, if the city in which the book is printed is a small one. If it is a large city, the agreement of the heads of that Community shall suffice provided the consent of three ordained Rabbis is obtained as said above. The names of the Rabbis and the heads of the Communities sponsoring the book shall be printed at the beginning of the volume. Otherwise no one shall be permitted to buy the book under penalty of a fine of twenty-five *scuti.* The fine shall be given to the charity fund of the city of the transgressor.[45]

The Ferrara decree seems to have been honored entirely in the breach, a result that is not entirely suprising given that, at the time, virtually all printers of Hebrew books in Italy were Christians.[46] But the Ferrara decree served as a model for similar enactments elsewhere in Europe where Jews were allowed to print Hebrew books and, hence, that do appear to have been enforced. Most significantly, the Council of Four Lands followed suit in 1594. It decreed that "no printer shall print any books without the consent of the rabbis and [lay] leaders," and that "should any printer disobey this order, then they [the rabbis and lay leaders] shall close down his printing establishment and excommunicate the printer, together with anyone who took part in the work."

Through this decree and subsequent edicts, the Council of Four Lands exerted far-reaching influence over the Hebrew book trade, especially as the geographical area of its jurisdiction came to constitute a large segment of the market for books printed in Amsterdam and Venice. Indeed, by its decree of 1594, the Council of Four Lands also asserted the authority to regulate the book trade between Italy and Poland. In addition to requiring rabbinic permission to print a book in Poland, the decree forbade the printing of any book in Italy that was already printed or being printed in Poland and, if such a book was nevertheless reprinted in Italy, the book was not to be sold in Poland for 10 years after its publication. As a sign of Eastern

45. Translation adapted from Finkelstein 1964: 304. For discussion, see Amram 1998: 285–86.

46. See Bonfil 1999: 157; Hacker 2011: 111–14. As Hacker elucidates, the Ferrara decree was preceded by a similar injunction formulated by a council of rabbis in Salonica in 1529, but, which appears never to have been implemented. Hacker 2011: 110.

European Jewish communities' continuing need for Hebrew books printed in Venice, and perhaps to avoid conflict with the Venetian rabbinate, the decree also provided that if a book was first printed in Italy, a Polish edition of the same book could not be sold for a certain period of time.[47]

The Council's decree served principally to delegate authority and responsibility for regulating Hebrew books to the rabbis and lay councils of the large communities within the Council's jurisdiction.[48] Accordingly, the *haskamot* issued pursuant to the decree were typically given by individual rabbis. Upon request, the *haskama* was then entered in the records of the Council, generally by representatives of the Council's rabbinic leadership, who assumed primary responsibility for regulating the book trade.[49] But following its decree of 1594, the Council itself, acting through its rabbinic leadership, issued a number of *haskamot* that included reprinting bans as well.[50] In 1617, for example, the Council issued this ban to Shabbetai bar Isaac, "scribe of the Jewish community of Przemysl," for his edition of the prayer book (an edition that Bar Isaac was apparently never able to bring to print):

> We therefore decree under pain of *ḥerem*, that no man in the world, either in our country or abroad, may print a prayer book, large or small, with or without commentary, based on the prayer book by the above-mentioned Shabbetai [Bar Isaac] and his emendations, until [said Shabbetai] will have sold [all the copies] of the prayer book he is printing, so that Shabbetai will not suffer any [economic] harm. And if, God forbid, any printer shall disobey this our decree, then our ban shall be in force from this day on and shall apply to anyone who calls himself a Jew; no one shall buy a prayer book [produced by such a printer]. The sixth day of Adar II, 1617, Lublin.[51]

Jewish communal authorities' regulation of the Hebrew book trade spread to other printing centers as well. In 1603, a rabbinic synod in Frankfurt am Main decreed that "no Jew shall print any new or old book in Basel or in any city in Germany without approval of three rabbinic judges."[52] Likewise, in 1638, the lay council of Portuguese Jewry in Amsterdam (called the *Ma'amad*) issued a decree that "no Jew may print in this city or elsewhere, in Ladino or in Hebrew, without the permission of the *Ma'amad*, so that said books shall be examined and corrected."[53] As noted above,

47. As such, the Council decree served to bolster the worldwide respect accorded to reprinting bans issued by Venetian rabbis.

48. Heilprin 1934.

49. Heilprin 1934: 106, 108.

50. The first of these was a one-year ban issued in 1614 for a new edition of the previously printed *Sliḥot Ve-Pizmonim* by Eliezer ben Eliyahu Ashkenazi. Benayahu 1971: 58.

51. Translation in Carmilly-Weinberger 1977: 192.

52. Benayahu 1971: 125; Hacker 2011: 113; Burnett 2006.

53. Benayahu 1971: 121–22.

in 1608 the lay council of Venice explicitly prohibited the publication or reprinting of any book without rabbinic permission.[54]

Like the decrees of Ferrara and the Council of Four Lands, these communal enactments aimed primarily at requiring rabbinic inspection of a book's content, not to provide protection against reprinting. But some who applied for the required rabbinic imprimatur also requested an exclusive reprinting ban.[55]

III. PROLIFERATION OF RABBINIC REPRINTING BANS

As the fulcrum of Hebrew printing moved from Venice to Amsterdam during the course of the seventeenth century, the Hebrew book trade became highly diverse and competitive. The first book issued by a Jewish publisher in Amsterdam was Menasseh ben Israel's 1626 edition of Yonah Gerondi's (d. 1263) medieval ethical work *Sefer Ha-Yirah*. The century following its publication saw over 300 Jewish printers active in the city.[56] Hebrew (and Yiddish) books printed in Amsterdam were marketed for export throughout the Jewish world, but primarily to the large Jewish population centers of greater Poland and Lithuania, where Jewish printing had been decimated in the turbulence of the Chmielnicki uprising and Swedish and Russian invasions during the mid-seventeenth century.[57] Toward the end of the seventeenth century, there was also a resurgence of the publication of Hebrew and Yiddish titles by Jewish publishers in Poland and Lithuania. Jewish printing houses were re-established in Lublin and Krakow, but were soon overshadowed by the press founded in Zolkiew by a leading Jewish printer from Amsterdam, Uri Fayvesh Halevi (1625–1715), who had obtained a royal license and the support of the Council of Four Lands.[58] (We will revisit that competition among the late seventeenth century Jewish printers in Poland below.) By the nineteenth century, Hebrew printing establishments had spread to multiple locations in central and eastern Europe. Additional centers of printing books of Jewish learning and liturgy included, at various times, Lemberg, Vilna, Frankfurt am Main, Prague, Slavuta, Shklov, and Zhitomir.

54. See Malkiel 2001: 137.

55. Early books printed in Amsterdam did not bear rabbinic bans. Printers were apparently satisfied with privileges from civil authorities in the various Dutch states. Benayahu 1971: 60–61. From 1648, however, they began to include rabbinic bans, typically for 10 years, in books printed in Amsterdam, albeit the signatories were initially rabbis from Poland and Ashkenaz, not Amsterdam. Benayahu 1971: 61.

56. Heller 2008: 218. See also Israel 1987: 109 (noting Amsterdam's supplanting of Venice as the center of Hebrew printing by 1650). The Amsterdam Booksellers and Printers Guild was one of the few guilds in Amsterdam that admitted Jewish citizens of the city as members. Even so, Jews had to pay higher fees and did not have same privileges as Gentile publishers. Fuks-Mansfeld 2004: 151.

57. Pilarczyk 2004. By the end of the seventeenth century, an estimated 350,000 Jews lived in Poland-Lithuania, making up almost half of all Jews living in Europe at that time. Israel 1998: 140.

58. Hundert 2006: 54–55.

Together with the emergence of multiple centers of Hebrew printing, the eighteenth century saw a dramatic increase in output; the number of Hebrew and Yiddish titles multiplied between three-to-fourfold over the previous century's production.[59] Not surprisingly, as indicated in Figure 5.1, this increase in titles also led to a dramatic growth in the number of books issued with a *haskama*.

I derive estimates for the number of titles and *haskamot* from the Bibliography of the Hebrew Book, an online database featuring bibliographical information covering approximately 90 percent of all books printed between 1470 and 1960 in the Hebrew language, as well as thousands of books printed in Ladino, Yiddish (with some Hebrew text), and other Jewish vernacular languages.[60] The Bibliograpy's searchable listings include information about whether any *haskamot* appears in the book and who issued them. The Bibliography probably underreports both the absolute number of Hebrew books as well as the number of books issued with *haskamot*. To avoid speculation about whether, when, and by whom a book was printed, the Bibliography features only books of which a copy still exists and has been examined by a Bibliography researcher. In addition, although the vast majority of rabbinic approbations and reprinting bans were printed in the book itself, that was not always the case. It was sometimes the practice merely to announce them from the pulpit in synagogue or to record them in a community registry.[61] Nonetheless, the Bibliography presents the best data we have on the number and percentage of Hebrew books printed with a *haskama*.

As reported in the Bibliography of the Hebrew Book, only 17 books bearing a *haskama* were printed before 1600. During the seventeenth century, 278 books were printed with a *haskama*, and in the eighteenth century the number of *haskamot* rose to 1,695. At the tail end of the nineteenth century, 750 books were printed with a *haskama* in just a single decade.

Yet, more tellingly than the increase in absolute numbers of *haskamot* is the sharp increase in the *percentage* of Hebrew books that were issued with a *haskama*. As indicated in Figure 5.2, the percentage of Hebrew books receiving a *haskama* (again based on the data collected in the Bibliography of the Hebrew Book) continued to grow from the beginning of the seventeenth century until the decline of Jewish communal autonomy in the late eighteenth and early nineteenth centuries. It reached its apex during the decade of 1760 to 1769, just as the Council of Four Lands was abolished by order of the Polish Sejm. The dramatic increase in the percentage of books printed with a *haskama* in the seventeenth and early eighteenth centuries is likely attributed to a variety of factors. They include regulations of the Council of Four Lands and other communal councils requiring rabbinic approval for newly printed books, market fragmentation of the Hebrew book trade, and concerted rabbinic efforts to suppress Sabbatean literature.

59. Gries states that the number of titles almost quadrupled. Gries 2007: 16. According to The Bibliography of the Hebrew Book, the number of titles increased from 2,161 in the seventeenth century to 6,465 in the eighteenth.

60. The Bibliography was produced by The Institute for Hebrew Bibliography, founded by The Hebrew University of Jerusalem, the Israel Ministry of Education and Culture, the Bialik Institute, and Goldman Publishers. It is available on the website of the National Library of Israel.

61. Benayahu 1971: 31 (discussing sixteenth-century Venice); Rakover 1991: 153–60.

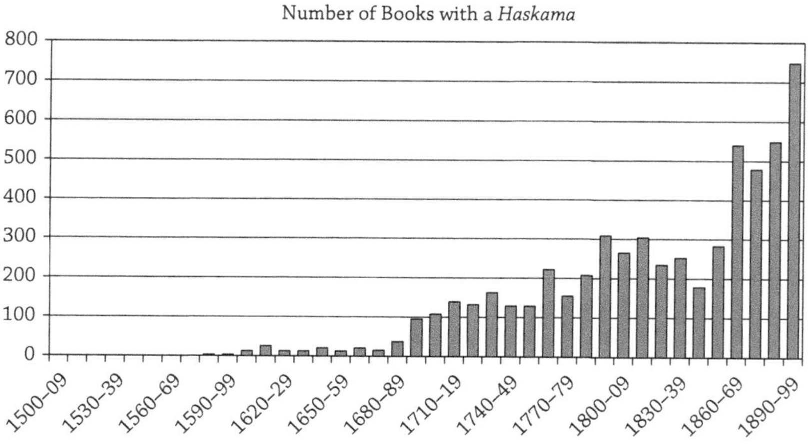

Figure 5.1
Number of Hebrew Books with a *Haskama*, 1500–1899.

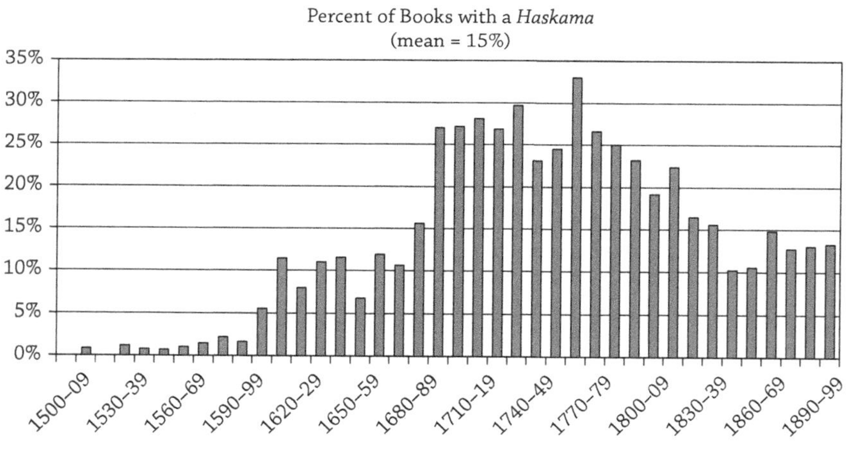

Figure 5.2
Percent of Hebrew Books with a *Haskama*, 1500–1890.

Not all *haskamot* included a reprinting ban. The percentage of *haskamot* that included a reprinting ban varied from place to place, time to time, and one issuing rabbi to another. Here I rely on my own investigation of *haskamot* issued in select times and locations, inasmuch as the Bibliography of the Hebrew Book does not specify which *haskamot* included a reprinting ban and which just an approbation. Most *haskamot* issued by the Venetian rabbis from the late sixteenth to late seventeenth centuries included a reprinting ban in addition to a rabbinic approbation. Similarly, just under half of the *haskamot* issued in Amsterdam during the 50-year period 1690 to 1740, the height of Hebrew printing in that city, prohibited reprinting. In contrast, only one-third of the *haskamot* issued directly by the Council of Four Lands included a ban. It is possible, however, that during certain periods, a Council of Four Lands' approbation was tantamount to a reprinting ban. The Council forbade printing any book without rabbinic approval, and it might have been understood that such approval would not be forthcoming when the applicant sought to compete with an existing publication. Finally, of the some 240 *haskamot* issued by Joseph Saul Nathanson, rabbi of Lemberg, between 1840 and 1875, one-third included a reprinting ban.

Like approbations, reprinting bans were not always printed in the book; as noted above, they were sometimes only read aloud in synagogue or recorded in a community registry.[62] Nonetheless, it is clear that although some *haskamot* include a reprinting ban, many others set forth only a rabbinic approbation. Why would rabbis issue an approbation without a reprinting ban?

As we have seen, sixteenth- and seventeenth-century Venetian rabbis apparently refused to issue reprinting bans for titles that had been previously printed. We see a similar reluctance to issue bans for previously printed books, particularly for classic books of Jewish law and liturgy, in other times and locations as well. A prime example is the 1716 decree of the Amsterdam rabbinic leadership that no more bans would be issued for prayer books.[63]

The reluctance to issue bans for previously printed titles was by no means a hard-and-fast rule, however. There have been numerous instances in which rabbis have issued reprinting bans for new printings of the Talmud, the *Shulḥan Arukh*, prayer books, and other foundational texts of Jewish law, learning, and liturgy. On some such occasions, the issuing rabbi has noted that the edition contains new commentary. But on others, the ban has been issued entirely to protect the publisher's investment in a high quality printing.

Otherwise, there seems to be no distinguishing characteristic that determined which books received bans and which only approbations. Virtually all books that received a *haskama* were Hebrew titles concerning Jewish law, learning, liturgy, ethical literature, homiletics, Kabbalah, or, occasionally, philosophy. Books that have received reprinting bans span those subjects as well and, at least in my limited study, no striking difference marks which subject categories were more likely to receive a *haskama* containing only an approbation versus those that received both a *haskama* and *ḥerem*.

Hence, aside from those instances in which bans were withheld from previously printed books, the reason many *haskamot* did not include a reprinting ban probably had more to do with the nature of reprinting bans than with distinguishing characteristics of the books for which *haskamot* were issued. Along these lines, there a number of possible explanations:

First, as I presently discuss, the halakhic justification for issuing reprinting bans was questioned by leading rabbinic decisors. This cloud of doubt might have led to a reluctance among some rabbis to issue reprinting bans as opposed to merely a statement of praise for a book and its pious author, editor, or publisher.

62. Benayahu 1971: 31 (discussing sixteenth-century Venice); Rakover 1991: 153–60.
63. Rakover 1991: 305–21.

Second, during certain periods, it was doubtful whether a ban would be respected outside the territory where it was issued. In those instances, in order to obtain financing and to gain market advantage over possible competitors, publishers would have had to rest content with the approbation of leading rabbis attesting to the book's superior quality.

Third, some publishers of Jewish books held monopolies or book privileges from secular authorities, and thus might have been inclined to look to rabbis merely to give their imprimatur to the book rather than seek a rabbinic reprinting ban as well.

Fourth, some authors and publishers were confident of their ability to recover their printing investment without a reprinting ban, which in any case typically lasted only until the holder of the ban had sold out his first edition. Jonathan Eybeschutz (1690–1764) expressed this sentiment in his introduction to *Kreti U-Plati*, his commentary on the *Yoreh De'ah* section of the *Shulḥan Arukh* published in Altona in 1763. Eybeschutz explains that he did not apply for a reprinting ban because doing so would provide no advantage: no one would reprint the book before he sold his first printing because his first printing would quickly satisfy virtually all consumer demand for the book—and after his first edition was sold, anyone would be free to reprint anyway.[64] In that vein, it was not uncommon for publishers to sell their print run through advance subscription before the book was printed. Approbations from distinguished rabbis would serve as a vital marketing tool for selling advance subscriptions. But unless a rival publisher tried to tempt subscribers to break their commitment and instead purchase the rival's hastily prepared competing edition—which did sometimes happen—a reprinting ban would be superfluous.

Finally, as part of secular governments' moves to diminish and ultimately abolish Jewish communities' juridical autonomy, beginning in western Europe in late eighteenth century and continuing in central and eastern Europe through the nineteenth century, secular authorities often forbade rabbis from issuing a *ḥerem*. Deprived of that ultimate power of enforcement, rabbinic reprinting bans came to be framed as requests to refrain from reprinting rather than mandatory rabbinic edicts, making them concomitantly less valuable to publishers and authors.

IV. RABBINIC REPRINTING BANS COMPARED WITH BOOK PRIVILEGES

Even if not all *haskamot* included a ban, rabbinic reprinting bans rapidly proliferated from the early seventeenth century on. As they did so, they evinced rabbinic sensibilities and concerns and, thus, traveled a distinct path from secular and ecclesiastical

64. Rakover 1991: 234. Eybeschutz was famously charged with being a closet Sabbatean and, although he was cleared by leading rabbinic authorities, suspicions lingered throughout his life. Perhaps that controversy made it more difficult for him to obtain a *haskama* and ban. Cf. Dynner 2006: 203 (noting that publishers of well-established Hasidic authors were typically "confident enough about sales not to feel compelled to undertake the arduous task of collecting *haskamot*.")

book privileges. We explore four areas related to bans and book regulation: (1) the need for halakhic justification, (2) territorial scope, (3) flexibility in interpretation and application, and (4) printing industry regulation and guilds.

A. Halakhic Justification

As we have seen, both the prohibition against reprinting and the rabbis' authority to issue such bans were understood to require halakhic justification. Over the centuries, indeed, rabbinic decisors have engaged in protracted debate about what that halakhic justification might be. And some leading halakhic scholars argued that, in their age, rabbis no longer had authority to issue reprinting bans.

In contrast, as discussed in Chapter 2, the Holy See and secular sovereigns typically asserted unquestioned authority to regulate the book trade and issue book privileges. Granted, in principle, the privileges could not be dispensed entirely as a personal favor. Since book privileges constrained non-recipients' freedom of trade, they required justification, typically that the recipient was worthy of the special privilege, given his substantial investment and contribution to the realm in creating and printing a useful book. Aside from reciting the worthiness of the recipient, however, the privileges do not evince any perceived need to justify the privilege-issuer's juridical authority to award an exclusive entitlement to print a book or to provide a legal foundation for the privilege. It was simply understood that the sovereign enjoyed the prerogative and largely unbridled discretion to regulate commercial activity and grant exclusive privileges for commercial endeavors, including book privileges.

Rabbinic bans sometimes express similar policy justifications to those we see in papal and secular book privileges. For example, a four-year ban given in Prague in 1615 for *Tosefot Yom-Tov*, commentaries on the Mishnah by a prominent early seventeenth-century Bohemian rabbi and Talmudist, Yom-Tov Lipman Ha-Levi Heller (1578–1664), sets out two reasons for the ban—so that the land would be filled with knowledge and so that the publisher should not suffer a large loss. But these policy arguments were not sufficient justifications for rabbinic bans. Rabbis did not have the same inherent authority as secular sovereigns to regulate the book trade. Nor did they have the authority to grant a special privilege in derogation of otherwise generally applicable law merely because the recipient was deserving of such a privilege.

Recall that the rabbis' need to provide halakhic justification for their reprinting bans appears from the very first ban of which we have a record. The Rome rabbis who issued the *ktav dat* regarding Eliyahu Bakhur's three books of Hebrew grammar grounded their reprinting ban in the halakhic prohibition against encroaching on another's livelihood. In so doing, the issuing rabbis took care to present themselves as faithful transmitters of venerable halakhic doctrine, not innovators of a new entitlement, and certainly not as members of a body with inherent authority to dispense commercial privileges. Moses Isserles's 1550 responsum set out further halakhic support for his reprinting ban in favor of the Maharam of Padua. Yet subsequent rabbinic authorities questioned the proffered halakhic bases for those bans. Some posited that book publishing falls within the rubric of the majority rule in Jewish law favoring free competition, and thus that a reprinter does not typically violate the prohibition of encroachment.[65] In particular they questioned whether Jewish law accords one publisher a superior, exclusive right over others to print a previously printed title; such a rule, they argued, would benefit one publisher while harming potential competitors and imposing higher prices on purchasers. Other rabbinic decisors insisted, contrary to the Rome rabbis, that the prohibition against encroaching on another's livelihood applies only when a newcomer sets up shop in the incumbent's geographic location, and thus does not govern the book trade, for which the market is the entire world.[66]

If reprinting bans are not simply mechanisms for restating and enforcing the long-standing halakhic prohibition against encroaching on another's livelihood, then what is their halakhic basis? Indeed, absent any grounding in preexisting halakhic doctrine, wherein would lie the rabbinic authority to prohibit reprinting?

Rabbinic decisors have proffered various alternative doctrines that both establish and delimit rabbinic authority to issue the bans. These include arguments that reprinting bans are grounded in rabbinic authority to issue regulations that govern commercial dealings, protect against harm those engaged in fulfilling *mitzvot* (religious obligations and good deeds), and promote the publication of books of Jewish learning so the knowledge of the Torah will not be diminished. Under centuries-old halakhic doctrine, rabbis had broad authority to regulate such matters, including the authority to order that property be transferred from one person to another. But Jewish law contains a precept that roughly parallels the Roman law prohibition, discussed in Chapter 2, against a ruler granting one person a privilege in derogation from generally applicable law when doing so would cause harm to another. The halakhic tenet, which rabbinic decisors have variously interpreted and applied, provides that a rabbinic regulation may not profit one person while causing loss to another.[67]

Rabbinic authority to issue reprinting bans has also been held to derive from the rabbis' broader authority to enforce community ordinances and printers' guild regulations. The halakha has long recognized the authority of lay community councils and

65. See, e.g., Mordekhai Banet (1753–1829), *Responsa Parshat Mordekhai*, Ḥoshen Mishpat, No. 7.

66. See, e.g., Aryeh Leib Zuenz (1768–1833), *Shalom Ve-Emet Le-Tivukh Ben Ha-Madpisim* (Peace and Truth for Settling Disputes between the Printers). See also Menaḥem Mendel Schneersohn (1789–1866), *Responsa Tzemaḥ Tzedek*, Yoreh De'ah, No. 195 (holding that even if the prohibition against encroachment does, in principle, apply to the book trade, it is not a violation to reprint in another country).

67. See Y. Cohen 1999: 308 (discussing the principle that rabbinic authority is limited by the rule that the rabbi may not profit one while causing loss to another); Rakover 1991: 342–45 (discussing particular claims that a reprinting ban should not be enforced because it causes another a loss). Some decisors have also subjected rabbinic authority to regulate in commercial matters to procedural constraints, such as that the regulation must be enacted by a duly constituted rabbinic court. See, e.g., Menaḥem Mendel Schneersohn (1789–1866), *Responsa Tzemaḥ Tzedek*, Yoreh De'ah, No. 295 (holding, on the basis of that general rule, that only a rabbinic court with expertise in the law of reprinting bans may issue a reprinting ban).

trade guilds to issue ordinances in commercial and other matters that are binding on members of their community or guild, provided that the ordinance is approved by a "distinguished person," typically a leading rabbi.[68] For that reason, unlike rabbinic reprinting bans, council decrees requiring that books be approved by rabbinic and lay leadership required no additional halakhic justification. Finally, rabbinic reprinting bans were said to be valid and enforceable in accordance with long-standing local custom, which the halakha also recognizes as a binding norm, or as a *ma'arufia*, a form of halakhically sanctioned commercial monopoly with medieval roots.[69]

Sometimes the arguments putting forth the halakhic basis for rabbinic reprinting bans have been set out in the text of reprinting bans themselves. More commonly, they appear in responsa or commentary. In either case, the debate over the halakhic justifications for rabbinic bans has loomed large in leading disputes. As such, competing theories regarding rabbinic authority and the justification of rabbinic reprinting bans have had far-reaching ramifications for delineating the nature, scope, and duration of halakhic protection against reprinting.

B. Territorial Scope

As we have seen, rabbinic reprinting bans differed from their secular counterparts (but not papal book privileges) in that they often purported to be without territorial limit. The ban issued in favor of Eliyahu Bakhur prohibited reprinting anywhere in the world. That worldwide scope was also a central feature of bans issued by the Venetian rabbinic court as well as those issued pursuant to the decree of the Council of Four Lands and by rabbinic authorities in Amsterdam. Bans that prohibited reprinting throughout the world stood on uncertain halakhic foundations, given the lack of precedent for prohibiting competition outside a specified locale and traditional limits on rabbis' authority to regulate conduct outside their local community. Nevertheless, the worldwide scope of rabbinic reprinting bans was largely accepted until the late eighteenth century. Beginning in the late eighteenth century, however,

68. See Elon 1997: 399–400 (guild regulation) 564–69 (community regulation); 607–14 (approval of a distinguished person or "adam ḥashuv").

69. See, e.g., Moses Sofer (1762–1839), *Responsa Ḥatam Sofer*, Ḥoshen Mishpat, No. 41 (custom and rabbinic regulation); Mordekhai Banet (1753–1829), *Responsa Parshat Mordekhai*, Ḥoshen Mishpat, No. 8 (printers' mutual consent); Rakover 1991: 150 (describing a ban, issued by Yeshaya Segal Horowitz in 1616, that stated that it was given so that the land would be filled with the work's knowledge and so that the publisher would not suffer a large loss); 185–87 (describing a disagreement regarding the juridical basis for reprinting bans among issuers of such bans for an edition of the Talmud printed in 1835, with Menaḥem Naḥum ben Yehuda Leib stating that the basis of his ban lay in guild regulation, not the prohibition against encroaching on another's livelihood, while Abraham bar Alef Gimmel stated that, in reality, no Jewish publishers have ever gathered to promulgate any guild regulation, and that the basis for the ban is, rather, the prohibition against encroachment). See also Y. Cohen 1999: 285–88, 308–10, 313, 333 (summarizing authorities for the view that rabbinic authority lies in guild regulation, community ordinance, rabbinic regulation, custom, and *ma'arufia*); Eidelberg 1953 (discussing *ma'arufia* in Rabbeinu Gershom's responsa).

a majority of leading halakhic decisors came to hold that rabbinic reprinting bans are not effective outside the country in which they have been issued.

The primary juridical basis for that dramatic retraction of bans' territorial scope was a centuries-old ruling by the medieval Spanish decisor and Talmudic authority Isaac ben Sheshet (1326–1408). Sheshet (known in Jewish tradition by the Hebrew acronym Rivash) ruled that a rabbi does not have authority to forbid the committing of an act that is otherwise permitted under halakha outside the territory of his country.[70] Those who invoked that ruling to limit the territorial scope of rabbinic reprinting bans assumed that, but for a ban, it would not be a wrongful encroachment on the livelihood of the original publisher, or any other violation of halakha, to reprint the publisher's book in another country.

Those who challenged the worldwide force of rabbinic reprinting bans reasoned further that changed circumstances required that bans be limited to the country where they are issued. First, as Aryeh Leib Zuenz opined, ever since the demise of the Council of Four Lands (in 1764), there was no longer a Jewish communal body that could be said to have the authority to regulate the book trade and enact an ordinance that authorized the issuance of rabbinic reprinting bans throughout much of the Jewish world.[71] (Under Jewish law, the regulatory power of a Jewish communal body extends only within the communal body's territory, but, at its height, the Council of Four Lands had either direct jurisdiction or influence over a large swath of the Jewish world.)

Second, the successive partitions of Poland, between 1772 and 1795, had the effect of dividing the bulk of European Jewry among three nations: Russia, Austria, and Prussia. Of particular significance to rabbinic reprinting bans, those countries each imposed strict control of the book trade, including sharp restrictions on book imports. For example, under Austrian censorship laws enacted shortly after the partition, any package coming in from another country was examined, and prohibited books were confiscated, while unknown titles were submitted to the censor for approval.[72] In addition, as part of its sustained campaign to suppress Ḥasidism and to Germanize the Jews of the formerly Polish region of Galicia, the Austrian authorities banned the printing of Ḥasidic and Kabbalistic books and generally prohibited the importation of Hebrew and Yiddish books.[73] In the face of those restrictions on cross-border shipments of Hebrew books, some rabbis reasoned that it would be counterproductive to enforce a rabbinic ban against reprinting a book in a different country when the original publisher could not export copies of his book into that country.[74] Under such

70. See Mordekhai Banet (1753–1829), *Responsa Parshat Mordekhai*, Ḥoshen Mishpat, No. 8, relying on the ruling by Rivash. See also Menaḥem Mendel Schneersohn (1789–1866), *Responsa Tzemaḥ Tzedek*, Yoreh De'ah, No. 195 (concluding that a rabbinic court's power to issue a reprinting ban is limited to the territory of that court's jurisdiction and that it is not wrongful encroachment on the publisher's livelihood to reprint in another territory).

71. Aryeh Leib Zuenz (1768–1833), *Shalom Ve-Emet Le-Tivukh Ben Ha-Madpisim* (Peace and Truth for Settling Disputes between the Printers). I discuss Zuenz's responsum further in Chapter 7.

72. Bachleitner 1997: 101–03.

73. Mahler 1961: 133–54.

74. Rakover 1991: 394–96.

circumstances, to enforce a reprinting ban in the foreign country would only deprive readers in that country of any access at all to the book in question.

Finally, as Aryeh Leib Zuenz also reasoned, publishers of previous generations had to reach a worldwide market of relatively small, widely dispersed Jewish communities in order to recover their investment. By the early nineteenth century, however, Jews were far more numerous. From Zuenz's perspective, therefore, domestic markets now sufficed to maintain publishers' viability.[75]

C. Flexibilities

As distinct from secular authorities, rabbis have long interpreted and applied rabbinic reprinting bans in a flexible manner, designed, in principle, to enable dissemination of affordable books so long as the publisher has recovered his investment. In particular, rabbis frequently allowed reprinting during the nominal term of the ban so long as the publisher had substantially sold out his first printing. As with secular book privileges, the term of years set forth in the ban was meant roughly to approximate the time needed for the publisher to sell out his first printing. Rabbinic bans varied from 3 to 25 years, and in rare instances even 30 years in duration, with the most common period being 10 years. But regardless of the nominal duration, rabbis frequently interpreted the term of years as a maximum period of protection. In this view, the ban expired when all (or substantially all) books were sold, even if before the expiration of the term of years enumerated in the ban.[76] At the same time, even if many unsold books remained at the end of the prescribed period, the ban would expire nonetheless. The publisher's sole recourse in that event was to petition for a second ban, and obtaining a renewal was far from certain. Thus, while secular book privileges came to be indefinitely renewable or even perpetual in many locations, rabbinic reprinting bans generally remained targeted, short-term entitlements.

Rabbis also narrowly interpreted reprinting bans when determining whether a given book constituted a prohibited "reprinting". Some decisors held that a ban on reprinting an edition of the Talmud did not extend to printing individual tractates, especially if the tractates were lower market versions produced primarily for students. For example, in 1720, Yaakov Ha-Cohen Poppers, the head of the rabbinic court of Frankfurt am Maim, granted a *haskama* for an individual tractate without certain commentaries, even though a previously issued rabbinic ban on printing the Talmud remained in force. Poppers reasoned that the tractate was just a "kuntras" (a pamphlet)

75. Aryeh Leib Zuenz (1768–1833), *Shalom Ve-Emet Le-Tivukh Ben Ha-Madpisim* (Peace and Truth for Settling Disputes between the Printers).

76. See, e.g., Barukh Teumim-Frankel (1760–1828), *Responsa Ateret Hakhamim*, Yoreh De'ah, No. 25 (citing previous authorities), discussed in Rakover 1991: 182–84. The question of whether a ban ceased to be of any force and effect once all copies of the book had been sold stood at the heart of the disputes in the first decades of the nineteenth century between the publisher of the Talmud in Slavuta and its competitors. Those disputes are the subject of Chapter 7.

and thus was not covered by a ban on printing the complete Talmud. Even further, a *haskama* for a small-format edition of the Talmud tractate *Niddah*, printed in Metz in 1770, stated that although an existing rabbinic ban extended to printing individual tractates as well as the entire Talmud, the rabbis who issued that ban could not have intended to prevent the printing of small, cheap volumes that were not part of a complete edition.[77]

Also telling is a *haskama* that Joseph Saul Nathanson issued in 1867 to Ḥaim Brait, a noted Galician collector of Hebrew manuscripts, for Brait's edition of a compendium of essays authored by the late Renaissance Italian Talmudist and Kabbalist, Menaḥem Azariah da Fano (1548–1620). As we shall later see, Nathanson was a staunch proponent of copyright in Jewish law. Nonetheless, Nathanson gave Brait his *haskama* even though Brait's compendium contained the entire content of another book, an anthology of a smaller set of da Fano's essays, for which Nathanson had granted a reprinting ban just three years previously. Nathanson justified his *haskama* for Brait's compendium on the grounds that it was a more complete edition than the earlier book that was the subject of Nathanson's reprinting ban: even though Brait incorporated the entire contents of the previous edition, some two-thirds of his compendium comprised essays that had not appeared in the earlier book.[78] Nathanson, indeed, not only gave his approbation for Brait's edition, but issued a reprinting ban for it as well.

Granted, reprinting bans were occasionally stated quite broadly. The ban given in Prague in 1615 for *Tosefot Yom-Tov* forbade not just reprinting the book itself, but also any edition of passages from the Mishnah with commentary, for a period of four years.[79] A ban given in Lublin in 1654 for a book about monetary laws forbade any other book about monetary laws without rabbinic permission. But such broad bans were an exception and typically stemmed from the era in which the Council of Four Lands assumed the all-encompassing authority to regulate the Hebrew book trade. Especially following the emergence of competing rabbinic authorities and the decline and eventual demise of the Council in the eighteenth century, rabbis commonly interpreted a previous ban narrowly when awarding a *haskama* for a new book that might be said to fall within the existing ban.

Finally, similarly to secular book privileges, we see numerous instances in which reprinting bans were made conditional on the actual printing of the book within a reasonable period of time and on the sale of the book at a reasonable price.[80] Indeed, reprinting bans sometimes set out a deadline for when the book had to be printed

77. Heller 2008: 102.

78. It was Menaḥem Mandel, who, alongside Nathanson, issued a *haskama* and ban for the Brait edition, who noted that two-thirds of it contained newly printed material. See Rakover 1991: 221–22. On Brait, see Encyclopedia of the Founders and Builders of Israel, Vol. 18, p. 5469, available at http://www.tidhar.tourolib.org/tidhar/view/18/5469.

79. Rakover 1991: 150–52.

80. For a detailed discussion of these conditions, together with examples of each, see Rakover 1991: 292–304 (requirement that the book be expeditiously printed), 322–25 (price regulation).

and a specific maximum price at which the book could be sold. On occasion, rabbis abrogated a ban on the grounds that the publisher had yet to bring the book to print, even when the ban did not contain an express condition that the book be expeditiously printed.

Underlying these conditions, like the narrow interpretation and limited duration of reprinting bans, was the rabbis' overriding concern for spurring both the production and the availability of books of rabbinic commentary, learning, ethics, and liturgy. Reprinting bans were designed, tailored, and flexibly interpreted to enable publishers (and occasionally authors) to recover their initial investment by selling out their first printing in the market for which their edition was aimed. Indeed, as rabbinic decisors repeatedly held, rabbis had no authority to issue reprinting bans for any greater extent or other purpose. So long as the publisher was protected from harm in his initial market, reprintings and multiple editions of the book were to be encouraged.

D. Printers' Guilds and Book Trade Regulation

By the dawn of secular copyright law in the eighteenth century, secular book privileges were inextricably bound up with printers' guilds. As discussed in Chapter 2, printers' guilds were established in every major printing center in Europe, including Venice, Amsterdam, Paris, Frankfurt, Leipzig, Prague, and London, typically at the behest of the sovereign government. The guilds, which operated as cartels, came to be the primary site for regulating the book trade. The guilds both controlled who was allowed to print books and allocated printing rights for particular titles and types of books among guild members. They also served as a tool for sovereign governments to control and censor print content, even if in some places guild self-regulation came to stand in tension with the prerogative of the sovereign to issue privileges directly to favored printers and authors.

Some rabbinic decisors have posited that rabbis have authority to issue reprinting bans as a means to enforce printers' guild regulations and/or trade custom in the printing industry. The Talmud provides that the people of a town may enact regulations for their common benefit that are binding on all current and future residents, provided that if a rabbi resides in the town, the townspeople must obtain his agreement to the regulations.[81] Rabbinic commentators extended that rule to members of a craft or trade, effectively treating them as townspeople—except that tradesmen must agree unanimously, while townspeople may enact a binding regulation by majority vote.[82] The rabbinic decisors who have invoked guild regulations or trade custom as the juridical basis for rabbinic reprinting bans have drawn upon that extended rule, as codified in the *Shulḥan Arukh*.[83] They posit that rabbis may issue reprinting bans to give halakhic force to, and to aid in the enforcement of, regulations that printers have explicitly or tacitly adopted for their common benefit.

81. *Babylonian Talmud, Baba Batra* 8b.
82. Tamari 1998: 149–50; Rapp 2010: 436–37.
83. *Shulḥan Arukh*, Ḥoshen Mishpat, 231: 28.

However, it is unclear whether and how that understanding applies with respect to non-Jewish printers' guilds—almost all of which prohibited Jews from becoming members—or whether rabbis surmised that Jewish printers had organized guilds and adopted guild regulations among themselves. As we will later see, the eminent early nineteenth-century rabbinic authority, Mordekhai Banet posited that, in the early days of print, the publishers of books of Jewish learning affirmatively requested that the rabbis institute the practice of issuing reprinting bans in order to enforce the printers' consensus agreement. In Banet's telling, those printers must have been Jewish; Christian printers would be highly unlikely to petition a rabbi to lend support for their guild regulations. But Banet's theory of events seems exceedingly unlikely to be accurate. As we have seen, there were very few rabbinic reprinting bans issued in the early days of print; rabbinic reprinting bans did not take hold until the second half of the sixteenth century. Moreover, the market for high-end books of Jewish liturgy and learning throughout most of the sixteenth century was dominated by a handful of leading publishers, who, except for Gershom Soncino, were Christians. Perhaps because of Banet's faulty factual premises, other rabbinic decisors apply the guild regulation rationale for rabbinic reprinting bans and Jewish copyright law based on what they view as a consensus in the printing trade generally, not just among Jewish publishers, whether today or in the early days of print.[84]

In basing their rulings upon what they perceive to be the general consensus within the publishing industry overall, those rabbinic decisors present yet another instance in which rabbis have incorporated external norms into Jewish copyright law. Indeed, this might also be the case when, like Mordekhai Banet, decisors have imagined that rabbinic reprinting bans derive from guild regulations of Jewish printers. Although Jews formed hundreds of their own craft guilds and artisan associations in early modern Europe, we have no record of any guilds of Jewish printers save one, a guild of Hebrew book printers established in Moravia in the seventeenth century.[85] At most, Jewish printers occasionally obtained membership in general, secular printers' guilds, even though secular printers' guild regulations, with the notable exception of Amsterdam's, typically prohibited Jews from joining. Hence, rabbinic rulings that purported to give halakhic imprimatur to regulations of Jewish printers' guilds rested almost entirely on a mythical ideal. Rabbis may have imputed to mythical Jewish printers' guilds what they understood of allocations of printing rights within printers' guilds generally.

Aside from the Moravian guild, the closest equivalent in the Hebrew book trade to the type of regulation effected by printers' guilds lay in efforts of the Council of Four Lands to divide up the market for Hebrew books in order to prevent what it regarded as ruinous competition. As we have seen, by its decree of 1594, the Council

84. See Batzri 1984–85: 181 (referring to trade custom among booksellers generally); Y. Cohen 1999: Kuntras, 560–63 (contending that because authors lobbied for international copyright treaties, those treaties today constitute guild regulation that is part of Jewish copyright law).

85. Jewish guilds included those of tailors, apothecaries, furriers, barbers, peddlers, weavers, silversmiths, goldsmiths, bakers, and other craftsmen. Kellenbenz 1977; Bauer 2008 (noting that Hebrew book printers, like tailors, furriers, weavers, and other crafts, organized guilds in Moravia in the seventeenth century); Wischnitzer 1965; Feldman 1982. In addition, Christian guilds sometimes set up separate sections for Jews and other non-Christians.

did not merely require rabbinic permission to print individual titles. It also forbade the printing of any book in Italy that was already printed or being printed in Poland and the sale in Poland of a Polish edition of any book first printed in Italy for 10 years after the book's initial publication.

The Council also dictated which tractates of the Talmud would be studied in *yeshivot* each year, such that all *yeshivot* in Greater Poland and Lithuania studied the same tractate. This practice served an educational function by focusing halakhic discourse on common themes and enabling students to transfer from one *yeshiva* to another. But the Council also provided local publishers with advance notice of which tractate would be required in the coming year, thus ensuring a market for their imprints. Further, by requiring a different tractate each year, the Council effectively gave backing to a printing of the complete set of the Talmud, issued in Lublin between 1617 and 1639.[86]

As noted above, the late the seventeenth century brought intense competition among incumbent Hebrew printing houses in Krakow and Lublin, and the house that the eminent Amsterdam printer, Uri Fayvesh Halevi, established in Zolkiew in 1692 with the Council's blessing and a privilege from the Polish king.[87] In response to complaints by Favyesh's competitors, the Council proceeded to tightly regulate the market for Hebrew books. At the Jaroslaw Fair in 1697, the Council appointed a committee composed of three members of the Council, each selected by one of the printing houses and chaired by Council notable Simḥa Menaḥem Miyona, to resolve the disputes among the printers and to put an end to competition among them.[88] The Council's decree divided the annual demand for Hebrew books used for study in synagogues and academies of Jewish learning. It permitted each of the three publishers to print no more than 700 copies of the study books per year, required that each copy bear the signature of the Council's auditor, and forbade synagogues from purchasing study books that did not bear the auditor's signature. The Council permitted the printing houses to publish as many copies of other types of books as they wished, but only in their own printing facilities. The Krakow and Lublin houses had been importing books and selling them out of their shops in order to compete with the Zolkiew house. The Council prohibited this practice.[89]

Two years later, the Council intervened once again. It issued a decree prohibiting the Krakow and Lublin publishers on pain of *ḥerem* and a large fine from importing any sacred books, large or small, that had already been printed by Fayvesh, and from importing small books, of fewer than 10 folded sheets per book, even if Fayvesh did not carry them. The Council also forbade the two publishers from printing large or small books outside Poland and bringing those books into Poland. It also prohibited Fayvesh from importing into Poland titles that had already been printed in Krakow

86. Heller 2008: 109; Heilprin 1934.

87. Heller 1999: 287. The privilege gave Uru Fayvesh Halevi permission to establish a Hebrew press and sell its output throughout Poland.

88. Heilprin 1934: 83.

89. In approximately 1685, the Council also banned all printing of books of sermons and other rabbinic texts. This ban appears to have originated in efforts to stem the rapid spread of Kabbalistic and Sabbatean texts, rather than for market regulation. Teller 2004: 391.

and Lublin. However, it was clear that the Council's edict was aimed primarily at the Krakow and Lublin publishers, whom the Council charged with printing books of inferior quality and accuracy and who had apparently continued to import books to compete with Uri Fayvesh despite the Council's unequivocal edict in 1697.[90]

In sum, the Council of Four Lands sought to engage in a form of structural regulation of the book trade, with some similarities to that achieved by the secular printers' guild regulations and printers' ordinances. But despite some rabbinic decisors' invocation of guild ordinances as a halakhic basis for reprinting bans, we see no evidence of any Jewish printers' guilds outside of Moravia.

90. Heilprin 1934: 84. See also Carmilly-Weinberger 1977: 268 n. 8, citing Pinkas Vaad Arba Artzot, pp. 242–43, no. 520.

CHAPTER 6

From a Yiddish Bible to a German Prayer Book

I. THE YIDDISH BIBLE AND THE COUNCIL OF FOUR LANDS

Before relocating to Poland, Uri Fayvesh Halevi (1625–1715) had been a leading Ashkenazic publisher in Amsterdam and one of only two Jewish members of the Amsterdam Booksellers and Printers Guild. In 1670, at the height of Amsterdam's dominance of the Jewish book trade, Fayvesh conceived a plan to publish the first-ever complete Yiddish translation of the Hebrew Bible unaccompanied by Hebrew text and commentaries.[1] Fayvesh's publication of the Yiddish Bible took a tortuous path, replete with Christian financers, broken promises, failed partnerships, and litigation in Dutch secular and rabbinic courts. The implosion of one partnership generated a competing edition of the Yiddish Bible, which, in turn, spawned rival rabbinic reprinting bans and secular book privileges. As the saga vividly illustrates, even at the height of Amsterdam's Jewish book trade, leading Jewish printers faced perilous financial risks, a heavy dependency on Christian financing, and the treacherous uncertainties of navigating among overlapping rabbinic and secular authorities in multiple jurisdictions.

1. My discussion of the Yiddish Bible dispute draws upon Aptroot 1993; Aptroot 1989; Fuks and Fuks-Mansfield 1987: 236–40, 269–70, 289–98, 319; Haberman 1978: 294–309; and Timm 1993. Fayvesh is also known as Phoebus. His Dutch name, under which he was registered in the Amsterdam Booksellers and Printers Guild, was Philips Levi.

To finance his Yiddish Bible, Fayvesh joined with a silent business partner, Borrit Jansz Smit, a local Christian merchant-bookseller and publisher of a 1662 edition of the Dutch Bible. On December 14, 1670, the two partners executed a written promise to pay Ḥaim ben Judah Leib of Pila, a Polish rabbi, 1,000 guilders for Leib to intercede on their behalf to obtain an approbation and reprinting ban from the Council of Four Lands for Fayvesh's "German Jewish" edition of the Bible. The partners' contract with Leib provided that the Council's *haskama* would be in Fayvesh's name, and that its reprinting ban would be of at least four years' duration.

Fayvesh wanted the Council's reprinting ban as an assurance of exclusivity in his primary market, the Yiddish-speaking Ashkenazic communities of the Kingdom of Poland, spanning from Pozen to Bratslav.[2] The elite rabbinic scholars and academies of Poland would have disdained a Yiddish Bible lacking the ancient Hebrew text. But for the vast majority of East European Jews, including virtually all women, the Bible was directly accessible only in Yiddish. Fayvesh hoped that the Council of Four Land's approbation and reprinting ban would assure him a large pool of potential buyers.

Leib proceeded to obtain two *haskamot* from the Council of Four Lands, the first signed in Lublin on April 5, 1671, and the second on May 22, 1671, issued by Yitzḥak ben Avram of Pozen during a meeting of the national council of greater Poland. In many respects, the Council's *haskamot* were exactly what Fayvesh and Smit wanted: the Council granted permission to print and distribute the Yiddish Bible and also forbade anyone from printing or buying a competing edition for a period of 10 years on pain of excommunication. But the Council's *haskamot* made no mention of Uri Fayvesh or his partner Borrit Smit. Rather they named only Fayvesh's translator, Yekutiel Blitz, a rabbi who hailed from Witmund in northern Germany, suggesting that Blitz alone was holder of the exclusive printing rights.

Fayvesh accordingly refused to pay Leib until he obtained a new *haskama* that would name Favyesh as its beneficiary. In turn, Leib refused to hand over the *haskamot* to Fayvesh. He finally did so in 1672, after receiving full payment in return for his promise to obtain a corrected *haskama,* a promise that he apparently never carried out.

By the time Fayvesh had the Council's *haskamot* in hand, the Dutch Republic had gone to war against England, France, and the Bishop of Munster, so its economy was in turmoil. In the wake of these developments, Fayvesh and Smit went bankrupt and their Yiddish Bible project stagnated. When the hostilities and recession ended, the partners renewed their efforts to publish the Yiddish Bible, but at that point they lacked sufficient financing for the expensive project. Accordingly, on February 10, 1674, they entered into a new contract for the printing of the Yiddish Bible with an additional Christian financial backer, Jan Otto van Halmael. Under that contract, van Halmael was to provide financing to print the Yiddish Bible as well as some Hebrew books.

Soon thereafter, on various dates between October 28, 1674, and August 23, 1675, Fayvesh obtained *haskamot* from the Ashkenazic and Sephardic rabbinic leadership

2. The Polish name for Pozen is Poznan. Bratslav is also called Breslov.

and lay councils of Amsterdam, this time expressly in favor of Fayvesh himself. The Amsterdam *haskamot* refer to the Council of Four Lands' *haskamot*, which Fayvesh submitted to the Amsterdam rabbis and councils in support of his petition. And like the Council of Four Lands, the Amsterdam rabbis prohibited other Jewish printers from printing a Yiddish Bible for a period of 10 years. Fayvesh also received a *haskama*, supporting those of the Amsterdam rabbis, from Meir Stern, a German rabbi whom Fayvesh had retained as his corrector. Stern's *haskama* was given on the condition that all proofs be submitted to him for editing and correction before the edition went to press.

Fayvesh's printing of Yekutiel Blitz's Yiddish translation began around January 1, 1675. It was supposed to be completed within a year, but by September 1675, less than half the initial print run had come off the press. Dissatisfied with the slow pace and quality of the printing, van Halmael insisted on bringing yet another partner into the venture: the renowned Sephardic publisher Joseph Athias, the first Jew to gain membership in the Amsterdam Booksellers and Printers Guild. Athias specialized in books for the non-Jewish world; his Hebrew publications were limited to those that Uri Fayvesh had not already published. But Athias had already achieved great commercial success in publishing editions of the Hebrew Bible in English and Spanish translation, as well as a Hebrew language edition with an introduction and annotations in Latin by the Christian Hebraicist Johannes Leusden. Van Halmael hoped that Athias would bring his considerable acumen in such endeavors to publishing the Yiddish Bible.[3]

Athias also agreed to make a substantial financial contribution to the venture. He pledged to pay paper costs and printers' wages up to a total of 12,000 guilders, of which he borrowed 5,000 guilders from van Halmael. Newly printed sheets were to be locked in a "neutral attic" for safekeeping and held as security for Athias's financial contribution. No one but Athias and van Halmael were to hold a key. The contract with Athias provided that Athias would receive one-third of the net profits, and that "around 6,300" copies of the Yiddish Bible would be printed.

That expanded partnership, too, was short-lived. By December 1675, Athias had become so unhappy with the quality of certain newly printed sheets that he suspended all payments, and all further printing, until Fayvesh corrected them. Apparently, the text had not been corrected after the first proof and was riddled with typographical errors. Unwilling to take on the cost of further corrections, Fayvesh charged that van Halmael had harassed him into accepting a disadvantageous agreement and that Athias was now blocking work even under that agreement. Fayvesh threatened to treat the entire contract as null and void, which led van Halmael and Athias to declare Fayvesh solely responsible for all consequences resulting from the rift. The partnership was officially dissolved on February 6, 1676.

Athias then seized the printed sheets that had been deposited in the "neutral attic" and presented them in support of his petition for an exclusive book privilege for the Yiddish Bible from the States of Holland and West Friesland. On March 18, 1676,

3. On Athias's English, Spanish, and Hebrew editions, see Haberman 1978: 294–300.

the States issued their 15-year exclusive privilege to Athias for the "Old Testament printed in the High German language in Hebrew characters, never before printed this way; which publication had already advanced to the fourth book of Moses, as emerged from the leaves shown to us." Armed with a book privilege under secular law, Athias and van Halmael proceeded with their own (now rival) edition of the Yiddish Bible. To complete the project, they hired a new translator, Joseph Witzenhausen, a typesetter from Witzenhausen in Hessen, Germany. They also hired away from Fayvesh the corrector and issuer of a *haskama* in favor of Fayvesh, Meir Stern.

Unwilling to cede the venture to his rivals, Fayvesh found yet another group of Christian investors. In April 1676, he entered into a publishing and financing contract with Willem Blaeu, an influential Amsterdam publisher and member of the city council, and the brothers Laurens and Justus Baeck, who were wealthy local merchants. Under that contract, the Christian partners would provide the financial backing for the project, while Fayvesh would print the Yiddish Bible and obtain a book privilege from secular authorities to prevent a rival publication of a similar edition, including Athias's edition in particular. Fayvesh would own one-quarter of the print run, but he could not sell his copies until his financiers had sold theirs.

In an attempt to acquire a secular book privilege, Fayvesh and his new partners brought a lawsuit challenging the privilege that the States of Holland and West Friesland had already granted to Athias for the Yiddish Bible.[4] They were unsuccessful. After prolonged litigation, the Dutch court apparently accepted Athias's argument that Fayvesh had bungled the work. The court was also convinced that, given Athias's demonstrated record of success in publishing and selling Bibles, a Yiddish Bible published by Athias would have a much better chance of selling, notwithstanding the rabbinic approbations and reprinting bans that Fayvesh had obtained.

By October 1676, Fayvesh's financial situation had greatly deteriorated. He was forced to cede title and control over his printing house to Willem Blaeu and Justus Baeck (Laurens had died), who had assumed Fayvesh's debts. Fayvesh could recover his printing establishment, including his inventory and machinery, only if he repaid his financiers the principal sum of his debt, with interest, within one year.

Around this time, Fayvesh also petitioned the Ashkenazic rabbinic court of Amsterdam for a ruling prohibiting Athias's translator, the Ashkenazi Joseph Witzenhausen, from continuing to prepare a Yiddish translation of the Bible in opposition to Fayvush's *haskamot*. On October 13, 1676, the Ashkenazic rabbis granted Fayvush's petition. Citing Fayvush's 10-year rabbinic reprinting ban, they enjoined Witzenhausen from preparing a translation for printing by a certain third party, a thinly veiled reference to Athias.

In the meantime, to further secure the prospects of recovering their investment, Fayvush's Christian partners, Blaeu and Baeck, petitioned King Jan Sobieski III of Poland for an exclusive privilege for the Yiddish Bible. Blaue and Baeck were granted a 20-year royal privilege for their "German Bible with Chaldean Characters," on October 17, 1677. The privilege made no mention of Uri Fayvesh or his translator, Yekutiel Blitz.

4. Fuks and Fuks-Mansfield 1987: 296–97.

By then, van Halmael, who had been a partner with both Fayvesh and Athias, had abandoned his rights in both editions, apparently by selling the sheets in his possession to Favyesh's new financier, Willem Blaeu. Athias, in turn, had a new financier of his own. Until 1672, Athias's principal financier had been his paper merchant, Christoffel van Gangelt. But when van Gangelt himself faced financial difficulties, he sold Athias's outstanding loans to his son-in-law, Josephus Deutz. Under their agreement, Deutz was to come into possession of all books that Athias had given to van Gangelt as security for payment of his debt. These included Athias's Yiddish Bible. In an apparent oblique reference to Athias's unbound copies, Deutz's records mention the deposit of "6,000 and more High-German Bibles," each worth three guilders, but still lacking the final sheets, for storage in his attic.

Finally, on September 21, 1677, and April 27, 1678, at its successive meetings at Jaroslaw and Lublin, the Council of Four Lands granted Joseph Athias a *haskama* prohibiting other printers from printing a Yiddish Bible for a period of 16 years from the issuance of the *haskama*. The Council also prohibited any Jew from assisting in any such publication. In its *haskama* for Athias, which appears in Illustration 5, the Council lauded Athias's Yiddish Bible for making it possible for women and young children to learn the Torah during times of leisure in the only language they could understand, while men (the Council supposed) would still study in the "difficult and holy language of Hebrew."

Athias's *haskama* appears to stand in direct opposition to the 10-year reprinting ban that the Council had purportedly granted in favor of Fayvesh's translator, Yekutiel Blitz, some six years earlier. Yet it makes no mention of that earlier *haskama*. Why would the Council so dramatically reverse course? It is possible that, as Athias charged, the twin *haskamot* purportedly obtained by Ḥaim Leib of Pila on behalf of Uri Fayvesh were out-and-out forgeries and thus that Leib was a swindler. However, that seems unlikely given subsequent laudatory references to Leib's character and his later involvement in the publishing and editing of Hebrew books. The ruling of the Ashkenazic rabbinic court of Amsterdam in Fayvesh's favor also weighs against that possibility, as does the Council's active support for Fayvesh to establish his printing house in Poland about 15 years later.

It appears, rather, that the Council now regarded its earlier *haskamot* as null and void. Perhaps that was because the Council believed that the Fayvesh-Blitz project had passed entirely into the hands of Favyvesh's Christian financiers—who had petitioned the King of Poland for a secular privilege in their name only.[5] Or, perhaps, Athias convinced the Council rabbis to disregard the *haskamot* they had granted six years earlier because Fayvesh had failed to print the Yiddish Bible in a reasonable time and, indeed, would be unable to do so during the four years remaining on his reprinting ban.

In any event, in late 1678—shortly after the Council had granted the second of its *haskamot* to Joseph Athias—Fayvesh and his partners finally succeeded in completing

5. Timm 1993: 55. On the other hand, the *haskama* in favor of Fayvesh is far more perfunctory than that given to Athias and states simply that Fayvesh's edition would be useful to men, women, children, and youths, without any differentiation among them. Unlike the Athias *haskama* and, for that matter, those of the Amsterdam rabbis in favor of Fayveh, the Council of Four Lands' *haskama* for Fayvesh makes no effort to justify awarding a *haskama* for a Yiddish-language Bible. Those characteristics do raise some questions about the *haskama*'s authenticity.

הסכמת כבוד האלופים הקצינים רוזני מנהיגי
ארבע ארצות יצ"ו בצירוף כבוד המאורות הגדולים הרבנים
מורי צדק בחרמות ושמתות ונדויים שלא ידפיס
שום אדם בעולם ספרי כ"ד תורה נביאים וכתובים בלשון אשכנז עד כלות ששה עשר
שנים מיום הדפסת כ"ד ספרים הנ"ל בלשון הנ"ל ע"י הנגיד השלם כמר יוסף עטיאש יצ"ו:

פה יערסלב

פה לובלין

Illustration 5
Council of Four Lands *Haskamot* for Athias Yiddish Bible, 1677 and 1678.
(courtesy National Library of Israel).

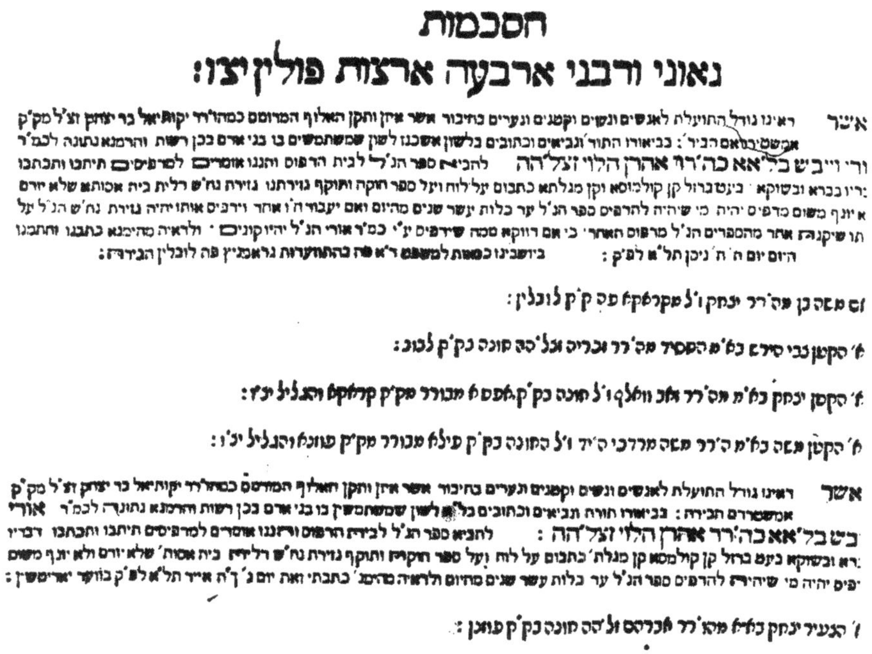
הסכמות
גאוני ורבני ארבעה ארצות פולין יצ״ו:

Illustration 6
Council of Four Lands *Haskama* as Altered in Fayvesh Yiddish Bible, 1678.
(courtesy National Library of Israel).

their Yiddish Bible, as translated by Yekutiel Blitz. Their edition included the Council of Four Lands' earlier *haskama* that had been issued in Blitz's name. But as printed by Fayvesh in his Yiddish Bible (and reproduced here in Illustration 6), the *haskama* states that it is issued in favor of Fayvesh, even if it still refers to the Blitz translation. Fayvesh, apparently, made that change on his own initiative. In his forward, he seeks to explain that, as originally issued, the *haskama* "contained by mistake an incorrect name, as is attested in the judgments I have obtained from the Amsterdam *geonim*." The Fayvesh-Blitz Bible was printed in approximately 6,000 copies.

The completed Athias-Witzenhausen Yiddish Bible was printed in 1679. It prominently displayed the *haskamot* that the Council of Four Lands awarded to Athias, insisting that Fayvesh's *haskama* from the Council of Four Lands was a forgery. The Athias-Witzenhausen Bible also contained 32 pages of the translation that Yekutiel Blitz had prepared for Uri Fayvesh: Athias had brazenly incorporated into his edition some of the sheets that had been deposited in the "neutral attic" during his partnership with Fayvesh.

Although Athias completed printing in 1679, few copies of his Bible were sold before 1686. It seems that Athias, seeing that most Amsterdam rabbis continued to support Fayvesh, initially decided to wait until the Amsterdam rabbis' 10-year reprinting ban in favor of Fayvesh had expired before putting his print run on the market. In 1686, however, Deutz's heirs began to sell their stock of Athias's Yiddish Bible to retailers. In turn, Athias printed new title pages, dated 1687, for his unbound inventory, and prepared to place his copies on the market as well. Athias apparently hoped to sell his copies in Germany; his new title pages bore a Latin dedication to the Elector of Brandenburg dated 1687.[6] But Athias was in such immediate need of cash that he soon offered his 3,000 Yiddish Bibles at auction in Amsterdam for a fraction of the original intended selling price.

Despite a large prospective readership, both editions of the Yiddish Bible were commercial failures. A number of factors contributed to their lack of commercial success. First, the combined 12,000-plus copies of the rival editions far exceeded what must have been the publishers' estimate of market demand for the Bible's first printing. Athias knew that Fayvesh and his partners intended to print some 6,300 copies. That was already a very large print run for the time, one expected to satisfy virtually all initial market demand for a Yiddish Bible.[7] Athias nevertheless printed a like number of copies of his own edition. He apparently banked on the assumption that he could wrestle market exclusivity out of his Council of Four Lands reprinting bans and Dutch book privilege. Yet as events actually transpired, large numbers of both editions of the Yiddish Bible haunted Amsterdam book auctions until well into the eighteenth century.

Second, neither edition was well suited to an Eastern European Jewish readership. The two translators, Blitz and Witzenhausen, were not great Hebrew scholars. Accordingly, in preparing their Yiddish translations, each made liberal use of Martin Luther's German translation and of the standard Dutch translation of the Bible. Further, although it was then standard practice to employ West European Yiddish in printing books, the Fayvesh and Athias Bibles contained instances of a distinctly Dutch-Northern German dialect of Yiddish. That dialect left, some passages incomprehensible to Jewish readers in Poland, although this is less the case for the Athias Bible as Athias hired the widely respected scholar, Shabbetai Bass of Prague, to correct Witzenhausen's translation by eliminating words in use by Dutch Jews that would not be understood by Jews of other countries. Both Blitz and Witzenhausen also sought dramatically to reform the traditional practice of translating Biblical passages into Yiddish; rather than meticulously translating word for word from the Hebrew original into the canonized, archaic Yiddish vocabulary for the Pentateuch known as *taytsch*, they changed the syntax and paraphrased where they deemed it necessary to produce an idiomatic text. Here, too, Witzenhausen ultimately cleaved closer to the traditional Eastern European practice, but, especially as Athias's Bible contained 32 pages that Athias had appropriated from Fayvesh, both Yiddish Bibles contained passages that would have appeared to their readership as unfamiliar and, possibly, inauthentic.[8]

Finally, the rival publishers might have been stymied by their conflicting privileges and reprinting bans. The privilege that Fayvesh's Christian partners obtained from the King of Poland likely imposed a significant constraint on Athias's efforts to export his Bibles into that country, as evidenced by Athias's plans to sell his copies in

6. Fuks and Fuks-Mansfield 1987: 297, 319.

7. By contrast, Athias's previous two printings of the Bible in Hebrew with Latin introduction and annotations, which Athias marketed to Christian Hebraicists as well as Jews, were in print runs of 3,000 and 5,000 copies. Haberman 1978: 294–96; Fuks and Fuks-Mansfield 1987: 292.

8. Aptroot 1989: 28–43, 333–34.

Germany. In that regard, Fayvesh's contract with a bookselling agent for the Polish market provided that the agent was to prevent "any Bibles of Christoffel van Gangelt and Josephus Deutz, printed by Athias here or elsewhere, from being imported and sold in Poland, but on the contrary make buyers and sellers pay the fines that had been specified by the aforesaid royal privilege." At the same time, the Council of Four Lands' reprinting ban in favor of Athias might have severely hindered Fayvesh and his partners in selling their Bibles to Polish Jews, even if we have a record that some copies of Fayvesh's edition—which, after all, bore the Council's purported *haskama* in favor of Fayvesh—were sold in Poland.

* * *

As the story of the rival Yiddish Bibles makes vividly clear, Jewish publishers faced perilous market uncertainty and, in central and western Europe, a heavy dependence on Christian financing, even at the apex of Hebrew and Yiddish printing in Amsterdam. Further, the need to obtain reprinting bans for each title from both the Council of Four Lands and the Amsterdam rabbis, and to hire agents for book sales in Poland-Lithuania, made the Hebrew and Yiddish book industry all the more precarious. It was for that reason—and, no doubt, others—that Uri Fayvesh relocated to Poland, where he established a new printing house in Zolkiew in 1692 with a privilege from King Jan Sobieski III and the support of the Council of Four Lands. In Poland, as we saw in the previous chapter, the Council strictly regulated competition in the Hebrew book trade to ensure that both Fayvesh and his principal rivals in Krakow and Lublin would enjoy a steady market for their books.

The Fayvesh-Athias dispute also sheds light on both the power and the limitations of the Council of Four Lands in the second half of the seventeenth century, a time when the Council's influence was near its height. When Fayvesh and Athias published Hebrew and Yiddish texts, the Jewish community of the Polish-Lithuanian Commonwealth was the largest in the world. Any significant publication that sought to reach that market required a *haskama* containing at least an approbation from the Council of Four Lands. And we see from the example of the Yiddish Bibles that the Council's *haskama* was perceived as a necessity not only for foundational rabbinic texts studied in *yeshivot*, but also for liturgical works in Yiddish aimed at a broad readership. At the same time, Jewish publishers in the centers of Hebrew printing in the Netherlands and Germany also regularly sought complementary *haskamot* from their local rabbinic authorities. They needed a set of rabbinic approbations and, preferably, reprinting bans in the jurisdiction where they produced their work even if their primary market was elsewhere, in the vast territory governed by the Council of Four Lands.[9]

Jewish publishers also sought privileges from secular rulers, although these were more commonly obtained from authorities in the place where the book was printed, not from the King of Poland. In the relatively unusual case in which the King of Poland issued a royal privilege for a book marketed by the Christian partners of a Jewish publisher, that privilege coexisted with any reprinting ban issued by the Council of Four

9. Schmelzer 2006: 51. With regard to the book trade, like other areas, the Council of Four Lands enjoyed considerable influence and moral authority, but not legal authority, beyond the borders of Poland. See, generally, Rosman 2010.

Lands. As we see from the Fayvesh-Athias case, the Council asserted the authority to issue a reprinting ban in favor of the rival of the printer who had obtained a privilege from the King of Poland. Of course, the Council could not countermand the royal privilege. But neither was the Council cowed by the contrary royal privilege issued to Fayvesh's Christian backers. Significantly, the king's power was itself circumscribed by the powerful Polish nobility, many of whom were protectors of Jews' communal autonomy in their respective territories. Hence, at the height of its power, the Council operated with authority over Jewish book distribution that, de facto, overlapped with that of secular powers, rather than being entirely subservient to those powers.

II. THE DEMISE OF JEWISH COMMUNAL AUTONOMY

A century later, however, that relative communal autonomy under the broad umbrella of the Council of Four Lands was no more. Plagued by increasing debt and division among its constituent local and regional councils, the Council of Four Lands met irregularly during the first half of the eighteenth century.[10] Then, on June 1, 1764, the Council was abolished by the Polish Sejm in a measure designed primarily to make tax collection more efficient by removing the mediation of an autonomous body that had applied some of the funds it collected to the internal needs of Jewish self-governance rather than paying the entire amount to the Polish treasury. Henceforth, taxes and other legal duties would fall directly on each individual Jewish subject, without the intermeddling of a communal authority that had acted as a buffer between Jewish subjects and the state.[11]

Shortly thereafter—and with even more monumental ramifications for the Jewish community—the Polish-Lithuanian Commonwealth was itself dismembered. Following three successive partitions, the first in 1772 and the last in 1795, the Commonwealth disappeared as an independent state. The heartland of European Jewry was now divided among the territories annexed by the Russian Empire, Austrian Empire, and Kingdom of Prussia.

The significance for Polish-Lithuanian Jewry was not merely that it no longer answered to the same overarching secular regime. Rather the partition of Poland also heralded the end of the semi-sovereign communal autonomy that had been central to European Jewish life throughout the medieval and early modern eras. Seventeenth-century Polish and Lithuanian Jewish communities had operated within a so-called "democracy of the nobility," characterized by a considerable dispersion of power among feudal magnates and the Crown. Although magnates and kings cabined the autonomy of Jewish lay and rabbinical councils to varying degrees, the rights of residence that they granted to Jews generally guaranteed the juridical authority of rabbinic courts and communal governing councils. Polish rulers were also dependent on Jewish governing bodies to collect taxes and manage internal affairs.[12] But by the end of the eighteenth century, that solicitude toward Jewish

10. Teller 2008: 355–56.
11. Bartal 2005: 29.
12. See generally Hundert 2006: 99–118.

communal autonomy had evaporated, together with the "democracy of the nobility" that anchored it—continuing the process begun by the Polish Sejm's abolition of the Council of Four Lands in 1764. In the partitioned territories of former Poland and elsewhere, the vast bulk of European Jewry now lived under monarchies that aspired to far more centralized administration and control, and that fluctuated between enlightened governance and reactionary absolutism.[13]

Beginning in the late eighteenth century, those monarchies, together with the various states and principalities of Germany and the territories conquered by Napoleon, systematically dismantled the juridical authority of Jewish community councils and rabbinic courts. They also eradicated rabbinic and lay authorities' primary tool of enforcement, the *ḥerem*, by either forbidding rabbis from issuing such a decree or sharply limiting its use.

Joseph II of Austria's Edicts of Toleration (Toleranzpatente), issued and applied in successive stages to Bohemia, Silesia, Vienna and lower Austria, Moravia, Hungary, and Galicia between 1781 and 1789, formed a model for the dismantling of Jewish communal autonomy. The Edicts contained various provisions designed to transform Jews into "useful subjects": Jews were restricted to "productive" occupations, Jewish children were required to receive a secular education, and Jewish young men were made subject to compulsory military service. Alongside these provisions, the Edicts also abolished the juridical autonomy of lay Jewish community councils in civil and criminal matters and eliminated rabbis' authority to adjudicate civil cases between Jews. They further prohibited rabbis from ordering the excommunication of those who flouted rabbinic decrees, the sole exception being the rabbis' authority to order *ḥerem* for failure to pay taxes, a vestigial rabbinic power that redounded to the benefit of the royal treasury.[14]

In Prussia, the 1797 General Regulation for Jews in South and New Eastern Prussia expressly abrogated rabbis' judicial authority in civil and religious matters. It also provided that Jews could not be punished for any offense they might commit against Jewish belief or ritual law within their own home. The Emancipation Edict of 1812 reiterated that Jewish communal bodies, rabbis, and community elders were prohibited from assuming any form of legal authority.[15]

In Russia, the Statute of 1804 abolished the exclusive jurisdiction of rabbinic courts in civil cases between Jews, providing that Jews "must in all lawsuits have recourse to the general courts." It also forbade rabbis from imposing a *ḥerem* or similar coercive measures. Jewish lay councils—the last vestige of juridical Jewish community autonomy—were formally abolished in 1822 in the Kingdom of Poland (a Russian protectorate established by the Congress of Vienna in 1815) and in 1844 in the Polish territories that had been directly absorbed into the Russian Empire.[16]

As we will now see, by the early nineteenth century, rabbis called upon to adjudicate disputes among printers of Jewish liturgical and rabbinic texts had to grapple with this stark new reality. As precarious as was the Hebrew book trade when

13. Bartal 2005: 24–25.
14. Miller 2011: 46–52.
15. Meyer 1997: 101.
16. Lederhendler 1989: 47–48, 180 n. 50.

Uri Fayvesh and Joseph Athias were in business, they could at least look to the Council of Four Lands to establish printing rights in the primary market for Hebrew and Yiddish books, and to exert great influence throughout the Ashkenazic world. But nineteenth century publishers and rabbis faced a far more treacherous landscape. By then, the major Jewish population centers of what had been the Polish Commonwealth were divided among three monarchies that imposed import barriers on Hebrew books and sharply curtailed Jewish communal autonomy, together with rabbis' state-backed juridical authority. These developments had a profound impact on Jewish life and—of particular relevance here—Jewish copyright law.

III. THE DISPUTE OVER *SEFER KROVOT*, THE "RODELHEIM *MAḤZOR*"

In the early nineteenth century, a set of holiday prayer books titled *Sefer Krovot Hu Maḥzor* became the subject of reprinting disputes that reached across the borders of German free cities and principalities into both the Habsburg Empire and the Kingdom of Prussia. The disputes erupted at the cusp of the monumental changes that brought the medieval and early modern governing institutions of European Jewry to an end. *Sefer Krovot* was printed in Rodelheim, a small town on the outskirts of Frankfurt am Main. It thus came to be known as the "Rodelheim *maḥzor*," meaning the holiday prayer book from Rodelheim. When *Sefer Krovot* was first printed, Jewish councils and rabbis still enjoyed juridical authority and autonomy, including the power of excommunication, in most of Germany. By contrast, the Habsburg Empire and Kingdom of Prussia—where, respectively, a Christian and a Jewish publisher reprinted the Rodelheim *maḥzor* without its author's permission—had already abolished those institutional prerogatives.

A. *Sefer Krovot*

In 1798, the renowned Hebrew grammarian and Masoretic scholar Wolf Heidenheim (1757–1832) established a Hebrew and German printing house in Rodelheim with the financial backing of a Jewish partner, "an energetic business man" named Barukh Baschwitz.[17] The pair obtained a license to establish the press from the local count, Graf Vollrath of Solms-Rodelheim. They named it the Orientalische und Occidentalische Buchdruckerei (the Oriental and Occidental Printing House).

Heidenheim published on a wide variety of subjects. But, like most Hebrew presses in Germany in that era, the publication of prayer books was his bread and butter.[18] *Sefat Emet*, his small prayer book for times other than holidays, went through more than 150 printings, and was long "distinguished for its correctness and typographical

17. Seligson 1906: 319; Temkin 2007: 763; Feffer 1956–1957.
18. Prayer books of all types made up about half of the production of Hebrew presses in Germany through the end of the eighteenth century. Breuer 1996: 226.

beauty."[19] He also printed a larger prayer book, *Safa Berura*, with a German translation in Hebrew characters.

Sefer Krovot Hu Maḥzor, the work that sparked the disputes described in this chapter, was a nine-volume edition of the *maḥzor*, the prayer book used for holiday worship over the annual cycle of the Jewish calendar. Like *Safa Berura*, it featured a translation of the Hebrew text into High German, but with the German transliterated in Hebrew characters. The holiday liturgy in its original Hebrew appeared alongside the German translation.

Heidenheim set the standard for high quality, typographically precise editions of traditional prayer books. Yet, as an early admirer of the *Bi'ur*, the German translation of the Bible and rabbinic commentary by the leading modernist reformer and polymath Moses Mendelssohn, Heidenheim also exemplified the complex brew of traditional rabbinic Judaism and modernist reform that characterized the late eighteenth- and early nineteenth-century proto-Haskalah (the Haskalah being often translated as the "Jewish Enlightenment").[20] *Sefer Krovot*, the first volume of which was published in 1800, featured a preface, interspersed with poetry by Solomon Dubno, a proto-*maskilic* Bible scholar and Hebrew poet who had partnered with Mendelssohn on the *Bi'ur* and had encouraged Heidenheim to produce his own critical edition of the Pentateuch.[21] In 1812, Heidenheim published *Divre Iggeret*, a tractate authored by the reformist rabbi Menaḥem Mendel Steinhardt. In that work Steinhardt defended a highly controversial ruling, which he and his fellow reformists at the Jewish consistory of Westphalia had issued, permitting Ashkenazic Jews to eat legumes on Passover. In his forward to Steinhardt's tract, Heidenheim expressed his own approval of the reformist school that the Westphalia consistory had established in Kassel. In his 1831 edition of the prayer book *Siddur Li-Venei Yisrael*, which presented his translation in German letters for the first time, Heidenheim omitted certain prayers and included a preface by the fervent proponent of "enlightened" education and theological reform, Michael Creizenach, which presented a historical and critical analysis of the prayers and advocated gradually modifying them in light of changing circumstances.

Sefer Krovot, of which we see the title page in Illustration 7, reflected Heidenheim's considerable investment of time and study. To compile the nine-volume *maḥzor*, Heidenheim did not simply reprint earlier editions or rely on the customary liturgy of his community. Instead, he produced a critical edition by scouring previous volumes and going back to the most ancient manuscripts he could locate, including one dating back to 1258. The project expanded beyond the liturgy practiced in neighboring Frankfurt to include notes annotating the traditions followed by Ashkenazic congregations throughout the world.[22] Indeed, Heidenheim produced two parallel

19. Temkin 2007: 763.

20. This paragraph draws on Kohler 2012: 39; Meyer 1988: 32–33; Reif 1995: 263–64; and Temkin 2007: 763. Moses Mendelssohn (1729–1796) was a German Bible scholar, translator, and leading proponent of combining Enlightenment philosophy with traditional Judaism.

21. Dubno discontinued his work with Mendelssohn before the *Bi'ur* was completed, possibly under pressure from traditionalist friends. But Mendelssohn nevertheless gave high praise to Dubno's work in his introduction to the *Bi'ur*. Levinger 2007: 34. On Heidenheim's relationship with Dubno, see Seligson 1906: 319.

22. Temkin 2007: 763.

Illustration 7
Sefer Krovot Hu Maḥzor Title Page Heidenheim edition, 1800.
(courtesy National Library of Israel).

editions: one following the "Ashkenazic" liturgical rite—that traditionally followed in Germany and northwestern Europe—and the other following the Polish rite, which included local customs originally introduced into the worship service by Jewish communities of Poland-Lithuania and which had been brought to Germany by the many Polish Jews who migrated westward in the seventeenth and eighteenth centuries.[23]

Bringing the *Sefer Krovot* manuscript to print was a substantial undertaking spanning several years. The nine volumes of the Ashkenazic rite edition were printed serially between 1800 and 1805. The Polish rite edition was printed between 1804 and 1807.

The liturgical value of *Sefer Krovot* to Heidenheim's contemporaries emerged from the numerous innovations that he pioneered. Most important, *Sefer Krovot* presented the first complete German translation of the holiday worship service—transliterated in Hebrew characters—to be published. The ability to read and understand Hebrew was rapidly diminishing among German Jews of the early nineteenth century even if worship services were still conducted in that language.[24] German Jews spoke and read Western Yiddish, a dialect of German that included many Hebrew words and was written with Hebrew characters. Many could also read High German when written in Hebrew characters, although few spoke High German fluently or were able to read in the German alphabet. *Sefer Krovot* thus enabled German Jews to understand the lexical meaning of the Hebrew liturgy that constituted their holiday worship service. *Sefer Krovot* also featured Heidenheim's textual corrections, based on his historical investigation of previous Hebrew editions published in Italy and Germany, and Heidenheim's own commentary, extending both to substantive explanations and descriptions of textual variations that he uncovered. The work went through numerous printings, in both the Ashkenazic and Polish rite editions, throughout the nineteenth and even into the twentieth century.[25]

B. Rabbinic Reprinting Bans for *Sefer Krovot*

Heidenheim obtained the *haskamot* of eight prominent rabbis for the first parallel editions of *Sefer Krovot*. With the exception of *haskamot* from Solomon Hirschell, chief rabbi of Great Britain, and Arieh Leib Breslau, chief rabbi of Rotterdam, all were issued by rabbis of principalities and free cities in Germany or Denmark. Evidently, Heidenheim's target market for his *maḥzor* consisted of communities of German-speaking Jews of north-central Europe. The absence of *haskamot* from rabbis in Prussia or Austria suggests that, given severe restrictions on the import of Jewish books into those territories, those German-speaking lands were, at best, secondary markets for Heidenheim, primarily served by copies that would be smuggled across the border.

23. On the westward migration of Polish Jews, see Shulvass 1971.
24. Meyer 1997: 92–95.
25. Seligson 1906: 320; Breuer 1996: 226; Temkin 2007: 763.

Heidenheim obtained four *haskamot*, including approbations and reprinting bans, prior to commencing printing. They appear in the Ashkenazic rite edition's first volume, the prayer book for the first six days of Passover, printed in 1800. Of the subsequent volumes printed in 1800, the volume for the first day of Rosh Hashana contains a note apprising the reader that the pertinent approbations and reprinting bans have already been published in the first volume, but the respective volumes for the seventh and eighth days of Passover and for Yom Kippur do not contain *haskamot* or any reference to those printed in the earlier volume. The four additional *haskamot* appear, respectively, in volumes printed in 1803 and 1805, but all refer back to the four *haskamot* printed in the first volume, and purport to apply to the entire nine-volume edition.

Sefer Krovot's primary *haskamot*, those appearing in the first volume printed in 1800, were issued, respectively, by Noaḥ Tzvi Ḥaim Berlin of Altona, Naftali Hirsch Katzenellenbogen of Frankfurt an der Oder, Arieh Leib Breslau of Rotterdam, and Moshe Tuvia Sontheim of Hanau. Following effusive praise for Heidenheim's piousness, knowledge, and meticulousness and the high quality of his and his partner's work, each pronounced a broad, 25-year reprinting ban. For example, Berlin's *haskama*, which appears in Illustration 8 below, forbade wrongful competition by reprinting, without the author's permission, one or more volumes of the *maḥzor* with or without the German translation or of the German translation standing alone, including with small changes in language, title, or quantity or quality of the text. Berlin's *haskama* likewise forbade any participation with non-Jews in printing such works. Violators of the reprinting ban, his *haskama* stated, would be subject to *ḥerem*. The other three *haskamot* were similar; indeed, Sontheim's contained some of the same formulaic language as Berlin's. Of note, Breslau added that it was also forbidden to buy or sell any *maḥzor* edition printed by a non-Jew that a Jew would be forbidden to print under the reprinting ban. Katzenellenbogen stated, similarly, that it was forbidden to buy any *maḥzor* printed in violation of the reprinting ban. Breslau also highlighted the importance of Heidenheim's *maḥzor*, observing that most European Jews need German translations in order to understand the holiday liturgy.

Pinḥas Horowitz (1730–1805), the chief rabbi of Frankfurt am Main, must have been among the first rabbis whom Heidenheim asked for a *haskama*. Horowitz was widely respected.[26] Further, at that time, Frankfurt was home to the third largest Jewish community among major cities in the German-speaking world, following Prague and Hamburg.[27] Frankfurt was also the primary market for Hebrew books printed in neighboring Rodelheim.

Horowitz gave his approbation and reprinting ban to *Sefer Krovot*, but not until 1803, three years after its initial volumes were printed. Horowitz's delay might have resulted from his concern that Heidenheim's German translation of the prayer book would serve a reformist agenda, similar to that of Moses Mendelssohn's German translation of the Pentateuch and rabbinic commentaries. Horowitz vigorously opposed the Haskalah

26. Y. Horowitz 2007b: 540–41.
27. In 1800, some 3,000 Jews resided in Frankfurt am Main, making up 7.5 percent of the city's population. Jersch-Wenzel 1997b: 55.

הסכמות וחרמות מגאוני הזמן נר"ו ·

מה יפו כעמי החכם. השלם המדקדק הגדול ה"ה התורני המופלא הר"ר
ואלך כ"ר שמשון היידנהיים אשר כל רז מרזי החכמה הנפלאה
הואת לא אנס לו, ואשר לו יד ושם בספרי ומדרשי חכמיט ז"ל אשר
באמלעותם חפן ס' ביהו הללית לבאר באר היטיב בלשון לח ונאה תפלות
וכיוטים יסדום באמונתם קדמונינו נוחי נפש, אשר ברכות השנים ובהעתקם
מכתב לכתב ומדפוס לדפוס כבו פניהם פרולים, ולאין מספר העלו קמשוגים,
ולהראות הוה חכנו אלקי' בחכמה ומדע, בהימן ודרדע, ולו יאתה לקרבה
אל המלאכה ולעשות אותה. ומבלעדי וה לשוני ממהרת לדבר לחות גם בלשון
אשכנו למען העתק החפלית והכיוטי' בלשון נאה ומהודר, ולהבינם לאינם
בקיאים בלשוננו העברית ולהורים מה ידברו, לא כהמעתקים הראשוני'
האשכנזים אשר בלעגי שפה וכמעט בלשון אחרת ידברו אל העם הזה, ותהי
להם חוות הכל כדכרי הספר החתום. והנה הלג לפני החכם המדקדק הנ"ל כרך
אחד מפיוטי המועדים אשר הדפיס בבית ועל הוללויתו המרוניו, ועברתי עליו
ומלאתי בתוכו את שאהבה נפשי, חדוו לא הכדיל תירוש המשמח אלקים ואכשים,
והטיח לכגדי רקנת לבבו מעובבני דברים אים מחת רעהו ויאכלו אחרי פרי
וגיעו, והטיתי אני למלאות בקשתו ולבלאת חוק מגדרי, ולהטיל גזרת כחש
על איש או אשה אשר יערב לבבו להסיא גבולו ולהדפיס אפילו כוך אחד או
יותר מספרי המחוורים עם הביחור ותרגום אשכנו שלו או עם כניאור לבד
או עם תרגו' אשכנו' לבד כן בל"ח והן בכל לשון ואפילו עם קלת שינו
בכמותו או באיכותו בשיכוי לשון או בשיכוי שם, כן ע"י גירי דילי' והן ע"י
הסתחפו' עם אחרי' אשר לא מבני ישראל המה, והעונר על זה להדפים
כרך אחד או יותר מהמחוורים הכ"ל על אחד מן האופנים בלתי ידיעת
והסכמת המחבר מהיום עד תום כ"ה שנים, יהי' כלבד בעונש חרם
ובלטותא דרבנן, ולהשומעים יונעם ותבוא אליהם ברכת טוב. כ"ד הכותב
והקותס פה ק"ק אלטונא ר"ח אדר תק"ס לפ"ק.

הק' נח חיים צבי בן מוהר"ר אברהם
מאיר ברלין ז"ל הקוונה פה ק"ק תק"ו יע"א.

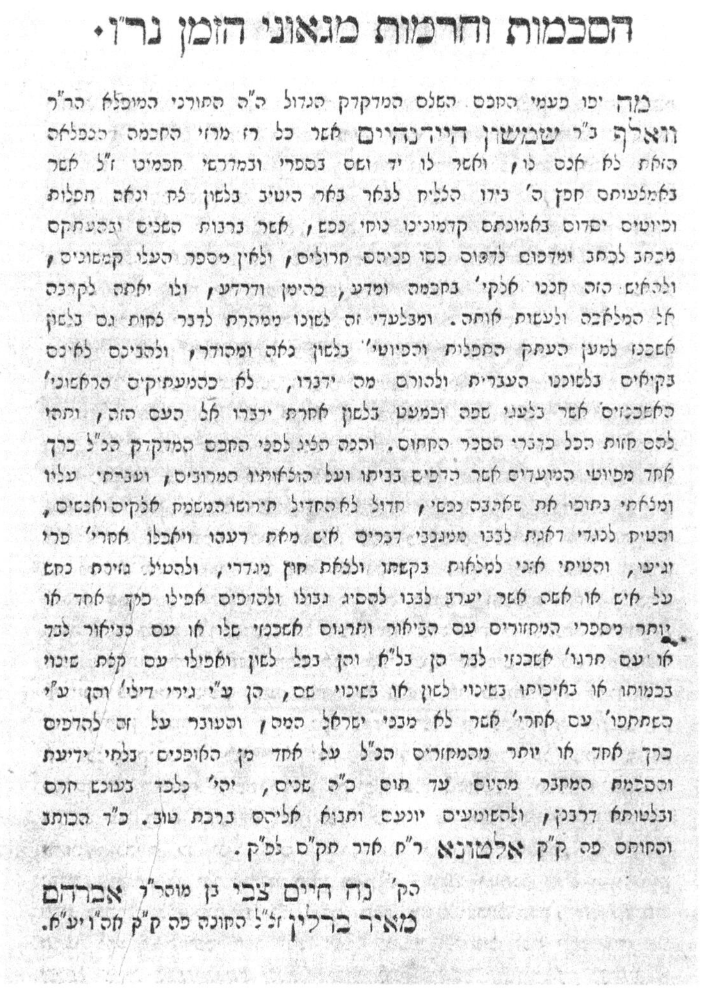

Illustration 8
Noaḥ Tzvi Ḥaim Berlin *Haskama* for Rodelheim *Maḥzor*, 1800.
(courtesy National Library of Israel).

movement and, in 1782, had famously preached a sermon denouncing Mendelssohn's *Bi'ur* as heretical. One might expect that the traditionalist rabbi would have held a similarly dim view of a German translation of the prayer book, especially given that such translations were a much-trumpeted, favored project of the proto-*maskilim* in Mendelssohn's circle.[28]

Whatever might have been his initial misgivings, Horowitz eventually gave his imprimatur to Heidenheim's German translation of the *maḥzor*. But before doing so he likely insisted upon inspecting the volumes that had already been printed. Horowitz

28. On the *maskilic* celebration of German language prayer books, see Gries 2007: 140–44.

also, no doubt, looked to the eminent rabbis who had already granted their *haskamot* in deciding to issue his own. Presumably, he relied particularly on the *haskama*, dated 19 Nissan 5560 (March 16, 1800), of Arieh Leib Breslau, whom Horowitz held in high regard as a Talmudic authority and to whom Horowitz repeatedly referred questions of Jewish law.[29] At any rate, following on Horowitz's approbation and those of the other Ashkenazic sages upon whom he relied, rabbinic traditionalists came to celebrate Heidenheim's *maḥzor* as a critical bulwark against reform, as a vital tool for enabling the mass of European Jews to understand the holiday liturgy while continuing to recite it in Hebrew. Decades later, in a responsum devoted to Jewish copyright law that we will shortly examine, the ardent traditionalist Moses Sofer lauded Heidenheim: "And were it not for him, our liturgical poems would have already been buried underground and, as is well understood, would not have been recited by these generations."[30]

Like the prior *haskamot* for *Sefer Krovot*, Horowitz's *haskama* and *ḥerem*, dated 12 Elul 5563 (August 30, 1803), extends to both Wolf Heidenheim and his partner, Barukh Baschwitz. Horowitz prefaced his statement by declaring that he was joining with rabbis who earlier gave their *haskamot* to Heidenheim's *maḥzor*. Horowitz then praised Heidenheim as a rabbi of great punctiliousness and lauded the fruits of Heidenheim's and Baschwitz's holy work. Finally, Horowitz pronounced a sweeping reprinting ban. He forbade anyone, on pain of *ḥerem*, from engaging in wrongful competition by printing or causing to be printed the Heidenheim-Baschwitz *maḥzorim*, with the commentaries and German translations, or the commentaries or German translations by themselves, whether in whole or in part. That ban, stated Horowitz, was to remain in force for the 25-year period set forth by the rabbis who had already issued reprinting bans.

When Horowitz died in 1805, his son Tzvi Hirsch Horowitz (1730–1817) succeeded him as rabbi of Frankfurt.[31] On September 7, 1807, the younger Horowitz issued a warning to Jews not to purchase copies of an edition of Heidenheim's *maḥzor* that a certain unnamed publisher had reprinted without Heidenheim's permission. Horowitz reiterated that Jews who violated the rabbinic bans issued for the *maḥzor*, particularly that of his father, would be subject to excommunication. Heidenheim published Tzvi Hirsch Horowitz's warning in subsequent editions of his *maḥzor*, together with the approbations and reprinting bans from the first edition, beginning with the respective second editions of the Ashkenazi and Polish rites, both printed in 1811.

C. The First Unauthorized Reprinting: Vienna

As Tzvi Hirsch Horowitz's 1807 warning made painfully clear, Heidenheim's *maḥzor* was reprinted without his permission almost before the ink was dry on his first edition—this despite the reprinting bans that Heidenheim had obtained. The "certain publisher" to whom Horowitz, no doubt, referred was the Viennese Christian printer,

29. "Breslau, Aryeh Löb Ben Ḥayyim," *The Jewish Encyclopedia* (1906).
30. Moses Sofer (1762–1839), *Responsa Ḥatam Sofer*, Ḥoshen Mishpat, No. 79.
31. Y. Horowitz 2007c: 545.

Anton Schmid. Schmid had established a Hebrew press in Vienna in the last decade of the eighteenth century under a royal license to print Hebrew books. Among his first publications was a 1795 edition of Mendelssohn's *Biur*, an undertaking which, above and beyond his reprinting of Heidenheim's *maḥzor*, would not likely have endeared him to rabbinic traditionalists. Schmid typically hired proto-*maskilim* from Galicia as his typesetters, editors, and correctors. He arranged special permits for them to live in Vienna, a city where Jews were otherwise forbidden to reside.[32]

When Schmid entered the Hebrew book trade, Austrian law forbade Jews from printing books. A royal ordinance enacted in 1800 prohibited Jews from importing Hebrew books as well. Yet, contrary to some commentators' descriptions, Schmid did not enjoy an absolute monopoly over the Hebrew book trade in Austria. He faced several rival Christian printers of Hebrew books in Vienna.[33] In addition, a number of Jewish-owned printing houses were active in Lemberg, the administrative center of the formerly Polish territory of Galicia, which the Austrian Empire had annexed as part of the first partition of Poland in 1772 and to which the prohibition on Jewish-owned printing houses did not apply. Nevertheless, Schmid profited handsomely from the regulatory restrictions on competition imposed by imperial authorities, particularly the prohibition on importing Hebrew books.[34] His Hebrew printing press reached a wide Jewish market, throughout the Austrian Empire and beyond. Over time, Schmid became a leading publisher of traditional rabbinic and liturgical texts, as well as *maskilic* works. As such, he garnered considerable acclaim among his Jewish readership.

Schmid published his reprinted edition of Heidenheim's *Sefer Krovot Hu Maḥzor*—without Heidenheim's permission—in 1806. Under Austrian law, that reprinting was perfectly legal. In Austria, indeed, such reprintings were actively encouraged. As implemented by Maria Theresa and reinforced by Joseph II, it was imperial policy to promote the Austrian book trade by allowing unhindered reprinting of foreign books and, at certain times, even prohibiting the importation of original foreign editions in order to protect the reprinters' domestic market.[35] Emperor Joseph II's Decree of January 13, 1781, which remained in force until 1837, provided, accordingly, that "the reprinting of approved foreign-published books is to be granted freely to every book printer as a commercial operation, even if exactly the same work happens to have already been (re-) published by one or several native book printers."[36] Joseph II's policies contributed to the resurgence of Austria's book trade and, in particular, to a flourishing reprint industry. Much to the consternation of publishers in other countries, Austrian reprinters served not only the domestic Austrian market, but reached

32. Wasserman 2007: 145; Wistrich 1989: 136–37.

33. In particular, Joseph Hraszansky, using a Frankfurt am Main font, opened a Hebrew press in Vienna, and printed a number of foundational rabbinic texts, including an edition of the *Babylonian Talmud* between 1791 and 1797 and the *Shulḥan Arukh* in 1810. See Lehman 2007: 523.

34. Grunwald 1936: 248–49, 501 (listing some of Schmid's many Hebrew publications).

35. Johns 2009: 13; Kawohl 2008a; Whittman 2004.

36. Austrian Statutes on Censorship and Printing, Vienna (1781), in *Primary Sources on Copyright (1450-1900)*.

readers across the Austrian border as well. Schmid's reprinted edition of *Sefer Krovot* was but a small part of that vibrant "pirate" industry, authorized and encouraged by imperial decree.

Heidenheim nonetheless responded aggressively to attempt to stifle Schmid's reprinted edition (of which the title page of the second reprint edition appears in Illustration 9). Having procured Tzvi Hirsch Horowitz's directive specifically prohibiting the purchase of such a reprint, Heidenheim turned to leading rabbinic authorities in the Austrian Empire. He (or, more likely, Horowitz on his behalf) sent the rabbis a written appeal, imploring them to enforce the rabbinic reprinting bans against any Jew who would sell, purchase, or otherwise lend assistance to Schmid's reprint.

Upon learning of Heidenheim's appeal, Schmid complained to the Austrian authorities, and on November 12, 1807, the Chancellor's Court ordered that the rabbinic reprinting ban for Heidenheim's *maḥzor* be suppressed. The Court's decree, issued to its regional offices in Bohemia, Moravia, Galicia, and elsewhere, declared:

> News has been received that after the domestic book publisher Schmid, with authorization from the state censor, reissued the Jewish prayer book and also printed a well-advised German translation in Hebrew letters prepared by a Rodelheim Jew by the name of Heidenheim, on behalf of the aforementioned Jew Heidenheim—who earlier had received an exclusive privilege to print this book from the Chief Rabbi of Frankfurt—an appeal to the Jewish people has been issued, and has been sent to some of the most respected rabbis in the Austrian monarchy by means of the postal service, proclaiming that several rabbis—and most notably the Chief Rabbi of Frankfurt, Pinḥas Levy Horowitz—pronounced a great excommunication order against the later publisher of the Jewish prayer book and his coworkers and assistants.
>
> The regional offices shall draw the rabbis' attention to this absurd measure so that if they encounter one of these writings, they will suppress and make no use of it, and in case any of their fellow believers have questions, they shall instruct them about the unlawfulness of such a measure, and they shall in no way dare to enforce any part of the excommunication order.[37]

On May 25, 1808, the Chancellor's Court took its ruling a step further: it commanded its regional offices to "prepare a specific circular to give notice, and in particular to direct the rabbis to clearly and emphatically explain the same in the synagogues of their fellow believers, that every excommunication order is not in force so long as the government does not recognize its legal force, and that whoever disseminates such an excommunication order by his hand, will pay a money penalty of 50 thalers, or based upon the circumstances will face corporal punishment."[38]

Foremost among the Austrian rabbis who had received Heidenheim's appeal—and the subsequent author of seminal responsa concerning Jewish copyright law

37. *Urkunden und Akten zur Geschichte der Juden in Wien* 1918: 172–73. The English translation is by Scott Dewey.

38. *Urkunden und Akten zur Geschichte der Juden in Wien* 1918: 173–74. The English translation is by Scott Dewey.

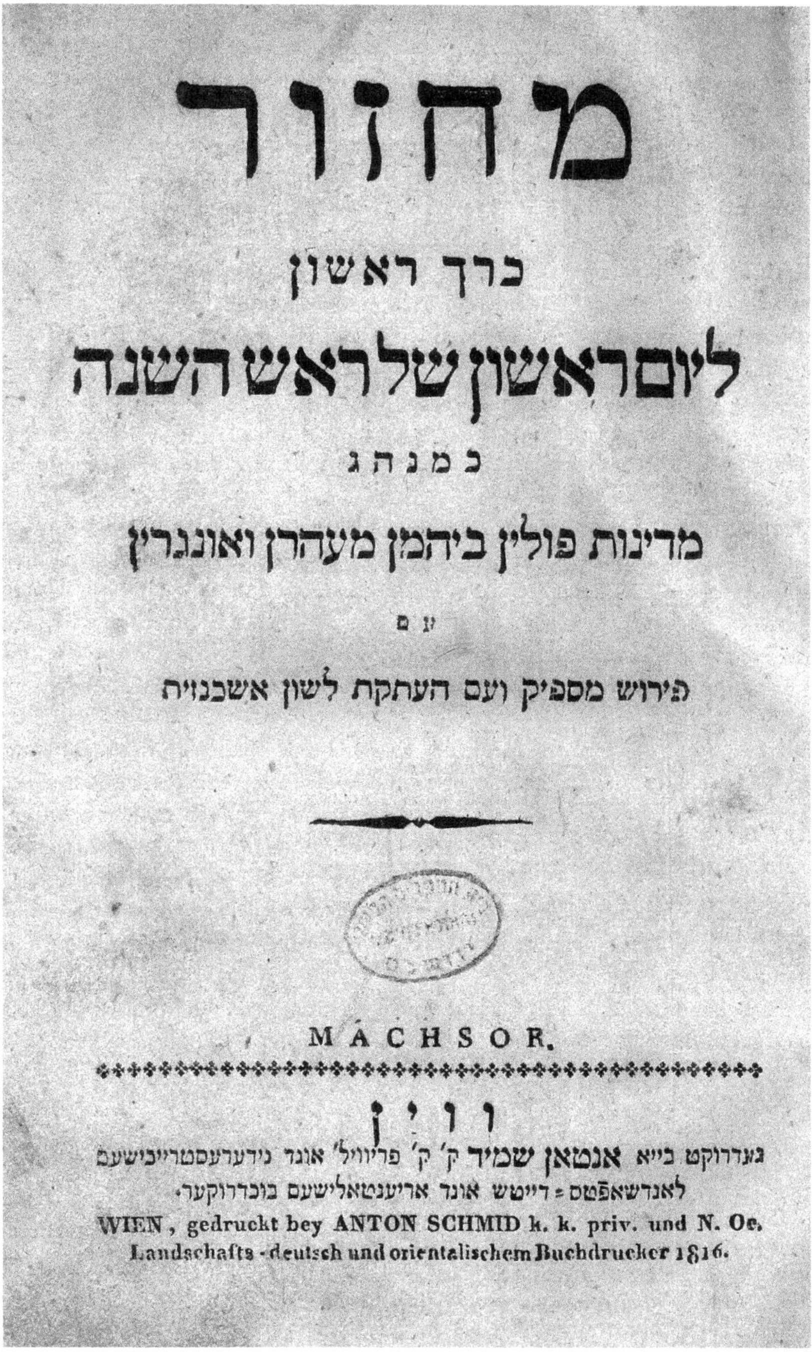

מחזור

כרך ראשון

ליום ראשון של ראש השנה

כמנהג

מדינות פולין ביהמן מעהרן ואונגרין

עם

פירוש מספיק ועם העתקת לשון אשכנזית

MACHSOR.

ווין

געדרוקט בייא אנטאן שמיד ק׳ ק׳ פריוויל׳ אונד נידערעסטרייכישעם
לאנדשאפטס = דייטש אונד אריענטאלישעם בוכדרוקער.

WIEN, gedruckt bey ANTON SCHMID k. k. priv. und N. Oe.
Landschafts-deutsch und orientalischem Buchdrucker 1816.

Illustration 9
Sefer Krovot Hu-Maḥzor Title Page, Anton Schmid 2nd Edition, 1816.
(courtesy National Library of Israel).

discussed below—was Mordekhai Banet (1753–1829).[39] Banet served for 40 years, beginning in 1789, as chief rabbi of Moravia, head of the rabbinic court of Nikolsburg (now Mikulov), and head of Nikolsburg's large and prestigious *yeshiva*. Like his mentor, Yeḥezkel Landau of Prague, Banet both excelled in traditional rabbinic scholarship and served as an outspoken presence in matters of public policy. He was a highly respected authority, whose influence extended well beyond Moravia.

Although Banet championed the rabbinic tradition, he also exhibited a moderate pragmatism towards the Haskalah, secular study, and the dictates of imperial authorities. A leading commentator has aptly put it: as "Moravian chief rabbi, [Banet] chose his battles wisely."[40] Banet resolutely opposed reformist rabbis' attempts to invoke halakhic precedent to justify lenient deviations from traditional legal norms, including eating legumes on Passover, travelling on the Sabbath, and eating sturgeon, a fish traditionally deemed unkosher. He also firmly rejected liturgical reform, most famously joining with some 20 of his traditionalist rabbinic colleagues in voicing staunch opposition to reformists' introduction of vernacular prayers and organ music in the Hamburg Temple.[41] Yet in other instances, Banet exhibited sympathies that some viewed as proto-*maskilic*. He spoke German, had considerable knowledge in several secular sciences, and encouraged others to attain certain types of secular knowledge so long as it remained subordinate to Talmudic study. It was even reported that Banet "would read the Bible with the German translation of Moses ben Menahem [Mendelssohn] and the commentaries of the Biurists."[42] Indeed, Banet gave his approbation to a new edition of Mendelssohn's *Bi'ur*, published in Vienna in 1817–1818.

Further, when confronting efforts by *maskilim* and the absolutist state to modernize Jewish education, Banet preferred compromise, engagement, and subtle resistance over open opposition. Banet, for example, accepted that he was powerless to block the Austrian government's policies requiring that Jews study secular subjects and that Jews' "ethical" study must be radically reformed to further the imperial goal of educating Jews to be "useful subjects." Rather than flat out oppose those directives, Banet sought to bring whatever traditionalist influence he could on government-approved textbooks.[43]

Banet's handling of Heidenheim's appeal to prohibit Jews from buying or selling the Schmid reprint exemplified his staunch support for traditionalism, coupled

39. My discussion of Mordekhai Banet draws on Miller 2010: 60–86; Ferziger 2008: 118–19.

40. Miller 2011: 60.

41. See Katz 1998b: 215–30.

42. Miller 2011: 80.

43. In that regard, Banet reluctantly gave his approbation to two decidedly modernist textbooks of the Jewish religion, *Imre Shefer* (published in 1808) and *Bnei-Tzion* (published in 1812). The textbooks were modeled on Christian catechisms and were authored by Herz Homberg, a *maskilic* scholar and Austrian government functionary, who was widely detested in the Jewish community. But, as a signal to the Jewish community of the half-hearted nature of his support for the latter book, he gave his approbation in German. In addition, 10 years later, Banet promoted a new catechism, authored by his son, which

with pragmatic compromise when necessary. He initially backed Heidenheim—and rabbinic authority over the Hebrew book trade—by publicizing the rabbinic reprinting bans.[44] But soon thereafter, in line with the Chancellor's Court decree and the Emperor's general prohibition on rabbinic enforcement of *ḥerem*, Banet was arrested by the Austrian authorities in Bruenn, the administrative capital of Moravia, and compelled to rescind his endorsement of the bans. As Banet later explained in one of his responsa on Jewish copyright law:

> And I tested this thing when the gentleman-publisher Schmid printed the Rodelheim *maḥzorim*. When I disseminated the bans of the sages on the buyers and the dealers to deter [their buying and selling of the work], the aforementioned publisher brought us up in court before the authorities in my country, in the city of Bruenn. I was positioned in a grave dispute from morning until evening and they spoke harshly to me and they saw my activities as wrongs and in this way said I was rebelling against the government, until the mercy of God came upon me and I was released in peace on condition that "the mouth that forbids will be the mouth that permits." And so I did . . .[45]

Banet, indeed, duly complied with the terms of release by affirmatively rescinding his support for the reprinting bans. In a letter addressed to Moses Loeb Tziltz (d. 1831), a rabbinic scholar and judge who served under Banet on the Nikolsburg rabbinic court, Banet affirmed:

> The rabbinical sages of Ashkenaz have granted an approbation and ban to all of the *maḥzorim* printed in Rodelheim and translated into the vernacular. And it is elucidated on the title page by the wise man, W. Heidenheim, that no other person may use the same format for twenty-five years; and I have said, lest there, therefore, be among the children of our nation who reside under the merciful wings of His Majesty, the Emperor, a man or woman whose heart will accordingly not wish to buy the *maḥzorim* that are being printed in the city of Vienna by Mr. Anton Schmid, that I hereby invalidate and declare that all of the words regarding bans and curses which have been issued, and which will be issued in the future by rabbis in other countries upon the next printing, are to be deemed nonexistent. . . .[46]

As I elucidate presently, Banet presented several halakhic justifications for his newly discovered position that the rabbinic reprinting bans issued for Heidenheim's

adhered far more closely to rabbinic tradition. Miller 2011: 72–76. On Homberg, see Wistrich 1989: 17–18.

44. Banet might have been predisposed to lending support to the Heidenheim appeal. Among his early mentors was the Ḥasidic master Shmuel Shmelke Horovitz of Nikolsburg, Tzvi Hirsch Horowitz's uncle and Pinḥas Horowitz's older brother.

45. Mordekhai Banet, *Responsa Parshat Mordekhai*, No. 8.

46. The letter is reproduced in *Milei D'Avot*, pt. 1, Ḥoshen Mishpat, ¶ 3 (Ezekiel Menashe Horowitz 1924).

maḥzor in other countries are "to be deemed nonexistent." It is obvious, however, that Banet's position was heavily colored by his painful realization of the profound limits of rabbinic authority under Habsburg rule. Indeed, Banet's halakhic justifications for holding rabbinic reprinting bans unenforceable expressly reflect his pragmatic understanding of the limits of rabbinic authority in a world of vanishing juridical autonomy for rabbinic courts and of secular governments' restrictions on the Hebrew book trade.

Yet, despite Austrian authorities' abrogation of the rabbinic reprinting bans and Banet's coerced about-face, the initial publication of the bans in Austria seems to have produced its desired effect: many Jews refrained from purchasing Schmid's reprinted edition. As a result, before issuing his next reprint edition of Heidenheim's *maḥzor*, Schmid took the trouble and money to acquire the rights of Heidenheim's (now former) partner, Barukh Baschwitz, in *Sefer Krovot*.[47] Evidently, Mordekhai Banet lent his assistance to Schmid in that endeavor. Schmid's next edition, printed in 1816, featured a letter from Banet, dated January 11, 1816, and no doubt intended for publication.[48] Banet's letter, which, as printed by Schmid, appears in Illustration 10, confirmed that Schmid had purchased from Baschwitz the right to reprint *Sefer Krovot*. Banet, in other words, publicly provided his imprimatur for Schmid's second edition based on the purchase by a seemingly recalcitrant Schmid of reprinting rights from a joint holder of those rights under the rabbinic reprinting bans that had originally been issued for *Sefer Krovot*. By ensuring that Jewish purchasers of the Schmid edition would see that, as confirmed by the Chief Rabbi of Moravia, Schmid had ostensibly acquiesced in the ban of the Ashkenazic sages by purchasing the reprinting rights from their rightful holder, Banet adeptly projected a measure of rabbinic authority over the Hebrew book trade. He did so even as he had, shortly before, relinquished the central pillar of that authority, the rabbinic power to issue reprinting bans that are enforceable by *ḥerem* across the Jewish world.

For his part, Heidenheim remained aggrieved by Schmid's reprinting. In his next edition of *Sefer Krovot*, published between 1815 and 1817, Heidenheim inserted an impassioned statement just below his reproduction of the original *haskamot* from 1800 to 1805 and Tzvi Hirsch Horowitz's warning to comply with them. Heidenheim began: "Who would believe that in the face of all of those rabbinic bans and warnings, someone would nevertheless have it in his heart to commit the villainous acts [forbidden by the bans] for nefarious profit?" Heidenheim then recited that "a certain printer" recently announced that he already has commenced a second reprinting of Heidenheim's *maḥzor* in Vienna without Heidenheim's consent, and that said printer gave the excuse that he had been given a written authorization for the reprinting from Heidenheim's former partner. Heidenheim further insisted that his erstwhile

47. Baschwitz had withdrawn from the partnership in 1806. Seligson 1906: 320.
48. Schmid's 1816 reprint also features an approbation from Moses Muenz (or Mintz) Me-Brody (1750–1831), rabbi and head of the rabbinic court of Oban (Obuda, Hungary; also called Altofen).

הסכמות מגאוני הזמן נר"ו

בע"ה יום ה' יוד טבת תקעו"ל

האדון הנכבד אנטאן שמיד!

אחרי ראותי תומתו ויושרו בהמודעה אשר הדפיס זה ימים לא כבירים ובה הודיע לאמר, כי קנה מאת המרומם ר' ברוך בכ"מ בשווין מנת חלקו אשר נפל לו בנעימים, בדבר המחזורים אשר הדפיסו הוא ורעהו איש חיל רב פעלים החכם השלם ר' וואלף היידנהיים, כאשר קימו וקבלו עליהם, בהפרדם איש מעל אחיו, להיות כל איש מהם נואל ידו להדפיסם שוב שנית, הן בעצמו, הן על ידי אחר אשר יאות אליו בדמות ותבנית הראשונים, ראיתי ונתתי אל לבי, לעורר את לבו להדפיס גם את ס' המפואר מאמר השכל להראב"ן ז"ל, אשר הדפיסו המשותפים הנ"ל לחלק העשירי מהמחזורים, ועתה בראותי כי נעשתה עצתי, וזה יצא ראשונה לאור, ותהי ראשית פרי מלאכתו קודש לה', כל אוכליו יאמרו אורו עיני, כי טעמתי מנופת דבש בעל הספר, הנותן אמרי שפר, אמרתי איעצהו נא גם בזאת, לבל יטה ימין ושמאל ממסלות הדקדוק אשר דרך בה החכם המדקדק ר' וואלף היידענהיים הן בפרשיות והפטרות, הן בפיוטים וחרוזים אשר עד הנה עלו כלן קמשונים, וכל זה שם החכם הנ"ל על לב, כאשר יעידון יגידון בהסכמותיהם גאוני ארצנו נבונים וחכמי לב. והיה כי ישמע לעצתי, וענתה בו צדקתו ביום מחר, כי יבוא על שכרו, כי כל רואיהם יגילו בראותם מעשה ידיו להתפאר, וכבכורה בטרם קיץ בעודה בכפו יבלענה.

ובכן ישלם ה' פעלו, ויכונן מעשה ידיו, והיה שלם ורענן היכלו וכבוד אומר כלו.

נ"ש ה"ק מרדכי בנעט חונה פה ק"ק
נ"ש והמדינה יע"א.

Illustration 10
Mordekhai Banet Letter/*Haskama* for Anton Schmid's Second Edition of *Sefer Krovot Hu-Maḥzor*, 1816.
(courtesy National Library of Israel).

partner Baschwitz had no authority to sell Heidenheim's own rights to others or to allow acts that were prohibited by the rabbinic bans. The rabbinic bans, Heidenheim asserted, were given to him for his sole benefit, as evident from the words of the sages who issued them and from the warning in support of the rabbinic bans that Tzvi Hirsch Horowitz issued in September 1807, at which time Baschwitz was no longer an ongoing stakeholder in Heidenheim's enterprise. Conspicuously absent from Heidenheim's statement was any indication that it was Mordekhai Banet, Chief Rabbi of Moravia, who confirmed the authenticity of Baschwitz's authorization and, on that basis, gave his imprimatur to Schmid.

D. The Second Unauthorized Reprinting: Dyhernfurth

In 1822 *Sefer Krovot* was again reprinted without Heidenheim's consent. This time the reprinter was Hirsch Warschauer, a Jewish publisher based in Dyhernfurth, a small town near Breslau, located in Prussian Silesia.[49] Dyhernfurth was then a hub of Hebrew printing. Its first Hebrew press—and, indeed, its first Jewish presence—was established around 1688, when the local magnate invited Shabbetai Bass to open a printing house in order to develop that recently founded town. (It will be recalled that Bass was the scholar who had edited Joseph Athias's Yiddish Bible.) In the ensuing 140 years, Jewish presses centered in Dyhernfurth published hundreds of Hebrew and Yiddish works.[50]

Warschauer printed the first volume of Heidenheim's nine-volume *Sefer Krovot* in 1822. His reprint appeared with the approbation, dated 7 Sivan 5581 (June 6, 1821), of Israel Yona Landau, head of the rabbinic court of Kempno, located in territory that had been annexed by Prussia in the 1793 Second Partition of Poland.[51]

No sooner had Warschauer printed the first volume than Heidenheim threatened to haul him before a rabbinic court for violation of Heidenheim's rabbinic reprinting bans.[52] In so doing, Heidenheim once again sought protection under Jewish law against a reprinting of his *maḥzor* that was entirely permissible under secular law. Unlike Austria, Prussia did not actively encourage reprintings undertaken without the original publisher's permission, and, indeed, periodically pressured other states to honor Prussian book privileges in their territories.[53] But in line with common practice in the early nineteenth century, Prussia did not forbid reprinting works of foreign authors and publishers absent a treaty with the foreigner's sovereign ruler

49. Dyhernfurth is now known as Brzeg Dolny. It is located in Lower Silesia (today southwestern Poland). Breslau is today known as Wroclaw.

50. Breuer 1996: 223–25.

51. Kempno, or "Kempen," as it was sometimes called, is now the Polish city of Kepno.

52. My account of the dispute is derived from letters that Akiva Eiger addressed to Zalman Tarir, head of the rabbinic court of Frankfurt am Main, and to Wolf Heidenheim in an attempt to mediate a compromise agreement. See Akiva Eiger (1761–1837), Letter in the Matter of the Printing of Maḥzorim of Roedelheim That Have Begun to Be Reprinted Without the Author's Authorization (1822).

53. Kawohl 2008n.

requiring protection against reprinting—and Prussia did not begin until later (1827) to sign such treaties with other states of the German Confederation, including the Grand Duchy of Hessen, where Rodelheim was located.[54]

Notwithstanding his freedom to reprint under secular law, Warschauer attempted to settle the dispute. He offered to give Heidenheim 30 reprinted "copies," presumably of the entire nine-volume *maḥzor*, in return for Heidenheim's consent to Warschauer's reprinting. He also pointedly reminded Heidenheim that, in any case, the 25-year period of Heidenheim's rabbinic reprinting bans was nearing its end.

Heidenheim evidently rejected Warschauer's settlement offer. Warschauer then turned to Akiva Eiger (1761–1837), rabbi of Pozen (also in Polish territory annexed by Prussia) and one of the most highly respected halakhic decisors of his generation. Warschauer relayed to Eiger that he had embarked on his reprinting of *Sefer Krovot* in good faith, pursuant to the rabbinic imprimatur of Israel Landau of Kempno. He also pleaded that he had invested heavily in the project and would go bankrupt if unable to complete it, or at least to sell the volume he had printed and a second volume for which he had already set the type. He added that, in any event, there was nothing he could do to stop the distribution of the copies he had already printed; he had borrowed from his non-Jewish partner to finance the reprinting, and if he were unable to repay the debt, the non-Jew would seize the printed copies and put them on the market.

In an effort to lend his weight to resolving the dispute, Eiger sent a written appeal, dated 1 Av 5582 (July 19, 1822), to Zalman Tarir, head of the rabbinic court of Frankfurt am Main, accompanied by a letter addressed directly to Wolf Heidenheim.[55] In addition to recounting Warschauer's good faith and dire financial straits, Eiger expressed his concern that if Heidenheim should enforce the reprinting bans against Warschauer, Warschauer's non-Jewish partner might bring an action before a Prussian court challenging the rabbinic bans—and "who knows what might sprout from that." In his letter to Heidenheim, Eiger warned further that an action by Warschauer's non-Jewish partner might lead Prussian authorities to enforce prohibitions on importing books into Prussia, and to impose fines on violators, just as the Emperor of Austria had directed as a result of a "similar case" in that country—a thinly veiled reference to Austrian authorities' sharp response to Heidenheim's efforts to enforce his rabbinic bans in Austria. Eiger added that were it therefore to become impossible to import copies of Heidenheim's *maḥzor* to Prussia, the Dyhernfurth publisher would readily find rabbis in Prussia who would give their approbations to the reprinting of *Sefer Krovot* in that country even absent Heidenheim's permission. Under those circumstances, indeed, he, Eiger, might well give his approbation as well. Eiger concluded his written appeal by personally guaranteeing the delivery of 40 copies of Warschauer's reprinted edition to Heidenheim in return for Heidenheim's written consent to Warschauer's reprinting.

54. Kawohl 2008o.

55. Akiva Eiger (1761–1837), Letter in the Matter of the Printing of Maḥzorim of Roedelheim That Have Begun to Be Reprinted Without the Author's Authorization (1822).

IV. AN EXTENDED COLLOQUY: MORDEKHAI BANET AND MOSES SOFER

Parallel to Eiger's effort to bring about a compromise settlement of Heidenheim's claim against Warschauer, the head of the rabbinic court in Dyhernfurth asked Mordekhai Banet for a ruling on whether Heidenheim's reprinting bans were enforceable against Warschauer. Perhaps Heidenheim had brought a complaint against Warschauer in that rabbinic court and the rabbi of Dyhernfurth then sought the opinion of a greater authority on the applicable halakha. Or perhaps the inquiry was sparked by Warschauer, seeking an approbation from the rabbinic court of Dyhernfurth, as he had received from the head of the rabbinic court of Kempno. Neither Banet's responsum nor the historical record gives an indication.

Banet's responsum addresses the Dyhernfurth rabbi as the "light of the Exile" and by other honorifics, but does not identify him by name. He was apparently Yaakov Yehuda Leib Falk (c. 1767–1838), who served as head of Dyhernfurth's rabbinic court and as a rabbinic judge in neighboring Breslau. Several years later, Falk granted an approbation for yet another reprinting of Heidenheim's *Sefer Krovot*, published by Leib Sulzbach in Breslau between 1829 and 1830.[56]

It would have been out of the ordinary for Falk, a rabbi of Dyhernfurth, to seek a ruling on such a matter from a rabbinic authority outside of his country. In his responsum, indeed, Banet initially expressed reluctance to respond, noting that he was unaccustomed to issuing a ruling to an inquirer from a different land, especially given the presence of preeminent rabbinic authorities in that land. Evidently, Falk chose to ask Banet for a ruling on the assumption that if anyone could authoritatively speak to the concerns that Akiva Eiger raised about the grave dangers of attempting to enforce Heidenheim's reprinting bans in Prussia, it would be Mordekhai Banet. And on that score, Falk could reasonably assume that Banet would incline favorably toward the Dyhernfurth printer. Banet had, after all, withdrawn his support for enforcing Heidenheim's reprinting bans in Austria following the Austrian authorities' sharp response to Heidenheim's enforcement efforts in that country.

If that was the Dyhernfurth rabbi's reason for posing his halakhic question to Mordekhai Banet, he was not to be disappointed. In his ruling, dated Thursday, 5 Elul 5582 (August 22, 1822), Banet took a decidedly narrow view of the protection to which Heidenheim was entitled under Jewish law.[57] In so doing, Banet exhibited a keen sense of the limits of rabbinic authority in a Jewish world divided among imperial powers that were bent on supplanting much of that authority—and that had decreed that reprinting foreign works was permissible under secular law.

But although Banet provided the assurance that Falk sought for Falk to back the Dyhernfurth printer, Banet's word was not the last on the subject in the annals of

56. Heidenheim's *maḥzor* was also reprinted by S. Arnstein & Soehne in Sulzbach (a town in Bavaria) in 1826.

57. Mordekhai Banet, *Responsa Parshat Mordekhai,* Ḥoshen Mishpat, No. 7.

Jewish copyright law. Six months after Banet's ruling, Moses Sofer (1762–1839), rabbi of Pressburg, at that time the most important Jewish community in Hungary, wrote a responsum addressed to Banet and directly taking issue with him. Sofer was Banet's junior; indeed, Banet had recommended Sofer for his first rabbinic post in Dresnitz in 1794. By this time, however, Sofer had already attained an exalted position in traditional rabbinic culture, a position cemented by his prominent role opposing the reformist Hamburg Temple some four years earlier.[58] In his responsum, dated 24 Adar 5582 (March 7, 1823), Sofer forcefully argued that Jewish law and long-standing rabbinic practice require that rabbinic reprinting bans be fully enforced throughout the Jewish world, including in a country other than the one where the ban was issued.[59]

As appears from its context and content, Sofer's initial responsum was evidently part of a private correspondence that he carried on with his senior colleague. It seems that Sofer initiated this exchange of letters by asking Banet to join him in granting *haskamot* for a forthcoming book, which Sofer identified as *Oryan T'litai*.[60] That request would have been quite routine; the two rabbis joined in granting approbations for several books, both before and after this exchange. Banet responded that that he would grant an approbation, but not a reprinting ban. That response would also not have been out of the ordinary; Banet had not granted a reprinting ban since he retracted his initial support for the bans for the Rodelheim *maḥzor* in 1807. But on this occasion, in a letter that Sofer quotes at the beginning of his responsum, Banet outlined his argument for why bans are unenforceable and should no longer be issued, and referred to the recent ruling he had given to the rabbi of Dyhernfurth.

Sofer responded by seeking to convince Banet that rabbinic reprinting bans were, indeed, a legitimate, enforceable exercise of rabbinic authority. In contrast to the ruling that Banet issued to the head of Dyhernfurth's rabbinic court, we have no reason to think that Sofer's letter to Banet would have been widely circulated at the time. Further, Sofer's responsa, a number of which consist of private correspondence, were not published until after his death.[61]

58. See Katz 1998b: 217–29.

59. *Responsa Ḥatam Sofer,* Ḥoshen Mishpat, No. 41. Of note, just over a year previously both Sofer and Banet had given approbations to an edition of the *Seder Mo'ed* (Order of the Festivals) of the Jerusalem Talmud printed in Vienna by Anton Schmid.

60. Sofer apparently referred to a collection of responsa and commentaries, entitled *Beit Aryeh*, authored by Aryeh Leibush Horowitz, of which the second section is entitled *Oryan T'litai. Beit Aryeh* was not published until 1834, more than a decade after Sofer's request that Banet provide a *haskama*. But its *Oryan T'litai* section was apparently written much earlier. *Beit Aryeh* contains approbations from Sofer and three other rabbis, but not Banet, who died in 1829. Sofer's undated approbation refers to the author's "previous composition," and another approbation, that of Eliezer Mintz is dated 23 Tevet 5588 (January 10, 1828)—some six years before the book was published, suggesting that the book was long in the making.

61. See Katz 1998b: 224 (describing a Sofer letter that was certainly not for public distribution, but that was posthumously published as one of his responsa), 404 (noting that Sofer never published a book in his life). Most of Banet's writings remained unpublished during his lifetime as well. Visi 2012: 177.

In any event, it is not entirely clear what inspired Sofer to respond to Banet. Apparently, Frankfurt rabbi Tzvi Hirsch Horowitz had asked Sofer to intercede on Heidenheim's behalf several years before, probably to endorse the ban against Jews lending, buying, or selling Schmid's reprintings. In a later responsum, in which Sofer further explicated his arguments for enforcing reprinting bans, he noted that Horowitz, who died in 1817, had informed him that Heidenheim had devoted considerable time to proofreading hymns and translating them into German, had gathered several existing texts for that purpose, and had expended a great deal of money, as to which he still remained accountable for unpaid debts.[62] Yet, in his 1823 responsum, Sofer also referred to a letter he received several months previously from Akiva Eiger, who was Sofer's father-in-law, complaining that a certain rabbi had claimed in writing that he, Eiger, had definitively stated that rabbinic reprinting bans are ineffective and thus are not to be enforced. Perhaps it was this letter that sparked Sofer's response to Banet. Indeed, Sofer stated in his responsum that he now suspected that the certain rabbi who had offended Eiger by overstating Eiger's position was the rabbi of Dyhernfurth.

If Sofer truly hoped to convince Banet to change his view of rabbinic reprinting bans, he was unsuccessful. Banet defended his position against Sofer in a responsum dated 7 Nisan 5587 (April 11, 1827).[63] Sofer then presented his counterarguments to Banet's defense in a lengthy exposition touching briefly on the Jewish law of wrongful competition before moving on to other grounds for supporting reprinting bans.[64] In contrast to Sofer's 1823 responsum, this later, undated responsum does seem to be intended for public circulation, perhaps for use in teaching at Sofer's *yeshiva*. It is not addressed to Banet, or to any other identified inquirer, and it is far longer than Sofer's typical responsa. In any case, the extended colloquy between Banet and Sofer presents in gripping detail the opposing arguments of two preeminent rabbinic scholars of the early nineteenth century on the nature of Jewish copyright law and the enforceability of rabbinic reprinting bans.

Equally, Banet's and Sofer's respective responsa both illuminate and are informed by those rabbinic leaders' contrasting approaches for how best to address the crisis of rabbinic authority that engulfed them. To be certain, these two luminaries of the early nineteenth-century central European rabbinic elite generally shared a devotion to rabbinic tradition, even while embracing study of certain secular subjects.[65] Further, Banet and Sofer both exhibited considerable adeptness—in extraordinarily difficult circumstances—in their dealings with imperial, ecclesiastical, and other political powers. They each responded with painful awareness of the need to

62. *Responsa Ḥatam Sofer,* Ḥoshen Mishpat, No. 79. As was—and is—common in traditional rabbinic culture, Sofer referred to Horowitz by the title of the book that Horowitz authored and for which he is known, *Maḥane Levi*.

63. *Responsa Parshat Mordekhai*, No. 8.

64. *Responsa Ḥatam Sofer,* Ḥoshen Mishpat, No. 79.

65. Like Banet, Sofer embraced the study of certain secular subjects, including medicine and mathematics, as part of traditional rabbinic education because, in his view, those subjects were essential to understanding central halakhic problems. Katz 1998b: 433; Schreiber 2006: 125–37.

cabin rabbinic authority within the sharp limits that absolutist governments had imposed, while seeking to enlist the support of secular political powers in preserving the hegemony of traditionalist rabbinic authority within the Jewish community in the face of reformist challenges.[66]

Yet even within this broad framework of common purpose, Sofer and Banet exhibited certain salient differences. First, Sofer exceeded Banet in the resoluteness and intransigence of his defense of rabbinic power and tradition—although it is important to stress that this was a difference in degree, not in kind. It was Sofer who made rigid adherence to immutable tradition an express, overriding principle. That principle is best encapsulated in Sofer's often-cited application of the Talmudic dictum *ḥadash asur min ha-Torah* to mean that any deviation from the traditional understanding of halakha, even if seemingly trivial, is strictly forbidden if for no other reason than that it is an innovation.[67] Sofer also held that rabbinic rulings and rabbinic-sanctioned local custom are no less an inherent part of that immutable tradition than are explicit biblical commandments.[68] The various elements of the rabbinic tradition thus constitute a single, organic whole, a sanctified body of rules and practices that must be observed in its entirety. For Sofer, as we shall see, rabbis' long-standing custom of issuing reprinting bans formed an integral part of that tradition.

For his part, Banet also insisted that the long-standing custom is as sacred and inviolable as biblical law, and thus may not be abrogated under any circumstances.[69] On the other hand, in his copyright responsa Banet seemed to draw a distinction between sacrosanct halakhic rules and custom, on one hand, and mutable rabbinic decrees, on the other. He also argued that the rabbinic practice of issuing reprinting bans did not rise to the level of binding custom.

Further, Sofer did not only erect a wall against innovation at the hands of Jewish reformers; he also adamantly opposed ceding authority to secular rulers over

66. Although Sofer regarded the obligatory conscription of Jewish boys into the Emperor's army with great anxiety, particularly given the impossibility for a Jew to observe religious strictures while in Austrian military service, he ruled, in a responsum issued in 1830, that the military conscription law was within the king's authority and that, accordingly, Jews were obligated to comply. For discussion see Graff 1985: 67–68; Katz 1998b: 417. With regard to seeking the support of political powers, Banet persuaded the Archbishop of Olmuetz to take a stand against Jewish reformers in Vienna, while Sofer appealed to imperial authorities to forbid Viennese Jews from transacting business on the Jewish Sabbath. Grunwald 1936: 374.

67. Sofer's principle is often misinterpreted. It does not mean that the halakha may not be applied to new circumstances in unprecedented ways, but only that the halakha must be interpreted and applied in such cases by learned rabbinic scholars who are fully steeped in and faithful to the rabbinic tradition. For example, Sofer expressed the view that the revelation of the truth of the Torah continues through the generations rather than being handed down just once in final concrete form at Mt. Sinai, and that learned rabbinic scholars of each generation will be directed to that truth by their deep immersion in Torah study even without being consciously aware of it. See Kahana 2007: 521–27 (describing the extended correspondence between Sofer and Tzvi Hirsch Ḥiyot (1805–1855) on that topic).

68. Katz 1998b: 431–32.

69. Miller 2011: 67–68.

traditional rabbinic domains.[70] For example, Sofer authored responsa insisting that halakhic rules regarding marriage and inheritance must take precedence over secular governments' regulation of those areas. He similarly declined to recognize the halakhic validity of wills drawn up in non-Jewish courts. As he cogently expressed it: "Heaven forbid that in such a case we will apply the rule that 'the law of the sovereign is the law' against the law of the holy Torah, for if [we were to do so], we would annul all the laws of the Torah."[71]

Hand in hand with his insistence on the principle of immutable rabbinic authority, Sofer came to hold a highly optimistic belief in his ability to convince secular rulers to support rabbinic traditionalists, especially vis-à-vis Jewish reformers who would undermine the power of the traditional rabbinic elite. As Sofer colorfully expressed:

> Secular rulers help and aid us and defend us in the maintenance of our religion, and they have absolutely no desire to abrogate even a single one of our commandments from the Torah. If in some countries the rulers have listened to the voice of these charmers, they have intended only to do good for us, for they do not know and have not been told that this contradicts the foundation of our faith. However, if they hear and understand that this thing is opposed to our Torah and that these persons possess no religion whatsoever, they pay them no heed them at all. And God is with us.[72]

As with the differences between Sofer and Banet regarding the defense of rabbinic power and tradition, Sofer's argument for the continued viability of rabbinic reprinting bans reflects his basic optimism about gaining the support of secular rulers, while Banet's response reflects considerable skepticism on that point. Both Banet and Sofer carefully grounded their disputation in halakhic precedent, as well as in their empirical assumptions about when and how the widespread practice of granting rabbinic reprinting bans came into being. But as we now see, their contrasting views of what degree of rabbinic authority it was possible to preserve and their contrasting approaches regarding how best to preserve that rabbinic authority heavily color their colloquy about Jewish copyright law.

A. Banet's Responsum to the Dyhernfurth Rabbi, August 22, 1822

In his initial responsum, Banet sets out a number of grounds why Heidenheim's reprinting bans were of no force. In so doing, he narrowly construes Moses Isserles's ruling in favor of the Maharam of Padua so as to avoid disagreeing with Isserles. The arguments that Banet adduces in his responsa boil down to several propositions:

70. Graff 1995: 52, 68, 110; Schwarzfuchs 1979: 168–70.
71. *Responsa Ḥatam Sofer*, Ḥoshen Mishpat, No. 142, discussed in Graff 1985: 52.
72. Sofer, Deroshot 1.113b, quoted in Katz 1998b: 437.

1. *Under the Jewish law of wrongful competition, a publisher does not generally have a right to prevent reprinting by a second publisher, certainly when the first publisher has already sold out his first print run.*

Banet devotes considerable attention to presenting and analyzing the various paradigm cases that provide the framework for the Jewish law of wrongful competition.[73] He begins with the basic rule favoring free competition absent grounds for a specific exception. Like the Rema, Banet's primary reference point is the Talmudic case of the Open Alley ("mavoy").[74] In that case, recall, the majority rejecting Rav Huna's contrary position ruled that a resident of an alleyway (or neighborhood) who is the first to establish a mill for commercial purposes in that alleyway may not prevent a local competitor from opening an adjacent mill. As Rashi (1040–1105) explains, the competitor may simply shrug off the incumbent merchant's complaint with, "Whoever comes to me, let him come; whoever comes to you, let him come." As we have seen, virtually all Talmudic authorities follow that majority rule, as do the *Mishneh Torah* and *Shulḥan Arukh*.[75]

Banet then canvasses four leading Talmudic cases presenting exceptions to the rule favoring free competition—and thus that are distinguished from the case of the Open Alley. They are the cases of (1) the Fish Who Lock Their Sight on the Bait (*sayara*), (2) the Dead End Alley (*mavoy satum*), (3) the Poor Man Reaching for a Crust of Bread (*ani ha-mehapekh ba-ḥarara*), and (4) the Poor Man Who Shakes an Olive Tree (*ani ha-menakef be-rosh ha-zayit*). The first and third cases were cited by the Rome rabbinic court in issuing its reprinting ban in favor of Eliyahu Bakhur. The second was invoked by Moses Isserles in his ruling in favor of the Maharam of Padua.

1) **The Case of the Fish Who Lock Their Sight on the Bait (*sayara*):** This case (which appears in the Talmud adjacent to the case of the Open Alley) involves two fishermen, each casting a net in order to catch fish. The Talmud rules that the second fisherman must keep his fishing nets away from a fish that has been targeted by the first fisherman for the full length of the fish's swim. The reason is *sayara* (the fish have set their "sight" on the food).

Rabbinic commentators provide different explanations for why this case differs from the Open Alley. Rashi explains that a fish has the tendency to go after the first thing that it sees. Therefore, when the first fisherman targets the fish, he can be justifiably confident that he will catch it, meaning that the fish is treated as if it already has been caught by the first fisherman. As a result, when the second fisherman interferes and deflects the fish, it is as if he has harmed the first fisherman by literally taking away "his" fish. By contrast, in the Open Alley, the potential customers of the mill are not considered to be "captured" by the first mill owner, but can go to whichever mill they choose.

Of course, every explanation generates its own disputation. The foregoing interpretation attributed to Rashi is not universally shared. In particular, Banet notes

73. My discussion draws on David Nimmer's early draft.
74. *Babylonian Talmud, Baba Batra* 21b.
75. *Mishneh Torah*, Sefer Kinyan, Hilkhot Shkhenim 6: 8; *Shulḥan Arukh*, Ḥoshen Mishpat 156: 5.

that the Rema understood Rashi differently. Under the Rema's interpretation, the difference between The Fisherman, in which one could justifiably limit competition and the Open Alley, in which competition could not be stopped, does not result from the first fisherman's confidence that he will capture the fish. Rather, the distinction between the two cases involves the certainty of the damage to be caused to the first actor. Because potential mill customers are able to choose to return to the first mill even after the rival mill has opened, damage is not certain; hence, it is not proper to limit competition. Say, for example, that Reuven operates the first mill and Shimon opens a rival shop. Even if Reuven's customers switch over to Shimon, nothing prevents them from later returning to Reuven. By contrast, because fish essentially have no choice regarding being captured by the fishnets, damage to the first fisherman is certain and competition properly may be limited.

Banet in addition adduces the view of Mordekhai ben Hillel (1250–1289), who invoked the doctrine of *ma'arufia* on this point. Dating from France and Germany in the tenth century, that doctrine refers to a recurrent Christian client (notwithstanding the Arabic etymology of the word itself).[76] It prohibits one Jew from attempting to "steal" another's established commercial client. The rationale for this principle is that the first Jew has invested time, money, and effort in order to achieve the special business ties that he has nurtured with his *ma'arufia*, and thus no one else should be permitted to interfere with the relationship. Jewish communities that follow the doctrine of *ma'arufia* (the custom is not universal) and rabbinic decisors who enforce it consider the Gentile client's patronage to be "certain," akin to a "fish that has set its eye on the bait," as it were.[77]

2) **The Case of the Dead End Alley (*mavoy satum*):** As also elucidated by the Rema in his ruling, this case is a variant of the case of The Open Alley, the paradigm favoring free completion. It was initially offered by *Avi'asaf*, a work consisting of commentary on the Talmud by German scholar Eliezer ben Joel Ha-Levi (1160–1235).[78] It involves the resident of a community who operates a mill at the terminus of a dead-end alleyway. According to many rabbinic authorities—even those who reject Rav Huna's minority position regarding the Open Alley—the first mill owner here *can* prevent a competitor from opening up a new mill near the open end of the dead-end alleyway.[79] These authorities explain that, because the two mills are located in an alleyway with only one entrance, customers cannot reach the first mill without passing by the door of its newly opened competitor, and therefore will end up doing business with this competitor rather than continuing on to the first mill. Under these circumstances, the first mill owner located inside the alleyway may prevent his competitor from entering the market and opening another mill closer to the entrance of the alley, given that damage to the first mill owner as a result of such competition is

76. The word comes from the Arabic meaning literally "a constant friend—in our context, a permanent business associate." Tamari 1998: 117–18.

77. Berenbaum and Skolnik 2007: 307; Tamari 1998: 119.

78. The text of *Avi'asaf*, Ha-Levi's commentary on the Talmud tractates Nashim and Nezikin, has been lost; we know of its contents only from reading later commentary regarding it. In this instance, Mordekhai ben Hillel attributes this point of view to *Avi'asaf*.

79. Hagahot Maimoniot, Hilkhot Shkhenim, pt. 6; Joseph Karo, *Beit Yosef*, Ḥoshen Mishpat, No. 156.

essentially "certain." In this case, the second mill owner is infringing upon another's business practices.

To summarize, the damage that occurs to the first fisherman when the second fisherman uses his nets to try to catch the same fish is considered "certain," because otherwise the fish would have automatically gravitated to the first fisherman's net. By contrast, in the Open Alley, the damage to the first mill owner is speculative, because a potential customer might choose to return to the equally proximate first mill owner after doing business with the new, competing mill. In the case of the Dead End Alley, however, inasmuch as every customer of the first mill now has to pass by the new shop, the damage again becomes virtually certain.

3) The Case of the Poor Man Reaching for a Crust of Bread (*ani ha-mehapekh ba-ḥarara*): This case (*Babylonian Talmud, Kiddushin* 59a) involves a poor man who finds a crust of bread that is ownerless and tries to take it. A second man comes along and grabs it first. The Talmud explains that, in this case, the second man is considered to be an "evildoer."

That phraseology is deliberate. Let us imagine that Reuven owns a crust of bread outright and Shimon comes along to take it. In that instance, Shimon is a *thief* and subject to the full force of Torah law, including restitution and a fine [Exodus 22:3]. Reverting to the instant case, by contrast, the second man who obtains the bread that was sought by the poor man is called an *evildoer* by analogy to a thief, but is not *actually* a thief. The difference, in practical terms, is that the usurper is subject to moral condemnation, but does not incur the monetary consequences that would attend outright theft.

4) The Case of the Poor Man Who Shakes an Olive Tree (*ani ha-menakef be-rosh ha-zayit*): This case (*Mishnah Gittin* 5:8) involves a poor man who climbs to the top of an ownerless tree to knock some olives to the ground, so that he may collect them after he comes down. But when the olives land on the ground, a second person appears on the scene to gather them before the first man can climb down to collect them. According to the sages of the Mishnah, the conduct of the second person, albeit not outright theft, is treated as such in an adjacent category, "theft because of the ways of peace." The rabbis reach that determination so as to avoid dissension, fighting, and hatred between people.

Under the minority view of Rabbi Yosi (a second-century sage typically mentioned in the Talmud without any patronymic), the second person, pursuant to rabbinic law, is treated no differently from an actual thief. Accordingly, the court may order the olives to be removed from the second person and returned to the poor man who shook the tree. Nevertheless, the majority view does not go that far. It disallows the poor man from affirmatively going to court to reclaim the olives; as a practical matter, therefore, it merely treats the second man as the same type of "evildoer" condemned in the previous case.

* * *

Having enumerated the paradigmatic exceptions to the rule favoring free competition, Banet proceeds to distinguish them from the case of the second publisher who wishes to reprint the first publisher's book. Banet initially suggests that one could learn from the Poor Man who Shakes the Olive Tree that the second publisher should be liable for "theft because of the ways of peace," giving due consideration to the toil and effort undertaken by the first publisher to produce his set of *maḥzorim*. Banet explains that the first publisher toiled hard to put together a definitive Hebrew text and to translate the *maḥzor* into the vernacular; now, the second publisher comes along in an attempt to benefit from the first person's effort.

Despite that wind-up, however, Banet concludes that the case before him is not like the Poor Man who Shakes the Olive Tree and therefore does not implicate "theft because of the ways of peace." Banet notes that, in both that case and the case of the Poor Man Reaching for a Crust of Bread, the second person wants to take the exact item that the poor man had toiled to obtain. By contrast, in the case of the publishers, the second is not taking from the first the same exact set of *maḥzorim* that the first had worked so hard to produce. Rather, the second is printing his own set of *maḥzorim*. The first publisher objects not because the second is taking an item from him but rather because potential customers of the first publisher will now purchase books from the second publisher instead.

Where have we ever seen, asks Banet rhetorically, that a person who works hard to produce an item acquires the *purchasers* of that item as a result of his hard work, such that another is forbidden from trying to convince those purchasers to acquire a competing item from him, rather than from the first actor? According to Banet, the notion that an individual has certain rights with respect to an item merely because of the effort he undertook in connection with that item applies only to the very item itself and not to prospective purchasers of that item. Therefore, this case is not like those of the Crust of Bread or the Olive Tree—for, in both those instances, the very crust of bread or olives that Reuven desired were scooped up by Shimon. In this case, however, the copies of the *maḥzor* printed by Reuven would not be sold by Shimon, as Shimon has printed up his own copies for sale to customers.

In addition, Banet notes that the case of the competing publishers is not one that involves certain damage or clear profit to the first publisher. The first publisher cannot say with certainty that the public would buy his *maḥzor*, particularly inasmuch as Heidenheim sold his *maḥzor* at a high price. For that reason, "the fish had not set their eye on the bait," as it were, allowing Banet to conclude that this case also is not like that of the Fisherman.

Banet puts forth yet another reason to distinguish the case before him from those of the Fisherman and the Olive Tree. He explains that the concept that the second person should not benefit from the first person's toil applies to those cases because, in each, the first person does not receive any benefit whatsoever from his efforts: the Fisherman loses out when the fish swims into the nets of the rival angler, and the Poor Man likewise comes up completely empty when the second person gathers up all the olives knocked off the tree. Here, by contrast, the first publisher has already benefited from his effort by selling out his first edition of the *maḥzor*. Why, asks Banet, should that first publisher be able to work to produce his first set of *maḥzorim*, profit from that work, and then profit again from later editions without any further work on his part, thereby causing a loss to others, that is, the second publisher, who would be barred from selling his own set of *maḥzorim*, in which he had invested a significant sum to publish?

> 2. *The Rema's ruling in favor of the Maharam of Padua concerned a special case and is not applicable beyond its highly particular facts.*

Banet's conclusion that the Jewish law of wrongful competition does not support the enforcement of a reprinting ban against the second publisher would appear to put him on a collision course with the Rema's seminal ruling in favor of the Maharam of Padua, discussed in Chapter 4. However, Banet carefully highlights distinct aspects of the Rema's ruling so as to distinguish it from most cases involving second publishers, including the dispute before Banet.

First, Banet asserts that once the Maharam of Padua received a license to publish the work of Maimonides, the Maharam could have been very nearly certain that others would purchase it because Maimonides's works were in great demand throughout the Jewish world. Therefore, the Maharam's case was similar to Rashi's explanation of that of the Fisherman—meaning that the Maharam was entitled to prevent his competitor, Giustiniani, from publishing an infringing edition.

Second, Banet maintains that Isserles ruled in favor of the Maharam because Giustiniani had announced in advance that he intended to sell his competing edition of the *Mishneh Torah* for one gold coin less than the Maharam, and Giustiniani, according to the Rema's ruling, was unusual in that he had the financial resources to sell his edition at that sharply reduced rate. Therefore, Banet explains, the Rema could bar Giustiniani's publication of his competing edition because it would have caused "certain damage" to the Maharam of Padua. In general, however, a competitor should be allowed to enter the marketplace and sell his competing product at a lower price. In the usual case, in which competing merchants do not have the resources to absorb losses from selling at a below-market rate, it is permissible to compete by selling at a lower price. As Banet notes, in the Open Alley case, the Talmud permitted a competing resident to open up a second mill, and was not concerned with the possibility that the second mill owner would sell his products at a lower price, thereby causing damage to the first mill owner.

Third, Banet contends that, in the case before Isserles, Giustiniani proclaimed that he would publish his competing version of the *Mishneh Torah* at a below-market price with the specific aim of causing financial ruin to the Maharam of Padua and his publisher—Giustiniani's rival, Alvise Bragadini. Therefore, the Rema's ruling can be conceptualized as providing protection to the Maharam against predatory pricing. Isserles was holding only that a publisher, like any other merchant, may not sell his works at a below-market price with the intent to drive his competitor out of business. Banet contends, in contrast, that the second publisher in the case before him had no intent to harm the first publisher, but merely was seeking to benefit himself. Therefore, the second publisher would not lower the price of his competing *maḥzor* if it would result in his suffering a loss (in contrast to Giustiniani). Alternatively, if the second publisher were able to lower his price, then the first publisher would also be able to reduce his price (in contrast to Bragadini), thereby reducing the overall market price for *maḥzorim*—and "may a blessing come upon both publishers" for such conduct! Banet therefore concludes that, in this case, where the second publisher actually seeks to publish his competing *maḥzor* without reducing his price, that attempt to enter the market does not result in "certain damage" to the first publisher and therefore should be permitted.

Fourth, Banet suggests that Isserles's ruling is limited to cases in which both publishers operate in the same location, and is thus inapplicable where the second publisher prints and sells his *maḥzor* in a different territory than the first. As Banet notes, according to Rav Huna's minority view, a resident of an open alleyway can prevent both a resident of a different alleyway and a resident of his own alleyway from opening up a competing business in the first resident's alleyway. However, even under Rav Huna's restrictive approach, a resident of one community may not prevent a resident of a different community from opening up a competing business in that second community. According to Banet, it is "possible" that the Rema's ruling was based on the fact that both the Maharam of Padua and Giustiniani were located in the same "alleyway" (i.e., Venice). Alternatively, Banet posits that, because the Maharam and Giustiniani were selling their competing editions of the *Mishneh Torah* to customers in the same territory (primarily Poland), it was *as if* both were doing business in the same alleyway. By contrast, Banet asks, what right does a person in one city (Rodelheim) have to prevent a person in a different city (Dyhernfurth) from engaging in a competing business? If a person possessed such a right, then all commerce would be nullified, and the first person who engaged in a particular business and sent his products to the marketplace would be able to bar all others from engaging in a similar business anywhere in the world.

Finally, Banet asserts that the two cases are distinguishable because government regulation differs in his own day from what it was three centuries earlier when Isserles ruled. Banet notes that governments in his own time give permits to those who want to engage in publishing and other forms of commerce. Through this system, the king collects taxes, people make a living, and the commercial world is able to function. Therefore, how would it occur to someone that one publisher would be able to prohibit another from competing with him when both hold permits from the king to publish their books? Such a prohibition would violate the "law of the sovereign," which permits such competition—and in commercial matters, Jewish law typically gives way before the law of the sovereign. Banet surmises (incorrectly) that, in Isserles's time, kings must not have overseen printing at all, and publishing was undertaken without permission or permits. Now, however, when everything is done with permission of the king, a person in one city does not have the right under Jewish law to prevent someone in a different city from engaging in acts of competition that the king has expressly permitted.

3. *Absent a violation of the Jewish law of wrongful competition, rabbis lack the authority to issue and enforce a reprinting ban unless doing so would not impose any loss on the second publisher.*

After determining that the unauthorized reprinters of the Rodelheim *maḥzor* do not violate the Jewish law of wrongful competition, Banet turns to another serious question raised by his analysis: If a competing publisher is neither guilty of "theft because of the ways of peace" nor considered an "evildoer," where did the sages of earlier generations derive the authority to issue bans that result in a benefit to the one person and a loss to his competitor? According to Joseph Colon ben Solomon Trabotto (c. 1420–1480), Italy's foremost Judaic scholar and Talmudist of the latter part of the fifteenth century, and known in Jewish tradition as the Maharik, even the greatest rabbi of the generation is not allowed to issue a regulation that results in a commercial benefit to one person and a loss to the other, except in exigent circumstances.[80] The Maharik's precept follows from that of some leading rabbinic authorities—and, as we have seen, roughly parallels a similar constraint on the ruler of a polity under Roman law.[81] But it was not the majority view; most medieval authorities permitted taking property from an individual pursuant to a regulation duly enacted by majority vote.[82] Nevertheless, Banet presents the Maharik's precept as the normative position and then seeks to elucidate why most reprinting bans are nevertheless permitted, whereas the bans on reprinting the Rodelheim *maḥzor* run contrary to the Maharik's precept and thus may not be enforced.

Banet first explains that the Rema could ban Giustiniani's competing version of the *Mishneh Torah* without violating the Maharik's precept because the Rema's ban did not cause Giustiniani any actual loss—for, were it not for the work of the Maharam in producing his edition of the *Mishneh Torah* (with the Maharam's original annotations, corrections, and additions of commentary), Giustiniani would have had nothing to begin with. The factual premise here is that Giustiniani's edition copied heavily from the Maharam's edition and thus that Giustiniani could not have prepared his edition of the *Mishneh Torah* unless the Maharam had first prepared his. (As discussed in Chapter 4, this factual premise—whether it is the Rema's or Banet's—is dubious; it seems that Bragadini copied as much or more from Giustiniani than vice versa.)

Proceeding to the case before him, Banet then asks how, given the Maharik's precept, one could possibly justify reprinting bans that rabbinic authorities have frequently issued for new editions of books that had previously been printed, such as the *maḥzorim* at issue in this case. The difficulty is that if the reprinting bans on the Rodelheim *maḥzor* are enforced, Heidenheim will benefit, but other publishers will be harmed. Banet explains that, prior to Heidenheim's preparation and publication

80. *Responsa Maharik*, root 1.

81. The Maharik cited the *Mordekhai* [a work authored by Mordekhai ben Hillel (c. 1240–1298)]. The *Mordekhai*, in turn, cites to Rabbeinu Tam [Jacob ben Meir (1100–1171)] for the proposition that rulers of a city may levy taxes only with universal consent—and, by analogy, nor may rabbis, even the rabbinic leaders of the generation, take property from one person and give it to another in contravention of Torah law. *Responsa Maharik*, root 1.

82. See Gershom ben Judah, (c. 960–1028? 1040?). *Responsa Rabbi Gershom Me'or Ha-Golah*, No. 63; Me'ir ben Barukh of Rothenburg (c. 1215–1293), *Responsa Maharam Me-Rotenberg*, No. 503 (presenting the position of Joseph Tov Alem ben Samuel Bonfils (c. 980–1050)); Isaac ben Jacob Alfasi (1013–1103), *Responsa Ha-Rif*, No. 13; Asher ben Yeḥiel (1250 or 1259–1327), *Responsa Ha-Rosh*, Nos. 6–8; Shlomo ben Aderet (1235–1310), *Responsa Ha-Rashba*, Part 3, No. 411, Part 5, No. 126.

of the Rodelheim *maḥzor*, publishers regularly printed older versions of the *maḥzor*. However, now that the Rodelheim *maḥzor* has been published, it has become the standard, such that no one would purchase a *maḥzor* that did not have the same content and format as the Rodelheim *maḥzor*. As a result, if the bans on reprinting the Rodelheim *maḥzor* are upheld, the other publishers will lose out entirely; they will both be prohibited from publishing the new standard version of the *maḥzor* and will be unable to sell the older versions that they had previously published but which consumers no longer want. To enforce the bans on reprinting the Rodelheim *maḥzor* would thus violate the Maharik's precept that rabbinic regulation may not benefit one person while causing monetary harm to another.[83]

Granted, Banet intimates, the Rodelheim *maḥzor* is a special case. In most instances, no particular edition of a previously printed book becomes the indispensable standard edition for that work. As a general rule, therefore, publishers do not suffer a loss if the publisher of a particular edition enjoys a reprinting ban for just that edition. Indeed, each publisher would benefit from a reprinting ban for his particular edition, while other publishers would be free to continue to market their editions. Sometimes publisher A would be the first printer and would be able to restrain B and C; when another work arose to be printed, B might be the printer, and could act to restrain A, and C; and, on another occasion still, C would be the one to benefit. Accordingly, Banet concludes, the sages of previous generations must have instituted the practice of issuing bans on reprinting new editions of previously printed books (as well as of newly authored books) because all publishers stood to benefit from that practice. In this way, the customary ban arose with consent of all concerned.

As Banet further elucidates (again citing the Maharik), there were many potential purchasers of the Rodelheim *maḥzor*, and the first publisher therefore would make a profit publishing this work. However, when the Rodelheim *maḥzor* established itself as the governing standard, no potential purchasers of the older versions of the *maḥzor* remained, and the publishers of those works thus would not make a profit. Moreover, given that the Rodelheim *maḥzor* has become the "must have" Jewish liturgy book of the day, one cannot even tell other printers to focus their energy on other publications. Accordingly, by contrast with the general rule justifying the practice of issuing reprinting bans, there could be no general consent in the affected industry to enforce this particular ban on reprinting the Rodelheim *maḥzor*.

4. *In any event, reprinting bans are meant only to secure investment in the publisher's first print run and thus may not be enforced after the publisher has sold his first print run.*

Banet next addresses the policy reasons that might justify rabbinic reprinting bans. The sages, he surmises, may have imposed bans (such as the one included in the Rodelheim *maḥzor*) to strengthen and protect from harm those who perform *mitzvot*

83. Banet implicitly distinguishes the case of Giustiniani, first, on the grounds that Giustiniani had not previously invested in publishing an edition of the *Mishneh Torah* and, second, by assuming that Giustiniani could have published and sold an alternative version if he had wished.

by publishing books of Jewish liturgy and learning. If a halakhically observant publisher (Heidenheim being the obvious example) face the prospect that his rivals may freely reprint whatever books they choose, he will be inhibited from publishing books of Jewish liturgy and learning. He will fear that, should he do so, he would suffer a loss from the subsequent cut throat competition. Reprinting bans imposed by the sages alleviate this fear and thus enable such publishers to invest in their initial printing. Banet adds, however, that if this is the purpose underlying reprinting bans, those bans should last only until the first publisher has sold out his initial print run. After all, selling out the initial print run is sufficient for the publisher to recover his investment. The imposition of a ban for a long period of time, which would prevent others from reprinting a book of Jewish liturgy or learning even after the first person sold out his print run, is inappropriate, and is not supported by the above rationale.

5. *Even if reprinting bans are enforceable, they are not enforceable outside the territory in which they were issued.*

Banet further concludes, citing a ruling of Isaac bar Sheshet Perfet, the fourteenth century sage known in Jewish tradition as Rivash, that a rabbinic court has no authority to issue a ban that purports to apply outside the court's territory.[84] Rivash's ruling followed earlier precedent that limited the force of halakhic rulings to the territory of the rabbi who issues the ruling.[85] According to Jewish tradition, the ancient Sanhedrin, a supreme court consisting of 71 judges that convened in Jerusalem, did have legal authority to issue rulings that were universally binding on the Jewish people. Further, following the dissolution of the Sanhedrin in the mid-fourth or early fifth century, rabbinic judges throughout the Jewish world generally recognized the central authority of the Babylonian Ge'onim, who headed the two leading academies of Jewish learning during the period 589–1040. Since that era, however, neither Jewish law nor rabbinic tradition has recognized any supreme rabbinic authority. Rather, halakhic interpretation and rabbinic regulation and decrees are binding only within the territory of the rabbis who issued them, even if certain rabbis exert considerable influence on their fellow decisors by virtue of the force of their reasoning, position, and personality.

According to Rivash, a fortiori, the power of a rabbinical court to issue a ban carrying a penalty of excommunication is limited to the territorial jurisdiction of the court. Hence, Banet concludes, following Rivash, that the reprinting bans issued for the Rodelheim *maḥzor* could have no force outside the territory of the rabbis who issued them, and were thus of no effect across the border in Prussia and Austria.

84. Isaac bar Sheshet Perfet (1326–1408), *Responsa Ha-Rivash*, No. 271.

85. See Nissim ben Reuven Gerondi (1320–1376; known in Jewish tradition as "Ran"), *Responsa Ran*, No. 48 (holding that one is obligated to follow the rulings of one's local rabbi).

6. *Reprinting bans that are merely printed in the book they aim to protect are not enforceable because a ban carrying a penalty of excommunication must be pronounced orally in a synagogue.*

Banet further attacks the validity of reprinting bans by citing authority that a *ḥerem*, like an oath, is effective only if pronounced orally in front of the community. A *ḥerem* that is promulgated only in writing, including in a printed form in a book, is void from the outset. The traditional rule requiring that a ban be pronounced orally in a synagogue provides further support for the understanding that bans are effective only in the local territory where they are issued. If a ban must be orally pronounced and heard in the community where it is issued, it will not have effect against someone who lives elsewhere and thus could not have heard it.

7. *Even if reprinting bans are enforceable in principle, they should not be enforced today, as the rabbinic bans cannot, in practice, be enforced against Christian publishers—therefore, enforcing them against Jewish publishers will only harm the Jewish publishers without benefiting the beneficiary of the ban.*

Banet also maintains that the factual realities of the publishing world in his age undercut the practical, and thus halakhic, basis for enforcing the ban on reprinting the Rodelheim *maḥzor*. Banet insists that, in his time, with a proliferation of non-Jewish publishers not obligated to follow any ban that a Jewish authority might impose on publishing, policy reasons in favor of such a ban lack force. A Jewish publisher who follows the reprinting ban loses out, whereas non-Jewish publishers are under no parallel disability. Therefore, the ban found in the Rodelheim *maḥzor* is both illogical and unenforceable.

Banet concedes that, in certain situations, the "Light of the Exile," Rabbeinu Gershom ben Judah (c. 960–1040?–1028?), had imposed a ban carving out exclusivity in certain retail markets in order to save Jewish store owners from the losses that would arise from mutual competition. But Banet adds that, even for Rabbeinu Gershom, if non-Jews—with no obligation to comply with the ban—engaged in competition with the Jewish store owner who was supposed to enjoy exclusivity, then other Jews were also permitted to enter the market. Any other rule would simply leave the field open to Gentiles.

In particular Banet addresses competition to obtain an *arenda* (from the Polish for "leasehold")—in essence, a concession that a person receives from the local sovereign authority for the sale of particular goods, typically a monopoly on estate management or distilling liquor.[86] Banet concludes, citing the precedent of earlier

86. Up to 80 percent of Jews were engaged in occupations related to the liquor trade during the previous century, leading to a wealth of responsa on point from which Banet and Sofer could draw. "The Jewish innkeeper, distiller, or brewer became a characteristic figure in the region, so much so that the terms *arendarz* (leaseholder) and 'Jew' became synonymous." Hundert 2006: 15, 53. For an extensive discussion of *arendy* (the plural in Polish), see Rosman 1990: 106–42 (underlining points that that arrendators could be either Jewish or Gentile—but the former were so common that the term was often used as

decisors, that no ban is imposed on such competition. The reason is that prohibiting Jews from competing against fellow Jews for an *arenda* would only leave the field open to Gentile competitors.

Likewise, in the case before him, if the right to print the Rodelheim *maḥzor* were denied to Heidenheim's Jewish rivals, then "this printer in Vienna," who faces no constraint imposed by rabbinic authorities, will simply grab the Jewish printer's market share by freely reprinting that *maḥzor* and distributing it throughout the world. Better, therefore, is a ruling that other Jews have the right to reprint the Rodelheim *maḥzor*, so that Schmid would not be able to walk into a wide open market. For, in either case, Heidenheim would lose business—either from the non-Jewish Viennese printer or from the other Jewish printers who would compete with him. Certainly, the sages would not impose a ban on reprinting the Rodelheim *maḥzor* when such a ban would just be counterproductive.

B. Sofer's Response to Banet, March 7, 1823

Sofer begins his response[87] by quoting in its entirety Banet's reply to Sofer's request that Banet join him in issuing an approbation and reprinting ban for the forthcoming book, *Oryan T'litai*. Banet's reply rehearses some of the principal arguments regarding the invalidity of reprinting bans that he set out in his responsum of August 22, 1822. Banet notes explicitly that he has recently written "in the same vein to the rabbi of the holy community of Dyhernfurth." Banet expresses skepticism about the need for approbations as well. He suggests that buyers of books know full well when a book is one of high quality and thus that rabbinic imprimatur is superfluous. The only reason for issuing *haskamot*, Banet states, is to decree a reprinting ban, but, for the reasons he enumerates, reprinting bans should not be issued. Banet concludes his letter by stating that "out of respect" (whether for the book's author or Sofer is unclear) he is nevertheless willing to issue an approbation for the book, but not a reprinting ban.

Sofer then responds to Banet with a number of arguments.

1. The practice of issuing approbations is necessary to ensure the integrity of texts of Jewish liturgy and learning.

Sofer expresses surprise that Banet seems to be prepared to eliminate the traditional practice of providing approbations and bans. Sofer insists, rather, that *haskamot* are vitally important even in connection with the printing of old and ancient books. Sadly, Sofer continued, the practice of securing *haskamot* has come to be disregarded,

a synonym for "Jew," and that a "large number of rabbinic responsa dealing with cases of *arenda* competition"). Banet must have been fully versed in the practice, as many Moravian Jews made their livelihood as arrendators, leasing distilleries, breweries, and taverns from the local landowners. Miller 2011: 34

87. *Responsa Ḥatam Sofer*, Ḥoshen Mishpat, No. 41.

and as a result two negative consequences have ensued. First, the Jewish people have become inundated with inaccurate and heretical texts. Second, publishers of new books name them with a title of an already published book, thus misleading readers who mistakenly think that they are buying the original book.[88] Thankfully, Sofer added, there are still God-fearing people who will only buy a new book if they see that it contains a *haskama* from an esteemed rabbi.

2. Reprinting bans are grounded in the Jewish law of wrongful competition.

Sofer then defends rabbinic reprinting bans. In a dramatic departure from Banet's positions, he argues that reprinting bans are a venerable rabbinic vehicle for protecting publishers against *hasagat gvul*, the type of wrongful competition that is prohibited in the Torah. Recall that the key biblical text here is: "Thou shalt not remove thy neighbor's landmarks" (Deut. 19:14). The simple meaning refers to moving the marker between two adjacent fields, essentially as a way of permanent trespass on that land. But later rabbinic law applied it generally to wrongful encroachment on another's means of earning a livelihood.

Along those lines, Sofer contended that "from the day that printing was established," rabbinical authorities issued a *gezeirat irin* or "heavenly decree"—a decree that is immutable and universal in scope—against all who would "trespass" on a publisher's livelihood by reprinting the publisher's recently issued book of Jewish liturgy or learning.[89] The rabbis did so in order to ensure that those who engage in mitzvot—in this case fulfilling God's commandments by disseminating the teaching of Jewish law—will not be harmed.

The prohibition against *hasagat gvul* set out in rabbinic reprinting bans, Sofer continues, is more critical and fundamental than the exclusive entitlements accorded under *arenda, ma'arufia*, and the principle of the Poor Man Who Shakes an Olive Tree. For with regard to those exclusive entitlements, if a merchant is unable to make a profit in one place due to ruinous competition in that location, he still might be able to make a profit by setting up his business elsewhere. For that reason, rabbis did not protect those exclusive entitlements by issuing a *ḥerem* against violators. In the case of publishers, however, it is impossible to publish a book without making a large initial investment of money and labor. As a result, reprinting without that publisher's permission will always cause the publisher a considerable loss. It was for this reason and on this doctrinal basis, grounded in the foundational law of the Torah, Sofer maintains, that the Rema forbade

88. On false attribution in Hebrew books, see Heller 2011: 269.

89. Sofer advanced a similar "heavenly decree" argument in another context: his opposition to the reformist Westphalian Consistory's proclamation that legumes may be eaten on Passover. Most traditionalist rabbis opposed that reform on the grounds that the prohibition on eating legumes, which had been extended throughout Ashkenazic communities by medieval authorities, was binding as matter of local custom. However, Sofer went further. He sought to give greater force to the ban against eating legumes on Passover by asserting that the prohibition arose from an immutable and universally binding decree issued by early medieval rabbis. See Katz 1998b: 431.

the reprinting of the *Mishneh Torah* by the Giustiniani, and that other rabbinic authorities have issued similar edicts forbidding reprinting, backed by the sanction of *ḥerem*.

3. Policy favors reprinting bans.

Sofer maintains further in his responsum that even if rabbinic reprinting bans were not grounded in the halakhic prohibition against wrongful competition, it would be fitting to issue a rabbinic edict banning reprinting. If we do not provide for such edicts, no one will enter the printing trade, and publishers of books of Jewish liturgy and learning will vanish. And if there are Gentile publishers who do not abide by such edicts, rabbinic authorities can prohibit Jews from buying books reprinted in violation of a ban. Such prohibitions on buyers, Sofer insists, will be an effective means of enforcing reprinting bans.

4. Reprinting bans are enforceable outside the territory where the ban was issued.

Sofer grants Banet's point that a rabbi may not generally issue a decree that is binding in another country. However, Sofer insists, there is an exception for reprinting bans. The rabbinic edicts establishing the universal enforceability of reprinting bans are of ancient origin. The reprinting bans were originally issued by our sages to be applied to all of Israel, wherever Jews may be.

5. Reprinting bans are valid and enforceable even in an age in which imperial and other secular authorities grant licenses for printing and forbid rabbinic bans.

Sofer's responsum vociferously challenges Banet's contention that reprinting bans should not be issued in an age in which imperial and secular authorities regulate business and forbid rabbinic bans. As Sofer dramatically puts it: "Is it really the case that I—a rabbinic authority—am just a mouthpiece for the King and a protector of the government that forbids us to place a *ḥerem* on anything? No, I am one who reminds others of their obligations under Jewish law to abide by the halakhic prohibition against wrongful competition."

In striking contrast to Sofer's resolute support for rabbinic reprinting bans in his response to Mordekhai Banet, elsewhere he advocated acquiescence in government-imposed restrictions on the rabbinic power of excommunication and public condemnation. In response to the reforms at the Hamburg Temple, Hamburg's traditionalist rabbinic court initially implored colleagues throughout Europe to join it in a public condemnation of the transgressors. Although agreeing that the reformers deserved public condemnation, Sofer expressed reservations about that course of action:

> And despite this I uphold the word of the king . . . for thus did the king, may he be exalted, command upon all the principals of his household and kingdom, to close the mouth of the lions, not to let them whisper or curse, and not to strike with the

> rod which does not draw blood. We are commanded by the Supreme Power not to transgress the law of the sovereign, and he has decreed, and who can undo it?

In light of Sofer's reticence to issue a ban and public condemnation against the Hamburg reformers, his embrace of continuing rabbinic authority to issue reprinting bans is puzzling. Perhaps Sofer viewed reprinting bans regarding books of Jewish liturgy and learning as more central to rabbinic prerogatives. Or perhaps he believed that government authorities would be more sanguine about local enforcement of rabbinic reprinting bans than they would about a public condemnation and ban on the Hamburg reformers jointly issued by leading rabbis from several countries.

One argument presented in Sofer's responsum points towards the latter. Sofer questions whether imperial authorities will perceive rabbinic reprinting bans as an affront to their prerogatives. The king, Sofer argues, earns tax revenue from publishers regardless of what books they publish. Thus, it should not matter to the king if publishers reprint a book or if, in order to comply with a reprinting ban, they must print a different book. The king will earn his revenue either way.

C. Banet's Response to Sofer, April 11, 1827

Sofer's letter drew a response from Mordekhai Banet. In his responsum, Banet directly took on Sofer's principal arguments.[90]

1. Sofer is incorrect about the origins of the reprinting ban.

Banet begins by countering Sofer's assumptions about the temporal and doctrinal origins of the reprinting ban. According to Banet, Sofer erred in stating that rabbinic authorities throughout the Jewish world joined in issuing reprinting bans to protect against wrongful competition at the birth of print. In fact, Banet counters, in most books published more than 100 years ago there is no mention of a reprinting ban. Rather, such bans have become prevalent only in recent times, having been sought by those who would "use the Torah as a spade." That reference to using the Torah as a spade is harsh. It follows a traditional rabbinic trope of condemnation—inasmuch as Torah occupies its own supernal realm, it is highly inappropriate to use it "as a spade," that is, as a mere instrumentality for personal profit.[91]

2. Reprinting bans do not serve the purpose of protecting from harm those who engage in mitzvot (i.e., Publishing books of Jewish liturgy and learning).

Banet also refutes Sofer's argument that, in protecting publishers of books of Jewish liturgy and learning from the harm of wrongful competition, reprinting bans serve

90. *Responsa Parshat Mordekhai,* No. 8.
91. Mishnah Avot 4: 5.

the goal of protecting those who engage in mitzvot from harm. That proposition is difficult to accept, Banet insists, "for are not the publishers that come afterwards equally engaging in a mitzvah by producing books that can be purchased at low cost?" Moreover, most printers are not intending at all to engage in a mitzvah, but instead are just out to make a profit. Perhaps, Banet concedes, someone who labors in his study to create a *new* book might qualify as one who engages in mitzvot, while those who merely reprint previously published books might not. After all, the reprinters are able to publish the book of Jewish learning only because of a mitzvah already performed by the first author-publisher. However, if a publisher is merely bringing out a second printing of his previously published book, he no more qualifies as one who engages in the mitzvah of disseminating the study of Torah than any other publisher who reprints that book.

3. The doctrinal basis for reprinting bans is consensus among those in the publishing trade, not wrongful competition.

Reiterating a point he made in his first responsum, Banet maintains that rabbinic authorities have never issued a sweeping edict against reprinting as a matter of rabbinic regulation per se. Rather, the rabbis of previous generations who instituted the practice of issuing reprinting bans did so upon the request of book publishers for the publishers' mutual benefit. The doctrinal basis for reprinting bans is thus something akin to trade guild regulations, not wrongful competition. Here Banet cites *Shulḥan Arukh*, Ḥoshen Mishpat 231:28, which sets forth the rights of members of a given trade to establish among themselves uniform norms—in essence guild regulations—and to sanction those who do not conform to those norms. As Banet explains, publishers agreed among themselves: "Today it will be profitable for this publisher to have an exclusive right for a period of years to publish a particular book and subsequently it will be profitable for another publisher to print his book with the protection of a reprinting ban."

As we have seen in Chapter 2, printers' guilds were indeed ubiquitous throughout the early modern period. However, as noted in Chapter 5 (and as Banet's detractors have been quick to point out), there is no evidence of any guild or industry-wide agreement of all Jewish publishers, and it is extremely unlikely that non-Jewish publishers would have requested that a rabbi issue a reprinting ban to support their agreements. On the other hand, as also noted in Chapter 5, the sole record we have of a Jewish printers' guild is of such a guild established in Moravia in the seventeenth century. Given that Banet was chief rabbi of Moravia, perhaps he drew upon lore about that guild in formulating his theory that a guild agreement served as the basis for rabbinic reprinting bans. He might have also extrapolated from his knowledge of non-Jewish printers' guilds. Or he might have simply hypothesized the historical existence of a Jewish printers' guild or industry-wide agreement without any particular evidence to support it.

In any event, Banet continues, the guild regulation or trade custom rationale for reprinting bans no longer applies in our day. For one, when rival publishers object to the issuance of reprinting bans, those bans are no longer an expression of uniform trade agreement and are thus of no force and effect. (Here Banet stands on firm doctrinal ground: medieval commentators held that only a unanimous agreement among tradesmen may take effect as binding regulation, a view adopted by the Rema in his commentary on the *Shulḥan Arukh*.) Moreover, Banet adds, today most publishers are non-Jews and thus not obligated to abide by rabbinic reprinting bans. Indeed, a growing number of Jews also flout the sanction of *ḥerem*. Under those conditions, enforcing reprinting bans would no longer be to the mutual benefit of all publishers. Rather, upholding the ban against a halakhically observant Jewish publisher who wishes to reprint a book would only harm that publisher, while doing nothing to ensure the profit of the first publisher, because Gentiles and non-observant Jews would still be free to reprint the book.

4. Rabbinic efforts to enforce reprinting bans will lead to confrontation with government authorities.

Banet takes particular issue with Sofer's contention that the government does not care which publishers have the right to print which books, so long as all publishers pay the applicable taxes to the government each year. Banet counters that he has personally tested the validity of that proposition. It is here that Banet recounts his bitter experience in being hauled before the Austrian authorities and threatened with prosecution for rebelling against the government when he initially publicized the reprinting ban on the Rodelheim *maḥzor*.

D. Sofer's Final Rebuttal (Undated)

Sofer's final rebuttal to Banet canvassed a number of arguments, ranging from wrongful competition to policy dictates.[92]

1. Reprinting bans protect publishers against wrongful competition.

Sofer begins his final rebuttal to Banet's arguments by stating, "I have now reviewed the laws of *yored l'omanut ḥavero*," meaning the various doctrines and cases that, together, make up the Jewish law of wrongful competition. Aside from providing citations and a mnemonic for anyone who wishes to study the cases outlined in Banet's first responsum and enumerated above, Sofer quickly moves on to other possible grounds for supporting rabbinic reprinting bans.

But Sofer later returns to the wrongful competition cases with the contention that publishers are especially worthy of protection under its aegis. Sofer first refers to the Case of the Fish Who Lock Their Sight on the Bait. Recall that Rashi and other authorities held that the reason competition may be limited in this case is that the first fisherman is certain to catch the fish when the second fisherman interlopes and takes it first. In contrast to Banet, who held that publishers cannot say with certainty that the

92. *Responsa Ḥatam Sofer*, Ḥoshen Mishpat, No. 79

public will buy their books, Sofer posits that, given the long-standing custom of granting reprinting bans, publishers have, indeed, come to be certain that no other publisher will come and encroach upon their livelihood by reprinting their books. Moreover, continues Sofer, the damage that would be caused to a publisher from such an encroachment would be far more severe than that caused to the fisherman or to the first to set up a mill on an open alley. Publishers typically invest large sums of their own savings in printing a book. They would thus suffer severe personal harm, not just a diminution in profit, from the encroachment. Finally, Sofer avers, the second publisher can always print a different book rather than reprinting the first publisher's book, just as the other fishermen can move their nets away from that of the first fisherman. In such circumstances, a reprinting ban, backed by a threat of *ḥerem*, is definitely warranted.

2. *The jealousy of scholars increases wisdom.*

Sofer concedes that even Rav Huna—whose minority view, it will be recalled, would accord the first merchant to set up shop in a neighborhood a right to prevent another from setting up a competing business in that location—permits unrestricted competition when it comes to those engaged in teaching Torah. The reason is the Talmudic dictum, set out in the same passage in which Rav Huna debates the majority who favor free competition, that the jealousy of scholars—and teachers—(literally "scribes") fosters greater wisdom: *kinat sofrim tarbeh ḥokhmah.*[93] In invoking this dictum, Sofer quotes a version of the Talmudic passage that puts it in context: "Perhaps we should fear [that the second scholar will put the first scholar out of business and then, without any competition] he will be indolent? And [the Talmud] then replied: 'the jealousy of scholars increases wisdom.'" Hence, we need not fear that intense market competition might harm the study of Torah when one competing teacher-scholar is able to drive his local rivals out of business. Even if only one teacher-scholar remains in a particular location, he, like all scholars, will be inherently driven to strive to exceed the knowledge and intellectual prowess of other scholars no matter where they are located.

Thus far, Sofer seems to be left with the majority rule that favors free competition, plus the admission, even among the minority, that there is no reason to hinder free market competition among Jewish scholars because even if all but one are driven out of business, the remaining scholar will still be driven to excel in learning and teaching Torah. Indeed, Sofer goes even further. He surmises that the rule favoring free competition should apply not just to teachers and scholars, but to all who engage in mitzvot, including publishers of books of Jewish liturgy and learning. Indeed, Sofer surmises, the rationale behind the rule should apply to all merchants and peddlers, for even merchants and peddlers who are not Jewish scholars are unlikely to abandon their business (i.e., become indolent) merely because they have successfully driven their competitors out of business.

The majority rule would thus seem to be that the principle of "the jealousy of scholars increases wisdom" supports free competition among publishers and thus stands contrary to granting any publisher the exclusive right to print a book of

93. *Babylonian Talmud, Baba Batra* 21a.

Jewish learning or liturgy. That is certainly how many nineteenth-century rabbinic decisors understood and applied that dictum to publishing. But Sofer then turns the proposition favoring free competition on its head. He draws from it the negative inference that Jewish law *does* restrict competition in those special cases in which there *is* reason to fear that a latecomer would drive an incumbent out of business and then become indolent. In those cases, Sofer argues, the rationale behind the "jealousy of scholars" rule does not apply, and we do give the incumbent merchant an exclusive right to engage in his trade.

The relevance of this negative inference to book publishers is quite attenuated, as Sofer nowhere argues that a publisher who drove his competitors out of business would then stop printing books. However, Sofer later states that, unless book publishers are protected by reprinting bans, they would become indolent for another reason: no publisher would invest in publishing books if any other publisher could come along and deprive the first of his profit by reprinting the book before the first has sold out his print run. Hence for that reason, it seems, Sofer concludes—contrary to other rabbinic authorities—that the maxim "the jealousy of scholars increases wisdom" does not apply to publishers of books of Jewish learning.

> 3. *Rabbis of early ages instituted a practice of issuing reprinting bans to forbid* hasagat gvul *and ensure that those who engage in mitzvot not be harmed.*

Sofer counters Banet's claim that reprinting bans are of recent vintage: "And I have scrutinized books and found proof of the custom of issuing *haskamot* for nearly 200 years, and it seems that this custom initially commenced after the Maharam of Padua printed the Rambam's books, and a certain Gentile trespassed upon his boundary, and the Rema issued his decree, as explicated in his responsum. From this time onwards, the rabbis began to erect fences in front of intruders and routinely inscribed in a *haskama* that those who engage in mitzvot will not be harmed." Moroever, Sofer continues, citing a number of related precedents, publishers qualify as persons who engage in mitzvot even if their motivation to print and sell books of Jewish learning is entirely to earn a living, and not to engage in a mitzvah in and of itself.

> 4. *Reprinting bans are not limited by territory, but, in order to protect publishers against wrongful competition, must have worldwide scope.*

Sofer argues that the conditions of the Hebrew book trade require that publishers be protected against wrongful competition throughout the world, not just in their own country. In essence, Sofer argues, even though the general rule is that an incumbent merchant may only prevent competitors who would deprive him of his livelihood from entering the merchant's own town, not engaging in business elsewhere, an exception to this territorial constraint must be made for book publishers. As Sofer states: "It is well known that it is impossible for a publisher to earn a livelihood if he does not print hundreds and thousands of books. But we, the nation of God, are a small minority in this country and thus it is impossible that publishers of Jewish books would be able to sell a sufficient amount of books if limited to a local market. Moreover, the books of the Talmud and the writings of rabbinic decisors and commentators are needed only by diligent rabbinic scholars and they, because of our many transgressions, are a small minority of the Jewish people . . . . Accordingly, where book publishers are concerned, the whole world is considered as one town . . . . And if another person shall reprint the first publisher's book within a short period—even at a distance of one hundred parsaot [approximately 4,500 kilometers]—the first publisher will not sell his books and he will lose that which belongs to him. Hence, unless protected by a reprinting ban, no person would be fool enough to draw near the printing of books."

Therefore, Sofer concludes, "it would have been appropriate to erect a fence to protect publishers against wrongful competition even if doing so were not dictated by halakhic doctrine and even if rabbis of earlier generations did not adopt such a decree *en masse* and as a unified group. In any event, issuing reprinting bans is the custom which everyone has adopted during the past several hundred years." Sofer then provides a litany of examples in which rabbis have issued reprinting bans for books of Jewish learning.

Recall that when the Moses Isserles forbade Jews from purchasing editions of the *Mishneh Torah* that competed with those of the Maharam of Padua, he limited the territorial scope of that ban to Poland. Sofer expresses puzzlement with that limitation and proffers a possible explanation for it. He hypothesizes that because the Rema's principle grounds for ruling in favor of the Maharam applied to Giustiniani's wrongful conduct, not obligations of buyers per se, the Rema "did not gather the courage to give his ruling application to scholarly buyers outside his territory." For Sofer, therefore, the territorial limitation of Isserles's decree has to do with the happenstance of how Isserles chose to frame his ruling. Sofer does not read Isserles's territorial limitation to stand for the proposition that reprinting bans must necessarily be limited to the territory of the rabbi who issues the ban.

5. Reprinting bans may be directed to prohibit Jews from buying reprints of books of Jewish liturgy or learning from non-Jewish publishers.

Sofer also invokes two secondary grounds for the Rema's ruling in favor of the Maharam of Padua: rabbinic authorities have ruled that Jews can be required to (1) buy from Jewish merchants rather than a Gentile merchant, even if the Gentile sells at a lower price; and (2) give preference to Jewish merchants who are rabbinic scholars. Although those injunctions are subject to various qualifications, Sofer maintains that both always apply when the merchants are selling books of Jewish liturgy or learning. In line with that precedent, Sofer holds, rabbinic reprinting bans may forbid Jews from buying a book that has been reprinted by a Gentile publisher in competition with a Jewish publisher. And what of Banet's harrowing experience in being hauled before the Austrian authorities for disseminating a reprinting ban against purchasing Anton Schmid's reprint of the Rodelheim *maḥzor*? Sofer makes no reference to Banet's testimonial. Rather, as he did in his initial response to Banet, Sofer expresses a steadfast refusal to give way before the constraints imposed by secular authorities: "We have thus learned that with regards to book publishers, even if he is a book publisher from the Nations [i.e., a Gentile] who is not required to carry out the rulings of the Sages of Israel; and moreover, even if the government has prohibited the import of books from outside of the country to within the country, and it is thus impossible to bring those books to the country," Jews may still be prohibited from purchasing the Gentile publisher's reprinted edition.

6. Wolf Heidenheim is deserving of protection.

Finally, Sofer relates that he had received a letter from Tzvi Hirsch Horowitz, praising Heidenheim and asking that the 25-year reprinting ban issued on Heidenheim's behalf be enforced. Quite possibly, that letter was the same written appeal that Horowitz had sent to Mordekhai Banet and other rabbinic authorities in 1807. But it would likely have borne special significance for Sofer, who had been a devoted pupil in his youth in Frankfurt am Main of Tzvi Hirsch Horowitz's father, Pinḥas Horowitz, issuer of one of the reprinting bans in favor of Heidenheim.[94] As Sofer recounts from the letter:

> [Heidenheim] devoted substantial time to proofreading religious hymns and translating them into the language of Ashkenaz [German]. Moreover, if it was not for him, the hymns would have already been absorbed [in the earth and forgotten] and, as is well understood, would not have been recited by these generations. [But] he labored and gathered a sufficient quantity of books for the hundreds [of worshippers] who need this undertaking, and he expended a great deal of money to produce his books, and [he] still remains accountable [for unpaid debts]. . . .
>
> And our pious *Geonim* and rabbis of Ashkenaz [Germany], may their righteous memories be blessed, have determined that his reward should consist of reserving the market for 25 years, so that no other person shall trespass upon his boundary, since he was unable to print a sufficient amount [of *maḥzorim*] for all of Israel, for 25 years, at a single moment in time. Hence, he prints and reprints [the books at various intervals], and he [may] secure his reward for all of [the merchandise].

Sofer concludes that "the other publishers should publish different *maḥzorim* or other books, for why should they benefit from that which he [Wolf Heidenheim] has created?" The other publishers are like the interloping fisherman in the Case of the Fish Who Lock Their Sight on the Bait. They should be required "to remove their nets the distance of a *parsa*," and must seek to catch other fish.

E. Conclusion

In sum, in his responsa, Mordekhai Banet holds that rabbinic reprinting bans were grounded in a consensus agreement among the publishing trade—essentially embodying guild regulations—that is no longer of force and effect given that the

94. On Sofer's continuing esteem for Pinḥas Horowitz, see Katz 1998b: 406–08.

conditions underlying the agreement have radically changed and the prior consensus among publishers has disintegrated. Concomitantly, rabbinic reprinting bans have no basis in the halakhic doctrine of wrongful competition. Nor do bans find support in rabbinic authority to protect those who engage in mitzvot, at least with respect to bans that would accord exclusivity for second and third printings of editions that have already been published and sold. Further, in the absence of any such halakhic justification, rabbis have no authority to issue a ban that enables one publisher to profit at another's expense. Indeed, even if rabbinic reprinting bans are valid exercises of rabbinic authority, they may not be enforced outside the territory in which they were issued or after the publisher has sold out his edition and thus recovered his investment. Finally, Banet asserts that reprinting bans are counterproductive because, by preventing Jewish publishers from reprinting, they merely leave the field open to non-Jewish publishers, who are not bound by the bans.

In contrast, Moses Sofer maintains that rabbinic reprinting bans serve to enforce a publisher's right against wrongful competition under fundamental tenets of halakha, not merely guild regulation. Further, even if publishers did not have such a right, rabbinic reprinting bans would be a necessary measure to promote the publication of books of Jewish liturgy and learning and to protect those who engage in the mitzvah of publishing such works. Moreover, given that publishers' markets extend across borders, bans must be enforceable throughout the Jewish world, not just in the territory where issued. Sofer also highlights the halakhic force of what he describes as the ancient custom of issuing bans that have effect throughout the world. Finally, bans may be enforced even in an age of competition from non-Jewish publishers and secular governments' contraction of rabbinic autonomy. Bans may prohibit Jews from *buying* illicit editions, and kings should not object so long as they receive tax revenue from the Jewish publisher who benefits from the rabbinic reprinting ban.

In their extended colloquy, Banet and Sofer also present contrasting interpretations of the Rema's seminal ruling regarding the Maharam of Padua. For Banet, the Rema's ruling stood only for the unique case in which an exceptionally well-heeled competitor may cause certain harm and, indeed, deliberately causes severe harm through predatory pricing. For Sofer, in contrast, the Rema's ruling is proof that rabbinic reprinting bans are grounded in the foundational halakhic doctrine of wrongful competition.

Sofer's responses to Banet were not his last word on the subject of copyright. Perhaps surprisingly, he later presented grounds to limit the scope of rabbinic reprinting bans. As we shall presently see, Sofer later declared that Heidenheim's *maḥzor* presented a special case. Most publishers, Sofer held, have an exclusive right to print only until they have sold out their first edition—and rabbis have no authority to issue a ban that extends beyond that time.

CHAPTER 7

Internecine Battles and the Slavuta Talmud

Soon after his colloquy with Mordekhai Banet, Moses Sofer was called upon to opine on yet another dispute involving Jewish copyright law. The dispute arose over two competing editions of the Talmud: one that the Shapira printing house began to print in Slavuta, Volhynia (in present day Ukraine), in 1835, and the second that the Romm press began to print in Vilna that same year. The dispute embroiled hundreds of rabbis and rekindled a smoldering internecine battle between rival streams within Judaism, the Ḥasidic movement and its traditional rabbinic opponents, the "Mitnagdim."

The dispute between the Slavuta and Vilna publishers erupted some two decades after a similar dispute between the Slavuta press and the Yaffe press in Kapust, which began printing its own edition of the Talmud in 1816. In each case, the Slavuta press insisted that its rival had violated the rabbinic reprinting bans issued for the Slavuta publishers' successive editions of the Talmud. And each of the Slavuta publishers' rivals argued that the ban against competing editions of the Talmud had automatically expired the moment the Slavuta press sold out its print run, even though the nominal term of years set forth in the ban had not yet come to an end. Moreover, the rivals further insisted, a ban does not apply outside the publisher's local market.

As rabbinic decisors grappled with those central issues regarding reprinting bans' duration and geographical scope, they engaged in a protracted and lively debate about the justifications and legal foundations for rabbinic reprinting bans.

I. THE SLAVUTA TALMUD

The Slavuta press was founded by Moses Shapira, the rabbi of Slavuta, in 1791, pursuant to an exclusive privilege granted by Duke Hariam Sangajski.[1] Shapira was a devout adherent of Ḥasidism, and his press was closely identified with that movement. The Slavuta press published hundreds of Ḥasidic titles, contributing to the widespread popularization of Ḥasidic beliefs, practices, and liturgy among Eastern European Jews.[2] It also published mainstream rabbinic and halakhic works, including the Talmud and the medieval code of Jewish law, the *Arba'a Turim*. The press's editions of the Talmud were exemplars of beauty, typographical clarity, and high quality paper, widely sought throughout the Jewish world.[3] "Who in Germany did not hear of the deluxe printing house in Slavuta?" asked a German-Jewish newspaper in 1840.[4]

The Slavuta press issued its first edition of the Talmud between 1801 and 1806. Shapira's silent partner in that venture was Shneur Zalman of Liady (c. 1745–1812), a rabbinic luminary who founded Ḥabad Ḥasidism.[5] Shneur Zalman invested in the production of the Talmud through two agents: his brother, Mordekhai Barukh, and son-in-law, Shalom Shakhna. The *haskama* and reprinting ban for the Slavuta Talmud issued by celebrated Ḥasidic leader Levi Yitzḥak of Berditchev (1740–1809), which is reproduced in Illustration 11, expressly names Barukh and Shakhna as the holders of the printing right. (The other *haskamot* simply refer to the Slavuta publishers without identifying them by name.) According to Shneur Zalman's agreement with Shapira, Shapira was to receive one-sixth of the proceeds from the sale of the Talmud, with the remainder due presumably to Shneur Zalman.

The *haskamot* issued for the first edition of the Slavuta Talmud pronounced a 25-year reprinting ban. They warned that violators would be deemed to have committed wrongful competition (*hasagat gvul*) and face the punishment of *ḥerem*. Along the lines of Moses Sofer's defense of rabbinic reprinting bans, the leading Ḥasidic rabbis who issued the ban stated that in prohibiting anyone else from printing the Talmud during the ban's term, they acted by authority of an age-old edict issued by sages of earlier generations.

The Slavuta press sold out its first edition well before 1826, when the initial 25-year period set out in the reprinting ban was set to expire. Indeed, the Slavuta house began to print its second edition in 1808 and completed it in 1813. Beginning with that edition, Shneur Zalman transferred his printing rights to Moses Shapira.[6] Shneur Zalman also reaffirmed the 25-year reprinting ban that had commenced with the printing of the first edition. Shapira's press soon sold out all—or substantially all—of its second edition as well.

1. Friedberg 1950: 104.
2. Stanislawski 2005: 100.
3. S. Ginsburg 1991: 30.
4. S. Ginsburg 1991: 30–31 (quoting *The Orient* (#3) (1840).
5. My discussion of the Slavuta printing house's first three editions of the Talmud and of the business arrangements that surrounded them draws heavily upon Levi Yitzhak Cooper's highly illuminating, and as yet unpublished, study. Cooper 2013.
6. Shneur Zalman (c. 1745–1812), *Mesirat Koaḥ Ve-Zkhut Al Hadpasat Ha-Shas Be-Slavita.*

הסכמות הרבנים הגאונים המפורסמים

הסכמת
הרב המאור הגדול המפורסם
החריף ובקי הגאון האמיתי
איש אלהי קדוש יאמר לו כבוד
שמו מוהר"ר יעקב שמשון אב"ד דק"ק סלאוויטא
ומצ"פ בק"ק שופעטיווקא ובק"ק באר ובק"ק אומן
והגליל אשר לע"ע מקום ישיבתו בארץ הקדושה
טבריא תוב"בא :

הסכמת
הרב המאור הגדול המפורסם
החריף ובקי הגאון האמיתי
איש אלהי קדוש יאמר לו מוהר"ר לוי יצחק אב"ד
דק"ק בארדיטשוב :

Illustration 11
Haskamot of Yaakov Shimshon of Slavuta and Levi Yitzḥak of Berditchev for Slavuta Talmud, First Edition, 1801.
(courtesy National Library of Israel).

II. THE KAPUST TALMUD

In 1816, another prolific Ḥasidic publisher, Israel Yaffe (c. 1749–1829), began to print an edition of the Talmud at his press in Kapust (today Kopys, Belarus). He did so even though the 25-year period set out in the rabbinic reprinting bans for the Slavuta Talmud had not yet expired.[7] To defend himself against possible claims by Shapira, Yaffe obtained seven *haskamot*. The *haskamot* presented several arguments why the Slavuta reprinting ban should be of no force and effect. The principal arguments were that (1) 25 years was an unprecedented, unreasonably long period of exclusivity; (2) the Slavuta press had already sold out its first and second printings, and thus there was no justification for the ban to continue in force; (3) all printers should be entitled to engage in the mitzvah of printing books of Jewish law and learning, free from a monopoly given to one printer because he was the first to print the book; and (4) the Slavuta reprinting ban did not apply outside the boundaries of the Russian administrative district of Volhynia, even to Kapust, which was located in a different administrative district of the Russian Empire.[8]

7. My summary of the dispute between Yaffe and Shapira draws upon the illuminating and more detailed discussions in Cooper 2013 and Mondshein 2003a.

8. Kapust was in White Russia. A number of the *haskamot* for Yaffe's Talmud are discussed and quoted at length in Rakover 1970: 57–64. The first argument of Yaffe's defenders was not entirely correct. Although rabbinic authorities initially issued reprinting bans that were far shorter than 25 years, longer bans became more common in the eighteenth

Of particular note, the rabbinic court of Shklov, a community near Kapust, issued a *haskama* for Yaffe's Talmud that expressly embraced Mordekhai Banet's holding that the legal basis for rabbinic reprinting bans lies in a centuries-old rabbinic decree that effectively codified Jewish publishers' guild regulations. In turn, the Shklov court posited, that decree was predicated upon a general understanding among publishers that reprinting bans would be applied to their mutual benefit. The condition of mutual benefit was not met in the case of Yaffe's Talmud, the rabbinic court held, because (1) Yaffe began printing his Talmud in reliance on evidence that the Slavuta press had already sold out its edition and thus he would suffer harm if prevented from completing and selling his Talmud, and (2) the Slavuta press sought the exclusive right to print the Talmud for a second and third time, which runs contrary to the assumption underlying the postulated guild regulation that one publisher would benefit from the first printing of a book and then another publisher would benefit from the next printing of that book.

In contrast, in his *haskama* for Yaffe's Talmud, Abraham Shor of Orsha insisted that Mordekhai Banet was wrong: there is no record of previous regulations issued by or on behalf of Jewish publishers.[9] Nor do the *haskamot* of earlier generations refer to any such guild regulation. Rather, the legal basis for rabbinic reprinting bans lies in the Jewish law of wrongful competition (*hasagat gvul*). Moreover, Shor contended—echoing Moses Sofer's earlier argument—that it can be wrongful competition to reprint a book even in a foreign territory because publishers must recover their investment by selling their books in several countries. Nonetheless, Shor concluded, a publisher's right against wrongful competition is not absolute. Rather it is limited to enabling the publisher to recover his initial investment. Therefore, Yaffe was entitled to print his Talmud after the Slavuta press had recovered its investment by selling all, or even substantially all, of its prior edition. In that vein, a reprinting ban is to be interpreted not by its literal language setting out a term of years, but in line with the intent of those who issued it—to enable the publisher to recover his investment. Moreover, given that wrongful competition is not an absolute right, rabbinic decisors have often limited the geographical scope of publisher's exclusive right to their own territory, which is typically the publisher's primary market. In that vein, it was not wrongful competition for Yaffe to compete with the Slavuta press in selling the Talmud when the volumes printed by that press do not typically reach Kapust.

The arguments of Yaffe's defenders were countered by a preeminent rabbinic authority of that era, Ephraim Zalman Margoliot (1760–1828).[10] Margoliot insisted that Yaffe was forbidden to print the Talmud because the reprinting ban given to the Slavuta press remained in effect for its full term of 25 years even if that press had sold its entire printing before the ban was set to expire. Margoliot's argument rested on the

and nineteenth centuries. As discussed in the previous chapter, in 1800 Wolf Heidenheim received 25-year reprinting bans for *Sefer Krovot*. Further, the Council of Four Lands enforced a 25-year ban issued in 1752, for the Proops Talmud, printed in Amsterdam. Rakover 1970: 30.

9. Shor's *haskama* is reprinted in Mondshein 2003a: 126–30.

10. See Rakover 1986-87: 836–37 (summarizing Margoliot's unpublished responsum as referenced by other rabbinic authorities of the nineteenth century).

age-old halakhic principle that anything that is forbidden by a rabbinic court may later be permitted only by a rabbinic court of equal or greater authority.[11] For Margoliot, a rabbinic decree forbidding reprinting for a number of years may be curtailed only by a rabbinic court of equal or greater authority, even if, arguably, the rationale for the reprinting ban no longer holds because the publisher has sold out his entire edition.[12]

Margoliot's thinly veiled inference was that the Shklov rabbinic court and other rabbis who awarded Yaffe *haskamot* were of lesser authority than those who had issued the original reprinting bans for the Slavuta Talmud. Margoliot's slight of Yaffe's rabbinic supporters bespoke the sectarian rivalry between Ḥasidim and Mitnagdim. Although Yaffe was a noted publisher of Ḥasidic literature, he was hard pressed to obtain *haskamot* from Ḥasidic rabbis after Ḥasidic luminaries, most notably Shneur Zalman of Liady and Levi Yitzḥak of Berditchev, had already lined up in favor of the Slatuva press. Almost all of those who gave Yaffe a *haskama*—and whom Margoliot deemed to be lesser authorities—were prominent Mitnagdim.[13]

In any event, Yaffe's fears of a possible challenge by Shapira were well founded. When Yaffe began to distribute exemplar pages of his edition of the Talmud to assist him in selling subscriptions for the purchase of a full multi-volume set, the Slavuta publisher charged that Yaffe had violated the 25-year reprinting ban. Shortly thereafter, in an arbitration agreement signed on July 22, 1816, before Shneur Zalman's son, Dov Be'er (1773–1827), the parties agreed to have the dispute heard before a rabbinic court in the vicinity of Slavuta.[14] There is no record that that agreed-upon proceeding ever transpired, however. Perhaps Shapira was cowed by the *haskamot* from leading rabbis that Yaffe had obtained. In any event, Yaffe amassed some 3,000 subscribers for his edition of the Talmud and proceeded to print the work one tractate at a time, completing the full set some 12 years later, in 1828.

Meanwhile, quickly following on Yaffe's initiatives, Shapira's Slavuta press proceeded to print its third edition of the Talmud. The first volume of that edition came off the press in 1817 and the final volume in 1822. Shapira was thus able to complete his third edition of the Talmud in just five years, less than half the time it took Yaffe to print his first. Even though Shapira appears to have dropped his claim against Yaffe in rabbinic court, in his third edition he again prominently displayed

11. The rule "kol davar she-be-minyan tzarikh minyan aḥer lehatiro" has roots in the Pentateuch and was further developed by Talmudic and medieval rabbinic authorities. It is not to be confused with a related rule, "a rabbinic court may not override the ruling of a sister court unless it is greater in wisdom and number." For discussion of that rule, see Elon 1997: 443–46.

12. As Yehoshua Mondshein concludes, it appears that, by reaffirming the original 25-year ban in his *haskama* for the second edition of the Slavuta Talmud, Shneur Zalman likewise took the position that a ban remains in force for its full nominal term even if the initial edition has been sold. See Mondshein 2003a: 124.

13. Mondshein 2003a: 125. An exception was Abraham Shor of Orsha, whose *haskama* is discussed above. Shor was a prominent figure in Ḥabad Ḥasidism and a close associate of Menaḥem Mendel Schneersohn, who assumed spiritual leadership of Ḥabad Ḥasidism in 1831 and subsequently authored a responsum in support of the Romm press against the Slavuta press's reprinting bans.

14. Cooper 2013: 5.

מסכת

פסחים

מן

תלמוד בבלי

עם פירש״י ותוספות ופסקי תוספות ורבינו אשר ופסקי הרא״ש ופירוש
המשניות מהרמב״ם ז״ל

וחילופי גרסאות ותוספות ישנים המה נצבים על מקומם הראוי בכל דף ובתוספת הגהות של הגאון
ר׳ ישעיה ברלין ז״ל הכל כאשר נדפס פה״ק בפעם שנית דף על דף ממש ובכל מעלות הנזכרים
שמה אתת מהנה לא נעדרה :

ועתה נדפס הש״ס פעם שלישית בתוספות מרובה לרכות כל בעלי חוברין לסמיכה סמיכת חכמים עטרת הפוסקים
וראשי המפרשים העמודים והמכונות אשר בית ישראל נשען עליהם למען לא יצטרכו חפש מחופש אחת הנה
ואחת הנה הלא המה

הרב אלפסי עם כל נושאי כליו לא נפקד דבר מן האלפסין הנדפסים פה״ק לבדם ;

וספר חכמת שלמה מהגאון מהרש״ל ז״ל : וספר מהרש״א חידושי
הלכות : וחידושי אגדות : ולמען כל רואים יכירום מה המה אלה הדפסנו חידושי אגדות באותיות קטנים

וספר מהר״ם מלובלין על כמה מסכתות הנמצאים בחיבורו :

ופירוש מעדני יום טוב ודברי חמודות מהגאון בעל תוספות יום טוב
על הרא״ש על כל המסכתות הנמצאים בחבורים הנ״ל והצבנו ציונים בתוך הרא״ש על סדר א״ב וציון הוא דבעי דרישה
בשני החוברות האלה ועל סדר נזיקין יהיה נדפס פירוש מספר פלפלא חריפתא שחיבר הגאון הנ״ל :

אלכסנדר פאוולאוויטש

בסלאוויטא

בשנת

Illustration 12
Slavuta Talmud, Shapira Press, Tractate Pesaḥim Title Page, Third Edition, 1817–1822.
(courtesy National Library of Israel).

the rabbinic reprinting bans that granted him exclusivity in printing and selling the Talmud. In particular, Shapira reprinted Shneur Zalman's transfer of rights and reiteration of the original 25-year reprinting ban. He also obtained and printed new *haskamot* that granted him an additional 15-year period of exclusivity that would begin to run only when he finished printing the entire third edition.[15] Given that Shapira finished printing his third edition of the Talmud in 1822, that stated period of exclusivity, lasting 15 years from completion, would not expire until 1837.

III. THE VILNA TALMUD

In 1834, a new, more serious competitor to the Slavuta press arose. That year, the well-heeled Romm printing house in Vilna, a press famous throughout the Jewish world for its publication of traditional rabbinic works—but decidedly not Ḥasidic literature, began to print its own edition of the Talmud.[16] The Romm house's principal justification for flouting the Slavuta press's still subsisting reprinting ban was essentially the same as that of Israel Yaffe: the Slavuta press had already sold out its third edition, so the 15-year reprinting ban granted for that edition was no longer in effect.[17] On those grounds, the Romm publishers were able to obtain *haskamot* in their favor from several leading rabbinic authorities in Vilna and elsewhere. These *haskamot* were not merely approbations, moreover; they also included reprinting bans lasting 15 years from the Romm house's completion of its edition of the Talmud.

As a result, the Slavuta press, now managed by Moses Shapira's two sons, did not only face rabbinic imprimaturs for its competitor's Talmud in derogation of its own ban. The Slavuta printers also had to contend with reprinting bans that forbade them from publishing another edition of the Talmud in competition with that of the Romm press. They responded much as their father had responded to Yaffe, both by immediately proceeding to print their next edition of the Talmud and complaining to various rabbinic authorities, including those who had issued *haskamot* for the Vilna Talmud, that the Romm press had violated the Slavuta press's reprinting ban.

The Slavuta press and its rabbinic supporters argued once again that the press's reprinting ban must remain in force for the entire period set out in the ban regardless of whether the press had sold out its print run. Furthermore, the Slavuta publishers maintained that they still had in inventory 37 unsold sets of their third edition of the Talmud. They contended, on that basis, that their ban remained in force in any event—even assuming for purposes of argument that reprinting bans do expire when the publisher has sold out his edition.

15. See Schneersohn, *Responsa Tzemaḥ Tzedek*, Yoreh De'ah, No. 295 (describing reprinting ban given to third edition of Slavuta Talmud).
16. Stanislawski 2005: 101.
17. Bayvel 2002: 118–19; Rabbinovicz 1951: 136–38.

Illustration 13
Vilna Talmud, Romm Press, Tractate Brakhot Title Page, 1835.
(courtesy National Library of Israel).

Following the Slavuta press's complaint, some of the rabbis who had initially supported the Vilna Talmud withdrew their *haskamot*. The dispute was then brought before the rabbinic court of Grodno, quite possibly by the Romm family, given that Grodno was where the Romm press had been founded in 1789.[18] The Grodno rabbinic court ruled in favor of the Romm press, but on the condition that prior to issuing their own edition of the Talmud, the Romm family would have to buy from the Slavuta publishers their remaining unsold inventory of the third edition.

The Slavuta publishers were unwilling to accept the ruling of the Grodno rabbinic court, which required that they—and not the Romm family—had to cease printing the Talmud.[19] They continued to press their claim against the Romm printing house. Eventually, the parties agreed to a mediation headed by three rabbinic judges. The mediation panel was duly constituted according to the traditional manner by which each party selected one judge and the two judges then chose the third. However, the mediation failed to produce a compromise upon which the parties could agree.

In the meantime, each printing house continued to amass *haskamot* and rabbinic rulings to support its position. Ultimately, over 100 rabbis lined up on the opposing sides. The alliances were largely along sectarian lines. The Mitnagdim, centered in Lithuania but also including the luminaries Akiva Eiger, rabbi of the East Prussian city of Pozen, and his son-in-law, Moses Sofer, rabbi of Pressburg, Hungary, largely sided with the Romm press. The Ḥasidim, hailing largely from Galicia, Congress Poland, and Volhynia, generally supported the Slavuta press.

IV. PRINCIPAL ARGUMENTS OF THE RABBINIC DECISORS

The rabbis who supported the Slavuta press adduced a number of arguments why its extended reprinting should be enforced. Primarily, they relied on Ephraim Zalman Margoliot's earlier ruling that a reprinting ban must remain in force for the number of years set out in the ban unless the ban is reversed by a rabbinic court of equal or greater authority than that which issued the ban. Along those lines, all of the rabbis who issued *haskamot* for the Slavuta press's fourth edition—foremost among them, Abraham Abele Posveller, head of the rabbinic court in Vilna and one of the leading Talmudists of his era—stated that they had previously given their imprimatur to the Vilna Talmud but had erred in doing so. They had not known, they explained, that the reprinting bans issued for the third edition of the Slavuta Talmud remained in force (whether because its nominal 15-year period of exclusivity had not yet expired or because 37 sets remained unsold). Other supporters of the Slavuta Talmud, including Barukh Mordekhai Ettinger (d. 1852), rabbi of Bobruisk and the Ḥasidic community of Vilna, held, citing precedent from the time of the Talmud, that—in contrast with the position of Mordekhai Banet—rabbinic courts in fact have the authority to issue

18. See Friedberg 1950: 107 (describing the proceedings); Stanislawski 2005: 100–1 (describing the establishment of the Romm press).
19. Rabbinovicz 1951: 136–38.

a regulation that benefits one person while harming another. Accordingly, they held, the reprinting ban for the Slavuta Talmud represented a valid exercise of rabbinic authority even if it favored the Slavuta press at the Romm publishers' expense.

Ettinger also argued that the Slavuta press could prevent reprinting under the halakhic doctrine of wrongful competition, above and beyond any rabbinic reprinting ban. For Ettinger, rabbinic reprinting bans are a means by which rabbis define and enforce rights to prevent wrongful competition, such as by determining the number of years that a printer shall enjoy exclusivity. But a publisher's right to prevent reprinting is grounded in foundational principles of halakha in and of themselves, not rabbinic regulation. Further, Ettinger contended, a failure to prevent the Romm press and other publishers from printing the Talmud during the period of the reprinting ban would discourage other publishers from undertaking the publication of new editions of the Talmud in the future.[20]

Finally, in a letter to Romm press supporter Akiva Eiger, Yitzḥak Meir Alter (1799–1866), the founder and spiritual leader of Gur Ḥasidism, argued that preference must be given to the Slavuta press as it had already demonstrated that it was capable of printing the Talmud, whereas the Vilna publishers were as yet untested. That difference is significant, Alter maintained, because many publishers in the past had proven unable to complete the considerable undertaking of publishing a complete edition of the Talmud.[21]

The rabbis who supported the Romm press left a more capacious record of their arguments and reasoning. Foremost among them was Moses Sofer, who, as we have seen in the previous chapter, so forcefully championed rabbinic authority to issue reprinting bans in his colloquy with Mordekhai Banet.

A. Moses Sofer

Sofer weighed in on the Slavuta Talmud controversy in a short, undated responsum.[22] In that ruling, Sofer situates his discussion of the controversy within the framework of his previous disputation with Mordekhai Banet.

Recall that Sofer had previously held that Wolf Heidenheim's 25-year ban for the Rodelheim *mahzor* remained in force for that full period even though Heidenheim had sold out his first printing.[23] Sofer reasoned that the rabbis who issued the 25-year ban for Heidenheim knew that Heidenheim lacked sufficient means to produce, in a single print run, a sufficient number of holiday prayer books for all of the worshippers who require a German translation in order to understand the prayers. Rather, the rabbis anticipated that Heidenheim would have to print multiple editions in order to satisfy that important need. Accordingly, Sofer posited, Heidenheim was

20. Rakover 1991: 190; Mondshein 2003b: 122–24 (reproducing Ettinger's *haskama* for the Slavuta Talmud).
21. Rakover 1991: 238.
22. *Responsa Ḥatam Sofer*, Likkutim, No. 57.
23. *Responsa Ḥatam Sofer*, Ḥoshen Mishpat, No. 79.

entitled to issue and sell out multiple editions of his *maḥzor* at various intervals during the 25-year period without giving cause for the ban to expire prior to the end of that period.

However, the reprinting ban for the Slavuta press's third edition of the Talmud was constructed differently than the ban issued for Heidenheim. The Slavuta ban ran 15 years from the Slavuta press's completion of that edition. The rabbis who issued that ban determined that it should last for 15 years after printing had been completed because they assumed that it would take that period of time for the Slatuva press to sell out the entire edition, not because the Slatuva press would have to use sale proceeds to print more volumes during that 15-year period. As it turned out, however, the Slavuta publishers did not need the entire period of the ban to sell out their edition. Accordingly, Sofer held, the ban is no longer in force. Indeed, Sofer stated, under those circumstances a reprinting ban automatically comes to an end upon the sale of the entire edition even if the issuing rabbis stated explicitly in their *haskamot* that the ban would last for the term of years set out in the ban. Rabbinic decisors Sofer ruled, have no authority to decree that a ban will remain in force for the full term of years even if the books have all been sold.

In explaining this holding, Sofer reiterates central themes from his earlier response to Banet, but also backs away from his previous position in some respects. He states that reprinting bans are not necessarily based on preventing wrongful competition or protecting a *ma'arufia*. Rather, reprinting bans serve to ensure that publishers will invest in books of Jewish learning and liturgy. Otherwise, without reprinting bans, the publishing of such books will cease—for no one would be fool enough to invest his savings in publishing a book when others can freely reprint—and the study of Torah will come to an end. Therefore, Sofer continues, our rabbinic forbearers did not institute reprinting bans for the good of the author, but rather for the sake of sustaining and expanding the study of Torah. And as such, rabbinic authorities in the early days of print established the principle of reprinting bans as a matter of binding halakha—not merely as rabbinic regulation. Accordingly, reprinting bans apply worldwide, to all the Jewish people wherever they are, and, furthermore, may forbid Jews from purchasing books printed in violation of the ban.

On the basis of that legal foundation for reprinting bans, Sofer then reasons that if, in fact, the Slavuta publishers have sold out their print run or if the Romm press purchases the remaining 37 sets of the outstanding volumes in accordance with the order of the Grodno rabbinic court, the Romm press is entitled to print its edition of the Talmud even though the term of years set out in the reprinting ban for the Slavuta Talmud has not run its course. The rabbis of earlier generations instituted reprinting bans in order to promote Jewish learning for the benefit of all of Israel, not to benefit publishers per se. For that reason, present-day rabbis have no authority to issue reprinting bans that do merely serve the interests of a particular publisher rather than benefiting all of Israel. Consequently, once the publisher protected by the ban has sold all of his books, the dictum that the jealousy of scholars increases the study of Torah applies and competition must be allowed. In those circumstances, competition among printers to be the first to issue the next edition of the work in question, whether it be the Talmud or another book of Jewish learning, will lead to greater availability of such books and greater study of Torah.

B. Menaḥem Mendel Schneersohn

Menaḥem Mendel Schneersohn (1789–1866), spiritual leader of Ḥabad Lubavitch Ḥasidism, was a notable exception to Ḥasidic support for the Slavuta publishers. Schneersohn authored a responsum in which he considered several possible legal foundations for rabbinic reprinting bans, including wrongful competition, rabbinic power to regulate, and guild regulation.[24] He finds in his responsum that none would prevent the Romm press from printing the Talmud.

Throughout his responsum, Schneersohn exhibits an overriding concern for achieving the greatest possible production and dissemination of the Talmud, even if the Slavuta publishers suffer some harm in the pursuit of that goal. He reasons, first, that the law of wrongful competition does not apply to publishers of books of Jewish law and learning. When it comes to Jewish publishing, rather, the general prohibitions against wrongful competition give way before the dictum that the jealousy of scholars increases wisdom, especially given that competition would lead to greater availability of books of Jewish law and learning. In any case, moreover, it is not wrongful competition to engage in a competing business in a far-away territory. Schneersohn further holds that rabbis lack the authority to favor one printer over all others without an explicit general agreement of all printers; trade custom short of an explicit agreement of the entire trade does not suffice. In any event, Schneersohn opines, rabbis lack authority to issue a reprinting ban that continues in force even after all copies of the book have been sold.

C. Yitzḥak Eizik Ḥaver

Yitzḥak Eizik Ḥaver (1789–1843) was a leading student of the Vilna Gaon. His essay *Concerning Reprinting Bans and Wrongful Competition in Book Publishing, as Is Customary Today*[25] offers a window into how yet another illustrious contemporary viewed the Jewish law of copyright.

Ḥaver begins his inquiry by asking on what possible basis any rabbi could issue a reprinting ban. Ḥaver considers various doctrinal grounds concerning wrongful competition before rejecting them all. He also rehearses the views of the Rema, along with the doctrines of *ma'arufia* and *arenda*, but presents his reasons rejecting these as well. In particular, following the dictum of *kinat sofrim*, the jealousy of scholars increases wisdom, Ḥaver argues, we should welcome competition among creators and publishers of books of Jewish learning, both to spur the production of such books and to bring about lower prices. Further, under ordinary circumstances, Ḥaver concludes, rabbis do not have the authority to issue regulations—even those favored by a guild—that benefit one person while harming another.

24. *Responsa Tzemaḥ Tzedek,* Yoreh De'ah, No. 295.

25. Yiẓḥak Eizik Ḥaver, Responsa Binyan Olam, *B'inyan Haskamot Vehasagat Gevul Bisfarim Hanidpasim Hanahug Beyameinu, Olat Shlomo,* Part II at 179–84 (Yeshivat Or Yisrael, Petach Tiqva (5749)[1989]).

Ultimately, Ḥaver maintains, there is no legal foundation for reprinting bans per se. Rather they are rooted in the inherent power of rabbinic leaders of each generation to act in the face of pressing social need. For example, it was originally forbidden to write down the oral law, but in the face of the widespread dispersion of the Jewish people following the destruction of the Second Temple, the sages permitted that practice to ensure that the law would not be forgotten. Similarly, Ḥaver continues, rabbinic leaders in the early days of print instituted a device—the reprinting ban—that met the need to reward printers for publishing works, lest Jewish learning be diminished. "It seems to me," he concludes, "that it is fitting and correct . . . to prohibit others from publishing in order not to cause the first publisher damage and so that mitzvah-doers not be harmed, God forbid." All publishers should support this innovation, as the publisher who faces a restriction today will be the one tomorrow who seeks exclusivity for his own book.

However, Ḥaver introduces a significant qualification to the publisher's exclusive reprinting entitlement. Given that the rationale for issuing reprinting bans is to promote the study of Torah, rabbis in every generation must calibrate the scope and duration of protection in a manner that would best foster the production of more works of Jewish learning. Concededly, past reprinting bans have run for a set course of years. But the nominal period of the bans was calibrated just to allow the publisher to sell out his first print run. In other words, it was an estimate of how much time seemed necessary to protect that publisher from loss. Accordingly, if it turns out that the first publisher has sold out the entire run sooner, then there is no need for any further protection until the end of the nominal time period of the ban.

Moreover, Ḥaver continues, in seeking to prevent the first publisher from suffering damage, we must guard against abuse. If the first publisher sells out his first edition and then prints a new edition shortly before expiration of the period of ban, then he himself would be the one causing damage were he to insist that his ban remains in force and thus continues to prohibit other publishers from printing the book. Reprinting bans were not instituted to create a continuing monopoly, but only to protect the publisher's initial investment.

It also follows from the above what procedure needs to be undertaken in order to set aside a prior rabbinic printing ban. Unlike an individual vow or a ruling by the Sanhedrin, which would require formal nullification to be set aside, a printing ban remains operative only while its rationale persists. Thus, the *ḥerem* that attached to the Slavuta Talmud persisted only so long as the first printing remained unsold. That ban ran out as soon as the reason that animated it evaporated. In contrast to Ephraim Zalman Margoliot's view, no formal nullification by another rabbinic court is required.

Especially now that a majority of sages of Lithuania have given their imprimatur to the Vilna Talmud, Ḥaver affirms, the previous ban applicable to the Slavuta Talmud is of no more moment. To the contrary, the Vilna publishers have invested their money and energy in this new enterprise, so the *haskamot* that apply to their edition deserve preeminence.

But what about the fact that the Slavuta printing house wishes to go forward and print the entire Talmud anew? Again, the same logic dooms their claim—the sages who gave their *haskama* to Slavuta wished to guard only the edition for which the ban was issued, not to protect subsequent printings. Indeed, one can go further: by seeking to print the Talmud anew, the Slavuta printers are effectively testifying that the time has come to put out a new edition—thus proving that they have not been damaged as to their initial print run! They are certainly not facing a loss. Rather, it is the Vilna printers who have now expended a tremendous sum to put out this new edition of the Talmud. They have merited the rights for themselves now, and the Slavuta press has no right to compete with them in that market.

D. Aryeh Leib Zuenz

Aryeh Leib Zuenz (1768–1833), known in Jewish tradition by the honorific Maharal Zuenz, was born in Poland, matured in Prague, and later resettled to Warsaw, where he lived out his life. His present-day disciples highlight that he promised, shortly before his death, to intercede in heaven on behalf of anyone who would reprint one of his many works; that same promise was engraved on his tombstone.[26]

Zuenz's deathbed request was not the first time that he spoke out about the domain of publishing. Toward the end of his life, he also penned an essay that addressed the Slavuta Talmud controversy, under the title *Peace and Truth for Settling Disputes between the Printers*.

Zuenz begins the essay by noting that he received a communication regarding the need to encourage the publication of certain books in order to abate the decline of the study of rabbinic texts. It sparked his interest in the ruminations of Moses Sofer on the legal foundations for reprinting bans, causing Zuenz to wonder whether reprinting bans truly stand on solid doctrinal ground.

Moving to those legal foundations, Zuenz first considers and rejects the Jewish law of wrongful competition as a doctrinal ground for reprinting bans. Even in those limited instances when Jewish law prohibits competition in a given locale, the principle of *kinat sofrim,* the jealousy of scholars increases wisdom, specifically permits— and, indeed, encourages, such competition among those who teach Torah. Even Rav Huna, who favored giving an incumbent merchant the right to prevent competition in the same neighborhood, agreed that free competition should thus apply to scholars, teachers, and scribes. The same principle, it would seem, should allow publishers to enter into competition with each other locally. All the more so should publishers in remote locations be allowed to compete. After all, the Jewish law of wrongful competition gives no prerogative to prevent commerce in another territory, and Jewish law certainly does not countenance preventing someone from engaging in a mitzvah far away.

How then could reprinting bans extend to activities taking place in other countries? Perhaps it is to save loss to first comers, Zuenz speculated. But that principle, he realized, encounters an immediate obstacle: both the first printer and the second printer are businessmen; they are not simply throwing away their money. The first printer acts to gain a profit, the second likewise acts to gain a separate profit. As the

26. See http://www.tzintz.org/system/scripts/front_page.cgi.

saying goes, "The world is big and can accommodate many books." There is room for each of them to gain without suppressing the other.

In short, the law of wrongful competition cannot be the legal foundation for reprinting bans, which have often purported to apply without territorial limit. Indeed, Zuenz concludes, there is no basis in halakha per se for restricting competition among publishers.

Instead, Zuenz finds legal foundation for reprinting bans in rabbis' inherent authority to regulate in the area of social and economic relations within the community, a power that could extend even to expropriating property. Granted, there are limits to that authority. Rabbis may not expropriate property unless there would be general consensus among the community that the expropriation serves the greater moral good. But the concern that, without reprinting bans, no one would publish books of Jewish learning and liturgy, and thus that Israel would forget the Torah, provides ample justification for the rabbis to issue such decrees.

Yet even if reprinting bans fall within rabbis' inherent regulatory authority, there remains the problem that rabbinic power to regulate typically extends only within a rabbi's local community. On what basis, then, can a rabbinic ban forbid publishers from printing books in another country?

Zuenz's answer to that conundrum is that rabbinic authority to prohibit reprinting throughout the Jewish world must trace back to the Council of Four Lands. The Council of Four Lands enjoyed plenary authority over the entire area of their jurisdiction, and, Zuenz imagines, effectively over the entire Jewish world, just as did the great rabbinical court, the Sanhedrin, in days of yore. Of course, Zuenz concedes, the Council of Four Lands has been disbanded. So how can today's rabbis still issue reprinting bans that are effective throughout the Jewish world?

The answer, Zuenz reasons, lies in the venerable principle of the extension of rabbinic authority as a kind of agency. In Talmudic times, the rabbinic sages posited that formal rabbinic ordination existed only in the Land of Israel, not in Babylonia. For some purposes, though, the Babylonian courts had to act in a manner that required formal rabbinic ordination. The solution that the sages employed was to invoke the principle of agency to allow courts in the latter to act as agents of the former.[27] A court in Pumbedita could be viewed as effectuating the dictates of a court in Yavneh, for example. With that legal device—what might be termed the principle of *geographic extension*—the Babylonian sages overcame the lack of their formal judicial authority.

By the medieval period, however, formal rabbinic ordination had been lost even in the land of Israel. Accordingly, medieval rabbinic decisors stretched the foregoing principle into one of *temporal extension*.[28] They declared themselves to be agents of rabbinic courts in the Land of Israel across time. Zuenz applies this principle to find rabbinic authority for issuing reprinting bans effective throughout the Jewish world

27. See *Babylonian Talmud, Baba Kama* 84b; *Gittin* 88b.
28. See Tosaphot HaRosh, Gittin ch. 9.

even though the Council of Four Lands has become defunct. Today's rabbis, he posits, continue to act under authority of the Council to issue worldwide reprinting bans for the salutary purpose of inducing publishers to print books and thereby increase the dissemination of works of Torah.

Like Yitzḥak Ḥaver, however, Zuenz insists that the rabbis the who issued reprinting ban under the auspices of the Council of Four Lands never intended to make books of Jewish law and learning artificially expensive. Instead, they must have assessed the duration of exclusivity that publishers needed to avoid incurring a loss, and then must have added a couple years just to make certain that the publishers could rest assured about entering into their venture. Each rabbi made his own assessment, on a case by case basis, about how long a term was needed for a particular publisher and book. For the entire aim was—and is—that publishers not desist from printing and distributing books of Torah.

Turning to the issue that stood at the heart of the disputes over the Slavuta Talmud, Zuenz then considers the scenario in which the publisher has sold out his entire print run earlier than anticipated—in the middle of the period of exclusivity set out in the reprinting ban. By this time, Zuenz surmises, the publisher has already made his expected profit. That being the case, the ban should be considered expired. Reprinting bans are intended only to promote the dissemination of Torah, and, for this book, that goal has now been accomplished. What does it matter if there are a lot of years left or a few?. Once the publisher is out of danger of suffering a loss, any ongoing need for the ban evaporates. Everyone else should be free to reprint the work in question.

Addressing another wrinkle in the Slavuta controversy, Zuenz adds that if a first publisher goes in search of new reprinting bans during the period of exclusivity previously granted to him, then his own mouth has testified that he sold out the first printing—the result being that nobody else is prevented from reprinting that volume. In that event, no further protection should inure to the Slavuta publishers. If such were allowed, the result would be permanent protection, as the first publisher could seek to continue the bans indefinitely. It is illegitimate to use subterfuge to extend one's rights into perpetuity; to the contrary, a publisher is affirmatively obligated to announce to the world that he has sold out his stock to give other publishers an opportunity to print the work, before seeking protection anew.

Zuenz closes with some ruminations about the market for books of Jewish law and learning in his own era. Even though Torah learning has diminished, he states, our generation has progressed because there are tenfold times as many buyers today. The result is that publishers can earn a profit that much more quickly. In earlier generations, there were fewer buyers, so it was not possible to recoup an investment without international protection. But in our own era, there are enough buyers in each country so that publishers can recoup their investments entirely from domestic demand, and will suffer no harm from printings of the same work in other countries. Each country has thus effectively become its own independent market. With respect to reprinting bans, that development supports a return to the normal principle of territoriality, whereby a ban is deemed to have no effect outside the borders of the country in which it is issued.

E. Summary

All in all, the prevailing view on both sides of the early nineteenth-century debates over rival publications of the Talmud was that rabbinic reprinting bans owe their legal force to the inherent rabbinic power to issue regulations and decrees as necessary to address pressing social needs or to give legal effect to publishers' guild regulations. The rabbis disagreed on the nature and limits to that rabbinic power. The supporters of the Slavuta press contended that rabbis may issue regulations and decrees that harm one person while helping another, and that once a rabbinic decree has been issued it may not be overturned except by a rabbinic body of equal or greater authority. The rabbinic supporters of the publishers of Kapust and Vilna Talmuds, in contrast, posited that the power of rabbis of their era to issue reprinting bans stems from the consensus of rabbinic authorities of earlier generations, supported by the community and by publishers generally; that such bans are necessary to promote Jewish learning; and that the bans serve that goal only if limited to the period required for the first publisher to recover his initial investment. Hence, once a ban's publisher-beneficiary has sold all of his books, the ban automatically expires.

The view of Barukh Mordekhai Ettinger that publishers have a foundational right in the halakhic doctrine of wrongful competition to prevent others from reprinting was not widely shared even among rabbinic supporters of the Slavuta press. Further, the rabbinic supporters of the Kapust and Vilna publishers expressed disagreement with that view on a number of grounds. They contended, first and foremost, that publishers of books of Torah have no such right, principally because the axiom that the jealousy of scholars increases wisdom dictates that the Jewish book market be fully competitive and thus that the normal strictures of the doctrine of wrongful competition do not apply. In that vein, Moses Isserles's ruling on wrongful competition was largely understood—or reinterpreted—to be limited to the unusual case of predatory pricing in which one publisher had the wherewithal and intent to drive his rival out of business. Even Moses Sofer, who had earlier sought to convince Mordekhai Banet that publishers have a right under the halakhic doctrine of wrongful competition to prevent reprinting, seemed to back away from that position in expressing his support for the Vilna publishers. He now came to rely instead on the argument that the age-old rabbinic edict that established reprinting bans for the purpose of preserving Torah study was itself a part of foundational halakha, not merely regulation. Moreover, the rabbinic opponents of enforcing the reprinting bans granted to the Slavuta press posited, in line with the argument of Abraham Shor of Orsha, that even if the doctrine of wrongful competition applies to publishers of books of Torah study, the doctrine does not generally prevent a rival publisher from reprinting in a different location or after the first publisher has sold out his first edition.

In sum, by the 1830s, we see a declining rabbinic confidence in the doctrinal foundations and territorial scope of rabbinic reprinting bans—a decline that mirrored the disintegration of Jewish communal autonomy and of rabbis' juridical authority. Rabbinic decisors of the sixteenth and early seventeenth centuries quite confidently asserted that rabbinic decrees banning reprinting served to protect publishers against acts of "actual misappropriation" prohibited under the Jewish law of wrongful competition and that, given the global reach of the Hebrew book trade, reprinting bans applied throughout the Jewish world. During its reign, the Council of Four Lands served as the foundation for rabbinic authority to regulate the Hebrew book trade throughout the vast area of the Council's jurisdiction and influence. But, as in the pointed exchange between Mordekhai Banet and Moses Sofer, rabbis who were drawn into the disputes between the Slavuta press and its rivals expressed sharply conflicting views about the halakhic justifications for rabbinic reprinting bans, rabbinic authority to issue such bans, and the bans' territorial and temporal scope.

As time went on, the institution of rabbinic reprinting bans increasingly appeared as a weakened, vestigial remnant of rabbinic authority of an earlier time. It was riven by territorial division, the absence of rabbic authority to sanction violators, and sectarian rivalry within the rabbinic world. Moreover, to the extent reprinting bans were grounded in rabbis' inherent power to regulate, that power generally fell into disuse following sovereign states' abolition of Jewish communal autonomy and the juridical authority of the rabbis.[29]

V. EPILOGUE

The fierce battle between the Vilna and Slavuta presses over the rights to print the Talmud came to a sudden end in 1836, with events that were a sharp blow for Jewish publishing. In 1835, a Gentile bookbinder employed by the Slavuta press was found hanged in his employers' plant.[30] The Shapira family claimed that he had committed suicide, but others alleged it to be murder, as the worker in question had reportedly denounced his bosses for publishing books without the required permission of the local state censor. The Russian authorities launched a formal inquiry, which led to the conviction of the Shapira brothers, followed by the imposition on them of harsh physical punishment and their deportation to Siberia. The authorities also closed the Slavuta press and burned its books-in-preparation.

That scandal followed decades of mutual recriminations among Mitnagdim, Ḥasidim, and Maskilic reformers and their periodic denunciations of their rivals to the Russian authorities. As such, it probably contributed to the decision of the Russian government, issued in 1836, to shut down all existing Hebrew presses in the Empire so as to better contain the fractious Jewish population.[31] The Russian clampdown on Jewish publishing was an extension of various measures, enacted in the wake of the coronation of Nicholas I in 1825, that were aimed, ultimately, at eradicating Jewish self-rule. Censorship and control over the importation of Jewish books were an integral part of these policies, which were punctuated by periodic efforts to tighten enforcement through greater centralization of the censorship apparatus.[32]

29. Elon 1997: 401.
30. In relating this incident, I draw heavily upon Stanislawski 2005: 100–01.
31. Stanislawski 2005: 101.
32. See Stanislawski 1983: xii, 35–42.

Nonetheless, the Vilna-Slavuta dispute might also have played its part in the closure of all Jewish presses in 1836 by "creating an impression of a situation dangerously, even violently, out of control."[33]

In the end, Russian authorities allowed only two Jewish printing houses to continue to function: one in Vilna, to serve the Mitnagdim and Maskilim, and another, originally in Kiev, but then moved to Zhitomir, to publish Ḥasidic works.[34] The monopolies were awarded through a bidding process in which the winning firm had to pay the government a stipulated tax in addition to customs duties on Hebrew and Yiddish books imported from abroad. The Vilna monopoly was obtained by the Romm family. In turn, the Zhitomir press was leased by the sons of the Shapira brothers, who began to issue books in 1847.[35]

In 1858, the Shapira press commenced publication of a new edition of the Talmud, which it completed in 1864. Once again, the Shapira house's principal competitor was the Romm publishing house in Vilna. The Romm house began to issue its own edition of the Talmud in 1859 and completed it in 1866. This time, neither rival bothered to obtain rabbinic reprinting bans.

33. Lederhendler 1989: 96–97.
34. Stanislawski 2005: 101–02.
35. Assaf 2010: 1702.

CHAPTER 8

Moving Beyond Reprinting Bans

From Property to the Law of the Sovereign

I. INTRODUCTION

To better compete with its Slavuta rivals, the Romm press of Vilna incorporated several commentaries in its Talmud that did not appear in the Slavuta editions. Among them was a new commentary by two preeminent Galician rabbinic scholars, the brothers-in-law Mordekhai Ze'ev Ettinger (1804–1863) and Joseph Saul Nathanson (1808–1875). The pair reportedly sold the rights in their commentary to the Romm press. In turn, in the printer's introduction to the tractate Sabbath, issued in 1836, the Romm publishers colorfully declared: "In addition to our exalted haskamot, which erect a fence against those who would commit *hasagat gvul* against us, we have yet another grounds for preventing intruders across our borders: we have placed upon this Talmud a glorious crown of valuable commentaries that have been given to us alone, and no stranger holds any part of or property in them. This Talmud, with those valuable commentaries, sprouts a great and exalted fruit of usefulness for the study of God's Torah—and on this ground, the rabbis of olden times have already strengthened the hands of publishers of that era against their fellows, as explained in the responsum of the Rema and the other responsa."

The Romm publishers were not unusual in invoking the tropes of property in support of their declaration of exclusive rights. After all, the term *hasagat gvul,* though rooted in trespass on land, has long been extended to those engaging in wrongful competition. Yet, in line with the plethora of rabbinic rulings issued on both sides of the Vilna-Slavuta controversy, the halakhic grounds that the Romm publishers pressed to support their claim of exclusive rights in the commentaries lay also in rabbis' inherent authority to regulate for the good of the community, particularly to foster the study of Torah.[1]

Twenty-four years later, Joseph Saul Nathanson played a far more direct—and far-reaching—role in the development of Jewish copyright law. Nathanson ruled in 1860 that authors enjoy a perpetual exclusive right to reprint their creative work. In essence, Nathanson characterized the author's right as a property right wholly independent of any rights under a rabbinic reprinting ban or, for that matter, any rights under the Jewish law of wrongful competition. For Nathanson, authors hold a perpetual property right to reprint their work, a right that arises under fundamental tenets of halakha, not rabbinic edict or regulation. Further, the author's perpetual right stands over and above a publisher's right to recover the investment in the work's first printing under a reprinting ban or the law of wrongful competition.

When Nathanson issued his ruling, he was rabbi of Lemberg (or Lvov), having been appointed to that post in 1857. Lemberg, then the capital of Galicia, a crown land of the Habsburg Empire, was a major center of Jewish printing and cultural life in the nineteenth century. Nathanson served as Lemberg's rabbi during times of momentous change for the Jewish community, which then comprised some 30 percent of Lemberg's total population. Jews faced special taxes and severe restrictions on their choice of occupation and housing when Nathanson assumed his post. But, together with their coreligionists throughout Galicia, they were given political emancipation in 1867.[2] Mirroring those developments, while Lemberg's Jews generally adhered to religious tradition—indeed Lemberg was a stronghold of Ḥasidism, they also included a vibrant *maskilic* movement.

Nathanson was widely recognized as one of the great Talmudic scholars of his generation. An esteemed member of the traditional rabbinic establishment, Nathanson also adeptly straddled the worlds of Galician *maskilim*, Ḥasidic devotees, and modern secular culture and politics. Nathanson had no formal secular education and, indeed, was able to assume the post of district rabbi of Lemberg only after the Austrian authorities dispensed with their previous requirement that no one could be appointed to the post unless he had passed university exams in philosophy and ethics.[3] Nathanson opposed educational reforms advanced by Jewish progressives, and when the Austrian government sought to compel Galician Jews to give their children a secular education, Nathanson joined forces with other traditionalist rabbinic leaders to lobby successfully for the edict's repeal.[4] Yet, Nathanson resolutely opposed schism within the Jewish community and maintained working relations with progressives as well as Ḥasidim. He also expressed openness to modern methods in his pragmatic halakhic rulings, including ordering a chemical analysis to determine the presence of forbidden matter in food and permitting the use of a new machine of German manufacture for baking matza. Finally, he united with Jewish progressives in campaigning for Jews to vote for a party favoring Polish national identification in elections for the Galician parliament.[5]

1. Actually, unlike other rabbinic decisors, the Rema did not explain or explicitly rest his ruling on rabbinic authority to regulate in order to foster the Torah.
2. Wierzbieniec et al 2000: 225–27, 232.
3. Bromberg 1960: 49.
4. S. Warhaftig 2007: 18–19.
5. Bromberg 1960: 57; Manekin 1999: 110.

Nathanson was also a major figure in the printing of books of Jewish learning and liturgy. He was renowned for issuing some 300 *haskamot*—and was highly regarded, no less, for actually reading and often commenting on the books he approved.[6] He also authored several halakhic works and helped some of his pupils establish publishing houses that specialized in rabbinic literature.[7] In so doing, Nathanson was motivated by a belief that, in his era, the dissemination of books of Jewish learning was vital to maintaining the integrity of rabbinic authority. In a responsum in which he supported the claim of a mediocre son of a great rabbi to inherit his father's post, Nathanson opined that "in our days, the number of books of Jewish law that have been published on every topic has increased, thank God, so that even a mediocre rabbi will not make errors."[8]

Nathanson's multifaceted commitment to rabbinic tradition, engagement with the secular world around him, and support for publishing of books for Jewish learning and liturgy are all manifest in his ruling on Jewish copyright law. Yet, despite Nathanson's prestige as a scholar and halakhic decisor, his innovative ruling proved to be controversial. As we shall see, indeed, it earned a blunt rebuke from Yitzḥak Schmelkes, a leading late nineteenth-century rabbinic authority, who had been Nathanson's student.

II. NATHANSON'S STRIKING INNOVATION

A. The Dispute

Nathanson gave his groundbreaking ruling in a dispute involving two editions of *Yoreh De'ah*, the section of the *Shulḥan Arukh* concerning Jewish dietary laws, various ritual matters, Torah study, and rabbinic bans. *Yoreh De'ah* served as a key text in nineteenth-century *yeshiva* study and, indeed, was the basis for examination for rabbinic ordination.[9]

Abraham Joseph Madpis was a Lemberg printer and the scion of a distinguished family of Jewish book publishers, extending back to the Amsterdam printer, Uri Fayvesh Halevi, whom we have previously encountered. In 1858 Madpis published part one of *Yoreh De'ah*. Madpis issued his edition under the traditional title for *Yoreh De'ah, Ashlei Ravrabi*, the Aramaic term for "great tamarisk trees," which poetically connotes the seminal sources of halakhic interpretation upon which one should rely.[10] Madpis's edition included a number of commentaries and annotations. Among

6. Nathanson's profusion of *haskamot* earned him the sobriquet *Sar Ha-Maskim*, meaning "Chief Approver" or "Prince of the Haskama Writers." That title represents a transposition of the reference to Pharaoh's chief butler, *Sar Ha-Mashkim*. Genesis. 40: 9. See Gries 2007: 117–18; S. Warhaftig 2007: 19.

7. Gertner 2008: 1253.

8. Stampfer 1999: 51 n. 21 (quoting Nathanson, *Shoel U-Meshiv*, Mahadura Tlitaa, 26, No. 154). Nathanson held, nonetheless, that a son did not have an automatic right to inherit his father's post.

9. Stampfer 2012: 41.

10. The reference stems from *Babylonian Talmud, Beitza* 27a.

them was *Pitḥei Teshuva*, authored by Avraham Tzvi Hirsch Eisenstadt (1812–1868), rabbi of Ottymia in Kovno.

Pitḥei Teshuva is widely regarded as the most useful index to the responsa and decisions of later authorities on the subjects treated in the *Shulḥan Arukh*. Madpis had purported to take assignment of Eisenstadt's rights in that work, which had first been published in an edition of the *Ashlei Ravrabi* printed in Vilna in 1836. It was *Pitḥei Teshuva* that lay at the core of the dispute that came before Nathanson.

Madpis issued his edition of *Ashlei Ravrabi* with a *haskama* from Nathanson's co-author (and brother-in-law) Mordekhai Ze'ev Ettinger, dated April 28, 1858, granting Madpis a 10-year reprinting ban. In his printer's introduction, Madpis also asserts that it is forbidden to reprint any part of his edition without his permission under Austrian law.

Meanwhile, Pinkhas Moshe Balaban had made preparations to issue his own edition of the *Ashlei Ravrabi*. Balaban was also a prominent Lemberg printer. He headed a press that his father had established in Bradi in 1830.[11] Balaban issued his edition of the *Ashlei Ravrabi* with financial backing from an apparent relation, Joseph Hirsch (Tzvi) Balaban. Of particular note, the Balaban edition also featured Avraham Tzvi Hirsch Eisenstadt's *Pitḥei Teshuva*.

Madpis and Balaban were already bitter rivals. In 1857, each printer had sued the other in a dispute involving their respective editions of *Korban Manḥe*, a holiday prayer book for women. Madpis issued his edition first, replete with a new Yiddish translation of the Hebrew prayers in which Madpis had acquired the rights. When Balaban issued his rival edition of the prayerbook in Yiddish translation, Madpis sued him in civil court.[12] That tribunal enjoined Balaban from further distributing the work and ordered him to pay Madpis compensation. Balaban then turned around and sued Madpis in a rabbinic court for return of the compensation that he had paid under civil compulsion. Balaban invoked a halakhic doctrine that generally prevents someone from having to pay another out of coercion, including the illicit coercion of Jews by Gentile authorities. He took the position that if Madpis wished to sue him, he should have sued him in rabbinic court, not civil court.

The dispute was brought to Joseph Saul Nathanson, who ruled in favor of Madpis.[13] Nathanson held that this was not a case of actionable coercion. Foreshadowing his views of copyright under Jewish law, Nathanson reasoned that the civil court's copyright ruling in favor of Madpis fully comported with justice and halakha, and thus that the halakhic doctrine of illicit coercion did not apply. Nathanson's support for the substance of the civil court's ruling was particularly striking given that Austrian law applicable in Galicia still forbade Jews from even testifying in civil court, a prohibition that was not lifted until 1859.[14]

11. Friedberg 1950: 84–85.
12. Friedberg 1950: 84 n. 4.
13. *Sho'el U-Meshiv*, No. 160.
14. Wierzbieniec et al. 2000: 231.

לפרט
זה שלחן הטהור
אשר לפני ה׳

ספר
אשלי רברבי
שלחן ערוך
יורה דעה

ערוך בכל טוב המפרשים והבאורים אשר עליו חונים . ושמורים
הדפים כאשר היו בדפוסים הראשונים . מוגה בתכלית השלימות
ונתוספו עתה הוספות רבות וחדשות כמבואר בשער השני .

ראה זה חדש הוא
חידושי רבי עקיבא איגר עם גליון רש״א וכללים מחודשים על כמה
סוגיות מבעל פרי מגדים : כמבואר בירעה החוברת :

לעמבערג
בשנת לא בא כבשם זה אף הפעם לפ״ק

חלק שני

JORE DEA.

Druck und Verlag von
Pessel Balaban.
in Lemberg. 1864.

בדפוס של הנגידה המפורסמת
אשת חיל מרת פעסיל
באלאבאן תחי׳

Illustration 14
Shulḥan Arukh, Yoreh De'ah (Ashlei Ravrabi) Title Page, Balaban Edition, 1864.
(courtesy National Library of Israel).

B. Initial Ruling: Shmuel Valdberg

In the wake of his loss to Madpis in their dispute over *Korban Manḥe*, Balaban took preemptive action when it came to *Ashlei Ravrabi*. He petitioned Shmuel Valdberg (1829–1907), head of the rabbinic court of Zolkiew, a center of Jewish printing just north of Lemberg, for a *haskama* and ruling that Madpis's reprinting ban was of no effect. Valdberg gave his *haskama* to Balaban, granting Balaban a 10-year reprinting ban for Balaban's edition of *Ashlei Ravrabi*.[15] Valberg also ruled that Madpis's reprinting ban was invalid.

According to Nathanson's responsum, which summarizes Valdberg's ruling, Valdberg posited that Madpis's rights were limited to those that he might have acquired from Avraham Tzvi Hirsch Eisenstadt under the law of the sovereign state. A rabbinic court would recognize Madpis's rights under secular copyright law, pursuant to the halakhic principle "the law of the sovereign is the law." But apart from that, Valdberg had ruled, Madpis had no rights under Jewish law. Valdberg reasoned that any reprinting ban in favor of the 1836 edition of *Ashlei Ravrabi* that contained the first printing of *Pitḥei Teshuva* is of no force or effect after its set term of years has expired, and if the ban were issued without a nominal time limit, if would be void ab initio. In any case, moreover, although the 1836 edition of *Ashlei Ravrabi* was issued with five *haskamot*, none of them included a reprinting ban. Accordingly, anyone may reprint *Ashlei Ravrabi* with *Pitḥei Teshuva*.

Nor, Valdberg ruled, would the Jewish law of wrongful competition dictate any recognition of exclusive rights in the work's author or assigns. Given that the author and first publisher have already sold the first edition, they suffer no cognizable harm from republication by another publisher. Indeed, even if Eisenstadt still had books left to sell, he could not prevent the reprinting and sale of *Pitḥei Teshuvah* outside the territory of the Russian Empire, where the work had initially been brought to print. Furthermore, the original 1836 edition in question was a small volume, which contained few commentaries, whereas Balaban's edition was a more expensive large volume, containing numerous commentaries and annotations in addition to *Pitḥei Teshuva*, and was targeted at a different market. Balaban's edition would not cause any significant harm to the author in that market because no one would purchase a large edition of the *Shulḥan Arukh* just to obtain *Pitḥei Teshuva*.

Valdberg's ruling was fully consonant with the weight of rabbinic authority, certainly at the time of the Vilna-Slavuta Talmud dispute two decades earlier, with regard to the temporal, territorial, and doctrinal limits to the protections against reprinting accorded by rabbinic bans and the Jewish law of wrongful competition. By the time the matter was brought to Valdberg, moreover, the 1836 edition of *Ashlei Ravrabi* featuring *Pitḥei Teshuva* had already been reprinted by two different publishers—in Warsaw in 1840 and Lemberg in 1852—each time bearing the original *haskamot* containing only approbations, and not reprinting bans. Another, different edition

15. Balaban also received a *haskama*, including a 10-year reprinting ban, from Meshalem Yissakhar Halevi Ish Horowitz, of Stanislav, dated June 16, 1861.

of *Ashlei Ravrabi*, but also containing *Pitḥei Teshuva*, was printed by yet another publisher in Zhitomir in 1852, the same year as the Lemberg reprint. It seems highly unlikely that any of these publishers acquired republication rights from Avraham Tzvi Hirsch Eisenstadt or his assigns, given that one edition came out just four years after the original, and the other two were issued in competition with one another in the same year—and none contained any claim to exclusive rights. In short, it seems to have been widely understood that anyone was free to include Eisenstadt's index in an edition of *Ashlei Ravrabi*.

C. Nathanson's Ruling

Nathanson's ruling on the Madpis-Balaban dispute, dated November 25, 1860,[16] is a detailed response to Valdberg. It is not clear from Nathanson's ruling how the matter came before him. Perhaps Valdberg or Balaban asked him to uphold Valberg's ruling by refusing to enforce Madpis's reprinting ban in Lemberg or by declaring it invalid. (Of possible relevance, Nathanson had had a falling out with his brother-in-law Mordekhai Ze'ev Ettinger, who had issued Madpis's ban.) It seems more likely, however, that Madpis petitioned Nathanson for a ruling that, contrary to that of Valberg, would affirm Madpis's exclusive right to reprint *Ashlei Ravrabi* with Eisenstadt's work. Not only had Nathanson ruled in Madpis's favor against Balaban over *Korban Manḥe*, but earlier in 1860, Nathanson also had given Madpis a 10-year rabbinic reprinting ban for an edition of the Ḥoshen Mishpat section of the *Shulḥan Arukh*.

In any event, Nathanson ruled to the contrary of "the incisive rabbi, our teacher, the head of the rabbinic court of Zolkiew." He concluded that Madpis had the exclusive right to print *Pitḥei Teshuva* under Jewish law by virtue of having acquired the author's exclusive, perpetual right in those works. In so ruling, Nathanson sought to distinguish between an author's rights in new works and a publisher's rights in existing works. For Nathanson, although publishers' rights under rabbinic reprinting bans and the law of wrongful competition are, indeed, subject to the temporal, territorial, and substantive limits that nineteenth-century rabbinic decisors had repeatedly imposed, authors enjoy exclusive rights that are perpetual and enforceable throughout the world.

But, of course, Nathanson's purported distinction between publishers and authors quickly breaks down. Under Nathanson's blueprint, authors' rights are fully assignable to publishers. Indeed it was a publisher, Madpis, who sought to enforce the author's rights in the dispute in which Nathanson issued his ruling. Consequently, Nathanson, in fact, propounded a vast new, perpetual exclusive right that could be enforced not only by authors, but by publishers and anyone else who has acquired the right anywhere in the world. Henceforth, publishers could squelch rival editions by taking assignment of the author's exclusive, perpetual rights. Publishers would no longer need to rely on rabbinic reprinting bans, with all their attendant limitations.

16. Joseph Saul Nathanson, *Sho'el U-Meshiv*, part 1, No. 44.

As such, Nathanson effectively sought to transform Jewish copyright from a prerogative derived from rabbinic regulation or, at most, a right against wrongful competition, to some manner of a natural right of property—a universal, perpetual, and fully assignable exclusive right that authors (and their assigns) enjoy wholly apart from any rabbinic regulation, decree, or reprinting ban or, for that matter, copyright under secular law. Nor is the right that Nathanson propounded limited to protecting the author—or publisher—against those who would prevent the author or publisher from recouping his investment by misappropriating his business opportunity to sell out his first edition. Nathanson's propounded right, rather, sounds as an author's right of literary property—an exclusive right that arises simply by virtue of having created a work and made it available to the public. Although Nathanson did not label the author's perpetual, exclusive right as "property" as such in his ruling on the Madpis-Balaban dispute, the import of his ruling was clear. Indeed, he did expressly refer to an author's right as *kinyan*, meaning "property," or *naḥala*, meaning "an asset," in a number of his subsequent *haskamot*.

1. *Authors' Rights*

The halakhic basis for Nathanson's enunciation of authors' rights is far from a paradigm of clarity. He cites no Talmudic proof text or rabbinic precedent for such a ruling and, given the weight of rabbinic authority that we have discussed, it seems unlikely that he could have found any. Rather, Nathanson presents the author's perpetual right simply as a self-evident, obvious proposition. As he puts it:

> [I]f an author prints a new book and he merits that his words are received all around the world, he obviously has an eternal right [to his work], because in any case if one prints or invents some type of craft, another person is not allowed to do so without his consent. And it is known that Rabbi Abraham Jacob of Harobshob, who invented a machine to do arithmetic,[17] received throughout his life payment from the government in Warsaw; and "Shall not our perfect Torah be no less than their idle chatter?" This is something that common sense rejects, and it is a daily occurrence that one who prints a work, he and those empowered by him, retain the rights.

For Nathanson, it seems, because secular law recognizes that inventors and authors have exclusive rights, and because our Torah, the source of Jewish law, is perfect (and complete), Jewish law must also recognize such exclusive rights. It could not be otherwise.

Nathanson's invocation of "our perfect Torah" as a reason for holding that Jewish law must equal the reach of secular law rule is all the more striking in that, within the rabbinic tradition, that phrase has traditionally stood for just the opposite: that

17. The individual in question was Abraham Jacob Stern (1762–1842). Tsar Alexander I was presented with the machine and decided that Stern should receive yearly payments from the treasury for life. Rakover 1991: 251 n. 6.

Jewish law is perfect, complete, and, indeed, fundamentally superior to Gentile law and thus that Jews' adoption of Gentile norms is problematic.[18] To be certain, rabbinic decisors have long recognized that Jews may follow customary practices and norms of the surrounding Gentile society in commercial matters so long as they do so for substantive reasons having to do with the specific transaction in question rather than out of an intent to supplant Jewish law. Under certain circumstances, indeed, local custom among Jews can be recognized as having halakhic force even if that custom stems from the norms of the surrounding Gentile community. However, Jewish merchants, communal bodies, and rabbinic decisors may not adopt Gentile norms on the basis that they are Gentile norms. In other words, Jews may not adopt Gentile norms if their fundamental purpose in doing so is to renounce, diminish, or cast aside the relevance of what would otherwise be Jewish law, or if the custom is fundamentally opposed to halakhic precepts.

Perhaps, then, Nathanson's primary point is that an author "obviously" has a perpetual right to his work. That, for Nathanson, is a self-evident proposition. In this interpretation of Nathanson's ruling, the fact that, according to Nathanson, secular law recognizes authors' rights just provides further evidentiary support that the author has such a right, in case any evidence were to be needed. Our perfect Torah must simply reflect the obvious, not adopt Gentile norms per se.

Or, more speculatively, perhaps Nathanson meant, obliquely, that the "daily occurrence" among Jewish authors and printers of respecting rights has halakhic force as custom, regardless of whether the practice originated natively within the world of Jewish publishing or arose from compliance with secular copyright law. However, Nathanson did not expressly refer to custom and did not cite the rabbinic precedents regarding custom in commercial matters. Moreover, as I presently discuss, an author's rights under secular copyright law were not, in fact, perpetual and universal, so a custom of adherence to secular copyright law would not be one that recognized perpetual and universal exclusive rights for authors.

Further, Nathanson gives but one example of the "daily occurrence" by which, he claims, authors—and their heirs—retain the exclusive right to print. And upon examination, that example does not actually support Nathanson's claim of a perpetual author's right under Jewish law. Nathanson's example is that of Shlomo Rabin-Shtein's reprinting of *Tzion L'Nefesh Ḥaya*, a work of commentary on the Talmud authored by the preeminent halakhic authority, Yeḥezkel Segal Landau (1713–1793), known in Jewish tradition as Noda Be-Yehuda. As Nathanson recounts, Rabin-Shtein's reprinted edition featured an express statement that Landau's sons had given their permission for the reprinting. Nathanson postulates that Rabin-Shtein had obtained their permission because "to do otherwise would violate an absolute prohibition."

The first complete edition of *Tzion L'Nefesh Ḥaya* was brought to print in 1799 by Yeḥezkel Landau's son, Israel (1758–1829), together with the Christian-owned

18. My discussion in this paragraph draws on Kleinman 2011: 19–21 and Broyde 2012.

Hebrew book publisher, the Elsenwanger Press.[19] That original edition features a statement by Israel Landau warning against reprinting. In his statement, Israel emphasizes that his father had forbidden anyone from reprinting the work for a period of 15 years from completion of the original printing.[20] Israel also indicates that he enjoys exclusive printing rights in the Austrian Empire by virtue of the Imperial Decree, dated January 13, 1781 (which protected native authors and publishers against reprinting even with regard to a book that was itself a reprint of a book previously published abroad). Further, Israel Landau continues, should anyone outside the Austrian Empire consider reprinting, that person should be warned that he, Israel Landau, holds reprinting bans from leading rabbis (both within and without the Austrian Empire), including Pinḥas Halevi Horowitz and Mordekhai Banet.

Shlomo Rabin-Shtein, together with the Gerson Letteres press, reprinted *Tzion L'Nefesh Ḥaya* in Zolkiew in 1824. The reprint, indeed, includes a statement on its title page that Landau's sons, the "great and famous rabbis," Israel, and Shmuel have given their permission for the reprinting.[21]

Yet, it is highly doubtful that the permission received from Landau's sons truly evidenced an understanding within the Jewish publishing world that it would "violate an absolute prohibition" to reprint a deceased author's work without the consent of the author's heirs. First, Israel Landau's own statement in the 1799 edition belies such an absolute prohibition; he grounds his claim to exclusive reprinting rights, not in an inherent right of the author's heirs and successors, but, rather in Austrian law, the 15-year reprinting ban issued by his father Yeḥezkel Landau, and the reprinting bans from leading rabbis.

Second, there were a number of other reprintings of *Tzion L'Nefesh Haya* that were published prior to Nathanson's ruling without any statement of permission from Landau's sons (or other heirs).[22] If reprinting without the heir's permission truly violated an "absolute prohibition," one would not expect such a blatant affront to the sons of one of the most prominent rabbis of his generation, sons who were preeminent rabbis in their own right.

19. The Elsenwanger Press, owned by Barbara Elsenwanger, was an active publisher of Hebrew books in Prague between 1788 and 1804. Under Yisrael Landau's influence, it published a number of *maskilic* texts as well as traditional rabbinic works.

20. On the occasional practice of rabbi-authors issuing reprinting bans for their own work, see Rakover 1991: 277–79.

21. The statement appears in the volume that presents Yeḥezkel Landau's commentaries on tractate *Brakhot*. A similar story involving the posthumous publication, in 1837, of Akiva Eiger's commentary on the Mishnah by his son Benjamin Wolf Eiger (1805–1890), in which Benjamin unsuccessfully sought to claim a perpetual exclusive right notwithstanding reprinting bans that were limited in years, is recounted in Urbach 1988: 574–76.

22. A first printing of a previously unpublished portion of *Tzion L'Nefesh Ḥaya* led to a dispute among Landau's descendants. Yosef Dov Be'er Soleveitchik (1820–1892) and Yitzḥak Elḥanan Spector (1817–1896), the rabbinic decisors who provided *haskamot* for the printing, respectively stated that Landau's grandchildren had no right in Landau's manuscript by virtue of being his heirs and, indeed, that the descendant who had already labored to prepare the manuscript for publication and to bring Landau's work to the world was entitled to prevent Landau's grandchildren from wrongfully competing with him by reprinting the book. See Rakover 1991: 269–70.

Third, Nathanson's statement that the permissions were required to avoid violating an absolute prohibition contradicts his own view of reprinting bans. As discussed below, Nathanson understood reprinting bans as a *waiver* of what would otherwise be a perpetual exclusive right to reprint the book. According to that view (which was not widely shared), when Israel Landau applied for reprinting bans that were limited to a term of years, his intent was to waive any right to prevent others from freely reprinting the work once the ban had expired.

Finally, even if Landau's sons, as the heirs of the illustrious Noda Be-Yehuda, did hold some sort of exclusive prerogative to reprint their father's book after his death, that does not mean that they held a perpetual property right that could be transferred to a publisher. One could imagine a customary practice that gave preference to an author's immediate heirs or recognized some sort of personal entitlement for them. Or, as present day rabbinic scholar and judge, Ezra Batzri hypothesizes, if there was, in fact, a customary practice that gave preference to an author's heirs, it might have been based on the Jewish law of wrongful competition, rabbinic reprinting bans, or secular copyright law.[23] In any event, a personal prerogative enjoyed by the author's immediate heirs would fall far short of embodying the fully transferable, perpetual property right that Nathanson propounded.

So why, then, did Rabin-Shtein obtain and display a statement of permission from Landau's sons even without "an absolute prohibition" requiring their consent? Most obviously, a statement of support by Landau's sons would establish the edition's authenticity and assist in its marketing. After all, Landau's sons had been involved in the original publication of their father's work and could be seen to speak on his behalf, as it were. Moreover, as the statement of permission notes, Landau's sons were also famous in their own right: Israel was a prominent publisher of Hebrew books, and Shmuel was head of the rabbinic court of Prague. Potential purchasers might well favor an edition that received their endorsement, without regard to whether their permission was actually needed as a legal matter.

2. Borrowing from Secular Law

In short, there appears to have been no customary practice or prior rabbinic precedent that recognized an author's perpetual, worldwide right to reprint his works. Instead, Nathanson must have come to his understanding that authors "obviously" have a property right in their works by drawing upon the secular copyright laws with which he was familiar. In the decades preceding Nathanson's ruling, the view that authors enjoy a natural property right in their creations had come to dominate European copyright law and thought. Indeed, the Austrian Law for the Protection of Literary and Artistic Property of 1846—to which Nathanson refers in his ruling and in some of his *haskamot*—expressly affirmed, in both its title and statutory text, that literary and artistic creations are the "property" of their author. Further, the Austrian Law vested the rights and property in the author, not the publisher, giving

23. Batzri 1984-85.

the author the "exclusive right of disposing of his work as he wishes" and the prerogative to "transfer this right to others wholly or partly."[24] As such, the Austrian Law followed on the Prussian Statute to protect the Property in Works of Scholarship and the Arts against Reprint and Reproduction of 1837, the Russian Copyright Law of 1828 and Decree of 1830, and the French Literary and Artistic Property Act of 1793, all of which replaced book privileges with a modern copyright law vesting a "property right" in the author.[25]

To be certain, in contrast to Nathanson's assertion of a perpetual property right as a matter of Jewish law, these secular copyright laws imposed durational limits on the author's exclusive rights. Under the Austrian Law, for example, the duration of the copyright term for printed works was the life of the author, plus 30 years.[26] And as Nathanson expressly noted in the introduction to a book he coauthored, first published in Vilna in 1839, his rights under the Russian copyright law of that time lasted for the life of the author plus 25 years (although in 1857 the copyright term in Russia was lengthened to the life of author plus 50 years).[27] Further, under secular copyright law, authors did not always have rights in other countries; that protection depended on whether the author's country had a treaty with the country where the author sought to prevent reprinting.

Nevertheless, Nathanson likely took inspiration from the secular copyright laws' conceptual and doctrinal embrace of authors' rights of literary property when he propounded a universal, perpetual, and transferable property right for authors under Jewish law. Legal transplantation commonly involves the modification of foreign legal concepts as they are incorporated into a new legal regime. Nathanson, it appears, creatively adapted the concept of literary property to comport with the framework of Jewish law.

In particular, Nathanson's decision to make the author's right perpetual and universal reflects his role as a halakhic decisor rather than a regulator. Nathanson purported to exercise his common sense to identify a property right that was a preexisting "obvious" feature of Jewish law. He did not frame his ruling as one in which he propounded a new right by exercise of the rabbinic power to regulate in local affairs for the overriding good of the community. As such, Nathanson had no real choice but to find that the property right of authors is perpetual. Property rights in Jewish law are perpetual; there are no property categories of limited duration. Hence, if

24. Austrian Copyright Act, 1846, §§ 1, 2, in *Primary Sources on Copyright (1450–1900).*

25. See discussion of Prussian and French laws in *Primary Sources on Copyright (1450–1900).* The full name of France's law was "Decree of the National Convention, of 19 July 1793, regarding the property rights of authors to writings of all kinds, of composers of music, of painters and illustrators (with the report of Lakanal)." On Russia's copyright law and decree, see Newcity 1978: 4. Despite its characterization of the author's rights as property, Russia's copyright law was not moved from the censorship statute to the property code until 1887. Newcity 1978: 5.

26. Austrian Copyright Act, 1846, § 13, in *Primary Sources on Copyright (1450–1900).*

27. Nathanson's reference to his rights under Russian copyright law appear in his introduction to *Meirat Einayim*, book that he co-authored with his brother-in-law Mordekhai Ettinger. On the extension of Russia's copyright term, see Newcity 1978: 5.

Nathanson were to have decreed that these particular rights—the exclusive rights of authors—are limited in time, he would have had to state expressly that he was propounding a new type of right. And he would have had to do so by resort to his rabbinic power to regulate, not by asserting that authors have a property right that is already "there," in halakha.

Nathanson had practical reasons for choosing to identify a property right within preexisting law rather than propounding a new right by decree or regulation. As we have seen, rabbinic regulations are far more limited than are interpretations of fundamental principles and tenets of halakha. In particular, unlike fundamental halakhic precepts, rabbinic regulations have no force outside the community of the rabbi who issues them. Hence, if Nathanson had promulgated a rule that authors must have transferable, exclusive rights for limited periods of time in order to spur the creation and publication of books of Jewish law and liturgy, that rabbinic decree or regulation would not have effect outside the territory of his jurisdiction. In contrast, by purporting to uncover a property right under basic principles of halakha—a right that is necessarily perpetual in Jewish law—Nathanson could insist that authors and their assigns may enforce such a right throughout the Jewish world.

3. Rabbinic Reprinting Bans as a Waiver of Right

If authors have a transferable, perpetual exclusive right to reprint their works, why have authors—and, for that matter, publishers who have acquired the rights of authors—petitioned rabbis for time-limited reprinting bans? According to Nathanson, it is not because they lack legal authority to bar republication forever, but for a different reason: the author himself usually wants his words to be disseminated widely after he has recouped expenses from the initial print run. In brief, "he wishes that his words will be spread all around the world." Hence, far from serving the goal of preventing rival publications, the rationale underlying rabbinic reprinting bans is the opposite. A rabbinic reprinting ban is a mechanism for the author to announce that he is staking a claim of exclusivity only for the time period set out in the ban—he is effectively waiving his exclusive right to print the work after that period has expired. Under Nathanson's logic, if a book is published without a reprinting ban, the author and his assigns enjoy a perpetual, exclusive right to print it. It is only when a book is printed with a reprinting ban, that the author's exclusivity expires with the ban.

4. Preserving the Centrality of Jewish Law

In rendering rabbinic reprinting bans superfluous to authors' exclusive rights, Nathanson also aimed, heroically, to preserve rabbinic oversight over the trade in books of Jewish liturgy and learning in the face of secular government's abrogation of rabbinic authority to issue and enforce reprinting bans. As yet another explanation for why Madpis could prevent Balaban from reprinting Avraham Tzvi Hirsch Eisenstadt's index even though Eistenstadt's work had originally been printed in Russia without a reprinting ban, Nathanson emphasizes that the Russian government had forbidden rabbis from issuing reprinting bans enforceable by the threat of excommunication. The *ḥerem* had traditionally been the sole effective means for rabbinic enforcement of such bans. Yet, as Nathanson puts it, in Russia, "it is forbidden for us to even mention a prohibition or ban or oath, and such terms cannot even be heard from our mouths." As a result, Nathanson notes, rabbinic reprinting bans had come to be framed as requests rather than enforceable rabbinic commands. Indeed, Nathanson states, "my own *haskamot* also do not contain any [binding] prohibition [on reproduction], but rather I am content with issuing [a non-binding] appeal to refrain from reproduction, for I have already written that we merely have the power to request [on the basis of] a teaching of the *Torah* that [one] should not trespass [upon another's right].")[28] Moreover, Nathanson continues, the Austrian Empire, where Lemberg was located, might well punish a publisher who sold copies of a book bearing notice of a rabbinic reprinting ban, rather than relying entirely on his rights under Austria's copyright law, enacted some 14 years earlier. Given that state of affairs, Nathanson laments, "[w]hat power does a Jewish court have" to rule that reprinting a book is forbidden only on the condition that its author or publisher has obtained a rabbinic reprinting ban?

Evidently, Nathanson also wished to maintain the direct relevance of Jewish law for Jewish publishing. If his sole concern had been to avoid conflict with secular authorities, he could have simply applied Austrian copyright law under the longstanding halakhic principle that "the law of the sovereign is the law." In other instances, Nathanson quite liberally applied that principle. He ruled, for example, that a purchase agreement between two Jews is enforceable under the law of the sovereign even if it does not meet the requirements of Jewish law per se.[29] Nathanson also ruled that an arenda, a monopoly in the sale of liquor or estate management issued by a king or noble to a Jewish merchant, is enforceable against putative Jewish competitors pursuant to the principle of the law of the sovereign is the law.[30]

For that matter, indeed, in a number of reprinting bans that Nathanson later granted for various books, he based the ban not only on Jewish law per se but also on the law and customs of the sovereign that Jews have accepted and followed. But when it came to his ruling on copyright, Nathanson instead recognized an author's perpetual property right within Jewish law. In so doing, he obviated the need to make recourse to external secular law through application of the tenet "the law of the sovereign is the law."

In characterizing copyright as a universal exclusive right, Nathanson also established a halakhic foundation for uniform protection for books of Jewish liturgy and learning throughout the widely dispersed communities of the Jewish Diaspora. Unlike the territorial limitations of rabbinic reprinting bans and secular law, an

28. For example, in the ban that Nathanson granted to a companion volume to the one at issue in his ruling, he stated, "I request of our brothers, the children of Israel, that they desist, without violation, from reprinting [this volume], whether as printed or with additions, for a period of ten years from the day of its completion." Nathanson's statement appears in his *haskama* for Abraham Joseph Madpis's edition of *Shulhan Arukh,* Ḥoshen Mishpat, published in Lemberg in 1860).

29. *Sho'el U-Meshiv*, Book 1, Pt. 1, No. 18, discussed in Shilo 1974: 169.

30. *Sho'el U-Meshiv*, Book 3, Pt. 1, No. 232, discussed in Shilo 1974: 418.

author's property right would be universally enforceable under Jewish law. As Nathanson posited, a publisher's rabbinic reprinting ban obtained in one country is not effective in another, especially when the sovereign authority of that other country prohibits importing Jewish books into that country. In contrast, "the author himself has the power to protest all over the world."

Finally, a universal proprietary right, independent of rabbinic reprinting bans, would avoid the communal strife and further erosion of rabbinic authority that sometimes ensued from conflicting bans. Nathanson was, of course, acutely aware of the bitter battles a couple of decades earlier involving competing editions of the Talmud that had rocked Eastern European Jewry and embroiled hundreds of rabbinic leaders in rancorous dispute, largely along internecine sectarian lines. A perpetual, universal proprietary right, anchored in Torah law rather than rabbinic reprinting bans, would accord authors and their successors with clear, unequivocal rights, no matter when or where their books were printed and sold.

D. Epilogue

Nathanson's ruling seems to have had no impact on the matter before him. Despite Nathanson's ruling in Abraham Madpis's favor, Pinkhas Moshe Balaban proceeded to publish *Ashlei Ravrabi*, in two parts, with *Pitḥhei Teshuva* included. Balaban published his edition in Lemberg. It included a *haskama* from Meshalem Yissakhar Halevi Ish Horowitz, from Stanislav, dated, June 16, 1861—in other words after Nathanson had issued his ruling—and an undated *haskama* from Shmuel Valdberg, which presumably preceded Nathanson's ruling. The *haskamot* included a 10-year exclusive reprinting ban, labeling any violation of Balaban's exclusive right as *hasagat gvul*.

Even more strikingly, Nathanson gave a *haskama* (just an approbation) for an edition of *Ashlei Ravrabi* with *Piṭhei Teshuva* published by A. J. Menkes & Solomon Sprecher in 1864. The Menkes/Sprecher edition received another *haskama*, from Shlomo Kluger, which indicates that Menkes and Sprecher did not trespass on a previous edition of the same work because their edition has different typesetting and arrangement, even though its content is the same. Kluger did not identify to which "previous edition" he referred. But a comparison of the Menkes/Sprecher edition of *Ashlei Ravrabi* with that of Abraham Madpis, published in two parts in 1858 and 1861, suggests that the "previous edition" was none other than that of Madpis. The Madpis and Menkes/Sprecher editions feature a different arrangement but virtually the same commentaries, including Nathanson's own commentary, *Yad Shaul*, which appeared in the second part of the Madpis edition. In contrast, the Balaban edition does not include Nathanson's commentary.

III. YITZḤAK SCHMELKES: "WITH ALL DUE RESPECT"

Yitzḥak Schmelkes, known in Jewish tradition as the *Beit Yitzḥak*, was the head of the rabbinic court of Przemyśl, in Austrian Galicia, in the late nineteenth century. A native of Lemberg, Schmelkes had been a student of Nathanson's. But Schmelkes authored two responsa that were sharply critical of Nathanson's recognition of perpetual author's rights.[31] Schmelkes addressed the first to Simon Sofer (1850–1944), the grandson of Moses Sofer.

A. Schmelkes's Responsum to Simon Sofer

At issue in this responsum was whether a manuscript featuring Torah novella (original commentary on matters of Jewish law) could be printed after the author's death without the consent of his heirs. Simon Sofer had taken the position that an author's prerogative to determine whether his teachings on matters of Torah will be released to the public is merely a "tovat hana'a"—a personal benefit lacking in monetary value, which cannot be bequeathed under Jewish law.[32] In contrast, Schmelkes opined that the prerogative to determine whether an unpublished manuscript will be published and disseminated to the public is descendible to the author's heirs. On that basis, Schmelkes concluded, the heirs may prevent another person from printing the manuscript even if that person had copied it during the author's lifetime.

Schmelkes begins his analysis with the example of those who hear someone expound Jewish teaching orally. In that case, unless the expounder told all listeners that they are prohibited from repeating his words, it should be assumed that he is indifferent to the possibility that listeners will tell others. And if thousands of disciples heard a rabbi declaiming, all may effectively disseminate his insights. In such a case, the listeners are actually fulfilling a mitzvah by spreading Jewish learning. Only if the teacher told his listeners that they should not pass on those insights to others are the listeners prohibited from repeating his words.

Schmelkes then moves from oral teachings to written works. If, Schmelkes opines, one copies from an unpublished manuscript with the author's permission, and if, in giving permission to copy, the author does not explicitly state that his written words may *not* be shared with anyone else, then the author in effect agrees that the one copying his words will teach those insights to others. This follows from the understanding predating the advent of print that when one entrusts holy books to a sage, he is allowed to read and copy from them, as that certainly was the original purpose of the loan. As the verse teaches, "People do not despise a thief if he steals to satisfy

31. *Beit Yitzḥak, Yoreh De'ah*, part 5, No. 75 (1899); *Beit Yitzḥak*, Ḥoshen Mishpat, Halakhot Nezikin, No. 80.

32. A contemporary authority, Yosef Dov Be'er Soleveitchik (1820–1892), widely regarded as one of the preeminent rabbinic decisors of his generation, agreed. He stated in a *haskama* issued in 1878 that an author's heirs have no exclusive right to print the author's manuscripts. See Rakover 1991: 269. Further, Naftali Tzvi Yehuda Berlin (1816–1893) (known in Jewish tradition by his acronym Netziv) held that the author's personal benefit is limited to selecting who will print his teaching; he has no prerogative to destroy or otherwise withhold his written teachings about Torah. For that reason, an author's heirs may publish their father's teachings even against the wishes he expressed during his lifetime. Naftali Tzvi Yehuda Berlin, *Responsa Meshiv Davar*, Part 1, No. 24.

his appetite when he is hungry." By the same token, one should not despise a person who "steals" words of Jewish learning and copies them.

For Schmelkes, however, copying and teaching are not the same as bringing a manuscript to print. Schmelkes posits that even when an author permits another to copy his manuscript, it is clear that the author allowed that person to copy only for his own personal study (or to orally convey his teachings), not to publish the manuscript or to use it for commercial advantage. Further, it is also in the nature of things that the children of an author are the ones to print and publish their father's teaching. If another does so without their permission, they will be deprived of the opportunity to perform the mitzvah of disseminating their father's teachings, and they will also suffer economic loss. Hence, concludes Schmelkes, "it is certainly forbidden for the other person to copy the manuscripts and print them without the consent of the heirs. Indeed, even if the author has already printed his book, so long as he has not sold his books it is surely forbidden for the other person to reprint [the book and thus cause] economic loss to the author or his heirs."

In sharp contrast to Nathanson, however, Schmelkes's recognition of an exclusive right in the author's heirs is limited to the right to print manuscripts and reprint books that have not yet been sold. But if the author has already sold his books, the situation is entirely different in Schmelkes's view. When copies of an author's book have been printed and sold, the author has already made his views public. Other people are then freely entitled to learn from and teach them. In Schmelkes's view, moreover, once the author has sold his books, the principle of "the jealousy of scholars increases wisdom" dictates that another may bring benefit to the people of his generation by printing and selling more books with the same content, but for a cheaper price.

B. Disagreement with Nathanson

We thus reach the nub of Schmelkes's disagreement with his former teacher. It is worth quoting his words at length:

> And I have seen the writings of the *Gaon* of Lemberg in his *Sho'el U-Meshiv*, where he discussed this issue extensively and concluded without hesitation that it is forbidden to reprint even when the original edition lacks a *haskama* and rabbinic reprinting ban and even though the author has already sold his books. [Nathanson further held that] the reason for the custom of the *haskama* and that the rabbis issue a decree that others will not be allowed to print for a certain amount of years is to *allow* the printing *after* the expiration of the set period; but absent a *haskama* and a decree, it is forbidden to print and the author has an *eternal right*.
>
> With all due respect to His Honorable Holy Torah [i.e., Nathanson], I see no proof for this opinion. For although a teacher's teachings about Jewish law are his, nevertheless my opinion is that once he lets another person learn from his written work or has sold the first printing of his books, he surely has permitted gratuitous use of them. As stated in Talmud Tractate *Nedarim*, Moses our Teacher was generous

with the *Torah* and gave it to Israel, and Scripture referred to him with the verse, "He who has a generous eye shall be blessed."

And for this reason ... rabbis' decrees that books may not be reprinted remain in effect for only a circumscribed number of years. And regarding what the *Sho'el U-Meshiv* wrote that if one invents a new craft, then another person is not allowed to practice that same craft without the former's consent, because "our perfect Torah should not be less than their idle chatter," this is not in accordance with what we learned about the Torah: "Just as I give it freely, so you shall give it freely." The Torah is not an axe to cut with [i.e., one should not teach the Torah for one's personal financial gain].

Moreover, regarding the tools of one's craft, if one does not possess a privilege from the government attesting that he owns an eternal right to his invention, I know of no prohibition whereby another may not practice the same craft [or reprint the same books].

Granted, one who teaches the Torah may be paid an "idleness payment"—what he might have earned in another profession were he not devoting all of his time to teaching Torah. But aside from that [subsistence payment], where is it allowed to take payment solely for an intangible right, even where there is no burden imposed? Plus, even if we would agree that it is permitted to receive such payment for an intangible right, who is empowered to prohibit another from printing a book based on the former's Torah knowledge until the one wishing to print pays for the right to do so? For the Torah is compared to water, from which one may draw freely with no charge.

C. Law of the Sovereign

Schmelkes adds that the "law of our country" forbids printing without government authorization and recognizes a copyright in printed works. Secular law thus diverges from Jewish law, which accords no right to prevent reprinting a published work that has already been sold. Nonetheless, Schmelkes continues, we must abide by secular copyright law.

The reason is twofold. First, it has become a firmly established custom among Jews to honor secular copyright law, and it thus behooves us to continue that custom. In invoking that custom, Schmelkes suggests that although secular copyright has a different rule than Jewish law, it does not fundamentally contradict halakhic principles. Accordingly, the customary practice among publishers and authors of following secular copyright law may take precedence over what would otherwise be the rule under halakha. Schmelkes, in other words, intimates what Nathanson did not: that publishers' and authors' long-standing practice of following secular copyright law is akin to a merchant custom in a commercial manner that has halakhic force.

Second, under the halakhic principle of *dina de-malkhuta dina*, "the law of the sovereign is the law," even when secular law runs contrary to the Torah, we must defer to secular law in commercial matters unless doing so would impose an economic loss. In a matter where applying secular law merely prevents someone from enjoying a financial profit that would otherwise be obtained, but does not impose an actual loss (as the terms "profit" and "loss" are understood in Jewish law), it is required on the basis of Jewish law to uphold secular law.

Finally, Schmelkes notes that, in contrast to Moses Sofer, who invited everyone to copy his books, the offspring of sages today are miserably poor and need to earn a livelihood from teachings about Torah. Nonetheless, if the offspring had to rely on halakha, publishers would not need to obtain their consent to reprint a book that has already been published. But in our country this does not matter, because secular law governs, pursuant to *dina de-malkhuta dina*.

D. Schmelkes's Second Responsum on Jewish Copyright

Schmelkes's second responsum concerned a question about territorial limits to copyright under Jewish law. It was addressed to Feivel Schreier, head of the rabbinic court of the small Galician community of Brodchin. In this responsum, dated 1891, Schmelkes considered a petition—akin to what Abraham Madpis had presented to Joseph Saul Nathanson—to prohibit reprinting in a different country from where the book in question had been initially published and sold. Indeed, the petitioner asked for a prohibition against reprinting everywhere in the world.

In his response, Schmelkes refers to earlier responsa on Jewish copyright and once again expresses his disagreement with Nathanson's view that authors have a property right in their published works. Schmelkes insists, in that regard, that an author of commentary on the Torah should not profit from this teaching. Rather, Schmelkes reiterates, published books of Jewish learning enjoy copyright protection only under the principle of *dina de-malkhuta dina*. And given that the rights of authors and publishers of such books derive entirely from secular law, their rights are limited to the territory of the country in which their book has been granted copyright protection under secular law.

Schmelkes concedes that there is a custom among Jewish publishers and rabbinic authorities of respecting the rights of authors and publishers under secular copyright law even across territorial borders. Hence, by force of that custom, perhaps reprinting should be prohibited throughout the world. However, Schmelkes concludes, there is no clear answer to the question of whether custom dictates a worldwide prohibition on reprinting, and the halakha itself does not recognize that universal right. Accordingly, Schmelkes denies the petition to forbid reprinting.

E. Conclusion

In sum, for both Joseph Saul Nathanson and Yitzḥak Schmelkes the mechanism and doctrine by which rabbinic authorities had pronounced, applied, and enforced Jewish copyright law since the sixteenth century had lost their force. In Nathanson's eyes, rabbinic reprinting bans, rabbinic regulation, and the halakhic doctrine of wrongful competition were fatally circumscribed by the temporal and territorial limitations of the protection they provided and by sovereign authorities' abolition of rabbinic power to issue orders of excommunication. And Schmelkes, ruling at the end of the nineteenth century, could simply find no basis in Jewish law in and of itself for recognizing copyright in a book of Jewish learning once the book had been published.

Accordingly, both Nathanson and Schmelkes looked to secular copyright law for a means by which authors and publishers of books of Jewish learning could have recourse to rabbinic authorities for protections against reprinting. Yet, the two rabbinic decisors took diametrically opposed positions on the role of secular copyright law in that endeavor.[33] Nathanson rejected Shmuel Valdberg's earlier ruling that, in the absence of an enforceable reprinting ban, an author and his assigns have rights only under secular copyright law. Instead, Nathanson took inspiration from secular copyright's recognition of an author's right of literary property and incorporated that principle into Jewish law. In so doing, Nathanson aimed to preserve the centrality of halakha in matters of copyright for books of Jewish law, learning, and liturgy. In contrast, Schmelkes gave recognition to secular copyright law without incorporating it into Jewish law per se. For him, the right to prevent reprinting lay only in secular law. And it was only by virtue of the Jewish law principle, the law of the sovereign is the law, together with the custom of respecting secular copyright law, that Jewish law would accord protection against reprinting.

Schmelkes's position that the halakha per se does not accord copyright protection for books of Jewish learning still left room for rabbinic prohibitions against reprinting. Schmelkes's rulings meant only that rabbinic courts would accord to authors of published books of Jewish learning whatever protections they enjoyed under secular copyright law—no more and no less. In that regard, by the end of the nineteenth century, secular copyright law in Austria and Russia provided for copyright terms of respectively, the life of the author plus 30 years and the life of the author plus 50 years. Further, pursuant to bilateral treaties requiring reciprocal copyright relations, the laws of those countries protected works of some foreign authors as well as domestic ones.[34] Hence, although Schmelkes denied authors and publishers of books of Jewish learning the perpetual, universal property right that Nathanson envisioned, his application to copyright of the Jewish law doctrine of the law of the sovereign is the law meant that such authors and publishers would generally have longer terms of protection over a more expansive territory than would have been the case if they had had to rely on rabbinic reprinting bans or on the Jewish law of wrongful competition.

As we will now see, contemporary rabbinic scholars generally accept neither Nathanson's nor Schmelkes's rulings. Although some rabbinic decisors follow Nathanson in positing that authors have a property right in their published works, most do not. And although contemporary rabbinic scholars often cite Schmelkes in support of the position that Nathanson's ruling is an outlier, without support

33. Elon 1997: 66 n. 87.
34. Bowker 1912: 405–06 (Austria), 409 (Russia).

in rabbinic precedent, they, like Nathanson, are unwilling to hold that "our perfect Torah" affords no copyright protection and thus that Jewish copyright law is entirely limited to applying secular copyright law under the doctrine of the law of the sovereign is the law. Contemporary rabbinic scholars endeavor, rather, to look for halakhic doctrine, native to Jewish law—and, purportedly, independent of the influence of secular law—to determine what are the rights to be accorded to authors and publishers.

CHAPTER 9

The Present-Day Debate

Is Copyright Infringement "Stealing"?

Viewed from the perspective of the centuries-long rabbinic debates about the halakhic basis of Jewish copyright law, the terse ruling of the Bnei Brak rabbinic court on Microsoft's petition, which we visited in Chapter 1, now begins to make sense. As the court held:

> We hereby emphatically announce in the matter regarding those who commit the act of copying computer disks and programs of various texts and selling them for a low price, and in so doing wrongfully encroach upon the business of those who invested years of labor and significant sums of money in developing those computer programs. Rabbinic authorities of the modern era have already expounded upon the prohibition of such wrongful competition at length, and every person who commits such act and copies any version is a transgressor. Moreover, each purchaser from such persons is an abettor of those who violate the law, and there is no excuse that such purchases are for the benefit of learning. The descendants of Israel shall not do wrong, and may all who obey the law find pleasantness.

We can now appreciate that the Bnei Brak court adopted Moses Isserles's characterization of a publisher's exclusive rights—that a commercial actor who reprints and undercuts the publisher's market price commits an act of wrongful competition by depriving the publisher of his livelihood—and not Joseph Saul Nathanson's pronouncement that authors own perpetual proprietary rights in their creations. The court also followed the centuries-old practice of forbidding the purchase of offending copies. Nonetheless, if Microsoft hoped to obtain a ruling that banned all unauthorized copying and distribution of its programs, including personal copying and noncommercial distribution, it could only have been disappointed by the rabbinic court's formulation.

Read closely, in fact, the rabbinic court's ruling might not reach Microsoft's software at all. The court condemns the copying and selling of "computer disks and programs of various texts." It seems that the rabbinic judges had in mind rabbinic texts in computer-readable format, such as collections of the Talmud and other foundational works, responsa, and rabbinic commentary on CD-ROM, not computer programs otherwise used in the operation of a computer, such as Microsoft Windows and Office.[1] Contemporary *ḥaredi* rabbis, including those who joined in the Microsoft ruling, have repeatedly banned most uses of computers. Indeed, shortly after they signed the Bnei Brak court's ruling, Nissim Karelitz and Ovadia Yosef joined other leading *ḥaredi* rabbis in issuing a decree warning of the terrible dangers of computers. The decree, which appears in Illustration 15, proclaims that the Internet is forbidden even for earning a living. It further announces that the grave prohibition on viewing videos set out in previous decrees outlawing television and movies applies equally to videos on CD-ROM even if they purport to be censored in accordance with religious strictures.

Notwithstanding their sweeping formulations, such rabbinic edicts have failed to stem the tide of Internet usage in Israel's *ḥaredi* community. According to a 2013 survey of Israel's Central Bureau of Statistics, 58 percent of self-described ultra-Orthodox Jews over the age of 19 reported using a computer during the previous three months, and 43 percent reported using the Internet, of which over 40 percent reported downloading files and 25 percent reported participating in chat groups.[2] Given the rabbinic prohibition against using the Internet, and the survey's limitation to respondents ages 20 and over, one would imagine that the numbers are actually considerably higher than those reported. Indeed, there are dozens of *ḥaredi* web portals and websites, even if they are periodically condemned by rabbinic leaders.

The Microsoft ruling must be understood within that context of repeated rabbinic efforts to impose severe limits on the use of computers within the *ḥaredi* community. The rabbis' grave concerns about licentious uses of computers and the Internet reinforce the understanding that, when the Bnei Brak rabbinic judges forbade the commercial piracy of computer programs "of various texts," they may well have intended to refer only to computer programs that they countenance, those that display rabbinic literature and teachings.

Yet, despite those limitations—and despite the ruling's doctrinal grounding in the Jewish law of wrongful competition rather than property—Microsoft nevertheless claimed that using unauthorized copies of software on one's computer is "stealing" under Jewish law. Illustration 16 is an advertisement that Microsoft's publicist

1. Contrary to that hypothesis, perhaps, when the same rabbinic court issued an edict in almost identical language in favor of the producers of the Bar-Ilan Responsa Project, which provides an electronic database of foundational works of halakha, it referred to "texts of Torah" rather than using the more general phrase "various texts" that appears in the Microsoft ruling. That edict is reproduced in Radzyner 2015: 173.

2. Central Bureau of Statistics of the State of Israel 2015: Table 9.7 (measuring computer and Internet use). In the Central Bureau of Statistics annual surveys, we see an ever increasing use of computers and the Internet among *ḥaredim* in Israel. That increase has continued apace despite periodic efforts by *ḥaredi* rabbis to clamp down on *ḥaredi* Internet portals, which previously proliferated with their qualified blessing. See Lynfield 2009: 34.

סכנה נוראה!

קריאת גדולי ומאורי הדור
בדבר הבעיות ההלכתיות והחינוכיות שבמחשב

מרחשון תשנ"ט לפ"ק

לאחרונה נתחדשו משחיתים חדשים שלא שיערום אבותינו, והיצה"ר בא להכניס לבתינו בדלת האחורית - באמצעות המחשב הביתי - רעל ממית, המאיים ח"ו למוטט את כל קדושת הבית היהודי, את עתידנו ואת עתיד ילדינו. ומחובת כל אחד ואחד - לעשות כל שביכולתו לבער נגע זה מקרבינו.

המחשב כולל בתוכו כמה סכנות:

א. **ה'אינטרנט'** - גם לצורך מסחר - לא יראה ולא ימצא בבתי ישראל, והוא מכיל רעל ממית אשר כל באיה לא ישובון, וכל המשתמש בו מכניס את עצמו לנסיונות עצומים. וכבר נחרבו ונהרסו בתים רבים מישראל ע"י שהכניסו ה'אינטרנט' בביתם לצרכי מסחר, ולא עמדו בנסיון. גם בבתי מסחר אסור השימוש ב'אינטרנט'. אולם אם אי-אפשר להם **בשום אופן** בלעדיו, אזי- אם יכולים להשתמש בו מבלי להכשל במראות שחץ, ויכולים גם לפקח כראוי שלא ישתמשו בזה לשם סקרנות (בזמן העבודה או לאחריה) - **אין בכוחינו לאסור.**

אולם, אם גם שלא בכוונה אפשר להכשל במראות שחץ תוך כדי חיפוש ב'אינטרנט' - **אין שום היתר בדבר גם לצורך פרנסה.**

ב. החרם החמור - חרם עולם- שהכריזו כל גדולי ישראל על מחריב האנושות - דהיינו הטלויזיה, **חל בכל תוקפו על מחשב שמותקנת בו אפשרות של צפיה בטלויזיה. וכמו"כ חל האיסור בכל תוקפו על סרטים** (גם המצונזרים והמבוקרים) **שרואים בתקליטורים במחשב או במכשיר הוידיאו** - אשר הם תמצית זוהמת הטלויזיה עצמה.

מלבד שכבר נתברר בבירור גמור שאי אפשר לצנזר סרטים בשום אופן, הנסיון הורה - שגם אלו המתרגלים לראות סרטים שהם 'כאילו' נקיים, סופם מתפתים ונגררים... ויורדים לדיוטא תחתונה, רח"ל. **ועל כן, חובה גמורה על ההורים ועל המחנכים, להחדיר שהמושג 'סרט' הוא טריפה ומוקצה מחמת מיאוס, ושכל סוגי הסרטים אין לצפות בהם**, כולל סרטי מחזות עלילות וערבי שירה.

ג. כל התקליטורים - כולל תוכנות מדעיות, לימודיות, אנציקלופדיות, גרפיקה ואוסף תמונות - מהוים סכנה חמורה, היות וצריכים בקורת מוסמכת על התכנים ועל מאגרי התמונות! - שלא יכנסו לבתי ישראל או למוסדות החינוך תמונות של פריצות, עניני עבודה זרה, כפירה, שפיכות דמים ואביזרייהו.

ד. הכנסת 'משחקי מחשב' - מהווה סכנה חמורה ביותר, ובמיוחד לצעירים, היות **ובמשחקי מחשב רבים** ישנם דברים המזיקים ושורפים כתבערת אש: תמונות מכוערות, קטעי סרטים, אלימות ומסרים גרועים אחרים - **הגם שאנשים באיצטלה חרדית מעידים עליהם שהם מצונזרים או מבוקרים - ואין להכניסם בבתי ישראל.**

הנסיון הוכיח, שגם משחקי מחשב נקיים, **שאין בהם שום מסרים שליליים, מביאים להתמכרות, מטמטמים את המוח וגורמים הרס חינוכי** - מלבד שהם מהוים פתח למשחקים ותקליטורים פסולים - **וכדאי מאד שלא יהיו בבית, כי בנפשם הדבר!**

ובודאי מי שיכול שלא להכניס מחשב לביתו, יציל בכך את עצמו ובני ביתו מנסיונות, מפיתויים וממכשולים חמורים, וגם יסייע לו לגדל את ילדיו לתורה וליראת שמים על טהרת הקודש.

ועל זה באנו עה"ח

א.י.ל. שטינמן
מיכל י. ליפקוביץ
שמואל אויערבך
שמואל הלוי ואזנר
ש. נסים קרליץ
חיים פינחס שיינברג
הק' משה יהושע בהה"צ מוה"ר ח.מ. זצלה"ה
הק' יוחנן סופר
אברהם יעקב פרידמן
הק' ישכר דב
אברהם מ. דנציגר
נתן גשטטנר
אלי' שמואל שמרלר
עובדיה יוסף
שמעון בעדני
משה צדקה

Illustration 15
Decree on the Terrible Danger of Computers, Issued by Leading *Ḥaredi* Rabbis of Israel, 1998.
(courtesy National Library of Israel).

placed in the *ḥaredi* press following the rabbinic court's ruling. The advertisement's bottom half displays a signed copy of the Bnei Brak rabbinic court ruling, while the upper half states that it is forbidden to use any computer that contains unauthorized copies of computer programs. And the large banner cutting across the middle of the advertisement features the Biblical admonition: "You Shall Not Steal."

Illustration 16
Microsoft Israel Publicist's Ad in *Ḥaredi* Press: You Shall Not Steal, 1998.

I. THE RABBINIC DEBATE OVER COPYRIGHT: CONTOURS AND RAMIFICATIONS

Even though the Bnei Brak court followed Moses Isserles's characterization of proto-copyright as protection against wrongful competition rather than Joseph Saul Nathanson's stronger formulation, Microsoft's "You Shall Not Steal" banner is not entirely without foundation in present-day rabbinic discourse. Leading contemporary rabbinic jurists in Israel have engaged in lively debate about Jewish copyright law's halakhic basis and applicability to Internet file trading, copying for personal use, and copying for classroom instruction, as well as commercial copying. Indeed, some of the rabbinic luminaries who signed the Microsoft ruling have issued individual rulings in other contexts that differ significantly from the Microsoft ruling—and from one another—in defining the doctrinal foundations for copyright under Jewish law.

A. Rival Schools

Among contemporary rabbinic jurists, there are two opposing schools of thought regarding the nature of authors' rights in their creations. One contends that Jewish law accords authors a right of ownership, akin to property rights in tangible chattel. I label this the "copyright-is-property school." The other views copyright under Jewish law as an amalgam of various rights arising from guild regulation, binding custom, protection against wrongful competition and unjust enrichment, mass market licenses that retain certain ownership rights in physical copies, rabbinic reprinting bans, and deference to secular law insofar as commercial matters are concerned. I refer to this as the "copyright-as-amalgam school." As we shall see, both schools bear influences of secular copyright law.

The copyright-is-property school draws support from three leading contemporary treatises on the Jewish law of copyright. The treatises—two authored by Lithuanian *ḥaredim* and the third by a National-Religious Orthodox rabbi—all recognize that there is a split of opinion about the nature of copyright in Jewish law, but each favors classifying copyright as property.[3] The copyright-is-property school cites the 1860 ruling of Joseph Saul Nathanson as its primary foundational authority. Nathanson, it will be recalled, held that authors have a perpetual, exclusive, and transferable right to print—and reprint—their works, independently of any secular or independently of Jewish communal copyright enactment and independently of rabbinic reprinting ban that might (or might not) have been issued. Nathanson did not explicitly use the terms "property" or "ownership" in his ruling. Nevertheless, given the nature of the authors' right he recognized, Nathanson clearly equated that right with the concept of property; indeed, he later referred to an author's exclusive rights as a form of property in rabbinic reprinting bans that he granted to various authors and publishers.[4] In any event, Nathanson's ruling is cited today as the leading authority for the proposition that authors have an ownership right in their works.

Despite treatise support for the idea that copyright is property, the copyright-as-amalgam school most probably represents the majority view of leading contemporary rabbinic jurists who have opined on the matter.[5] In addition to the Microsoft ruling, of

3. The two treatises authored by *ḥaredi* rabbis are: Y. Cohen 1999 and Weisfish 2002. The third is by a National-Religious Orthodox rabbi, law professor, and attorney with Israel's Ministry of Justice who has authored numerous books and articles about Jewish law, often in support of incorporating various facets of Jewish law into modern, secular Israeli law: Rakover 1991.

4. As noted in Chapter 8, in those reprinting bans, Nathanson referred to authors' rights as *kinyan* ("property") or *naḥala* (an "asset").

5. See, e.g., Shlomo Zalman Auerbach (1910–1995), Rulings and Answers, in Weisfish 2002: 121–22 (the source of the prohibition of infringing copyright is wrongful competition, not a right of ownership); Ezra Batzri, Zkhuyot Yotzrim, Ruling in Arbitration No.

special note here is the rabbinic ruling on a petition brought by the Israeli association of composers. It held that performing songs at weddings without the composer's permission is wrongful because the halakhic precept that "the law of the sovereign is the law" requires deference to secular Israeli copyright law, not because authors have a right of literary property under Jewish law. The copyright-as-amalgam school cites to rulings of Mordekhai Banet, Moses Sofer, and Yitzḥak Schmelkes.[6] As we have seen, Banet and Sofer engaged in a lengthy debate about the nature and scope of authors' rights. In the course of that back-and-forth, each expounded a number of possible bases in Jewish law for something approximating what we call copyright. But neither even considered the possibility that authors have a perpetual, exclusive right, let alone a "property right," in their works.

As discussed in Chapter 8, Schmelkes explicitly rejected Nathanson's ruling that authors have a perpetual exclusive right in their work, although the precise doctrinal bases and breadth of his rejection remain in dispute. Schmelkes conceded that an author and his heirs have an exclusive right to publish an unpublished manuscript. He held, however, that after the work has been published and the first edition sold (i.e., after the author or heirs have recovered their investment), anyone is free to print the book, subject to any rights the author or heirs may have under secular copyright law pursuant to the Jewish law rule that "the law of the sovereign is the law."[7] Rabbinic jurists of the copyright-is-property school contend that Schmelkes meant only to carve out an exception from the author's perpetual right of ownership for books of new commentary on Jewish law and religion. In contrast, those of the copyright-as-amalgam school read Schmelkes to hold that even the author's exclusive rights to publish the manuscript and sell the first edition do not derive from a proprietary copyright in the text. Those rights flow, rather, only from the Jewish law of wrongful competition or from the author's right to condition access and use of the physical chattel—the manuscript—in which the author holds a property right.

B. Doctrinal Ramifications

Secular copyright law has also seen protracted debate—ever since modern copyright statutes were enacted—about whether copyrights are property rights. Yet, in present-day common law and civil law jurisdictions, the question whether copyright qualifies as property carries virtually no immediate doctrinal consequences. With few exceptions,

42/3575181 (noting the disagreement and split of authority and thus relying on custom and "the law of the sovereign" in forbidding copying); Shmuel Ha-Levi Wosner, *Shevet Ha-Levi*, Pt. 4, Ḥoshen Mishpat, No. 202; Silman, *Darkhei Ḥoshen*, in Weisfish 2002: 180; Tzvi ben Hayim Yitzḥak Shpitz, *Responsa Minḥat Tzvi*, Hilkhot Shkhenim No. 18, *reprinted in* Weisfish 2002: 176; Navon 2001; Ishun 2001; Ganot 2001; Nehurai 1994–1995; Y. Landau 1998–1999; Int'l Beis Hora'ah of the Institute for Dayanim 2010.

6. See, e.g., Silman, *Darkhei Ḥoshen*; Wosner, *Shevet Ha-Levi*, Pt. 4, Ḥoshen Mishpat, No. 202; Navon 2001.

7. Yitzḥak Schmelkes (1828–1906), *Beit Yitzḥak*, Yoreh De'ah, Part. 5, No. 75.

the copyright holder's rights are what they are under copyright law regardless of whether copyright is deemed to be a property right.[8] Rather, the spirited debate over whether copyright is "property" has import for secular copyright doctrine primarily because of the rhetorical force of labeling a right as "property" in the popular imagination and its consequent impact on legislators and judges in applying copyright law. Those who characterize copyright as "property" in secular law typically do so to counter arguments that copyrights are—and should be—subject to robust exceptions to allow fair use, private copying, and mass digitization by public libraries. The "copyrights are property" trope is also invoked in opposition to various compulsory licenses under which copyright holders have rights to receive remuneration but no right to prevent the licensed use.

To label copyrights as "property" has rhetorical force in debates over copyright law and policy because contemporary political discourse typically imbues the term "private property" with a connotation of absolute right. In American culture, "property" encapsulates an individualistic, almost libertarian, vision: what is mine is mine and no one can take it away. (Although, in fact, property rights are subject to numerous constitutional, regulatory, and common-law limitations.) In Europe as well, "property" has historically carried connotations of a natural, pre-political entitlement, in the German idealist sense of an object completely subject to the "will" of its owner, even if present-day European constitutions explicitly place property in the service of the public good.[9] Hence, to denote copyrights as "property" is an effective rhetorical device to override their limited reach and public benefit character. The symbolic force of the absolute dominion ideal fosters lawmakers' intuition that if copyrights are "property," they should embody exclusive rights of broad scope, long duration, and relative imperviousness to exceptions and limitations. Indeed, if copyrights are property, copyright infringement becomes akin to theft, an egregiously immoral and even criminal act, even if the infringer has creatively modified or added to what he copied.[10]

In Jewish law, the doctrinal consequences of categorizing copyright as property fall along similar lines. If copyright is property, it is typically understood to be of

8. One possible exception is that if copyright is deemed "property," copyright holders might enjoy the benefit of constitutional protections against legislative enactments that substantially diminish the scope or duration of existing copyrights. But no U.S. court has ever ruled that a retroactive contraction of a copyright holder's rights is a "taking" of property under the Fifth Amendment. Further, European courts that have characterized copyrights as constitutionally protected "property" have qualified that protection on the grounds that, like all property rights, copyright must sometimes give way to a "fair balance" between private rights and the public interest. See, e.g., French Constitutional Council Decision, CC decision no. 2009-580, June 10, 2009, J.O. [Official Gazette of France], June 13, 2009, p. 9675 (Fr.); School Book [Privilege] Case (*Schulbuchprivileg*), Federal Constitutional Court, July 7, 1971, 31 Entscheidigung des Bundesverfassungsgericht [BVerfGE] 229 (F.R.G.).

9. On the historical force of denoting authors' right as "property," see Pfister 2005. On the German idealist view of property as an object completely subject to individual will, see Gordley 2006: 55–56, 69–70. The German Constitution provides, for example, that "Property entails obligations. Its use shall also serve the public good." GG art. 14, translated in Wolfrum and Grote 2007.

10. See Netanel 2007b: 11–12; Lemley 2005.

broader scope, longer duration, and greater imperviousness to doctrinal or regulatory limitation than if it is grounded in wrongful competition, trade regulation, custom, reprinting ban, or some other non-property doctrine.

In Jewish law, however, the repercussions of categorizing copyright as property flow from a perceived doctrinal mandate, not from the rhetorical force of some idealized model or theoretical construct of "property." The "copyright is property" trope lacks symbolic force within rabbinic debate because Jewish law does not contain any counterpart to secular jurisprudence's understanding of property as a repository of individual liberty and sovereignty. Indeed, Jewish law has no ideologically charged model or overarching theory of property. Jewish law, for that matter, lacks even a general definition of "property." As one leading commentator notes:

> "What is ownership?" is a question which is nowhere directly or abstractly put in any writings which are included under the description of Jewish law, early or late, and one will therefore search in vain in the mass of Jewish legal writings of recognized authority for a definition of ownership. Jewish jurisprudence was too pragmatic and concrete in tendency to occupy itself with the definition of legal terms without immediate reference to a practicable point.[11]

Put more broadly, unlike current secular common law and civil law, Jewish law has not undergone the fundamental conceptual transformation from a regime that provides subject-specific responses to novel problems, including reasoning by analogy from narrow, preexisting doctrinal categories, to a regime framed by abstract general categories, such as property, contract, and tort, that are applied to incorporate new subject matter deemed to share essential qualifying characteristics of the pertinent general category.[12] Accordingly, much like Roman law and early common law, Jewish law has no comprehensive category of "property" into which all existing and emerging variants of rights in things are seen to fit.[13] Even the Hebrew words traditionally used to connote forms of property or assets have narrower, more particular meanings than the modern English word "property," infused as it is with the connotation of absolute dominion. For that reason, perhaps, when contemporary rabbinic jurists debate how copyright should be characterized, they generally use a term from modern Hebrew, *ba'alut*, meaning ownership in the general sense, rather than the traditional word, *kinyan*, which can connote either dominion or lesser proprietary rights

11. Herzog 1980: 71. Isaac Herzog was the first Chief Rabbi of Ireland and later the first Ashkenazic Chief Rabbi of the State of Israel.

12. See Sherman and Bently 1999: 17–18 (describing the transformation of common law). The move to systematize the common law took place over the nineteenth and twentieth centuries, as the common-law writs were abolished and replaced with the general categories of property, tort, and contract. See Gordley 2006: 44.

13. See Herzog 1980: 65–67, 72–74. On the absence of an overarching concept of "property" in Roman law, see Bouckaert 1990: 781–84. On the particularistic, narrow forms of property in the common law that Blackstone described at length in the Commentaries, see Schorr 2008: 107–11.

and which primarily refers to the mode of acquisition of an object of property rather than the right itself.[14]

In sum, the terms property and ownership in Jewish law are essentially terms of classification of sundry rights that share common doctrinal precepts. Unlike "property" in common and civil law, property in Jewish law is not an independent archetype or ideal form with a defined set of essential attributes, and certainly not one freighted with the ideology of possessive individualism as in secular Western jurisprudence. Nor, for that matter, does one find in the rabbinic debate any hint of the view, which has historically found expression in Lockean and German idealist copyright theory, that authors' works are the unique, newly created products of mental labor, ingenuity, and personality, and thus the "first and most sacred of all properties."[15] To say that an author owns his work in Jewish law means simply that, as a doctrinal matter, the author's rights are governed by a set of rules and precepts that are generally understood to attach to chattel, land, and other things sometimes labeled as "property."

Yet, whatever the formalist, doctrinal character of the rabbinic debate, to classify copyright as "property" or a "right of ownership" in Jewish law typically yields the result that the rules and rights applicable to other forms of "property" also apply to copyright. That doctrinal result is roughly akin to that sought by the ideologically charged "copyright is property" argument in common and civil law, even though rabbinic adherents of the copyright-is-property school arrive at that result for very different reasons. The rabbinic jurisprudence contains a number of striking examples:

1. Following Nathanson, present-day rabbinic jurists assume that, if authors have a right of ownership in their works, that right is perpetual, descendible, and transferable.[16] In keeping with the under-theorized nature of property in Jewish law generally, rabbinic jurists do not explain why those characteristics necessarily attach to the author's right of ownership per se. Instead, they apparently flow by analogy to rules applicable to things typically treated as property under Jewish law.
2. Also following Nathanson, an author's right of ownership is what secular scholars would term pre-political and what in Jewish law terms is "*de-oreita*," a right grounded in the Pentateuch as opposed to a subsequent rabbinic regulation. In other words, the author and his heirs have the perpetual exclusive right to print even if they have not received a rabbinic reprinting ban, and even in the absence of secular law

14. See Herzog 1980: 72–73 (discussing the adoption of the modern word *ba'alut* in contemporary rabbinic jurisprudence generally); Webber 1928: 84 (discussing the meaning of *kinyan*).

15. Victor Hugo, Speech to the Council d'Etat (Sept. 30, 1849), quoted in Boyle 2008: 31.

16. See Weisfish 2002: 38–39; Weiss 2009; Y. Cohen 1999: Kitzurei Dinim le-Ma'aseh 1–2, Kuntras 1–8. Cohen ultimately concludes that copyright is not transferable given the inability to transfer incorporeal things in Jewish law, although authors may grant exclusive licenses to use their works. But the rabbis do not generally distinguish between an author's assertion of copyright and his publisher's or another transferee's assertion. Indeed, as highlighted in Chapter 8, Nathanson's seminal ruling involved a case in which the publisher had purchased the author's rights.

providing for such a right. In that vein, for example, the eminent rabbinic authority Yosef Shalom Eliashiv posited (in contrast to the Microsoft ruling that he signed) that the author has a right of ownership in his work that continues in perpetuity regardless of the limited copyright term prescribed under secular law.[17]

3. If copyright is property, the copyright holder's exclusive rights are universal, rather than being confined within local or national borders. In contrast, rabbinic reprinting bans, guild and community regulation, custom, and whatever secular law might be recognized according to the Jewish-law rule that the "law of the sovereign is the law" are all limited to particular territorial jurisdictions and may vary from one jurisdiction to another.[18] That limitation is of particular importance in Israel because some leading ultra-Orthodox rabbinic jurists posit that the "law of the sovereign" rule does not apply to the laws of the State of Israel and thus cannot be relied on as a basis for copyright protection in Israel.[19]
4. If copyright arises from the Jewish law of wrongful competition, rather than being a right of ownership, it is generally not a violation of the author's rights to make and distribute copies without permission to the extent that the author has already recovered his initial investment in creating and distributing the work (traditionally understood as selling out the first edition).[20] The reason is that the Jewish law of wrongful competition protects an incumbent only against a new entrant who would deprive the incumbent of his livelihood, not merely cause the incumbent to earn lesser profits.[21] In contrast, if copyright is property, the author's exclusive rights arise independently of whether unlicensed copying causes the author material monetary harm. Under Jewish law, a property owner may generally prevent conversion or unauthorized use of his property that would result even in relatively

17. Yosef Shalom Eliashiv, *Rulings and Answers*, in Weisfish 2002: 115. Before his death in 2012, at the age of 102, Eliashiv was a widely respected rabbinic authority both within and outside ultra-Orthodox circles. Unlike most other ultra-Orthodox rabbis of his day, he served as a *dayan* (rabbinical judge) in the Chief Rabbinate of the State of Israel, including on its Supreme Rabbinical Court, until the early 1970s.

18. For further discussion of the issue of the geographical limitations of copyright and reprinting bans under Jewish law, see Rakover 1991: 393–416; Navon 2001: 35, 37. As noted in Chapter 8, Yitzḥak Schmelkes posited that the law of the sovereign is in force only in the country where the law was enacted and thus that it cannot serve as a basis for forbidding reprinting in another country, at least absent custom to the contrary.

19. See, e.g., Yehuda Silman, *Darkhei Ḥoshen*, in Weisfish 2002: 180; Tzvi ben Ḥayim Yitzḥak Shpitz, *Responsa Minḥat Tzvi*, Hilkhot Shkhenim, No. 18. Other rabbinic jurists accept that the "law of the sovereign" rule applies in Israel, but strongly prefer to rely on internal sources of Jewish law if at all possible because reliance on external law suggests that Jewish law is incomplete. See, e.g., Navon 2001: 43–44.

20. See Y. Cohen 1999: 601; Weisfish 2002: 38.

21. Ephraim Zalman Margoliot (1762–1828), *Responsa Beit Ephraim,* Ḥoshen Mishpat, No. 27. For contemporary applications related to copyright, see Shmuel Ha-Levi Wosner, *Shevet Ha-Levi*, Part 4, Ḥoshen Mishpat, No. 202 (holding that an author's loss in profits resulting from multiple copying of portions of a book for classroom instruction is not sufficient harm to support a claim for wrongful competition); Shlomo Tana, *Responsa Brakhat Shlomo,* Ḥoshen Mishpat, No. 26, at 189, 192 (1986) (holding that sale of a rival edition of the Vilna Talmud would not be sufficiently ruinous to the business of the plaintiff publisher to constitute wrongful competition).

trivial monetary harm.[22] Under the copyright-is-property school, accordingly, the author may enforce his right of ownership even if he has already earned a substantial profit. Indeed, according to some commentators, unlicensed copying may infringe the author's right of ownership even absent any monetary harm at all.[23]

5. Following further from the Jewish law conception of wrongful competition, if copyright is a right against wrongful competition rather than a right of ownership, a number of jurists posit that it is not a violation of the author's rights for someone to engage in copying that does not cause the author material monetary harm and/or does not entail commercial competition, even if the author has yet to recover his investment. Under that view, the author typically has no claim against an individual who engages in private copying, a teacher who makes multiple copies for his classroom use, or even an Internet file trader (or anyone else) who copies a work and gives the copies away for free, although some jurists suggest that such copying is permissible only if the copyist or recipient would not otherwise buy a copy of the work.[24] In contrast, such copying would typically be an impermissible abridgment of the author's right of ownership, regardless of its noncommercial character and, presumably, even absent monetary harm.[25]
6. Some halakhic scholars posit that authors and publishers can overcome the inability to prevent private and other noncommercial copying under the Jewish law of wrongful competition by selling copies of their work partially or conditionally, with an explicit reservation to themselves of the exclusive right to make further copies.[26] That theory follows from the Talmudic doctrine of the right of *shiur*,

22. See Shilo 1980: 51 (discussing unjust enrichment).

23. See Ishun 2001: 59 (describing but rejecting that view).

24. See Y. Cohen 1999: Kuntras 387–90 (summarizing the contrasting approaches to private copying); Y. Cohen 1999: Kuntras 574 (arguing that there is always a danger that private copying will deprive the author of fair profits); Yehuda Silman, *Darkhei Ḥoshen*, excerpted in Weisfish 2002: 181 (arguing that if one copies only for oneself, that is not prohibited as "wrongful competition"); Weisfish 2002: 121 (quoting Shlomo Zalman Auerbach stating that it is not legally forbidden to copy a sound recording for oneself, but it is morally reprehensible to do so if one would have otherwise purchased the sound recording); Bar-Ilan 1985/1986: 367 (arguing that private copying even of an entire book is permitted if the copier would not have otherwise purchased the book, as the author's right is only one against monetary harm, not an absolute property right); Int'l Beis Hora'ah 2010 (concluding that private copying is permitted under Jewish law unless prohibited by the law of the sovereign); see also Nehurai 1994/1995: 50–51 (arguing that it is permissible to make a personal copy of a book or sound recording that one owns because the author's sole right is against unjust enrichment, and only economic harm caused by commercial piracy gives rise to a claim under that right).

25. See Eliashiv 2002: 116 (stating that personal copying of a work made for purposes of profit and that bears the legend, "all rights reserved," is prohibited); Moshe Feinstein (1895–1960), *Responsa Igrot Moshe*, Oraḥ Ḥaim, Part. 4. No. 41, para. 19 (copying a sound recording without permission of the person who made the recording is theft); Weiss 2009: 1 (opining that it is theft to copy a work in which the owner has reserved for himself the right to copy).

26. See, e.g., Goldberg 1984/1985: 186–94; Ishun 2001: 54 (at least where the copy is "leased" as opposed to sold). Similarly, some decisors propose "leasing" a copy for the explicit purpose of reading or listening to it and without any right to make copies. See Radzyner 2015: 174–76, 185–88 (presenting examples and questioning the efficacy of such an approach).

meaning "residual right," pursuant to which a person who sells an item of property, be it land or a chattel, may retain some aspect of that item for himself by explicitly informing the buyer of his intention to do so. For example, the seller of a house may reserve to himself the air above the house (essentially the right to build a unit on top of the house).[27] Some jurists posit that the reservation of the right to make copies must be set out in a formula akin to a provision of a standard form "shrink-wrap" license accompanying a compact disk bearing a computer program. Others, including Yosef Shalom Eliashiv, hold that printing the words "No Copying" or "All Rights Reserved" on the physical copy is sufficient.[28] However, a number of scholars question the efficacy of the reservation of right, largely because of the distinction between reserving a right in a particular item of tangible property and reserving part of a copyright. Shmuel Barukh Ganot and others question whether it is possible to reserve an incorporeal right—the right to make copies—that is not an integral part of the physical artifact that has been sold and, indeed, has nothing directly to do with control over that physical artifact.[29] Likewise, as Yair Wasserteil points out, the author who reserves to himself the right to reproduce a particular copy of his work has actually just reserved a negative right—to prevent the owner of the copy from making a copy—as the author has no continued access to the physical copy that he has sold and no practical way to make further copies from it.[30] It is at best unclear whether the right of *shiur* would apply in such a case. Finally, the reservation of right lies only against the purchaser of a particular tangible copy. It would not prevent a third party from making further copies of a work that has been uploaded to the Internet. Nor could the author reserve rights in a work that he has placed on the Internet; the right of *shiur* requires the sale of the work in a tangible, physical medium inasmuch as the reservation is in the property right in that physical item, not the intangible work embedded in it. In contrast, if copyright is itself a property right, the copyright owner may prevent copying without having to resort to the right of *shiur* and even if that right is limited to a reservation of right in tangible property.

7. Under Jewish law, copyright's doctrinal categorization determines whether the author has a claim against someone who creates what U.S. copyright law terms a "derivative work," such as abridgments, simplified versions, edited versions, a movie version of a story, recordings of a song, translations, and other adaptations that are based on the author's work. If copyright is property, the author's ownership rights include the exclusive right to create those derivative works.[31] In contrast, those who posit that copyright is a right against wrongful competition (or is based in custom or guild regulation) typically hold that an author has a claim against the creator of a derivative work only if the dissemination of the derivative work might harm the market for the underlying original, or if the custom in the

27. *Shulḥan Arukh*, Ḥoshen Mishpat, 209: 7; 212: 3.
28. Wasserteil 2011.
29. Ganot 2001: 44–46; Int'l Beis Hora'ah 2010.
30. Wasserteil 2011.
31. See Y. Cohen 1999: Kitsurei Dinim le-Ma'aseh 103–07; Weisfish 2002: 46.

pertinent industry is that the author's exclusive rights extend to the particular type of derivative work in question.[32]

8. The issue of whether authors have a right of ownership may bear upon whether they enjoy protection against unlicensed copyists under the Jewish law doctrine of unjust enrichment (*ze neheneh ve-ze ḥaser*). A number of contemporary rabbinic jurists view copyright as protection against unjust enrichment in that the unlicensed copyist unfairly benefits from the author's and publisher's labor and investment. But others argue that, under Jewish law, protection against unjust enrichment can apply *only* when one person benefits from using another's property, as opposed to benefiting from another's labor or investment.[33] In this view, if the author, in fact, has no right of ownership in exploiting his work, a copyist is not unjustly enriched under Jewish law because, although he might harm the author's market, he benefits from the author's work and investment, not from using the author's property.
9. Some jurists maintain that Jewish law does not recognize a non-Jew's claim of wrongful competition or unjust enrichment, and thus hold that if copyright is grounded in one of those doctrines, rather than a right against conversion of property (or secular law pursuant to the "law of the sovereign" rule), it does not protect Gentile authors or publishers per se, even if Jews must compensate Gentiles where failure to do so would result in *ḥilul ha-Shem*, the desecration of God's name.[34] Such discriminatory rules are the vestige of an age in which intense inter-communal rivalry, mercantilism, and Gentile government prohibitions on Jews engaging in most trades were the norm. Yet, they remain within the corpus of Jewish law. When the Bnei Brak rabbinic court ruled, in response to Microsoft's petition, that copying and selling software for a low price is wrongful competition under Jewish law, it did so only after being presented with evidence that Microsoft officer and principal shareholder, Steven Ballmer, qualifies as a Jew under Jewish law.[35]

Rabbinic jurists, therefore, frame their debate regarding copyright's nature, scope, and duration in terms of specific applications of rules pertaining generally to property, wrongful competition, unjust enrichment, reservation of rights, and other doctrines. In line with the legal formalist approach that characterizes much of Jewish law, the legal category into which copyright is placed almost entirely and invariably determines the doctrinal rule-set that applies (even if, as noted above, the legal categories in Jewish law tend to be narrower and more concretely tied to specific

32. See Y. Cohen 1999: Kuntras 103–06, 269–75.

33. See, e.g., Navon 2001: 38; see also Goldberg 1984/1985: 194–97, 207 (noting disagreement on that issue, but ruling that unjust enrichment does apply when one benefits from another's investment).

34. See Y. Landau 1998/1999: 813; Goldberg 1984/1985: 207 (concluding that the question of whether a non-Jew can claim unjust enrichment under Jewish law requires further examination); Int'l Beis Hora'ah 2010.

35. Telephone Interview with Yonatan Schreiber, Microsoft Isr. Mktg. Consultant (August 12, 2007). Steven Ballmer's mother is Jewish, which makes him a Jew under Jewish law. Jewish law presents diverse views, applicable in various contexts, on the legal status of corporations and the extent to which a corporation stands as an independent entity, separate and apart from the human beings who are its shareholders. See Broyde and Resnicoff 1997.

instances than the broad, abstract categories of common and civil law). Accordingly, the rabbinic debate centers almost entirely on how copyright should be categorized, not on whether copyright is sui generis or a subcategory that warrants special rules. The result is that, if copyrights are categorized as "property" or a "right of ownership" under Jewish law, they encompass considerably broader rights than the copyright-as-amalgam school would recognize.

C. Meanings of Copyright as Property under Jewish Law

That is not to say, however, that property or copyright-defined-as-property in Jewish law resembles the "sole and despotic dominion" that William Blackstone famously presented as the mythic ideal of property.[36] To the contrary, in some respects, the Jewish law and understanding of property deviate even more substantially from that ideal than does the common law. According to rabbinic tradition, indeed, the primary sin committed by the people of Sodom was to insist on the absolute primacy of property, declaring that "what is mine is mine and what is yours is yours," and thus refusing to share or countenance another's use of one's property that benefits the user but causes no harm to the owner.[37] Such spiteful, miserly behavior is regarded not merely as morally reprehensible; under certain circumstances, Jewish law affirmatively requires a property owner to allow another to benefit from using his property free of charge, so long as the property owner suffers no (other) loss from the use. Concomitantly, neither does Jewish law regard benefiting from another's property without causing any loss to the owner as unjust enrichment.[38]

As applied by rabbinic jurists, the rule against acting like a Sodomite gives rise to three possible limitations on copyright, even assuming that copyright is property. First, if an author has created and disseminated his work with no intention of profiting from it, he might be acting like a Sodomite were he to insist upon payment after the fact.[39] Second, the rule against Sodomite behavior supports the view of some rabbinic jurists that private copying is permitted so long as the copyist would not have otherwise purchased the

36. Blackstone 1825: *1. Despite his proverbial description, Blackstone and his contemporaries clearly understood that property rights were far from a "sole and despotic dominion" in positive law. See Schorr 2008.

37. Tamari 1998: 52 (quoting Mishnah, *Avot*).

38. For a detailed discussion of that principle, see Kirschenbaum 1991: 185–252; Shilo 1980; Dagan 1997: 112–27.

39. Cohen does not make this argument explicitly, but he treats the harm caused by unlicensed copying entirely as economic harm, and distinguishes the author's desire to prevent uncompensated and unlicensed copying from the classic case of Sodomite behavior in which the property owner had no intention of making a profit, yet nevertheless extorts money from another for agreeing to allow the use of his property. See Y. Cohen 1999: Kuntras 404–06. But cf. Shlomo Tana, *Responsa Brakhat Shlomo*, Ḥoshen Mishpat, No. 26: 177 (holding that the rule against acting like a Sodomite does not apply to forbidding another to print and distribute an out-of-print book because the unlicensed use harms the author's successors' potential licensing market).

copy and thus causes the author no loss.[40] Third, the rule might be the basis for limiting copyright's duration for published works. In his seminal ruling rejecting a perpetual, proprietary copyright while conceding that authors have an exclusive right to print their unpublished manuscripts, Yitzḥak Schmelkes reasoned that copying causes the author no damage (as distinct from forgone profit) once the first edition has been sold, and thus that the rule against Sodomite behavior negates any continuing claim the author might have to enforce an exclusive right following the sale of the first edition.[41]

In addition to the limitations on property, and therefore on copyright-defined-as-property, imposed by the rule against acting like a Sodomite, there are other ways in which recognizing copyright as property in Jewish law yields lesser rights than those that are often understood to flow from characterizing copyright as property in secular common and civil law. First, some jurists maintain that Jewish law regarding the abandonment of property permits the unlicensed copying and distribution either of old works whose rights holders are unknown ("orphan works" in secular copyright parlance) or of works that the rights holders have let fall out of print.[42] Under Jewish law, lost property is presumed abandoned, and therefore free for anyone to appropriate, either when the owner renounces ownership or under circumstances in which the owner is deemed to have given up hope of recovering the item.[43] The claim that orphan and out-of-print works are abandoned is fairly straightforward.[44] Yet, some jurists apply that rule even to in-print works that are so easily and pervasively copied that copyright enforcement appears to be impossible. That category of abandoned works has been held to include widely pirated software, songs broadcast on the radio, and works that are available for Internet downloading with or without the author's permission.[45] As one commentator puts it,

> because in reality there is no control over materials on the Internet nor any practical possibility of enforcing copyright, and anyone can download as he wishes, such

40. Y. Cohen 1999: Kuntras 437–62 (discussing this view, but ultimately presenting a doctrinal argument to reject it); cf. Moshe Feinstein (1895–1986), *Responsa Igrot Moshe,* Oraḥ Ḥaim, pt. 4, no. 40, para. 19 (holding that one who produces a cassette recording of Torah-teaching with the intent to earn a profit does not act like a Sodomite by affixing a notice that it is forbidden to copy the recording).

41. Schmelkes, *Beit Yitzḥak*, Yoreh De'ah, Part 5, No. 75.

42. See, e.g., Silman, *Darkhei Ḥoshen* in Weisfish 2002: 181 (ruling that one may distribute copies without permission when the author or publisher is neither distributing nor about to distribute the work).

43. Herzog 1980: 281–98.

44. Joseph Saul Nathanson explicitly held, however, that an author does not lose his exclusive right to reprint merely because the book is out of print. Nathanson presumed that the author must intend to issue a new printing to meet demand for the book, but is temporarily unable to do so due to insufficient capital. Nathanson, *Sho'el U-Meshiv,* pt. 1, No. 44.

45. Lior 2006/2007; Silman, *Darkhei Ḥoshen* in Weisfish 2002: 181 (holding that one may make a personal copy of a computer program that has been "breached" and widely copied); see also Y. Cohen 1999: Kuntras 601–03 (conceding that copyright owners in musical works who allow their works to be played on the radio knowing that some listeners will record the songs might have knowingly abandoned their property).

materials resemble a lost item that is swept away in a river, and thus any person is permitted to download for himself pursuant to the law of abandoned property.[46]

Second, even if we accept that copyright is property under Jewish law, the violation of that right is not necessarily "stealing." In the secular copyright world, those who characterize copyright as property have reflexively labeled copyright infringement as "theft."[47] Indeed, Congress denominated legislation providing for criminal penalties for Internet file trading as the "No Electronic Theft Act,"[48] and a U.S. district court invoked the commandment, "Thou Shalt Not Steal," in an opinion announcing that it would forward for criminal prosecution the copyright infringement claim against a hip hop artist who had sampled the copyright owner's music.[49] Likewise, rabbinic jurists seem typically to assume that if copyright is property, copyright infringement is tantamount to theft.[50] However, a couple of leading proponents of the copyright-is-property school conclude that unlicensed copying is actually an unlawful *use* of that property for the copyist's benefit, not an unlawful *conversion* of property.[51] According to this view, unlicensed copying is actionable under the Jewish law of unjust enrichment (*ze neheneh ve-ze ḥaser*), not theft. In turn, if unlicensed copying is unjust enrichment, Jewish law imposes doctrinal limitations to liability that do not apply to theft (or conversion), primarily the requirement that the author be harmed by the copying, and the possible ineligibility of Gentiles to assert claims for unjust enrichment. In addition, the monetary remedy for unjust enrichment under Jewish law, namely disgorgement of the copyist's benefit, will often be less than that for theft (although, in various ways that I cannot address here, the civil remedies for theft in Jewish law are themselves considerably more lenient than under contemporary secular law).[52]

Finally, some jurists posit that Jewish law circumscribes what would otherwise be an author's perpetual, proprietary copyright specifically with respect to certain works of signal importance to traditionally observant Jewish communities. These works are books, recordings, or videos of *ḥidushei Torah,* that is, new exegeses of

46. Lior 2006/2007 (applying the doctrine of "zuto shel yam"). But see Int'l Beis Hora'ah 2010 (asserting that the claim of abandonment due to Internet copying applies only when the copyright owner has undoubtedly given up hope of enforcement).

47. That rhetoric has a venerable pedigree, extending back to the beginning of the eighteenth century. See Loewenstein 2002: 215 (quoting Daniel Defoe's characterization, in 1704, of printing another's manuscript without permission as "a sort of Thieving").

48. Pub. L. No. 105–47, 111 Stat. 2678 (1997).

49. Grand Upright Music Ltd. v. Warner Bros. Records, Inc., 780 F. Supp. 182, 183 (S.D.N.Y. 1991).

50. See, e.g., Eliashiv 2002: 115; Moshe Feinstein (1895–1986), *Responsa Igrot Moshe,* Oraḥ Ḥaim, Part 4, No. 40, para. 19; Weiss 2009: 1.

51. One reason is that, under Jewish law, conversion requires physical appropriation, and these jurists are unwilling to extend physical appropriation as a metaphor for unlicensed copying. In addition, unlicensed copyists do not deprive the author of the intangible corpus of his property right, but only use it to their benefit. See Y. Cohen 1999: 391–403; Shlomo Tana, *Responsa Brakhat Shlomo,* Ḥoshen Mishpat, No. 26: 172.

52. For further discussion, see I. Warhaftig 1984/1985.

foundational Jewish texts, often relating to how traditional rabbinic literature and doctrine apply to current issues or circumstances.[53] Rabbinic tradition recognizes a fundamental public interest in making these teachings freely available to a community in need of knowledge and guidance about how Jewish law applies to contemporary life. Partly for that reason, as we have seen above, Jewish law has long prohibited rabbinic scholars from profiting from teaching Jewish law and religion.[54] Some jurists argue, accordingly, that authors of *ḥidushei Torah* may not assert a right to profit from the sale of such works.[55] Others mitigate that rule by distinguishing between the intangible work, that is the actual *teaching* presented in the book, on one hand, and the author's *labor and investment* in reducing his teaching to writing, and in printing, reproducing, and distributing the copies of his work, on the other.[56] The author may not profit from, and has no property right in, the teaching itself, but is entitled to receive the full, customary salary for his labor and investment in preparing the manuscript and in producing and distributing copies. (The same applies to the making and distributing recordings of sermons.)

According to some present-day accounts, Yitzḥak Schmelkes's holding that the author's exclusive right expires after he has sold his first edition represents a manifestation of this rule.[57] The works at issue in Schmelkes's rulings were books of *ḥidushei Torah*, and Schmelkes invoked the rule against profiting from teaching Torah in rejecting Nathanson's position that authors have perpetual exclusive rights. As such, Schmelkes might have seen the author's exclusive right to print and sell the first edition as a rough vehicle for providing the author with the full, customary salary for his labor and investment in preparing and printing the manuscript.[58]

On this reading of Schmelkes's ruling, it is also unclear what he would have held had the books before him been secular works rather than *ḥidushei Torah*. Some jurists of the copyright-is-property school contend that Schmelkes did not deny that authors generally have a right of ownership (even though he explicitly called Nathanson's holding into question on this point). Rather, Schmelkes meant only to carve out an exception from the author's right of ownership when the work is one of *ḥidushei Torah*.[59] In Schmelkes's day, however, virtually all newly authored works that rabbis

53. See Sacks 1992: 146–49.

54. That prohibition has been narrowly applied to enable scholars to earn a livelihood from teaching and fulfilling other rabbinic functions. For further discussion, see Netanel 2007a: 862.

55. For a discussion of the various positions on this issue, see Y. Cohen 1999: Kuntras 43–70.

56. See, e.g., Shlomo Tana, *Responsa Brakhat Shlomo,* Ḥoshen Mishpat, No. 26.

57. See, e.g., Y. Cohen 1999: Kuntras 30–34; Shlomo Tana, *Responsa Brakhat Shlomo,* Ḥoshen Mishpat, No. 26. But see Jachter 2000: 120 n. 4 (2000) (concluding that Schmelkes's rejection of authors' property right applies to all works, not just *ḥidushei Torah*).

58. I refer here to the author's exclusive right that Schmelkes seemed to recognize under Jewish law per se, not to copyrights under secular law that, according to Schmelkes, must be recognized under the "law of the sovereign" rule. But see Silman, *Darkhei Ḥoshen* in Weisfish 2002: 181 (contending that the author of *ḥidushei Torah* is entitled only to a set amount, not to any proceeds from book sales that might exceed that sum).

59. See, e.g., Y. Cohen 1999: Kuntras 2; Weisfish 2002: 40.

considered when determining authors' rights were *ḥidushei Torah*. With isolated exceptions, rabbinic jurists have applied Jewish copyright to secular works, such as computer programs and music, only in recent years.[60]

D. Summary: Ramifications of Categorizing Copyright

In sum, to categorize copyright as property in Jewish law largely determines copyright's shape and duration as a matter of doctrinal mandate by way of application of rules that govern property generally. For example, if property is perpetual and freely transferable, but can be deemed abandoned under certain circumstances, and if copyright is property, ergo copyright is also perpetual and freely transferable, and can be abandoned when analogous circumstances are deemed to apply. It may take some juridical work to interpret and apply property doctrine to the subject matter of copyright law. But we need not and, indeed, may not undertake any further analysis of the particularities or special policies involving authors' expressive works to develop rules that apply specifically to copyright. We may not consider, for example, whether, as in secular copyright, authors' rights should be subject to various limitations, such as fair use, that do not arise from property doctrine generally.

The holding of some jurists that property rules do not apply to *ḥidushei Torah* is a notable exception to this understanding that, if copyright is property, then copyright law is a direct instantiation of property doctrine. Under the *ḥidushei Torah* exception, the rule prohibiting profiting from teaching Torah, as well as the limitations on that rule designed to enable rabbinic scholars to earn remuneration from producing *ḥidushei Torah*, take precedence over property rules that would otherwise be applicable to an author's expressive works. These jurists thus carve out a sui generis regime specifically tailored to *ḥidushei Torah*, in part to promote public access to new rabbinic teachings.

II. RATIONALES FOR COPYRIGHT'S CATEGORIZATION UNDER JEWISH LAW

The secular law debate over whether copyright is property presents a richly colored canvas of deontological and consequentialist arguments grounded in a broad spectrum of ideologically charged claims about the nature of creativity, authorship, human personality, democratic society, social welfare, natural justice, freedom of speech, economic efficiency, liberty, and the institution of property. Deontological arguments loomed especially large in early common-law and civil-law copyright. In

60. Historically, the principal if only occasional, exceptions from the rabbis' singular focus on *ḥidushei Torah* and other books of Jewish law, learning, and liturgy have been newly authored books about mathematics, science, Hebrew grammar, or medicine. See Feiner 2004: 25 (describing eighteenth-century rabbinic approbations issued for books of geometry, anatomy, and astronomy).

eighteenth-century England and nineteenth-century France, leading jurists debated whether incorporeal creations can qualify as the subject of property, and whether the dictates of moral reason and natural justice require that authors have a right of property in their expressive works.[61] Although consequentialist discourse subsequently came to dominate Anglo-American copyright, deontological postulates about the nature of authorship and property continue to underlie today's aptly named "authors' rights" laws of Continental Europe.[62] Yet, in both regimes, modern-day scholars present intensive, methodical argumentation regarding such issues as the desirability of enhancing public access to existing works, supporting classroom teaching, avoiding holdouts and deadweight loss, giving authors greater ability to build upon existing works in creating new ones, authors' prerogatives to prevent unwanted modifications to their creations, and the value of remix culture.

As we have noted, rabbinic jurisprudence is devoid of the politically and ideologically freighted polemic regarding the meaning of authorship and property that has long marked Anglo-American and Continental European discourse. Despite the significant doctrinal consequences that flow from categorizing copyright as property in Jewish law, modern rabbinic jurists also devote remarkably little attention to weighing policy concerns when debating whether copyright should be categorized as property. Certainly, from a secular copyright scholar's perspective, the rabbinic debate is overwhelmingly characterized by formalist, doctrinal reasoning and a priori, essentialist supposition lacking in policy analysis and broader theoretical grounding.

However, one must not mistake the largely formalist character of rabbinic jurisprudence in this area for a lack of awareness of the political, social, and economic context in which Jewish law operates. Rabbinic sensitivity to the context—and consequence—of shaping copyright doctrine is particularly pronounced in rabbinic rulings and responsa from the era prior to political emancipation, when rabbinic courts and Jewish communal institutions still enjoyed a measure of lawmaking autonomy backed by the state. As we have seen, for example, in their extended colloquy in the early nineteenth century, Mordekhai Banet and Moses Sofer raised policy arguments that would be familiar to the secular legal academy today. In arguing for a limited scope of rabbinic reprinting bans and wrongful competition protection for existing books, Banet assessed the relative economic interests of rival publishers and held that the first publisher's investment of labor in producing a new edition did not justify granting him an exclusive right to market his work to potential purchasers of the work. In so holding, Banet emphasized that competition would benefit the public by bringing down the price of books and should thus be encouraged, except in those relatively rare cases in which the rival publisher could sell at a loss to drive the first out of business. In contrast, Sofer supported rabbinic authority to issue exclusive reprinting bans on the grounds that, if book publishers are not accorded exclusive

61. See Sherman and Bently 1999: 11–42 (discussing England); Pfister 2005 (discussing France).

62. See Sherman and Bently 1999: 39–40 (describing the turn to consequentialist thinking in English copyright); Netanel 1994 (describing deontological claims in civil-law copyright).

rights to print their editions, the threat of ruinous competition would induce them to stop publishing books, and the study of Jewish law and religion would greatly suffer.

For his part, in recognizing an author's universal and perpetual copyright under Jewish law, Joseph Saul Nathanson sought to propound a rule that would transcend the fragmented, fragile state of rabbinic and Jewish communal autonomy in mid-nineteenth century Eastern and Central Europe. Further, despite his sub rosa reference to secular copyright as one model for his perpetual exclusive right, Nathanson endeavored to maintain a vital, independent role for Jewish law—and thus of rabbinic decisors of halakha—rather than simply applying secular law under the doctrine "the law of the sovereign is the law." In so doing, he aimed to preserve rabbinic capacity and authority to foster the publication of books of Jewish law, learning, and liturgy.

Yet, despite Nathanson's grappling with the juridical and political realities of his day, his ruling is devoid of any explicit discussion of the potential consequences for Jewish publishing of recognizing perpetual copyrights, as opposed to merely a right against wrongful competition or a right derived from trade custom, both of which, following Jewish law precedent, would be limited in duration.[63] Nathanson, indeed, presents virtually no analytical reasoning or precedential support for his holding. He relies, rather, on what he presents as a self-evident conclusion: "If an author prints a new book and he merits that his words are received all around the world, he obviously has a perpetual right [to his work]."[64] As discussed in Chapter 8, Nathanson provides no convincing explanation for why that rule is obvious. He does recount that secular law protects authors and inventors, and then insists that "common sense rejects" the possibility that Gentile authorities protect authors and inventors, but "our wholesome Torah" would not. But here, too, he provides no proof text or precedential support beyond "common sense" for Jewish law's recognition of an author's perpetual, proprietary right.

Recall that, in rejecting Nathanson's ruling, Yitzḥak Schmelkes chided, "with all due respect to the Esteemed Scholar, I see no proof for this."[65] Other rabbinic jurists surmise that, in the absence of a proof text or Jewish law precedent for authors' right of ownership, Nathanson probably meant only that no one should print the author's work without permission as a matter of proper and ethical behavior, not that unlicensed printing is halakhically prohibited.[66]

Despite the persistent doubts about Nathanson's perfunctory ruling, leading present-day rabbinic proponents of the view that copyright is a property right echo Nathanson's a priori argument, while citing his responsum as supporting precedent.

63. See Moses Isserles (1520? 1530?–1572), *Responsa Rema*, No. 10 (holding that an author-publisher had the exclusive right, pursuant to the Jewish law of wrongful competition, to print the work in question until he sold out his first edition).

64. Joseph Saul Nathanson (1808–1875), *Sho'el U-Meshiv,* Part 1, No. 44.

65. Yitzḥak Schmelkes (1828–1906), *Responsa Beit Yitzḥak*, Yoreh De'ah, Part. 5, No. 75.

66. See, e.g., Jachter 2000: 120; Navon 2001: 42–43. But see Weiss 2009: (suggesting that, with respect to recognizing an author's rights, the dictates of justice and honesty constitute an independent grounds for imposing an obligatory legal norm).

For example, when asked, "Does an author have ownership in his work, and what is the source for this right?," Yosef Shalom Eliashiv answers: "He has ownership, and that is very solid reasoning, something that reason requires—see [Nathanson's responsum] . . .—and thus one who harms the author's right commits theft in violation of the Torah."[67] Asher Weiss similarly concludes, citing Nathanson, that it is axiomatic that one owns what one creates.[68]

Opponents of categorizing copyright as property in Jewish law avoid the converse peremptory conclusion that reason "obviously" requires that copyright is to be construed as something other than property. They thereby escape criticism for being the mirror image of Nathanson. However, like Nathanson, their argument remains almost entirely within the strict constraints of rabbinic precedent and analogies to preexisting doctrine. Notably, their writings and rulings on the issue contain no more hint than Nathanson's of the type of normative arguments for limiting authors' rights that populate modern-day secular debate or that infused the interchange between Mordekhai Banet and Moses Sofer in the early nineteenth century.

For example, Yehuda Silman, a member of the rabbinic court that ruled on Microsoft's petition, holds that copyright is a right against wrongful competition, rather than a right of ownership, for the reason that the rabbinic scholars who have contended that copyright is the former are of far greater stature than those who maintain that copyright is latter.[69] Such bare reliance on the preeminence of earlier jurists, without delving into the force of their reasoning regarding the issue at hand, is not at all unusual. Indeed, it is understood to be incumbent upon rabbinic judges to weigh the stature of conflicting authorities, as well as myriad other factors, in deciding disputes.[70]

Aside from their view that precedential support for recognizing authors' right of ownership is lacking, opponents of categorizing copyright as property rely heavily on the assumption that Jewish law can never recognize an incorporeal thing as property.[71] Since Talmudic times, Jewish law has provided that a thing with no substance, such as light or the air, is not susceptible to legal acquisition or transfer of ownership

67. Eliashiv 2002: 115.

68. Weiss 2009: 1. Cohen concedes that Nathanson's curt reasoning is vulnerable to challenge, but principally because Nathanson does not explain how an author can acquire ownership in an intangible creation given the long-standing view in Jewish law that only tangible objects can be acquired. Y. Cohen 1999: Kuntras 1–7, 247–48.

69. Silman, *Darkhei Ḥoshen* in Weisfish 2002: 180.

70. Waxman 1992: 218–19.

71. See Y. Cohen 1999: 206 (stating that this assumption is the primary argument of those who reason that copyright is not property). Opponents to classifying copyright as property in secular common and civil law have also sometimes invoked an essentialist argument that property cannot apply to intangible things. As Justice Yates famously expounded in *Millar v. Taylor*, "And it is well known and established maxim, (which I apprehend holds true now, as it did 2000 years ago,) that nothing could be object of property, which has not a corporeal substance." Millar v. Taylor, 98 Eng. Rep. 201, 232 (K.B. 1769); see also Epstein 2010: 3 (bemoaning what he deems to be the essentialist distinction between tangible and intangible property that is "almost a point of conventional wisdom" among present-day scholars and judges). On civil law's traditional restriction of property to physical things and the corresponding view that author's intangible creations cannot be objects of property, see Bouckaert 1990: 796–97; Pfister 2005: 122.

except in conjunction with the land or some other corporeal object to which it is attached.[72] That provision relates to the formal requirements of acquisition and transfer, not to the nature of property per se;[73] but, given that the ability to transfer title is so central to rights in things understood to fall within the rubric of "property," rabbinic scholars often state the provision more broadly to mean that incorporeal things, including author's creations and inventor's inventions, cannot be property.[74] Others reason, in addition, that since the Jewish law of theft and conversion applies only to depriving the owner of possession of tangible chattel, and since copying an author's work does not disturb the author's possession of his copy of the work, any prohibition of copying under Jewish law must lie in some doctrine other than the prohibition against stealing property, such as wrongful competition or community regulation.[75]

Finally, Ḥaim Navon, a National Orthodox rabbi, posits that recognizing a proprietary copyright of some shape or form would be desirable, but concludes reluctantly that existing Jewish law doctrine cannot be interpreted or judicially modified to provide for it.[76] He recommends rabbinic legislation to achieve the desired result.

Those familiar with rabbinic jurisprudence would not be surprised by the fact that the rabbinic jurists conduct their debate over whether copyright is property without presenting broad policy arguments. Rabbinic jurists, to be certain, have for centuries proven adept at adapting doctrine as required by changing social, economic, political, and technological circumstances, whether in deciding particular cases or issuing regulations.[77] At times, rabbinic decisors even expressly tailor their halakhic rulings

72. See *Mishneh Torah*, Sefer Kinyan, Hilkhot Mekhira 22: 13–14; *Shulḥan Arukh*, Ḥoshen Mishpat 203: 1, 213: 1–2.

73. But see Bleich 2010: 58 (arguing that the formal requirements for acquisition and transfer evince the metaphysical character of property rights' attachment only to choate, tangible objects and thus provide substantive support for the absence of intellectual property in Jewish law).

74. Cohen and Weiss counter the view that an author cannot acquire ownership in his intangible creations, by analogy to Jewish law doctrine providing that the owner of a tree acquires ownership in the fruits of the tree and that a craftsman acquires ownership in a new object that he has created. See Y. Cohen 1999: Kuntras 1–7, 247–48, 206; Weiss 2009: 1.

75. See, e.g, Y. Landau 1998/1999: 810 (noting the absence of authority for recognizing a property right in an incorporeal thing, and that a copier does not "steal" an author's creation because the author still has possession of it and can still use it); Tzvi ben Ḥayim Yitzḥak Shpitz, *Responsa Minḥat Tzvi*, Hilkhot Shkhenim, No. 18, in Weisfish 2002: 177 (same); Int'l Beis Hora'ah 2010 (concluding that copying does not fall within the prohibition against stealing or conversion). As noted above, other jurists agree that copying does not constitute stealing, but argue nonetheless that an author's creations are his property and that unlicensed copying constitutes an illicit use of that property under the Jewish law doctrine of unjust enrichment.

76. See Navon 2001: 48.

77. See Fram 1997 (presenting in-depth studies of instances in which leading rabbinic jurists adapted Jewish law to pressing economic and communal issues of the day through legal fictions and reinterpretations of textual authority); Katz 2000: 52–62 (discussing rabbinic rulings regulating and partly accommodating previously forbidden activities, including charging interest and dealing in non-kosher wine and food, in response to prevailing economic pressures).

to achieve a general policy aim or desired result in a particular case.[78] Nevertheless, the normative ethos of rabbinic jurisprudence, both in issuing rulings and writing commentary, is heavily tied to the integrity and coherence of the rabbinic tradition.[79] The fundamental precepts of the Torah are understood to be eternal and immutable, and yet fully capable of addressing new circumstances. As such, even the boldest rabbinic jurists almost always couch innovation firmly within authoritative precedent, proof texts, and reasoning by analogy from traditional sources and doctrine. As a leading present-day authority observes, "[t]here is a difference between the considerations [the rabbinic jurist] may formally cite in justification of his ruling, and those that may, consciously or intuitively, play a part in his judgment that this ruling is not merely justifiable but also correct."[80] The jurist leaves himself open to substantial challenge if he departs from this model; Joseph Saul Nathanson's perfunctory recognition of authors' proprietary rights is a case in point.

Moreover, rabbinic jurists' unwillingness to engage in the policy implications of their rulings might be more pronounced today than in the era prior to political emancipation. Unlike today, rabbinic decisors of that era still exercised considerable responsibility for Jewish communities' semiautonomous rule and thus had no choice but to weigh the consequences of their rulings.[81] For that reason, perhaps, as sociologists and historians of Jewish law have observed, present-day rabbinic jurists, particularly those whose authority is centered in ultra-Orthodox educational institutions, tend to follow a style of legal reasoning and ruling that focuses on foundational legal texts to the exclusion of practice and custom, which in previous generations constituted a vital source for Jewish law norms.[82] In the view of some critics, indeed, today's ultra-Orthodox rabbinic jurists have so elevated insular textual authority that they have lost sight of the practical import of their rulings.[83]

In addition, in tandem with that turn to the stringency and insularity of authoritative text, today's rabbinic jurists exhibit at best a highly ambivalent attitude toward the Internet and digital media that so occupy secular copyright scholars. "Modern" or "National" Orthodox rabbinic jurists generally permit Internet use.[84] As noted above, however, many ultra-Orthodox rabbinic jurists resolutely condemn all secular entertainment as well the media platforms used to communicate it. For them, the Internet

78. See generally Zohar 2012 (setting out a number of examples of what he labels "teleological decision making in halakha").
79. See generally Sacks 1992.
80. Sacks 1992: 152.
81. I thank Melech Westreich for highlighting the possible significance of this phenomenon for rabbinic commentary on copyright law.
82. See Friedman 1995; Soloveitchik 1994; L. Kaplan 1992: 1.
83. See, e.g., L. Kaplan 1992: 8 (lamenting the ultra-Orthodox view that "it is the rabbis who are completely immersed in the world of Torah and seemingly removed from the outside world," who, alone, can "draw upon the 'spirit of tradition' in order to formulate the policies needed to meet [contemporary] challenges and needs").
84. Baumel-Schwartz 2009: 2 (noting that Modern Orthodox rabbis permit Internet use other than visiting sites featuring pornography or other content forbidden by Jewish law). "Modern Orthodox" encompasses the "National Religious" stream of Judaism in Israel, but extends to the Diaspora as well.

is the "world's leading cause of temptation."[85] Nonetheless, the Internet and digital media have made significant inroads in ultra-Orthodox communities, including their use in the proliferation of rabbinic texts and teaching (not to mention blogs aimed at fellow believers), a fact that even those ultra-Orthodox rabbinic jurists who oppose all Internet use cannot ignore.

At bottom, despite the general trend toward insularity, ultra-Orthodox as well as Modern Orthodox rabbinic jurists regularly opine on copyright issues involving works in digital media, and make numerous explicit assumptions about the markets, practices, and social norms that characterize Internet use. For example, the ultra-Orthodox rabbinic court in Bnei Brak ruled on Microsoft's petition regarding copying computer programs and, in line with that ruling, one judge on the court elsewhere opined that personal copying of programs is permitted on grounds of abandonment when the program has been "breached" and unlicensed copies are ubiquitous.[86] In a like vein, as noted above, several commentators suggest that authors abandon their copyrights in works released on the Internet, with or without their permission, given the seemingly insurmountable obstacles of copyright enforcement in that medium. In addition, Asher Weiss qualifies his conclusion that authors have a property right in their creations by stating that he has heard from experts in the field of music recordings that many artists and composers implicitly consent to having their recordings freely copied, because if they were to insist on preventing copying, consumers would just listen to the recordings of others that can be freely copied and would thus lose interest in those who seek to enforce their copyrights.[87] Similarly, Shlomo Ishun posits that copying for one's own use from the radio is permitted because radio stations pay royalties that take such private copying into account.[88] As these and numerous other examples attest, rabbinic jurists take judicial notice of contextual facts as they understand them, even if their style of argumentation is fundamentally formalist, and some of them only grudgingly acquiesce in the use of digital media in their community.

III. THE INFLUENCE OF SECULAR COPYRIGHT LAW

Like many of their predecessors, contemporary rabbinic jurists evince an acute awareness of, and receptivity to, secular copyright law, even if they seem largely oblivious to secular copyright's precise contours and doctrinal intricacies. The most obvious example of this phenomenon is contemporary rabbinic jurists' repeated use of the modern Hebrew term for copyright, *zkhuyot yotzrim*, literarlly meaning "authors' rights," to refer to halakhic doctrine pertaining to exclusive reprinting rights. That term has no native foundation in Jewish law and was never used by rabbinic decisors until the past couple decades.

85. See Barzilai-Nahon and Barzilai 2005.
86. Silman, *Darkhei Ḥoshen*, in Weisfish 2002: 181.
87. Weiss 2009: 1.
88. Ishun 2007/2008: 44.

In line with their adoption of the term *zkhuyot yotzrim*, present-day halakhic scholars often invoke their general understanding of secular copyright law as the metric against which they measure and compare Jewish copyright law—and they often find Jewish copyright law failing. Echoing Nathanson, present-day rabbinic commentators note repeatedly that because the nations of the world accord authors exclusive rights, then Jewish law must as well. Even if the halakha does not recognize a right of literary property per se, it must accord authors a rough equivalent of copyright, grounded in some combination of rabbinic enactment, custom, wrongful competition, the reservation of property rights in physical copies, and moral dictate.[89] It often seems that rabbinic commentators are probing and, at times, stretching traditional halakhic doctrines in order to accord authors with rights to prevent copying that the rabbis believe to be roughly equivalent to those prevailing under secular copyright law. In so doing, contemporary halakhic scholars often present a preference for finding a "solution" to the phenomenon of unauthorized copying and distribution of an author's works within the halakha proper. They wish to avoid having to apply the principle of "the law of the sovereign is the law," with its tacit admission that native Jewish law might have no means of addressing a digital-age problem.[90]

Given that most rabbinic jurists, from the Rome rabbis who granted Eliyau Bakhur and his publishers a 10-year reprinting ban to the Bnei Brak rabbinic court that ruled on Microsoft's petition, do not recognize that Jewish law accords authors proprietary rights akin to secular copyright, the influence of secular copyright today is quite striking. Perhaps the rabbinic jurists have internalized secular understandings that an author morally deserves to own what he creates, a view that entered Jewish law with Nathanson's mid-nineteenth century ruling following on the heels of the enactment of statutes recognizing authors' right of literary property in Austria and other European countries. Alternatively, perhaps contemporary rabbinic jurists view what they believe to be uniform human practice as evidence of what logic and reason must demand, at least in the absence of any venerable Jewish law norm to the contrary. In that vein, Yaakov Avraham Cohen posits that because authors lobbied for the multilateral copyright treaties (such as the Berne Convention for the Protection of Literary and Artistic Works) that, today, require most countries in the world to accord robust copyright protection lasting at least for the life of the author plus 50 years, the provisions of those treaties constitute authors' guild regulations and are thus binding within Jewish law as well.[91]

Finally, many contemporary rabbinic authorities do not wish to give non-Jews cause to view the Jewish religion as less than ethical and just. It is a venerable principle of Jewish tradition that Jews, as individuals and as a group, are obligated to avoid

89. See, e.g., Navon 2001: 43–44, 47–48; Weiss 2009: 1. But see Nehurai 1994/1995: 51 (noting that personal copying is permitted under Jewish law, and that a careful examination reveals no clear rule under secular law regarding the permissibility of personal copying).

90. See, e.g., Navon 2001: 43–44.

91. Y. Cohen 1999: Kuntras, 560–63.

ḥilul ha-Shem—the desecration of God's name—by acting in an immoral manner that brings God, the halakha, and the Jewish people into ill repute among other nations. In the rabbinic tradition, to cause *ḥilul ha-Shem* is a grave moral sin. Present-day rabbinic commentators, who struggle to find ways within Jewish law to recognize some fashion of a copyright akin to secular copyright, express concern that the nations of the world, as well as secular Israelis, will look disdainfully at Jewish religious belief and at the halakha if religiously observant Jews make uses of authors' works that, the rabbis believe, would not be permitted under secular copyright law. In his online lesson about Jewish copyright law, Yair Wasserteil, of the National-Religious Orthodox Beit El *Yeshiva* Center, bemoans that the State of Israel stands among the "leading" countries in the area of software piracy, and that that fact is reported in the international press and at conferences the world over—a matter that leads to *ḥilul ha-Shem*.[92] In his ruling that Jewish law requires wedding halls to pay royalties to the Israeli association of composers for music performed at the venue, Ovadia Yosef, then the foremost living rabbinic authority for Israel's Mizraḥi Jews, noted that secular Israeli law requires that such royalties be paid. Accordingly, Yosef ruled, Jewish law also requires such payment under the rule that "the law of the sovereign is the law." Further, Yosef held, wedding hall owners who are religiously observant Jews have a particular obligation to pay copyright royalties, lest non-observant Israelis and others think that they act immorally, thus causing *ḥilul ha-Shem*.

Like the view that multilateral treaty requirements constitute binding authors' guild regulation, the concern over *ḥilul ha-Shem* stands in some tension with the long-standing majority view that Jewish law prohibits copying only when it prevents the author and publisher from recovering their initial investment. Under that view, as we have seen, copying and distribution are generally permitted unless they truly substitute for sales that are needed for the author and publisher to recover their initial investment. Accordingly, Jewish copyright law as traditionally understood may well permit individuals to (1) copy or download for one's own use, at least when one would not otherwise purchase a copy; (2) distribute copies on the Internet when the author and publisher have no realistic prospect of enforcing copying on the Internet; (3) copy for classroom teaching when one's students would not otherwise buy a copy; and (4) even engage in commercial copying and distribution once the author and publisher have recovered their initial investment. Yet, the rabbinic concern over *ḥilul ha-Shem* leads some rabbinic jurists, even those of the copyright-as-almagam school, to be far more restrictive regarding the permissibility of unauthorized copying than what traditional interpretations of Jewish copyright law might otherwise suggest. (At times, indeed, those rabbinic pronouncements are even more restrictive than secular copyright law itself, which actually contains numerous exceptions and limitations to the copyright holder's rights, such as fair use and the private copying privilege.)

92. Wasserteil 2011. See also I. Warhaftig 2006/07 (decrying that there is "no greater *ḥilul ha-Shem*" than the fact that the State of Israel is known as having one of the highest rates of software piracy in the world).

We thus see in contemporary Jewish copyright law a continuing influence of secular copyright law within the ongoing debate about how, if at all, Jewish copyright law should be interpreted and applied given the sometime precarious place of rabbinic authority and Jewish communities vis-à-vis the non-Jewish world. We find in present-day rabbinic commentary echoes of debates of earlier centuries regarding what might be the halakhic justifications for rabbinic reprinting bans; territorial limits to rabbinic authority; the role of *dina de-malkhuta dina*; and Joseph Saul Nathanson's incorporation of the secular copyright model of literary property into Jewish law. And, notwithstanding their generally formalist approach to halakhic questions, present-day rabbinic jurists are considerably more forthright in adopting secular copyright norms in order to avoid *ḥilul ha-Shem* than were their early modern and nineteenth century predecessors.

IV. POSTSCRIPT

Gidi Dar is a secular Israeli film director. Dar directed *Ushpizin*, a critically acclaimed 2004 film that was a box office hit in Israel. The film, which was shot in Jerusalem, was written by Shuli Rand, an Israeli *ḥaredi*. Notably, Rand had turned away from his religious upbringing in his youth, only to return to religious observance some years later, becoming an ultra-Orthodox Breslov Ḥasid.[93] In addition to writing the script, Rand and his wife acted in the film, playing its central characters, an impoverished, childless, Breslov Ḥasidic couple, who had become religious observant as adults.

Ushpizin is a heartwarming story about the Ḥasidic couple's prayers for a child, the love and caring between them, and their willingness to accept a pair of escaped convicts, one of whom knew the husband during his earlier, nonreligious life, as traditional guests ("ushpizin") in their sukkah on the Jewish holiday of Sukkot. Dar, who had initially worked with Shuli Rand when Rand was secular, wanted to make a film that portrayed the humanity of a *ḥaredi* couple. He and Rand wished to counter the tendency among many secular Israelis to demonize ultra-Orthodox Jews. The two aimed to foster mutual understanding between religious and nonreligious Israelis.

Ushpizin was not marketed to *ḥaredi* audiences, who, as noted above, are forbidden from watching video, whether in theaters, on television, or on computer screens. Indeed, it was a condition of the rabbi from whom the Rands received permission to make the movie that it be exhibited only to non-*ḥaredi* audiences.[94] However, illicit copies of the movie were heavily downloaded by *ḥaredim* even before the movie appeared in theaters in non-*ḥaredi* neighborhoods. In Dar's eyes, such downloading was nothing short of the theft of his property, his intellectual creation.

Dar sought to publish an advertisement in a leading *ḥaredi* newspaper, *Yated Ne'eman*, announcing that copying and viewing his movie without payment is a violation of Jewish law. The advertisement he prepared provided a telephone number

93. Paris 2006: 45.
94. Paris 2006: 46.

and address that downloaders and viewers could use to pay him via credit card. Much to Dar's anger, however, the newspaper editors refused to run the ad on the grounds that doing so would countenance forbidden conduct—the watching of movies. Dar was astounded that the editors regarded watching movies as a worse transgression than what he regarded as stealing his intellectual property.

Ultimately, Dar spliced into the opening credits of *Ushpizin* a screen shot of the Bnei Brak rabbinic court's ruling on the Microsoft petition. He also distributed wall posters in Bnei Brak bearing the content of his rejected advertisement, plus a copy of the Microsoft ruling. Dar may have been unaware that the ruling addresses only commercial piracy, not personal downloading and viewing, and, indeed, that it refers only to rabbinic texts on computer-readable media, not forbidden movies. Heaven only knows whether Dar's invocation of the Microsoft ruling had any impact in the *ḥaredi* community.

BIBLIOGRAPHY

PRIMARY SOURCES: JUDAICA

Responsa are generally available in digital format in the database of the Bar-Ilan Responsa Project.

Aderet, Shlomo ben (1235–1310). *Responsa Ha-Rashba*, Part 3, No. 411; Part 5, No. 126.

Auerbach, Shlomo Zalman (1910–1995). Rulings and Answers, in Weisfish, Naḥum Menashe, 2002. *Mishnat Zkhuyot Ha-Yotzer; Im Tshuvot Ve-Psakim Me-Gedolei Ha-Dor* [The Doctrine of Copyright; with Responsa and Rulings of the Leading Rabbis of Our Generation], 121–22. Jerusalem: Hekhal Naḥum.

Banet, Mordekhai (1753–1829), *Responsa Parshat Mordekhai*, Nos. 7 and 8.

Barukh, Meir ben (1215–93). *Responsa of Ha-Maharam Me-Rotenberg*, Nos. 503 and 677.

Batzri, Ezra. 1984/85. Zkhuyot Yotzrim [Copyright], Ruling in Arbitration No. 42/3575. *Teḥumin* 6: 169–203.

Berlin, Naftali Tzvi Yehuda (1816–93). *Responsa Meshiv Davar*, part 1, no. 24.

Eiger, Akiva (1761–1837). Letter in the Matter of the Printing of Maḥzorim of Roedelheim That Have Begun to Be Reprinted Without the Author's Authorization. In Shlomo Sofer, *Igrot Sofrim: Kovetz Mikhtavei Geonei Mishpaḥat Eiger-Sofer* [Scribes' Letters; Collection of Letters of the Sages of the Eiger-Sofer Family]. Vienna 1929: Joseph Schlesinger, Verlag. Part I, pp. 60–61.

Eliashiv, Yosef Shalom (1910–2012). Rulings and Answers from the Great Rabbi Eliashiv. In Weisfish, Naḥum Menashe, 2002. *Mishnat Zkhuyot Ha-Yotzer; Im Tshuvot Ve-Psakim Me-Gedolei Ha-Dor* [The Doctrine of Copyright; with Responsa and Rulings of the Leading Rabbis of Our Generation], 115–20. Jerusalem: Hekhal Naḥum.

Feinstein, Moshe (1895–1960). *Responsa Igrot Moshe*, Part 4, No. 40.

Goldberg, Zalman Neḥemia. 1984–85. Ha'ataka Me-Kaseta Le-Lo Reshut Ha-Ba'alim [Copying from a Cassette Without the Owners' Permission]. *Teḥumin* 6: 185–207. [Arbitration Ruling].

Ḥaver, Yiẓḥak Eizik (1789–1843). B'inyan Haskamot Ve-hasagat G'vul Bi-sfarim Hanidpasim Hanahug Beyameinu [Concerning Reprinting Bans and Wrongful Competition in Book Publishing, as is Customary Today], Olat Shlomo, Part II at 179–84 (Yeshivat Or Yisrael, Petakh Tikva (5749)[1989]).

Horowitz, Aryeh Leibish (1847–1909). *Sefer Beit Aryeh*. Zholkva: Saul Dov Meyerhoffer. 1835.

Isserles, Moses (Rema) (1520? 1530?–1572). *Darkhei Moshe*.

———. *Responsa Rema*, Nos. 7, 10, 25, 38, and 73.

———. *Torat Ha-Olah*.

Judah, Gershom ben (c. 960–1028?1040?). *Responsa Rabbi Gershom Me'or Ha-Golah*, No. 63.

Karo, Joseph (1488–1575). *Shulḥan Arukh*.

———. *Beit Yosef*, Ḥoshen Mishpat.

Katzenellenbogen, Meir (1482–1565). *Responsa Maharam of Padua*, Nos. 13, 19, and 78.

Leon, Judah Messer (1420?–1490). *Haskama for Landau, Yaacov Bar Yehuda*. Naples. Azriel Gunzenhauser.
Maimonides, Moses (1135–1204). *Mishneh Torah.*
Margoliot, Ephraim Zalman (1762–1828). *Responsa Beit Ephraim* , Ḥoshen Mishpat, No. 27.
Nathanson, Joseph Saul (1808–75). *Shoel U-Meshiv,* Nos. 18, 44, 160, and 232.
Pinkas Va'ad Arba Artzot [Council of Four Lands Minute Book] 1945. Ed. Israel Heilprin. Jerusalem: Mossad Bialik.
Reuven Gerondi, Nissim ben (1320–76). *Responsa Ran*, No. 48.
Schmelkes, Yitzḥak (1828–1906). *Beit Yitzḥak*, Yoreh De'ah, Part 5, No. 75.
———. *Beit Yitzḥak,* Ḥoshen Mishpat, Hilkhot Nezikin, No. 80.
Schneersohn, Menaḥem Mendel (1789–1866). *Responsa Tzemaḥ Tzedek*, Yoreh De'ah, No. 295.
Sheshet, Isaac bar (1326–1408). *Respona Ha-Rivash*, No. 271.
Shpitz, Tzvi ben Hayim Yitzḥak. 1987. *Responsa Minḥat Tzvi*, Hilkhot Shkhenim, No. 18.
Silman, Yehuda. *Darkhei Ḥoshen*, Part 1. Excerpted in Weisfish, Naḥum Menashe, 2002. *Mishnat Zkhuyot Ha-Yotzer; Im Tshuvot Ve-Psakim Me-Gedolei Ha-Dor* [The Doctrine of Copyright; with Responsa and Rulings of the Leading Rabbis of Our Generation], 180-83. Jerusalem: Hekhal Naḥum.
Sofer, Moses (1762–1839). *Responsa Ḥatam Sofer,* Likutim, Nos. 14, 57.
———. *Responsa Ḥatam Sofer*, Ḥoshen Mishpat, Nos. 41, 79.
Tana, Shlomo. 1986. *Responsa Brakhat Shlomo,* Ḥoshen Mishpat, No. 26.
Wosner, Shmuel Ha-Levi. 2001. *Shevet Ha-Levi,* Part. 4, Ḥoshen Mishpat, No. 202.
Zalman, Shneur (c. 1745–1812). c. 1806. *Mesirat Koaḥ Ve-Zkhut Al Hadpasat Ha-Shas Be-Slavita* [Transfer of Power and Right on the Printing of the Talmud in Slavuta]. In *Igrois Koidesh: Admur Hasoken, Admur Ha'emtza'ee, Admur Atzemach Tzedek*, 133-34. Brooklyn: "Kehot" Publication Society.
Zuenz, Aryeh Leib (1768–1833). *Shalom Ve-Emet Le-Tivukh Ben Ha-Madpisim* [Peace and Truth for Settling Disputes between the Printers].

PRIMARY SOURCES: SECULAR AND PAPAL LAW

Unless otherwise indicated, all sources in this section are found in their original language and in English translation in *Primary Sources on Copyright (1450–1900)*, eds. L. Bently and M. Kretschmer. http://copy.law.cam.ac.uk/cam/index.php.

Ariosto's Printing Privilege, Venice (1515).
Austrian Copyright Act (1846).
Austrian Statutes on Censorship and Printing, Vienna (1781).
Basel Printers' Statute (1531).
Bernardo Giunti's Privilege for Machiavelli's works, Vatican (1531).
Blackstone, William. 1825. *Commentaries on the Laws of England*, 16th ed., vol. 2, 405–406. London: T. Cadell & J. Butterworth & Son.
Decree Establishing the Venetian Guild of Printers and Booksellers, Venice (1549).
Elector of Saxony, Mandate Against Offensive Works, Lampoons, Copper Engravings and Pamphlets, as well as Concerning the Censorship of Books, the Reprinting of Privileged Ones, and the Sending in of Copies in Due Course of Time, 27 February 1686. In *Electoral Saxon Printing and Censorship Acts from 1549 to 1717*, Leipzig (1724).
Electoral Saxon Printing and Censorship Acts from 1549 to 1717, Leipzig (1724).
French Literary and Artistic Property Act, Paris (1793).
Imperial Privilege for Aloysius Blumauer's Travesty of Virgil's "Aeneid," Vienna (1785).
Imperial Privilege for Arnolt Schlick, Speyer (1511).

Imperial Privilege for Eucharius Rösslin, Strasbourg (1513).
Johannes of Speyer's Printing Monopoly, Venice (1469).
Mackeldey, Ferdinand, trans. 1883. *Handbook of the Roman Law*. T. & J. W. Johnson & Co.
Marco Antonio Sabellico's Printing Privilege, Venice (1486).
Encyclopedia Article on "The Reprinting of Books," Leipzig and Halle (1740).
Order of Christian II, Elector of Saxony, Whereby Booksellers Are to Be Earnestly Admonished to Send Copies of Privileged Books to the Superior Consistory, 18 August 1609. In *Electoral Saxon Printing and Censorship Acts from 1549 to 1717*, Leipzig (1724).
Pezzana e Consorti Case: Supporting Documents, Venice (1780).
Prussian Copyright Act, Berlin (1837).
Pütter: The Reprinting of Books, Gottinggen (1774).
Saxon Copyright Act, Dresden (1844).
Schott v. Egenolph, Strasbourg (1533).
Venetian Decree on Author-Printer Relations, Venice (1545).
Venetian Decree on Press Affairs, Venice (1517).
Venetian Decree on Privileges for New Books and Reprints, Venice (1603).

CASES

United States Courts

Feist Publications v. Rural Telephone Service, 499 U.S. 340 (1991).
Fogerty v. Fantasy, 510 U.S. 517 (1994).
Grand Upright Music v. Warner Bros. Records, 780 F. Supp. 182 (S.D. N.Y. 1991).
Stowe v. Thomas, 23 F. Cas. 201 (E.D. P.A. 1853).

English Courts

Millar v. Taylor, 98 Eng. Rep. 201 (1769).

French Courts

Conseil constitutionnel [CC] [Constitutional Court] decision No. 2009-580, June 10, 2009, J.O. June 13, 2009, p. 9675.

German Courts

Bundesverfassungsgericht [BVerfGE] [School Book Privilege Case], July 7, 1971.

SECONDARY LITERATURE: JUDAICA, HEBREW AND YIDDISH BOOK TRADE, AND CHRISTIAN HEBRAICISTS

Abrahams, Israel. 1896. *Jewish Life in the Middle Ages*. New York and London: MacMillan & Co.
Albeck, Shalom. 2007. Oppression. In *Encyclopedia Judaica*, 2nd ed., vol. 15, 452–53. Detroit: Macmillan Reference USA.
Amram, David Werner. 1988. *The Makers of Hebrew Books in Italy*. London: Holland Press.
Aptroot, Marion. 1989. *Bible Translation as Cultural Reform: The Amsterdam Yiddish Bibles (1678–1679)*. Unpublished doctoral dissertation, University of Oxford.
———. 1993. "In galkes they do not say so, but the taytsch is as it stands here." Notes on the Amsterdam Yiddish Bible Translations by Blitz and Witzenhausen. *Studia Rosenthaliana*, 27: 136–58.
Aranoff, Deena. 2009. Elijah Levita: A Jewish Hebraist. *Jewish History* 23: 17–40.
Assaf, David. 2010. Shapira Family. In *YIVO Encyclopedia of Jews in Eastern Europe*, ed. Gershon David Hundert, vol. 2, 1701–702. New Haven: Yale University Press.

Bar-Ilan, Naftali. 1985/86. Ha'atakat Sefarim o Kasetot [Copying Books or Cassettes]. *Teḥumin* 7: 360–67.
Bartal, Israel. 2005. *The Jews of Eastern Europe, 1772–1881*, trans. Chaya Nor. Philadelphia: University of Pennsylvania Press.
Baruchson, Shifra (sub nom Zipora). 1986. Yediot Al Ha-Mishar Be-Sefarim Ivrim Ben Italia Ve-Ha-Imperia Ha-Ottomanit Be-Mea Ha-16 [Information about the Book Trade Between Italy and the Ottoman Empire in the 16th Century], 53–76. In *Mi-Mizraḥ le-Ma'arav* [From East to West], eds. A. Bashan et al. Ramat Gan: Bar Ilan University Press.
———. 1990. Money and Culture: Financing Sources and Methods in the Hebrew Print Shops in Cinquecento Italy. *La Bibliofilia* 92: 23–39.
———. 1993. *Sefarim Ve-Korim: Tarbut Ha-Kreeya Shel Yehudei Italia Be-Shlahei Ha-Renaissance* [Books and Readers: The Reading Interests of Italian Jews at the Close of the Renaissance]. Ramat Gan: Bar-Ilan University Press.
Baruchson-Arbib, Shifra and Gila Prebor. 2007. Sefer Ha-Ziquq (An Index of Forbidden Hebrew Books): The Book's Use and Its Influence on Hebrew Printing. *La Bibliofilia* 109: 3–31.
Barzilai-Nahon, Karine and Gad Barzilai. 2005. Cultured Technology: Internet and Religious Fundamentalism. *The Information Society* 21: 25–40.
Bauer, Ela. 2008. Guilds. In *The Yivo Encyclopedia of Jews in Eastern Europe*, ed. Gershon David Hundert, vol. 1, 639–40. New Haven: Yale University Press.
Baumel-Schwartz, Judy Tydor. 2009. Frum Surfing: Orthodox Jewish Women's Internet Forums as a Historical and Cultural Phenomenon. *Journal of Jewish Identities* 2: 1–30.
Baumgarten, Jean. 2005. *Introduction to Old Yiddish Literature*. Ed. and trans. Jerold C. Frakes. New York and London: Oxford University Press.
———. 2009. The Printing of Yiddish Books in Frankfurt-on-the-Main (17th and 18th Centuries). *Bulletin du Centre de recherche français de Jérusalem* 20: 1–22.
———. 2010. *Le Peuple Des Livres; Les Ouvrages Populaires dans la Société Ashkénaze XVIe–XVIIIe Siècle*. Paris: Albin Michel.
Bayvel, Rachel. 2002. Closed Down by Two Tsars: A Short Note from a Family Archive. *Jewish Culture and History* 5(2), 114–27.
Bell, Dean Phillip. 2008. *Jews in the Early Modern World*. Plymouth: Rowman & Littlefield.
Benayahu, Meir. 1971. *Haskamot Ve-Reshut Be-Defusei Venetzia* [Copyright, Authorization and Imprimatur for Hebrew Books Printed in Venice]. Jerusalem: Makhon Ben Tzvi and Mossad Ha-Rav Kook.
Benbassa, Esther and Aron Rodrigue. 2000. *Sephardi Jewry: A History of the Judeo-Spanish Community, 14th–20th Centuries*. Berkeley: University of California Press.
Ben-Sasson, Haim Hillel. 2007. Maimonidean Controversy. In *Encyclopedia Judaica*, 2nd ed., vol. 13, 371–81. Detroit: Macmillan Reference USA.
Ben-Sasson, Jonah. 1984. *Mishnato Ha Iyunit Shel Ha-Rema* [The Philosophical System of R. Moses Isserles]. Jerusalem: Israel Academy of Sciences and Humanities.
Berenbaum, Michael, and Skolknik, Fred. 2007. Ma'arufya. In *Encyclopedia Judaica*, 2nd ed., vol. 13, 307. Detroit: Macmillan Reference USA.
Berger, David. 2002. Jacob Katz on Jews and Christians in the Middle Ages. In *The Pride of Jacob*, ed. Jay M. Harris, 41–64. Cambridge, MA: Harvard University Press.
———. 2004. Judaism and General Culture in Medieval and Early Modern Times. In *Judaism's Encounter with Other Cultures: Rejection or Integration?*, ed. Jacob J. Schacter, 60–140. Lanham, Maryland: Rowman & Littlefield Publishers.
Berger, Shlomo. 2004. An Invitation to Buy and Read: Paratexts of Yiddish Books in Amsterdam, 1650–1800. *Book History*, vol. 7, 31–61.

Berkovitz, Jay R. 1995. The French Revolution and the Jews: Assessing the Cultural Impact. *AJS Review* 20: 25–86.

Biale, David. 2002. A Journey Between Two Worlds: East European Jewish Culture from the Partitions of Poland to the Holocaust. In *Cultures of the Jews: A New History*, ed. David Biale, 799–860. New York: Schocken Books.

Birnhack, Michael and Guy Pessach, eds. 2009. *Yotzrim Zkhuyot: Kriyot Be-Ḥok Zkhut Yotzrim* [Authoring Rights: Readings in Copyright Law]. Srigim: Nevo Press.

Bleich, Judah/Yehuda David. 1985. Current Responsa, Decisions of Bate Din and Rabbinical Literature. *Jewish Law Annual* 5: 65–79.

———. 1991. Jewish Law and the State's Authority to Punish Crime. *Cardozo Law Review* 12: 829–57.

———. 1995/96. Hasagat Gvul Be-Dinei Yisrael Ve-Be-Dinei B'nei Noah [Wrongful Competition in Jewish Law and Noaḥide Law]. *Or Ha-Mizraḥ* 44: 42–53.

———. 2010. The Metaphysics of Property Interests in Jewish Law: An Analysis of Kinyan. *Tradition* 43: 49–67.

Blidstein, Ya'akov. 2003. Ha-Halakha—Olam Ha-Norma Ha-Yehudi [The Halakha—Universe of the Jewish Norm]. In *Masa El Ha-Halakha—Iyunim Ben-Teḥumim Be-Olam Ha-Ḥok Ha-Yehudi* [The Quest for Halakha; Interdisciplinary Perspectives on Jewish Law], ed. Amichai Berholz, 21–58. Tel Aviv: Yedioth Ahronoth.

Bloch, Joshua. 1976. Venetian Printers of Hebrew Books. In *Hebrew Printing and Bibliography*, ed. Charles Berlin, 65–88. New York: The New York Public Library and Ktav Publishing House.

Bonfil, Robert/Roberto. 1990. *Rabbis and Jewish Communities in Renaissance Italy*, trans. by Jonathan Chipman. Oxford, UK, and Portland, OR: Litman Library of Jewish Civilization.

———. 1994. *Jewish Life in Renaissance Italy*, trans. Anthony Oldcorn. Berkeley and Los Angeles: University of California Press.

———. 1999. Reading in the Jewish Communities of Western Europe in the Middle Ages. In *A History of Reading in the West*, eds. Gugliemo Cavallo and Roger Chartier, trans. Lydia G. Cochrane, 149–78. Amherst: University of Massachusetts Press.

———. 2001. A Cultural Profile. In *The Jews of Early Modern Venice*, eds. Robert C. Davis and Benjamin Ravid, 169–90. Baltimore: Johns Hopkins University Press.

———. 2003. Ashkenazim in Italy. In *Yiddish in Italia: Yiddish Manuscripts and Printed Books from the 15th to the 17th Century*, eds. Chava Turniansky and Erika Timm, 172–73. Milano: Associazione Italiana Amici Dell'Universita di Gerusalemme.

Breger, Jennifer. 1995. Competition in the Hebrew Book Market. *AB Bookman's Weekly* Feb. 27, 1995: 940.

Breuer, Mordechai. 1996. The Early Modern Period. In *German-Jewish History in Modern Times: Volume 1 Tradition and Enlightenment 1600–1780*, eds. Michael A. Meyer and Michael Brenner, 79–260. New York: Columbia University Press.

Brisman, Shimeon. 2000. *A History and Guide to Judaic Dictionaries and Concordances.* Hoboken, NJ: Ktav Publishing House.

Bromberg, Avraham Yitzhak. 1960. *Ha-Gaon Rabbi Yosef Shaul Natanzon mi Lvov* [The Great Rabbi Yosef Shaul Natanzon of Lvov] Jerusalem: Hasidic Institute.

Broyde, Mettatiyahu/Michael J. 1998. Hovatam shel Yehudim le'oded Shmirat Sheva Mitzvot B'nei Noah al-Yadei Nokhrim: Skira Teoretit. [The Obligation of Jews to Encourage the Non-Jews to Abide by the Seven Commandments of the Sons of Noah: A Theoretical Survey] *Dinei Yisrael* 19: 87–111.

———. 2010. Public and Private International Law from the Perspective of Jewish Law. In *The Oxford Handbook of Judaism and Economics*, ed. Aaron Levine, 363–87. New York: Oxford University Press.

———. 2012. Custom as a Source of Jewish Law: Some Religious Reflections on David J. Bederman's *Custom as a Source of Law*. *Emory Law Journal* 61: 1037–44.

Broyde, Michael J. and Steven H. Resnicoff. 1997. Jewish Law and Modern Business Structures: The Corporate Paradigm. *Wayne Law Review* 43: 1685–818.

Broyde, Michael J. and Michael Hecht. 2000. The Gentile and Returning Lost Property According to Jewish Law: A Theory of Reciprocity. *Jewish Law Annual* 13: 31–45.

Burnett, Stephen G. 1998. The Regulation of Hebrew Printing in Germany, 1550–1630: Confessional Politics and the Limits of Jewish Toleration. In *Infinite Boundaries: Order, Disorder, and Reorder in Early Modern German Culture*, eds. Max Reinhard and Thomas Robisheaux, 329–48. Kirksville, MO: Truman State Univ. Press.

———. 2005. "Spokesmen for Judaism": Medieval Jewish Polemicists and their Christian Readers in the Reformation Era. In *Reuchlin und Seine Erben*, eds. Peter Schaefer and I. Wandrey, 41–51. Ostfildern: Thorbecke.

———. 2006. German Jewish Printing in the Reformation Era (1530–1633). In *Jews, Judaism, and the Reformation in Sixteenth-Century Germany*, eds. Dean Phillip Bell and Stephen G. Burnett, 503–27. Leiden, Boston: Brill.

———. 2012. *Christian Hebraism in the Reformation Era (1500–1660); Authors, Books, and the Transmission of Jewish Learning*. Leiden, Boston: Brill.

Carlebach, Elisheva. 2011. *Palaces of Time: Jewish Calendar and Culture in Early Modern Europe*. Cambridge, MA: Harvard University Press.

Carlton, Dennis W. and Avi Weiss. 2001. The Economics of Religion, Jewish Survival, and Jewish Attitudes Toward Competition in Torah Education. *The Journal of Legal Studies* 30: 253–76.

Carmilly-Weinberger, Moshe. 1977. *Censorship and Freedom of Expression in Jewish History*. New York: Sepher-Hermon Press.

Central Bureau of Statistics of the State of Israel. 2015. Table 9.7—Persons Aged 20 and Over by Use of Computer and Internet, and by Selected Characteristics. In *Statistical Abstract of Israel 2015*. Jerusalem.

Chavel, Charles B, trans. 1971. *Commentary on the Torah*. New York: Shilo Publishing House.

Cohen, Jeremy. 1999. *Living Letters of the Law: Ideas of the Jew in Medieval Christianity*. Berkeley: University of California Press.

Cohen, Yaakov Avraham. 1999. *Emek Ha-Mishpat, vol. 4: Zekhuyot Yotzrim* [Valley of the Law, vol. 4: Copyright]. Netanya: Makhon Shefa Ḥaim.

Cohn, Haim Hermann. 2007. Ḥerem. In *Encyclopedia Judaica*, 2nd ed., vol. 9, 10–16. Detroit: Macmillan Reference USA.

Cohn, Haim Hermann and Sinai, Yuval. 2007. Practice and Procedure. In *Encyclopedia Judaica*, 2nd ed., vol. 16, 434–46. Detroit: Macmillan Reference USA.

Cooper, Levi Yitzḥak. 2013. *Slavuta Neged Kapust: R' Shneur Zalman Me-Liady Ve-Ha-Maḥkoket Al Ha-Zkhut Lehadpis Et Ha-Talmud* [Slavuta v. Kapust: R' Shneur Zalman of Liady and the Dispute over the Right to Print the Talmud]. Unpublished paper (September 30, 2013).

Cooperman, Bernard Dov. 2004. Theorizing Jewish Self-Government in Early Modern Italy. In *Una Manna Buona per Mantova. Man Tov le-Man Tovah. Studi in onore di Vittore Colorni per il suo 92° compleanno*, 365–80. Florence: Olschki.

———. 2006. Ethnicity and Institution Building among Jews in Early Modern Rome. *AJS Review* 30: 119–45.

Coudert, Allison P. 2004. Five Seventeenth-Century Christian Hebraists. In *Hebraica Veritas?*, eds. Allison P. Coudert and Jeffrey S. Shoulson, 286–308. Philadelphia: University of Pennsylvania Press.

David, Abraham. 1973. Le-Berur Zehuto shel Rav Yisrael Ashkenazi Me-Yerushalayim [Towards a Clarification of the Identity of Rabbi Yisrael Ashkenazi of Jerusalem]. *Zion* 38: 170–73.

Davidson, Herbert A. 2005. *Moses Maimonides: The Man and his Works*. New York: Oxford University Press.

Deutch, Sinai. 1993–94. Business Competition and Ethics: Predatory Pricing in Jewish Law. *Dinei Israel* 17: 7–33.

Dweck, Yaacob. 2011. *The Scandal of Kabbalah: Leon Modena, Jewish Mysticism, Early Modern Venice*. Princeton: Princeton University Press.

Dynner, Glenn. 2006. *Men of Silk: The Hasidic Conquest of Polish Jewish Society*. Oxford, UK, and New York: Oxford University Press.

Ehrman, Arnost. 1980. Pretium Iustium and Laesio Enormis in Roman and Jewish Sources. *Jewish Law Annual* 3: 63–73.

Eidelberg, Shlomo. 1953. Maarufia in Rabbenu Gershom's Responsa. *Historia Judaica* 15(1): 59–66.

Elbaum, Jacob. 1990. *Petihut Ve-Histagrut: Ha-Yetsira Ha-Ruḥanit Ha-Sifrutit Be-Polin U-Be-Artsot Ashkenaz Be-Shilḥe Ha-Me'ah Ha-Shesh-Esrey* [Openness and Insularity: Late-Sixteenth-Century Jewish Askhenazic Literature in Poland and Ashkenaz]. Jerusalem: Magnes Press.

Elon, Menachem. 1997. *Ha-Mishpat Ha-Ivri: Toldotav, Makorotav, Ekronotav* [Jewish Law: History, Sources, Principles], Third Enlarged Edition. Jerusalem: Magnes Press.

———. 2007a. Codification of Law. In *Encyclopedia Judaica*, 2nd ed., vol. 4, 765–81. Detroit: Macmillan Reference USA.

———. 2007b. Hassagat Gevul. In *Encyclopedia Judaica*, 2nd ed., vol. 8, 448–53. Detroit: Macmillan Reference USA.

———. 2007c. Mishpat Ivri: Jewish Law—A Law of Life and Practice. In *Encyclopedia Judaica*, 2nd ed., vol. 14, 341–44. Detroit: Macmillan Reference USA.

Feffer, Solomon. 1956–57. The Literary Contributions of Wolf Heidenheim (1757–1832). *Jewish Book Annual* 14: 70–73.

Feiner, Shmuel. 2004. *The Jewish Enlightenment*, trans. Chaya Naor. Philadelphia: University of Pennsylvania Press.

Feldman, Eliyahu. 1982. *Ba'ale Melakha Yehudim be-Moldaviya* [Jewish Artisans in Moldavia]. Jerusalem: Magnes Press.

Ferziger, Adam S. 2008. Banet, Mordekhai ben Avraham. In *The YIVO Encyclopedia of Jews in Eastern Europe*, ed. Gershon David Hundert, vol. 1, 118–19. New Haven and London: Yale University Press.

Finkelstein, Louis. 1964. *Jewish Self-Government in the Middle Ages*. 2nd ed. New York: Philipp Feldheim.

Fishman, David E. 1997. Rabbi Moshe Isserles and the Study of Science Among Polish Rabbis. *Science in Context* 10: 571–88.

Frakes, Jerold C. 2009. *Early Yiddish Texts 1100–1750: With Introduction and Commentary*. Oxford, UK, and New York: Oxford University Press.

Fram, Edward. 1996. Jewish Law from the Shulhan Arukh to the Enlightenment. In *An Introduction to the History and Sources of Jewish Law*, eds. N. S. Hecht et al., 359–77 Oxford, UK, and New York: Oxford University Press.

———. 1997. *Ideals Face Reality: Jewish Law and Life in Poland*. Cincinnati: Hebrew Union College Press.

Friedberg, Chaim Dov. 1950. *Toldot Ha-Dfus Ha-Ivri be Polania* [History of Hebrew Typography in Poland]. 2nd ed. Tel Aviv: Baruch Freidberg.

Friedman, Menachem. 1995. Life Tradition and Book Tradition in the Development of Ultraorthodox Judaism. In *Israeli Judaism: The Sociology of Religion in Israel*, eds. Shlomo A. Deshen et al., 235–55. Piscataway: Transaction Publishers.

Fuks, Lajb and Renate G. Fuks-Mansfield. 1987. *Hebrew Typography in the Northern Netherlands 1585–1815, Part Two*. Leiden: E.J. Brill.

Fuks-Mansfeld, Renate G. 2004. The Role of Yiddish in Early Dutch-Jewish Haskalah. In *Speaking Jewish—Jewish Speak: Multilingualism in Western Ashkenazic Culture*, 147–55. Louvain: Peeters.

Gamoran, Hillel. 2008. *Jewish Law in Transition: How Economic Forces Overcame the Prohibition Against Lending on Interest*. Cincinnati: Hebrew Union College Press.

Ganot, Shmuel Barukh. 2001. Ha'atakat Kaletot Ve-Tokhniot Maḥshev [Copying Cassettes and Computer Programs]. *Tzohar* 9: 41–52.

Gertner, Haim. 2008. Yosef Sha'ul Natanson. In *The Yivo Encyclopedia of Jews in Eastern Europe*, ed. Gershon David Hundert, vol. 2, 1253. New Haven: Yale University Press.

Ginsburg, Christian D. 1867. *The Massoreth Ha-Massoreth of Elias Levita: Being an Exposition of the Massoretic Notes on the Hebrew Bible or the Ancient Critical Apparatus of the Old Testament, in Hebrew with an English Translation and Critical and Explanatory Notes*. London: Longmans, Green, Reader & Dyer.

Ginsburg, Saul Moiseyevich. 1991. *The Drama of Slavuta*, trans. Ephraim H. Prombaum. Lanham: University Press of America.

Goitein, Shlomo Dov. 1980. The Interplay of Jewish and Islamic Laws. In *Jewish Law in Legal History and the Modern World*, ed. Bernard S. Jackson, 61–77. Leiden: Brill.

Goldberg, Jacob. 1985. *Jewish Privileges in the Polish Commonwealth; Charters of Rights Granted to Jewish Communities in Poland-Lithuania in the Sixteenth to Eighteenth Centuries*. Jerusalem: Israel Academy of Sciences and Humanities.

Goldish, Matt. 2008. *Jewish Questions: Responsa on Sephardic Life in the Early Modern Period*. Princeton, NJ: Princeton University Press.

Graff, Gil. 1985. *Separation of Church and State: Dina De-Malkhuta Dina in Jewish Law, 1750–1848*. Tuscaloosa: University of Alabama Press.

Grafton, Anthony. 2014. The Jewish Book in Christian Europe: Material Texts and Religious Encounters. In *Faithful Narratives: Historians, Religion, and the Challenge of Objectivity*, eds. Andrea Sterk and Nina Caputo, 96–114. Ithaca: Cornell University Press.

Gray, Hillel Charles. 2009. *Foreign Features in Jewish Law: How Christian and Secular Moral Discourses Permeate Halakhah*. Unpublished dissertation, University of Chicago Divinity School.

Grendler, Paul F. 1978. The Destruction of Hebrew Books in Venice. *Proceedings of the American Academy for Jewish Research* 45: 103–36.

Gries, Ze'ev. 2007. *The Book in the Jewish World 1700–1900*. Oxford, UK, and Portland, OR: Littman Library of Jewish Civilization.

———. 2008. *Printing and Publishing Before 1800*. In *The Yivo Encyclopedia of Jews in Eastern Europe*, ed., Gershon David Hundert, vol. 2, 1454–58. New Haven: Yale University Press.

Grunwald, Max. 1936. *Vienna*. Philadelphia: Jewish Publication Society.

Haberman, Abraham Meir. 1978a. *Perakim Be-Toldoth Ha-Madpissim Ha-Ivrim We-Inyanei Sefarim* [Studies in the History of Hebrew Printers and Books]. Jerusalem: Ruben Mass.

———. 1978b. *Ha-Madpis Daniel Bomberg U-Reshimat Sifre Beit Dfuso* [The Printer Daniel Bomberg and the List of Books Published by His Press]. Zefat: Museum of Printing Art.

Hacker, Joseph R. 2011. Sixteenth-Century Jewish Internal Censorship of Hebrew Books. In *The Hebrew Book in Early Modern Italy*, eds. Joseph R. Hacker and Adam Shear, 109–20. Philadelphia: University of Pennsylvania Press.

Halbertal, Moshe. 1997. *People of the Book; Canon, Meaning, and Authority*. Cambridge, MA: Harvard University Press.

Heilprin, Israel. 1934. Haskamot Va'ad Arba Artsot be-Polin [Approbations of the Council of Four Lands in Poland]. *Kiryat Sefer* 11: 105–10.

Heller, Marvin J. 1999. *Printing the Talmud; A History of the Individual Treatises Printed from 1700 to 1750*. Leiden: Brill.

———. 2004. *The Sixteenth Century Hebrew Book: An Abridged Thesaurus*. 2 volumes. Leiden: Brill.

———. 2006. Earliest Printings of the Talmud. In *Printing the Talmud: From Bomberg to Schottenstein*, eds. Sharon Liberman Mintz and Gabriel M. Goldstein, 62–79. New York: Yeshiva University Museum.

———. 2008. *Studies in the Making of the Early Hebrew Book*. Leiden and Boston: Brill.

Herzog, Isaac. 1980. *The Main Institutions of Jewish Law: The Law of Property*. Brooklyn: Soncino Press.

Hildesheimer, Meir. 1994. "The Attitude of the Hatam Sofer Toward Moses Mendelssohn." *Proceedings of the American Academy for Jewish Research* 60: 141–87.

Hirschler, Gertrude, ed. 1988. *Ashkenaz: The German Jewish Heritage*. New York: Yeshiva University Museum.

Horowitz, Elliott. 1992. Speaking of the Dead: The Emergence of the Eulogy among Italian Jewry of the Sixteenth Century. In *Preachers of the Italian Ghetto*, ed. David Ruderman, 129–62. Berkeley and Los Angeles: University of California Press.

———. 2002. Families and Their Fortunes: The Jews of Early Modern Italy. In *Cultures of the Jews: A New History*, ed. David Biale, 573–636. New York: Schocken Books.

Horowitz, Yehoshua. 2007a. Eliezer ben Joel Ha-Levi of Bonn. In *Encyclopedia Judaica*, 2nd ed., vol. 6, 326–27. Detroit: Macmillan Reference USA.

———. 2007b. Horowitz, Phinehas (Pinhas) ben Ẓevi Hirsch Ha-Levi. In *Encyclopedia Judaica*, 2nd ed., vol. 9, 540–41. Detroit: Macmillan Reference USA.

———. 2007c. Horowitz, Ẓevi Hirsch ben Phinehas Ha-Levi. In *Encyclopedia Judaica*, 2nd ed., vol. 9, 545–45. Detroit: Macmillan Reference USA.

Hundert, Gershon David. 2006. *Jews in Poland-Lithuania in the Eighteenth Century; A Genealogy of Modernity*. Berkeley: University of California Press.

Hurvitz, Mark. 1978. *The Rabbinic Perception of Printing as Depicted in Haskamot and Responsa*. Unpublished rabbinic thesis. Cincinnati: Hebrew Union College.

Idel, Moshe. 1990. *Kabbalah: New Perspectives*. New Haven: Yale University Press.

———. 1992. Judah Muscato: A Late Renaissance Preacher. In *Preachers of the Italian Ghetto*, ed. David B. Ruderman. Berkeley: University of California Press.

———. 2011. *Kabbalah in Italy, 1280–1510: A Survey*. New Haven: Yale University Press.

———. 2014. Printing Kabbalah in Sixteenth-Century Italy. In *Jewish Culture in Early Modern Europe; Essays in Honor of David B. Ruderman*, eds. Richard I. Cohen et al., 85–96. Cincinnati: Hebrew Union College Press.

Iggers, Wilma Abeles. 1992. *The Jews of Bohemia and Moravia*, ed. Wilma Abeles, trans. Wilma Abeles et al. Detroit: Wayne State University Press.

Int'l Beis Hora'ah of the Institute for Dayanim. 2010. *Zkhuyot Yotzrim, Ha-atakat Kaletot Ve-Tokhniot Maḥshev Be-Halakha* [Copyright, Copying Cassettes and Computer Programs in Jewish Law]. http://din.org.il/2010/07/15.

Ishun, Shlomo. 2001. *Zkhuyot Yotzrim Be-Halakha—Tguva Le-Ma'amaro Shel Ḥaim Navon* [Copyright in Jewish Law—Response to the Article by Ḥaim Navon]. *Tzohar* 7: 51–61.

———. 2007/08. *Horadat Shirim Me-Ha-Internet Ve-Haklatat Shirim Me-Ha-Radio* [Downloading Songs from the Internet and Recording Songs from the Radio], *Keter* 6: 36–44.

Israel, Jonathan I. 1987. The Jews of Venice and their Links with Holland and with Dutch Jewry (1600–1710). In *Gli Ebrei e Venezia; secoli XIV–XVII*, 95–116. Milano: Edizioni Comunita.

———. 1998. *European Jewry in the Age of Mercantilism 1550–1750*, 3rd ed. Oxford, UK, and Portland, OR: Littman Library of Jewish Civilization.

Jachter, Chaim/Howard. 2000. *Gray Matter; Ve-Zot Le-Yehuda*. Teaneck: H. Jachter.

———. 2010. Interloping Behavior in the Marketplace in Jewish Law. In *The Oxford Handbook of Judaism and Economics*, ed. Aaron Levine, 255–68. New York: Oxford University Press.

Jackson, Bernard S. 1980. History, Dogmatics, and Halakhah. In *Jewish Law in the Legal History and the Modern World*, ed. Bernard S. Jackson, 1–26. Leiden: Brill.

Jersch-Wenzel, Stefi. 1997a. Legal Status and Emancipation. In *German-Jewish History in Modern Times: Volume 2 Emancipation and Acculturation, 1780–1871*, ed. Michael A. Meyer, 7–49. New York: Columbia University Press,

———. 1997b. Population Shifts and Occupational Structure. In *German-Jewish History in Modern Times: Volume 2 Emancipation and Acculturation, 1780–1871*, ed. Michael A. Meyer, 50–89. New York: Columbia University Press.

Kahana, Ma'oz. 2007. Hatam Sofer: Ha-Posek Be-Einei Atzmo [Hatam Sofer: The Self-Image of a Rabbinic Decisor]. *Tarbitz* 76: 519–56.

———. 2010. *From Prague to Pressburg: Halakhic Writing in a Changing World from the Noda BeYehuda to the Ḥatam Sofer*, 1730–1839, unpublished Ph.D. Thesis. English abstract.

Kaplan, Yosef. 2000. *An Alternative Path to Modernity: the Sephardi Diaspora in Western Europe*. Leiden: Brill.

Kaplan, Lawrence. 1992. Daas Torah: A Modern Conception of Rabbinic Authority. In *Rabbinic Authority and Personal Autonomy*, ed. Moshe Z. Sokol, 1–60. Northvale, NJ: Jason Aronson.

Kaplan, Zvi Jonathan. 2007. The Thorny Area of Marriage: Rabbinic Efforts to Harmonize Jewish and French Law in Nineteenth-Century France. *Jewish Social Studies* 13: 59–72.

Katz, Jacob. 1961. *Exclusiveness and Tolerance: Studies in Jewish-Gentile Relations in Medieval and Modern Times*. London: Oxford University Press.

———. 1973. *Out of the Ghetto: The Social Background of the Jewish Emancipation, 1770–1870*. Cambridge, MA: Harvard University Press.

———. 1998a. *A House Divided: Orthodoxy and Schism in Nineteenth-Century Central European Jewry*. Hanover, NH: Brandeis University Press.

———. 1998b. *Divine Law in Human Hands; Case Studies in Halakhic Flexibility*. Jerusalem: Magnes Press.

———. 1998c. Ideological Differences over the Status of the Kehilla: The Jewish Community in the Age of Emancipation. In *Perspectives on Jewish Thought and Mysticism*, eds. Alfred L. Ivry, Elliot R. Wolfson, and Allan Arkush, 457–70. Amsterdam: Harwood Academic Publishers.

———. 2000. *Tradition and Crisis: Jewish Society at the End of the Middle Ages*, trans. Bernard Dov Cooperman. Syracuse: Syracuse University Press.

Kellner, Menachem. 2006. *Maimonides' Confrontation with Mysticism*. Oxford, UK, and Portland, OR: Littman Library of Jewish Civilization.

Kirschenbaum, Aaron. 1991. *Equity in Jewish Law; Formalism and Flexibility in Jewish Civil Law*. New York: Ktav Publishing House.

Kleinman, Ron S. 2011. Civil Law as Custom: Jewish Law and Secular Law—Do They Diverge or Converge? *The Review of Rabbinic Judaism* 14: 11–36.

Kohler, George Y. 2012. *Reading Maimonides' Philosophy in 19th Century Germany: The Guide to Religious Reform*. Dordrecht: Springer.

Kozinets, Matthew I. 1995. Copyright and Jewish Law: The Dilemma of Change. *UC Davis Journal of International Law & Policy* 1: 83–103.

Krauss, Samuel. 1929. "Merkwurdige Siddurim." In *Studies in Jewish Bibliography and Related Subjects in Memory of Abraham Solomon Freidus (1867–1923)*, 128–40. New York: The Alexander Kohut Memorial Foundation.

Lamm, Norman and Aaron Kirschenbaum. 1979. Freedom and Constraint in the Jewish Judicial Process. *Cardozo Law Review* 1: 99–134.

Landau, Yisrael. 1998–99. Berur Dvarim Be-Din Neheneh Me-Hokhmat Ḥavero (Be-Inyan Ha'atakat Tokhniot Ve-Kaletot Le-Shimush Prati She-Lo Me-Daat Ha-Ba'alim) [Clarifying Writings Concerning the Law of Benefiting from Another's Wisdom (Regarding Copying Computer Programs and Cassettes for Personal Use Without the Owners' Permission)]. *Bekhorim* 2: 809–14.

Lederhendler, Eli. 1989. *The Road to Modern Jewish Politics; Political Tradition and Political Reconstruction in the Jewish Community of Tsarist Russia*. New York and Oxford, UK: Oxford University Press.

Lehman, Israel O. 2007. Vienna: Hebrew Printing. In *Encyclopedia Judaica*, 2nd ed., vol. 20, 523–23. Detroit: Macmillan Reference USA.

Lev-On, Azi and Rivka Neriya Ben-Shahar. 2009. A Forum of Their Own: Views About the Internet Among Ultra-Orthodox Jewish Women Who Browse Designated Closed Forums. *Media Frames: Journal of the Israel Communications Association* 4: 67–106.

Levin, Leonard. 2008. *Seeing with Both Eyes: Ephraim Luntshitz and the Polish-Jewish Renaissance*. Leiden: Brill.

Levinger, Jacob S. 2007. Dubno, Solomon ben Joel. In *Encyclopedia Judaica*, 2nd ed., vol. 6, 34. Detroit: Macmillan Reference USA.

Levy, B. Barry. 1990. *Planets, Potions, and Parchments: Scientifica Hebraica from the Dead Sea Scrolls to the Eighteenth Century*. Montreal and Buffalo, NY: McGill-Queen's University Press.

———. 2001. *Fixing God's Torah; The Accuracy of the Hebrew Bible Text in Jewish Law*. New York: Oxford University Press.

Lichtenstein, Aaron. 1995. *The Seven Laws of Noah*, 3rd ed. New York: Rabbi Jacob Joseph School Press.

Lieberman, Yehoshua. 1989. *Taḥarut Iskit B'Halakha* [Business Competition in Jewish Law]. Ramat Gan: Bar-Ilan University Press.

Lifshitz, Berachyahu. 1996. The Age of the Talmud. In *An Introduction to the History and Sources of Jewish Law*, eds. N. S. Hecht et al., 169–95. Oxford, UK, and New York: Oxford University Press.

Lior, Dov. 2006/07. Bama Toranit—Ha-im Mutar Le-Ha'atik Tokhnot Maḥshev, Diskim, Ve-Kaletot? [Torah Podium—Is It Permissible to Copy Computer Programs, Disks, and Videos?]. *Komemiyut* 32. http://www.netlaw.co.il/it_itemid_3879_desc__ftext_.htm: 32–x.

Lowenstein, Steven M. 2005. The Beginning of Integration: 1780–1870. In *Jewish Daily Life in Germany*, ed. Marion A. Kaplan, 93–171. New York: Oxford University Press.

Lynfield, Ben. 2009. Rabbis Rage Against Net "Abominations." In *The Independent*, Dec. 11, 2009. http://www.independent.co.uk/news/world/middle-east/rabbis-rage-against-net-abominations-1838204.html.

Mahler, Raphael. 1961. *Ha-Ḥasidut Ve Ha-Haskala* [Hasidism and the Jewish Enlightenment Movement]. Israel: Sifryat Poalim.

Malkiel, David J. 2001. The Ghetto Republic. In *The Jews of Early Modern Venice*, eds. Robert C. David and Benjamin Ravid, 117–42. Baltimore: Johns Hopkins University Press.

Manasseh, David Ben and David Darshan. 1984. *Shir Hama'a Lot L'David* [In Defense of Preachers]. Cincinnati: Hebrew Union College Press.

Manekin, Rachel. 1999. Politics, Religion, and National Identity: The Galician Jewish Vote in the 1873 Parliamentary Elections. In *Polin: Studies in Polish Jewry, Focusing on Galicia*, eds. Israel Bartal and Antony Polonsky, vol. 12, 100–19. Oxford, UK, and Portland, OR: Littman Library of Jewish Civilization.

———. 2008. Galicia. In *The Yivo Encyclopedia of Jews in Eastern Europe*, ed. Gershon David Hundert, vol. 1, 560–67. New Haven: Yale University Press.

Marx, Alexander. 1935. Texts by and about Maimonides. *Jewish Quarterly Review* 25: 371–428.

Marx, Moses. 1935. *Gershom (Hieronymus) Soncino's Wanderyears in Italy, 1498–1527.* Cincinnati: Hebrew Union College Annual.

Meyer, Michael A. 1997. Jewish Communities in Transition. In *German-Jewish History in Modern Times: Volume 2 Emancipation and Acculturation, 1780–1871*, ed. Michael A. Meyer, 90–127. New York: Columbia University Press.

———. 1988. *Response to Modernity: A History of the Reform Movement in Judaism.* New York and Oxford, UK: Oxford University Press.

Miller, Michael Lawrence. 2011. *Rabbis and Revolution: The Jews of Moravia in the Age of Emancipation.* Stanford: Stanford University Press.

Mondshein, Yehoshua, 2003a. Piskeihem Shel Rabbanei Ḥabad Be-Pulmusei Ha-Madpisim Kapust-Slavuta-Vilna, Part I [Rulings of Ḥabad Rabbis in the Dispute of the Publishers Kapust-Slavuta-Vilna, Part I]. *Or Yisrael*, Year 8, 4(32): 122–35.

———. 2003b. Piskeihem Shel Rabbanei Ḥabad Be-Pulmusei Ha-Madpisim Kapust-Slavuta-Vilna, Part II [Rulings of Ḥabad Rabbis in the Dispute of the Publishers Kapust-Slavuta-Vilna, Part II]. *Or Yisrael*, Year 9, 1 (33): 115–27.

Morell, Samuel. 1971. The Constitutional Limits of Communal Government in Rabbinic Law. *Jewish Social Studies* 33: 87–119.

———. 2004. *Studies in the Judicial Methodology of Rabbi David Ibn Abi Zimra*. Lanham, MD: University Press of America.

Navo, Asaf. 2009. Ha-Rav Ovadia: Hova Leshalem Tamlugim Al Shimushim Be-Zkhuyot Yotzrim. Mako, August, 17, 2009. http://www.mako.co.il/music-news/local/Article-aaf46827ba72321006.htm&sCh=f6750a2610f26110&pId=1950692751

Navon, Ḥaim. 2001. Zkhuyot Yotzrim Be-Halakha [Copyright in Jewish Law]. *Tzohar* 7: 35–49.

Nehurai, Meir. 1994–95. Ha-Zkhut Ha-Kalkalit Shel Ha-Yotzer Be-Yaḥas Le-Yetzirato [The Author's Economic Right Regarding his Creation]. *Mishlav Gal* 27: 39-51.

Netanel, Neil Weinstock. 2007a. Maharam of Padua v. Giustiniani: The Sixteenth-Century Origins of the Jewish Law of Copyright. *Houston Law Review* 44: 821–70.

Netanel, Neil Weinstock and David Nimmer. 2011. Is Copyright Property? The Debate in Jewish Law. *Theoretical Inquiries in Law* 12: 217–51.

Nielsen, Bruce. 2011. Daniel van Bombergen, a Bookman of Two Worlds. In *The Hebrew Book in Early Modern Italy*, eds. Joseph R. Hacker and Adam Shear, 56–75. Philadelphia: University of Pennsylvania Press.

Nimmer, David. 2009a. In the Shadow of the Emperor: The Hatam Sofer's Copyright Rulings. *Torah U-Madda Journal* 15: 24–67.

———. 2009b. Rabbi Banet's Charming Snake. *Hakirah* 8: 69–108.

Novak, David. 1983. *The Image of the Non-Jew in Judaism: A Historical and Constructive Study of the Noahide Laws.* New York: E. Mellen Press.

Parente, Fausto. 2001. The Index, the Holy Office, the Condemnation of the Talmud and Publication of Clement VIII's Index. In *Church, Censorship, and Culture in Early Modern Italy*, ed. Gigliota Fragnito, trans. Adrian Belton, 163–93. Cambridge, UK, and New York: Cambridge University Press.

Paris, Dov. 2006. A Conversation with Shuli and Michal Rand. *Jewish Action; The Magazine of the Orthodox Union* Fall 2006: 44–48.

Pilarczyk, Krzysztof. 2002. Printing the Talmud in Poland in the Sixteenth and Seventeenth Centuries. In *Polin: Focusing on Jewish Religious Life, 1500–1900*, ed. Antony Polonsky, 59–64. Oxford, UK, and Portland, OR: Littman Library of Jewish Civilization.

———. 2004. Hebrew Printing Houses in Poland Against the Background of their History in the World. *Studia Judaica* 7: 2004 nr 2(14), 201–21.

Polonsky, Antony. 2010. *The Jews in Poland and Russia 1350–1881*. Oxford, UK, and Portland, OR: Littman Library of Jewish Civilization.

Popper, William. 1899. *The Censorship of Hebrew Books*. New York: Knickerbocker Press.

Posner, Raphael and Israel Ta-Shema. 1975. *The Hebrew Book: An Historical Survey*. Jerusalem: Keter Publishing.

Pribram, A. F., ed. 1849. *Urkunden und Akten zur Geschichte der Juden in Wien: Erste Abteilung, Allgemeiner Teil 1526–1847* [Documents and Records of the History of the Jews in Vienna: First Section, General Part 1526–1847]. Wien: W. Braumuller.

Pullan, Brian. 1983. *The Jews of Europe and the Inquisition of Venice, 1550–1670*. Oxford, UK: Basil Blackwell.

Rabbinovicz, Raphael Nathan Nata. 1951. *Maamar Al Hadpasat Ha-Talmud: Toldot Hadpasat Ha-Talmud* [Article on the Printing of the Talmud: History of Printing the Talmud]. Jerusalem: Mosad Rav Kook.

Radzyner, Amiḥai. 2015. Ha-Mevukha Ha-Ruḥanit: Halakha Bat Zmaneinu U-She'elat Ha-Hagana Al Zkhuyot Ha-Yotzrim [The Intellectual Ambivalence: Contemporary Halakhah and the Question of the Defense of Copyright]. In *Intellectual Property Law: Interdisciplinary Analysis*, eds. Miriam Bitton and Lior Zemer, 169–214. Srigim: Nevo Press.

Rakover, Naḥum. 1970. *Ha-Haskamot Le-Sfarim Ke-Yesod Le-Zkhut Ha-Yotzrim* [The "Haskamot" for Books as a Basis for Copyright]. Jerusalem: State of Israel Ministry of Justice.

———. 1986–87. Pekiyat "Haskama" She-Nitna Le-Sefer Le-Aḥar Ha-Mekhira [Expiration of a Haskama Given for a Book after the Sale]. *Sinai* 100: 833–51.

———. 1991. *Zkhut Ha-Yotzrim Be-Mekorot Ha-Yehudim* [Copyright in Jewish Sources]. Jerusalem: Moreshet ha-Mishpat be-Yisrael.

Rapp, Dani. 2010. The Employee Free Choice Act, Unions, and Unionizing in Jewish Law. In *The Oxford Handbook of Judaism and Economics*, ed. Aaron Levine, 429–44. New York: Oxford University Press.

Ravid, Benjamin. 1979. The Prohibition against Jewish Printing and Publishing in Venice and the Difficulties of Leone Modena. In *Studies in Medieval Jewish History and Literature*, ed. Isadore Twersky, 135–53. Cambridge, MA: Harvard University Press.

———. 2001. The Venetian Government and the Jews. In *The Jews of Early Modern Venice*, eds. Robert C. Davis and Benjamin Ravid, 3–30. Baltimore and London: Johns Hopkins University Press.

Raz-Krakotzkin, Amnon. 1999. Print in Jewish Cultural Development. In *Encyclopedia of the Renaissance*, vol. 5, 161–69. New York: Charles Scribner's Sons.

———. 2004. Censorship, Editing, and the Reshaping of Jewish Identity: The Catholic Church and Hebrew Literature in the Sixteenth Century. In *Hebraica Veritas? Christian Hebraists and the Study of Judaism in Early Modern Europe*, eds. Allison P. Coudert and Jeffrey S. Shoulson, 125–55. Philadelphia: University of Pennsylvania Press.

———. 2007. *The Censor, the Editor, and the Text: The Catholic Church and the Shaping of the Jewish Canon in the Sixteenth Century*, trans. Jackie Feldman. Philadelphia: University of Pennsylvania Press.

———. 2014. Persecution and the Art of Printing; Hebrew Books in Italy in the 1550s. In *Jewish Culture in Early Modern Europe; Essays in Honor of David B. Ruderman*, eds. Richard I. Cohen et al., 97–108. Cincinnati: Hebrew Union College Press.

Reif, Stefan C. 1995. *Judaism and Hebrew Prayer: New Perspectives on Jewish Liturgical History*. Cambridge, UK: Cambridge University Press.

Reiner, Elchanan. 1997. The Ashkenazi Elite at the Beginning of the Modern Era: Manuscript versus Printed Book. In *Polin: Studies in Polish Jewry, Jews in Early Modern Poland*, ed., Gershon David Hundert, vol. 10, 85–98. Oxford, UK, and Portland, OR: The Littman Library of Jewish Civilization.

Resnicoff, Steven H. 2006. Jewish Law and Socially Responsible Corporate Conduct. *Fordham Journal of Corporate & Financial Law* 11: 681–96.

Rosenthal, Avraham. 1987. Daniel Bomberg and his Talmud Editions. In *Gli Ebrei e Venezia; secoli XIV–XVII*, 374–416. Milano: Edizioni Comunita.

Rosman, Moshe. 1990. *The Lords' Jews*. Cambridge, MA: Harvard University Press.

———. 2002. Innovative Tradition: Jewish Culture in the Polish-Lithuanian Commonwealth. In *Cultures of the Jews: A New History*, ed. David Biale, 519–70. New York: Schocken Books.

———. 2007. *How Jewish Is Jewish History?* Oxford, UK, and Portland, OR: The Littman Library of Jewish Civilization.

———. 2009. The Authority of the Council of Four Lands Outside Poland-Lithuania. In *Polin: Studies in Polish Jewry, Social and Cultural Boundaries in Pre-Modern Poland*, eds. Adam Teller, Magda Teter, and Antony Polonsky, vol. 22, 83–108. Oxford, UK, and Portland, OR: Littman Library of Jewish Civilization.

Rothkoff, Aaron. 2007. Finzi-Norsa Controversy. In *Encyclopedia Judaica*, 2nd ed., vol. 7, 40–41. Detroit: Macmillan Reference USA.

Rothstein, Gidon. 2004. Involuntary Particularism: What the Noahide Laws Tell Us about Citizenship and Alienage. *Georgetown Immigration Law Journal* 18: 543–66.

Rudavsky, T. M. 2010. *Maimonides*. West Sussex: Wiley-Blackwell.

Ruderman, David B. 1995. *Jewish Thought and Scientific Discovery in Early Modern Europe*. New Haven, CT: Yale University Press.

———. 1988. The Hebrew Book in a Christian World. In *A Sign and a Witness: 2,000 Years of Hebrew Books and Illuminated Manuscripts*, ed. Leonard Singer Gold, 101–13. New York: New York Public Library and Oxford University Press.

———. 2010. *Early Modern Jewry; A New Cultural History*. Princeton: Princeton University Press.

———. 2014. The People and the Book: Print and the Transformation of Jewish Culture in Early Modern Europe. In *Faithful Narratives: Historians, Religion, and the Challenge of Objectivity*, eds. Andrea Sterk and Nina Caputo, 83–95. Ithaca: Cornell University Press.

Sacks, Jonathan. 1992. Creativity and Innovation in Halakhah. In *Rabbinic Authority and Personal Autonomy*, ed. Moshe Z. Sokol, 123–68. Northvale, NJ: J. Aronson. Pages.

Samet, Moshe. 1988. The Beginnings of Orthodoxy. *Modern Judaism* 8: 249–69.

Schmelzer, Menachem H. 2006. Hebrew Printing and Publishing in Germany, 1650–1750. On Jewish Book Culture and the Emergence of Modern Jewry. In *Studies in Jewish Bibliography and Medieval Hebrew Poetry; Collected Essays of Menachem Schmelzer*, 38–57. New York and Jerusalem: Jewish Theological Seminary.

Scholem, Gershom. 1978. *Kabbalah*. New York: Meridian.

Schreiber, Aaron M. 2003. The Hatam Sofer's Nuanced Attitude Towards Secular Learning, Maskilim, and Reformers. *Torah U-Madda Journal* 11: 123–73.

Schrijver, Emile G. L. 2007. The Hebraic Book. In *A Companion to the History of the Book*, eds. Simon Eliot and Jonathan Rose, 153–63. Malden, MA: Blackwell Publishing.
Schwarzschild, Steven S. 2007. Noachide Laws. In *Encyclopedia Judaica*, 2nd ed., vol. 15, 284–87. Detroit: Macmillan Reference USA.
Schwarzfuchs, Simon. 1979. *Napoleon, the Jews and the Sanhedrin*. London and Boston: Routledge & Kegan Paul.
Seligson, Max. 1906. Wolf Heidenheim. *The Jewish Encyclopedia*, Vol. 6, 319–20. New York: Funk and Wagnalls.
Shamir, Avner. 2011. *Christian Conceptions of Jewish Books: The Pfefferkorn Affair*. Copenhagen: Museum Tusculanum Press.
Shapiro, Marc B. 2003. Of Books and Bans. *The Edah Journal* 3(2): 46–61.
———. 2004. *The Limits of Orthodox Theology: Maimonides' Thirteen Principles Reappraised*. Oxford, UK, and Portland, OR: Littman Library of Jewish Civilization.
Shilo, Shmuel. 1974. *Dina De-Malkhuta Dina* [The Law of the State Is the Law]. Jerusalem: Jerusalem Academic Press.
———. 1980. Kofin al Midat S'dom: Jewish Law's Concept of Abuse of Rights. *Israel Law Review* 15: 49–78.
Shochetman, Eliav. 1992–93. Ma'amadam Ha-Halakhti Shel Batei Ha-Mishpat Be-Medinat Yisrael [The Halakhic Status of Israeli Courts]. *Teḥumin* 13: 337–70.
Shulvass, Moses A. 1951. The Jewish Population in Renaissance Italy. *Jewish Social Studies* 13: 3–24.
———. 1952. Ashkenazic Jewry in Italy. *YIVO Annual of Jewish Social Science* 7: 110–31.
———. 1971. *From East to West: The Westward Migration of Jews from Eastern Europe in the Seventeenth and Eighteenth Centuries*. Detroit: Wayne State Press.
Simonsohn, Shlomo. 1988. *The Apostolic See and the Jews*. Toronto: Pontifical Institute of Mediaeval Studies.
Sinai, Yuval. 2010. *Ha-Shofet Ve-Ha-Halikh Ha-Shiputi Be-Mishpat Ha-Ivri* [The Judge and the Judicial Process in Jewish Law]. Srigim: Nevo Press.
Smith, Jerry C. 2003. *Elia Levita Bachur's Bovo-Buch: A Translation of the Old Yiddish Edition of 1541 with Introduction and Note*. Tucson: Fenestra Books.
Soloveitchik, Haym. 1994. *Rupture and Reconstruction: The Transformation of Contemporary Orthodoxy. Tradition* 28: 64–130.
Spiegel, Yaakov Shmuel. 1996. *Amudim Be-Toldot Ha-Sefer Ha-Ivri; Ha-Gahot Ve-Magi'im* [Chapters in the History of the Jewish Book; Scholars and their Annotations]. Ramat-Gan: Bar-Ilan Press.
Stampfer, Shaul. 1999. Inheritance of the Rabbinate in Eastern Europe in the Modern Period: Causes, Factors and Development over Time. *Jewish History* 13: 35–57.
———. 2012. *Lithuanian Yeshivas of the Nineteenth Century: Creating a Tradition of Learning*. Oxford, UK, and Portland, OR: Littman Library of Jewish Civilization.
Stanislawski, Michael. 1983. *Tsar Nicholas I and the Jews; The Transformation of Jewish Society in Russia 1825–1855*. Philadelphia: Jewish Publication Society of America.
———. 2005. The "Vilna Shas" and East European Jewry. In *Printing the Talmud: From Bomberg to Schottenstein*, eds. Sharon Liberman Mintz and Gabriel M. Goldstein, 97–102. New York: Yeshiva University Museum.
Stern, David. 2011. The Rabbinic Bible in Its Sixteenth-Century Context. In *The Hebrew Book in Early Modern Italy*, eds. Joseph R. Hacker and Adam Shear, 76–108. Philadelphia: University of Pennsylvania Press.
Stern, Sacha. 1994. Attribution and Authorship in the Babylonian Talmud. *Journal of Jewish Studies* 45: 28–51.
Stone, Suzanne. 1991. Sinaitic and Noahide Law: Legal Pluralism in Jewish Law. *Cardozo Law Review* 12: 1157–214.

Ta-Shma, Israel M. 1998. The Law Is in Accord with the Later Authority—Hilkhata Kebatrai: Historical Observations on a Legal Rule. In *Authority, Process, and Method: Studies in Jewish Law 101*, eds. Hanina Ben-Menahem and Neil S. Hecht, 101–28. Amsterdam: Hardwood Academic Publishers.

———. 2006. *Creativity and Tradition: Studies in Medieval Rabbinic Scholarship, Literature and Thought*. Cambridge, MA, and London: Harvard University Press.

———. 2007. Moses ben Jacob of Coucy. In *Encyclopedia Judaica*, 2nd ed., vol. 14, 549–50. Detroit: Macmillan Reference USA.

Tal, Shlomo. 2007a. Meir ben Isaac Katzenellenbogen. In *Encyclopedia Judaica*, 2nd ed., vol. 12, 19–20. Detroit: MacMillan Reference USA.

———. 2007b. Jacob ben Joseph Pollack. In *Encyclopedia Judaica*, 2nd ed., vol. 16, 355. Detroit: MacMillan Reference USA.

Tamari, Meir. 1996. *Al Chet: Sins in the Marketplace*. Northvale, NJ: Jason Aronson.

———. 1998. *With All Your Possessions: Jewish Ethics and Economic Life*. Northvale, NJ: Jason Aronson.

Teller, Adam. 2008. Councils. In *The YIVO Encyclopedia of Jews in Eastern Europe*, ed. Gershon David Hundert, vol. 1, 352–57. New Haven and London: Yale University Press.

———. 2004. Rabbis Without a Function? The Polish Rabbinate and the Council of Four Lands in the Sixteenth to Eighteenth Centuries. In *Jewish Religious Leadership*, ed. Jack Wertheimer, vol. 1, 371–400. New York: Jewish Theological Seminary of America.

Temkin, Sefton D. 2007. Heidenheim, Wolf. In *Encyclopedia Judaica*, 2nd ed., vol. 8. 763. Detroit: Macmillan Reference USA.

Teter, Magda and Edward Fram. 2006. Apostasy, Fraud and the Beginnings of Hebrew Printing in Cracow. *AJS Review* 30: 31–66.

Timm, Erika. 1993. Blitz and Witzenhausen. In *Studies in Jewish Culture in Honour of Chone Shmeruck*, eds. Israel Bartal et al., 39–66. Jerusalem: Zaman Shazar Center for Jewish History.

Tirosh-Samuelson, Hava. 2003. Philosophy and Kabbalah: 1200–1600. In *The Cambridge Companion to Medieval Jewish Philosophy*, eds. Daniel H. Frank and Oliver Leaman, 218–57. Cambridge, UK, and New York: Cambridge University Press.

Tishby, Isaiah. 1967–68. Ha-Polmus Al Sefer Ha-Zohar Be-Mea Ha-Shesh-Esrey Be-Italia [The Controversy over the Book of the Zohar in the Sixteenth Century in Italy]. *Perakim* 1: 131–82.

Turniansky, Chava and Erika Timm. 2003. *Yiddish in Italia: Yiddish Manuscripts and Printed Books from the 15th to the 17th Century*. Milan: Associazione Italiana Amici Dell'Universita di Gerusalemme.

Twersky, Isadore. 1983. Talmudists, Philosophers, Kabbalists: The Quest for Spirituality in the Sixteenth Century. In *Jewish Thought in the Sixteenth Century*, ed. Bernard Dov Cooperman, 431–59. Cambridge, MA, and London: Harvard University Press.

Urbach, Ephraim A. 1988. *Me'Olam Shel Ḥakhamim* [The World of the Sages]. Jerusalem: Magnes Press, Hebrew University.

Vinograd, Yeshayahu. 1995. *Otzer Ha-Sefer Ha-Ivri* [Thesaurus of the Hebrew Book], 2 volumes. Jerusalem: Institute for Computerized Bibliography.

Visi, Tamás. 2012. A Moravian Defense of Orthodoxy: Mordecai Benet and the Rabbinic Literary System. *Jewish Culture and History* 13: 173–93.

Warhaftig, Itamar. 1984–85. D'mei Shimush Be-Nekhes Gazul [Compensation for Use of Stolen Property]. *Teḥumin* 6: 235–51.

Warhaftig, Shillem. 1990. *Dinei Misḥar Be-Mishpat Ha-Ivri* [Jewish Commercial Law]. Jerusalem: Zur-Ot Press.

———. 2007. Nathanson, Joseph Saul. In *Encyclopaedia Judaica*, 2nd ed., vol. 15, 18–19. Detroit: Macmillan Reference USA.

Wasserman, Henry. 2007. Schmid, Anton von. In *Encyclopedia Judaica*, 2nd ed., vol. 18. 145. Detroit: Macmillan Reference.

Wasserteil, Yair. 2011. Copying Software and Cassettes. Yeshiva.org.il, The Portal to the World of Torah. The Beit El Yeshiva Center, Beit El. August 7, 2011. http://www.yeshiva.org.il/midrash/shiur.asp?id=16589.

Waxman, Chaim L. 1992. Towards a Sociology of Pesak. In *Rabbinic Authority and Personal Autonomy*, ed. Moshe Z. Sokol, 217–38. Northvale, NJ: Jason Aronson.

Webber, George J. 1928. The Principles of the Jewish Law of Property. *Journal of Comparative Legislation and International Law* 10: 82–93.

Weinryrb, Bernard D. 1973. *The Jews of Poland: A Social and Economic History of the Jewish Community in Poland from 1100–1800*. Philadelphia: Jewish Publication Society of America.

Weisfish, Naḥum Menashe. 2002. *Mishnat Zkhuyot Ha-Yotzer; Im Tshuvot Ve-Psakim Me-Gedolei Ha-Dor* [The Doctrine of Copyright; with Responsa and Rulings of the Leading Rabbis of Our Generation]. Jerusalem: Hekhal Naḥum.

Wierzbieniec, Wacław et al. 2000. The Processes of Jewish Emancipation and Assimilation in the Multiethnic City of Lviv During the Nineteenth and Twentieth Centuries. In *Lviv: A City in the Crosscurrents of Culture*, ed. John Czaplicka, 223–50. Cambridge, MA: Harvard Ukranian Research Institute.

Weiss, Asher. 2009. *Ha-Tokef Ha-Hilakhti Shel Patent Rashum* [The Legal Force of a Registered Patent in Jewish Law]. In *Me-Saviv Le-Shulkhan*, Feb. 19, 2009, at 1–3.

Westreich, Elimelech. 2002. *T'morot Be-Maamad Ha-Isha Be-Mishpat Ha-Ivry; Masa Ben Mesorot* [Transitions in the Legal Status of the Wife in Jewish Law; A Journey among Traditions]. Jerusalem: Hebrew University Magnes Press.

———. 2010. Elements of Negotiability in Jewish Law in Medieval Christian Spain. *Theoretical Inquiries in Law* 11: 411–40.

Wischnitzer, Mark. 1954. Origins of the Jewish Artisan Class in Bohemia and Moravia, 1500–1648. *Jewish Social Studies* 16: 335-350.

———. 1965. *A History of Jewish Crafts and Guilds*. New York: Jonathan David Company.

Wistrich, Robert S. 1989. *The Jews of Vienna in the Age of Franz Joseph*. New York: Oxford University Press.

Zimmels, H. J. 1958. *Ashkenazim and Sephardim; Their Relations, Differences, and Problems as Reflected in the Rabbinical Responsa*. London: Oxford University Press.

Ziv, Asher. 1957. *Ha-Rema; Rabbi Moshe Isserles*. Jerusalem: Mosad Rav Kook.

———. 1968. Maharam Me-Padua. *Hadarom* 28: 160–95.

Zohar, Zvi. 2012. Teleological Decision Making in Halakha: Empirical Examples and General Principles. In *"Wisdom and Understanding"; Studies in Jewish Law in Honour of Bernard S. Jackson*, eds. Leib Moscoitz and Joseph Rivlin, 331–62. Liverpool: Deborah Charles Publications.

SECONDARY SOURCES: PAPAL AND SECULAR

Armstrong, Elizabeth. 1990. *Before Copyright: The French Book-Privilege System 1498–1526*. Cambridge, UK: Cambridge University Press.

Bachleitner, Nobert. 1997. The Politics of the Book Trade in Nineteenth-Century Austria. *Austrian History Yearbook* 28: 95–111.

Baldwin, John W. 1959. *The Medieval Theories of Just Price*. Philadelphia: American Philosophical Society.

Banham, Rob. 2007. Industrialization of the Book 1800–1970. In *A Companion to the History of the Book*, eds. Simon Eliot and Jonathan Rose, 273–89. Oxford, UK: Blackwell Publishing Ltd.

Benton, Lauren. 2002. *Law and Colonial Cultures: Legal Regimes in World History 1400–1900*. Cambridge, UK: Cambridge University Press.

Biagoli, Mario. 2006. From Prints to Patents: Living on Instruments in Early Modern Europe. *History of Science* 44: 139–86.
Birn, Raymond. 1971. The Profits of Ideas; Privileges en librarie in Eighteenth-Century France. *Eighteenth-Century Studies* 4: 131.
Birnhack, Michael. 2001. The Idea of Progress in Copyright Law. *Buffalo Intellectual Property Law Journal* 1: 3–58.
Borghi, Maurizio. 2003. *Writing Practices in the Privilege and Intellectual Property Systems.* Available at: http://papers.ssrn.com/sol3/papers.cfm?abstract_id=1031639.
———. 2010. A Venetian Experiment on Perpetual Copyright. In *Privilege and Property; Essays on the History of Copyright*, eds. Ronan Deazley et al., 137–55. Cambridge, UK: OpenBook Publishers.
Bouckaert, Boudewijin. 1990. What Is Property? *Harvard Journal of Law & Public Policy* 13: 775–816.
Bowker, Richard Rogers. 1912. *Copyright: Its History and Its Law.* Boston and New York: Houghton Mifflin Company.
Boyle, James. 2008. *The Public Domain: Enclosing the Commons of the Mind.* New Haven: Yale University Press.
Bracha, Oren. 2008. "Commentary on John Usher's Printing Privilege" (1672). *Primary Sources on Copyright (1450–1900)*, eds. L. Bently and M. Kretschmer. http://copy.law.cam.ac.uk/cam/index.php.
———. 2010. The Adventures of the Statute of Anne in the Land of Unlimited Possibilities: The Life of a Legal Transplant. *Berkeley Technology Law Journal* 25: 1427–74.
Brown, Horatio F. 1891. *The Venetian Printing Press.* New York: G.P. Putnam's Sons.
Calisse, Carlo. 1928. *A History of Italian Law*, vol. 8, trans. L. B. Register. Boston: Little, Brown.
Chartier, Roger. 1994. *The Order of Books*, trans. Lydia G. Cochrane. Stanford: Stanford University Press.
Cresswell, Julia. 2009. *The Insect that Stole Butter? Oxford Dictionary of Word Origins* (2nd ed.). Oxford, UK, and New York: Oxford University Press.
Dagan, Hanoch. 1997. *Unjust Enrichment: A Study of Private Law and Public Values.* Cambridge, UK, and New York: Cambridge University Press.
———. 2006. Property and the Public Domain. *Yale Journal of Law and the Humanities* 18: 84–93.
Deazley, Ronan. 2004. *On the Origin of the Right to Copy; Charting the Movement of Copyright Law in Eighteenth-Century Britain (1695–1775).* Portland, OR: Hart Publishing.
———. 2008. "Commentary on the Stationers' Royal Charter" (1557). *Primary Sources on Copyright (1450–1900)*, eds. L. Bently and M. Kretschmer. http://copy.law.cam.ac.uk/cam/index.php.
Dondi, Cristina. 2010. The European Printing Revolution. In *The Oxford Companion to the Book*, eds. Michael F. Suarez and H. R. Woudhuysen, vol. 1, 53–61. Oxford, UK, and New York: Oxford University Press.
Edwards, Scott. 2012. *Repertory Migration in the Czech Crown Lands, 1570–1630.* Unpublished doctoral dissertation, University of California at Berkeley.
Eisenstein, Elizabeth L. 1979. *The Printing Press as an Agent of Change.* Cambridge, UK, and New York: Cambridge University Press.
———. 1983. *The Printing Revolution in Early Modern Europe.* Cambridge, UK, and New York: Cambridge University Press.
Elson, Louis Charles. 1912. Schlick (Arnolt). In *University Musical Encyclopedia* 10: 593. New York: The University Society Publishers.
Epstein, Richard. 2010. What Is So Special About Intangible Property? The Case for Intelligent Carryovers. *John M. Olin Law & Economics Working Paper No. 524.* Available at http://ssrn.com/abstract=1659999.

Feather, John. 1980. The Book Trade in Politics: The Making of the Copyright Act of 1710. *Publishing History* 8: 19.

———. 1984. The Commerce of Letters: The Study of the Eighteenth-Century Book Trade. *Eighteenth-Century Studies* 17: 405.

———. 2006. *A History of British Publishing*, 2nd ed. Oxon, Canada, and New York: Routledge.

Febvre, Lucien and Henri-Jean Martin. 1984. *The Coming of the Book; The Impact of Printing 1450–1800*, trans. David Gerard. London: Verso.

Flood, John L. 2010. The History of the Book in Germany. In *The Oxford Companion to the Book*, eds. Michael F. Suarez and H. R. Woudhuysen, vol. 1, 223–36. Oxford, UK, and New York: Oxford University Press.

Gehl, Paul F. 1995. The 1615 Statutes of the Sienese Guild of Stationers and Booksellers: Provincial Publishing in Early Modern Tuscany. *I Tatti Studies in Italian Renaissance*. 6: 215–53.

Ginsburg, Jane C. 1990. A Tale of Two Copyrights: Literary Property in Revolutionary France and America. *Tulsa Law Review* 64: 991–1024.

———. 2013. Proto-Property in Literary and Artistic Works: Sixteenth-Century Papal Printing Privileges. *Columbia Journal of Law and the Arts* 36: 345–78.

Gómez-Arostegui, H. Tomás. 2008. What History Teaches Us About Copyright Injunctions and the Inadequate-Remedy-at-Law Requirement. *Southern California Law Review* 81: 1197–280.

Gompel, Stef Van. 2010. Copyright Formalities and the Reasons for their Decline in Nineteenth Century Europe. In *Privilege and Property: Essays on the History of Copyright*, eds. Ronan Deazley et al., 157–206. Cambridge, UK: OpenBook Publishers.

Gordley, James. 2006. *Foundations of Private Law; Property, Tort, Contract, Unjust Enrichment*. Oxford, UK, and New York: Oxford University Press.

Gordon, Wendy J. 2009. Trespass-Copyright Parallels and the Harm-Benefit Distinction. *Harvard Law Review Forum* 122: 62–79.

Grafton, Anthony. 2011. *The Culture of Correction in Renaissance Europe*. London: The British Library.

Grendler, Paul F. 1977. *The Roman Inquisition and the Venetian Press, 1540–1605*. Princeton, NJ: Princeton University Press.

Grotius, H. 1964. *De Jure Belli Ac Pacis*, trans. Francis Willey Kelsey. New York: Oceana.

Hesse, Carla. 1990. Enlightenment Epistemology and the Laws of Authorship in Revolutionary France, 1777–1793. *Representations* 30: 109–37.

Hirsch, Rudolf. 1967. *Printing, Selling and Reading 1450–1550*. Wiesbaden: Otto Harrassowitz.

Hofri-Winogradow, Adam S. 2010. A Plurality of Discontent: Legal Pluralism, Religious Adjudication and the State. *Journal of Law and Religion* 26: 57–89.

Hoftijzer, Paul G. 1997. "A Sickle unto thy Neighbour's Corn": Book Piracy in the Dutch Republic. *Quaerendo* 27: 3–18.

———. 2010. The History of the Book in the Low Countries. In *The Oxford Companion to the Book*, eds. Michael F. Suarez and H. R. Woudhuysen, vol. 1, 212–22. Oxford, UK, and New York: Oxford University Press.

Holborn, Hajo. 1982. *A History of Modern Germany: The Reformation*. Princeton: Princeton University Press.

Horodowich, Elizabeth. 2008. *Language and Statecraft in Early Modern Venice*. Cambridge, UK: Cambridge University Press.

Hunt, Arnold. 1997. Book Trade Patents, 1603–1640. In *The Book Trade and Its Customers 1450–1900*, eds. Arnold Hunt et al., 27–54. Kent, UK: St. Paul's Bibliographies.

Johns, Adrian. 1998. *The Nature of the Book; Print and Knowledge in the Making*. Chicago: University of Chicago Press.

———. 2009. *Piracy: The Intellectual Property Wars from Gutenberg to Gates*. Chicago: University of Chicago Press.

Kant, Immanuel. 1887. *The Philosophy of Law: An Exposition of the Fundamentals of Jurisprudence as the Science of Right*, trans. W. Hastie. Edinburgh: T. & T. Clark.

———. 1913. Von der Unrechtmassigkeit des Buchernachdruckes. In *Immanuel Kants Werke*, ed. Ernst Cassirer. Berlin: B. Cassirer.

Kawohl, Friedemann. 2008a. Commentary on the Austrian Statutes on Censorship and Printing (1781). *Primary Sources on Copyright (1450–1900)*, eds. L. Bently and M. Kretschmer. http://copy.law.cam.ac.uk/cam/index.php.

———. 2008b. Commentary on German Federal Copyright Directives (1837–1869). *Primary Sources on Copyright (1450–1900)*, eds. L. Bently and M. Kretschmer. http://copy.law.cam.ac.uk/cam/index.php.

———. 2008c. Commentary on Imperial Privileges for Arnolt Schlick (1511). *Primary Sources on Copyright (1450–1900)*, eds. L. Bently and M. Kretschmer. http://copy.law.cam.ac.uk/cam/index.php.

———. 2008d. Commentary on Imperial Privileges for Conrad Celtis (1501–02). *Primary Sources on Copyright (1450–1900)*, eds. L. Bently and M. Kretschmer. http://copy.law.cam.ac.uk/cam/index.php.

———. 2008e. Commentary on Imperial Privilege for Eucharius Rösslin (1513). *Primary Sources on Copyright (1450–1900)*, eds. L. Bently and M. Kretschmer. http://copy.law.cam.ac.uk/cam/index.php.

———. 2008f. Commentary on German Federal Copyright Directives (1837–1869). *Primary Sources on Copyright (1450–1900)*, eds. L. Bently and M. Kretschmer. http://copy.law.cam.ac.uk/cam/index.php.

———. 2008g. Commentary on German Federal Copyright Directives (1837–1869). *Primary Sources on Copyright (1450–1900)*, eds. L. Bently and M. Kretschmer. http://copy.law.cam.ac.uk/cam/index.php.

———. 2008h. Commentary on German Printers' and Booksellers' Ordinances and Statutes. *Primary Sources on Copyright (1450–1900)*, eds. L. Bently and M. Kretschmer. http://copy.law.cam.ac.uk/cam/index.php.

———. 2008i. Commentary on Leopold Josef Neustetel, *The Reprinting of Books* (Heidelberg, 1824). *Primary Sources on Copyright (1450–1900)*, eds. L. Bently and M. Kretschmer. http://copy.law.cam.ac.uk/cam/index.php.

———. 2008j. Commentary on Schott v. Egenolph, Strasbourg (1533). *Primary Sources on Copyright (1450–1900)*, eds. L. Bently and M. Kretschmer. http://copy.law.cam.ac.uk/cam/index.php.

———. 2008k. Commentary on the Basel Printers' Statute (1531). *Primary Sources on Copyright (1450–1900)*, eds. L. Bently and M. Kretschmer. http://copy.law.cam.ac.uk/cam/index.php.

———. 2008l. Commentary on the Privilege Granted by the Bishop of Wurzburg. *Primary Sources on Copyright (1450–1900)*, eds. L. Bently and M. Kretschmer. http://copy.law.cam.ac.uk/cam/index.php.

———. 2008m. Commentary on Schott v. Egenolph (1533). *Primary Sources on Copyright (1450–1900)*, eds. L. Bently and M. Kretschmer. http://copy.law.cam.ac.uk/cam/index.php.

———. 2008n. Commentary on the Reprinting Provisions in the Prussian Statute Book (1794). *Primary Sources on Copyright (1450–1900)* eds. L. Bently and M. Kretschmer. http://copy.law.cam.ac.uk/cam/index.php.

———. 2008o. Commentary on Copyright Treaties between Prussia and Several German States (1827). *Primary Sources on Copyright (1450–1900)*, eds. L. Bently and M. Kretschmer. http://copy.law.cam.ac.uk/cam/index.php.

Kellenbenz, Hermann. 1977. The Organization of Industrial Production. In *The Cambridge Economic History of Europe, Volume V—The Economic Organization of Modern Europe*, eds. E.E. Rich and C.H. Wilson, 462–548. Cambridge UK: Cambridge University Press.

Keyl, Stephen Mark. 1989. *Arnolt Schlick and Instrumental Music Circa 1500*. Durham: Duke University Press.

Khoury, Amir H. 2003. Ancient and Islamic Sources of Intellectual Property Protection in the Middle East: A Focus on Trademark. *IDEA Journal* 43: 151–206.

Kilgour, Frederick G. 1998. *The Evolution of the Book*. New York: Oxford University Press.

Kostylo, Joanna. 2008a. Commentary on Aldus Manutius's Warning against the Printers of Lyon (1503). *Primary Sources on Copyright (1450–1900)*, eds. L. Bently and M. Kretschmer. http://copy.law.cam.ac.uk/cam/index.php.

———. 2008b. Commentary on the Decree of the Council of Ten Establishing the Guild of Printers and Booksellers. *Primary Sources on Copyright (1450–1900)*, eds. L. Bently and M. Kretschmer. http://copy.law.cam.ac.uk/cam/index.php.

———. 2008c. Commentary on Venetian Decree on Author-Printer Relations (1545). *Primary Sources on Copyright (1450–1900)*, eds. L. Bently and M. Kretschmer. http://copy.law.cam.ac.uk/cam/index.php.

———. 2008d. Commentary on the Venetian Senate's Decree on Press Affairs (1517). *Primary Sources on Copyright (1450–1900)*, eds. L. Bently and M. Kretschmer. http://copy.law.cam.ac.uk/cam/index.php.

———. 2008e. Commentary on Marco Antonio Sabellico's Printing Privilege (1486). *Primary Sources on Copyright (1450–1900)*, eds. L. Bently and M. Kretschmer. http://copy.law.cam.ac.uk/cam/index.php.

———. 2008f. Commentary on the Venetian Senate's Decree on Press Affairs (1517). *Primary Sources on Copyright (1450–1900)*, eds. L. Bently and M. Kretschmer. http://copy.law.cam.ac.uk/cam/index.php.

———. 2010. From Gunpowder to Print: The Common Origins of Copyright and Patent. In *Privilege and Property; Essays on the History of Copyright*, eds. Ronan Deazley et al. Cambridge, UK: OpenBook Publishers.

Krek, Miroslav. 1979. The Enigma of the First Arabic Printed Book from Movable Type. *Journal of Near Eastern Studies* 38: 203–12.

Landau, David and Peter Parshall. 1996. *The Renaissance Print: 1470–1550*. New Haven: Yale University Press.

Landau, Norma. 1999. Indictment for Fun and Profit: A Prosecutor's Reward at Eighteenth-Century Quarter Sessions. *Law and History Review* 17: 507–36.

Langbein, John H. 1974. *Prosecuting Crime in the Renaissance*. Cambridge, MA: Harvard University Press.

Langer, Maximo. 2004. From Legal Transplants to Legal Translations: The Globalization of Plea Bargaining and the Americanization Thesis in Criminal Procedure. *Harvard International Law Journal* 45: 1–64.

Lemley, Mark A. 2005. Property, Intellectual Property, and Free Riding. *Texas Law Review* 83:1031–75.

Leuschner, Eckhard. 1998. The Papal Printing Privilege. *Print Quarterly* 15: 359.

Loewenstein, Joseph. 2002. *The Author's Due: Printing and the Prehistory of Copyright*. Chicago: The University of Chicago Press.

Lowry, Martin. 1979. *The World of Aldus Manutius: Business and Scholarship in Renaissance Venice*. Ithaca: Cornell University Press.

Maclean, Ian. 2012. *Scholarship, Commerce, Religion: The Learned Book in the Age of Confessions 1560–1630*. Cambridge, MA: Harvard University Press.

McCormack, Alan. 1997. *The Term "Privilege": A Textual Study of Its Meaning and Usage in the 1983 Code of Canon Law*. Rome: Gregorian University Press.

McKitterick, David. 2003. *Print, Manuscript and the Search for Order, 1450–1830*. Cambridge, UK, and New York: Cambridge University Press.

Mellot, Jean-Dominique. 2007. Counterfeit Printing as an Agent of Diffusion and Change: The French Book-Privilege System and Its Contradictions (1498–1790). In *Agent of Change: Print Culture Studies after Elizabeth L. Eisenstein*, eds. Sabrina Alcorn Baron, Eric N. Lindquist, and Eleanor F. Shevlin, 42–66. Amherst: University of Massachusetts Press.

Mosley, James. 2010. Technologies of Print. In *The Oxford Companion to the Book*, eds. Michael F. Suarez and H. R. Woudhuysen, vol. 1, 89–104. Oxford, UK, and New York: Oxford University Press.

Netanel, Neil Weinstock. 1994. Alienability Restrictions and the Enhancement of Author Autonomy in United States and Continental Copyright Law. *Cardozo Arts & Entertainment Law Journal* 12: 1–78.

———. 2007b. Why Has Copyright Expanded? Analysis and Critique. In *New Directions in Copyright Law*, ed. Fiona Macmillan, vol. 6, 1–34. Cheltenham, UK: Edward Elgar.

———. 2008. *Copyright's Paradox*. New York: Oxford University Press.

Newcity, Michael A. 1978. *Copyright Law in the Soviet Union*. New York: Praeger Publishers.

Nimmer, David. 2000. A Riff on Fair Use in the Digital Millennium Copyright Act. *University of Pennsylvania Law Review* 148: 673–742.

———. 2003. *Copyright: Sacred Text, Technology, and the DMCA*. The Hague and New York: Kluwer Law International.

Orenstein, Nadine. 1995. Prints and the Politics of the Publisher: The Case of Hendrick Hondius. *Simiolus: Netherlands Quarterly for the History of Art* 23: 240–50.

Pennington, Kenneth. 2000. The Ius Commune, Suretyship, and Magna Carta. *Rivista Internazionale di Diritto Comune*. 11: 255–74.

Pettegree, Andrew. 2010. *The Book in the Renaissance*. New Haven, CT: Yale University Press.

Pfister, Laurent. 2005. Is Literary Property (a Form of) Property? Controversies on the Nature of Author's Rights in the Nineteenth Century. *Revue Internationale du Droit D'Auteur* 205: 116–209.

———. 2010. Author and Work in the French Print Privileges System: Some Milestones. In *Privilege and Property; Essays on the History of Copyright*, eds. Ronan Deazley et al., 115–36. Cambridge, UK: OpenBook Publishers.

Piotraut, Jean-Luc. 2006. An Authors' Rights-Based Copyright Law: The Fairness and Morality of French and American Law Compared. *Cardozo Arts & Entertainment Law Journal* 24: 549–615.

Pullan, Brian. 1964. Wage-Earners and the Venetian Economy, 1530–1630. *Economic History Review* 16: 407–26.

Putnam, George Haven. 1897. *Books and Their Makers During the Middle Ages*. New York: G.P. Putnam's Sons.

Rasterhoff, Claartje 2014. The Spatial Side of Innovation: the Local Organization of Cultural Production in the Dutch Republic, 1580-1800. In *Innovation and Creativity in Late Medieval and Early Modern European Cities*, eds. Karel Davids and Bert De Munck, 161-88. Surrey: Ashgate Publishing.

Richardson, Brian. 1994. *Print Culture in Renaissance Italy: The Editor and the Vernacular Text 1470–1600*. Cambridge, UK, and New York: Cambridge University Press.

———. 1999. *Printing, Writers, and Readers in Renaissance Italy*. Cambridge, UK, and New York: Cambridge University Press.

Rose, Mark. 1993. *Authors and Owners; the Invention of Copyright*. Cambridge, MA: Harvard University Press.

———. 2003. Nine-Tenths of the Law: The English Copyright Debates and the Rhetoric of the Public Domain. *Law and Contemporary Problems* 66: 75–87.

Sawyer, Jeffrey K. 1988. Judicial Corruption and Legal Reform in Early Seventeenth-Century France. *Law and History Review* 6: 95–117.

Schorr, David B. 2008. How Blackstone Became a Blackstonian. *Theoretical Inquiries in Law* 10: 103–26.

Shaw, James E. 2006. *The Justice of Venice; Authorities and Liberties in the Urban Economy 1550–1700*. Oxford, UK, and New York: Oxford University Press.

Shaw, William Arthur. 1896. *The History of Currency 1252–1894*. New York: G.P. Putnam's Sons.

Sherman, Brad and Lionel Bently. 1999. *The Making of Modern Intellectual Property Law: The British Experience, 1760–1911*. Cambridge, UK, and New York: Cambridge University Press.

Sichelman, Ted and Sean O'Connor. 2012. Patents as Promoters of Competition: The Guild Origins of Patent Law in the Venetian Republic. *San Diego University Law Review* 49: 1267–82.

Spooner, Frank C. 1972. *The International Economy and Monetary Movements in France, 1493–1725*. Cambridge, MA: Harvard University Press.

Taylor, Charles. 1989. *Sources of the Self: The Making of the Modern Identity*. Cambridge, MA: Harvard University Press.

Treiger-Bar-Am, Kim. 2008. Kant on Copyright: Rights of Transformative Authorship. *Cardozo Arts & Entertainment Law Journal* 25: 1059–103.

Urban, Sylvanus. 1819. *On the Crown Privilege of Printing*. London: John Nichols and Son.

Vera, Eugenia Roldan. 2010. The History of the Book in Latin America. In *The Oxford Companion to the Book*, eds. Michael F. Suarez and H. R. Woudhuysen, vol. 1, 408–17. Oxford, UK, and New York: Oxford University Press.

VerSteeg, Russ. 2000. The Roman Roots of Copyright. *Maryland Law Review* 59: 522–52.

Vliet, Rieje van. 2007. Print and Public in Europe 1600–1800. In *A Companion to the History of the Book*, eds. Simon Eliot and Jonathan Rose, 247–58. Oxford, UK: Blackwell Publishing Ltd.

Waldron, Jeremy. 2005. Foreign Law and the Modern Ius Gentium. *Harvard Law Review* 119: 129–47.

Weedon, Alexis. 2010. The Economics of Print. In *The Oxford Companion to the Book*, eds. Michael F. Suarez and H. R. Woudhuysen, vol. 1, 105–14. Oxford, UK, and New York: Oxford University Press.

Weidhass, Peter. 2007. *A History of the Frankfurt Book Fair*, trans. C. M. Gossage and W. A. Wright. Toronto: Dundurn Press.

Whittman, Reinhard. 2004. *Highwaymen or Heroes of the Enlightenment? Viennese and South German Pirates and the German Market*. Unpublished paper presented at Conference on the History of Books and Intellectual History, Center for the Study of Books and Media, Princeton University, Dec. 2004.

Witcombe, Christopher L.C.E. 2004. *Copyright in the Renaissance: Prints and the Privilegio in Sixteenth-Century Venice and Rome*. Leiden and Boston: Brill.

Wolfrum, Rudiger and Rainer Grote, eds. 2007. The Federal Republic of Germany: Constitution. In *Constitutions of Countries of the World*. New York: Oceana.

Woodbine, George E. 1924. The Origins of the Action of Trespass. *Yale Law Journal* 33:799–816.

Zanden, Jan L. Van. 1999. Wages and the Standard of Living in Europe, 1500–1800. *European Review of Economic History* 3: 175–97.

GLOSSARY AND BIOGRAPHIES

Some Terms of Relevance to the Jewish Law of Copyright

Aḥaronim. Literally "the last ones," this term refers to the rabbinic sages of the modern era, whose interpretations became authoritative starting with the advent of printed Jewish texts and continuing to the present. After the era of the **Rishonim**, the publication of the **Shulḥan Arukh** in 1565 heralded the change from those "first ones" to these "last ones."

Arenda. Derived from the Polish for "leasehold," it is a concession that a person receives from the government or a nobleman for the sale of particular goods, typically a monopoly on distilling or estate management. A person who holds this interest is called an **arendator**.

Ashkenazic and Sephardic. The Bible refers to two lands called *Ashkenaz* and *Sepharad*. By the late medieval period, those monikers were applied to refer respectively to Germany and Spain. By the early modern period, world Jewry became divided between those two primary poles, with those who traced their roots to Germany, Poland, and Central Europe being labeled **Ashkenazim** and those who traced their roots to the Iberian peninsula and neighboring lands (such as southern France) being labeled **Sephardim**. The two strains follow different customs, rituals, and interpretations of certain halakhic doctrines.

Babylonian Talmud (abbreviated, BT, and sometimes referred to simply as the Talmud). A multi-volume compilation of the debates, teachings, and stories of the rabbinic authorities from the third to the fifth centuries. The Babylonian Talmud was redacted in about the year 500. It consists of the **Mishnah**, a collection of rabbinic teachings redacted at the beginning of the third century, and the Gemara, which consists of rabbinic elaborations and commentary on the **Mishnah**. The Babylonian Talmud is distinct from the Jerusalem (or "Palestinian") Talmud, which is a different compilation of rabbinic teachings, redacted about two centuries earlier. Between the two, the Babylonian Talmud presents the normative rabbinic teachings that are reflected in authoritative codes of Jewish law such as the **Mishneh Torah** and **Shulḥan Arukḥ**.

Ban. See **Ḥerem**.

Beit Din. A rabbinic court that adjudicates disputes between litigants pursuant to **halakha** and that also might handle questions of status under Jewish law (e.g., conversion).

Council of Four Lands. The central governing body of Jewry within Poland, starting in 1580. It initially exerted far-reaching legislative and judicial authority over the Jews of Poland, Lithuania, and Galicia, but later met only irregularly before finally being abolished by the Polish Sejm in 1764.

Decisor. See **Posek**.

De-oraita. Aramaic for "of the Torah," it refers to a foundational rule that rabbinic literature understands to be mandated by the Pentateuch or otherwise deemed to have been given to Moses at Mount Sinai. In contrast, a **de-rabbanan** rule, Aramaic for "of the sages," refers to a rule that is rabbinically mandated, often by way of a specific rabbinic regulation or enactment. Given that **de-oraita** rules include rabbinic interpretations and applications of foundational rules to new situations, rabbinic decisors sometimes disagree on whether a given rule or precept is actually **de-oraita** or **de-rabbanan**.

Dina de-malkhuta dina. A principle of **halakha** that looks outward to adopt local law as governing within the system of Jewish law. Translated as "the law of the sovereign is the law," it means that, within prescribed limits, a **posek** or **Beit Din** may derive governing standards from those that apply under the secular law of the nation in which the disputants are located. That deference to the law of the sovereign state arises principally in commercial matters.

Excommunication. See **Ḥerem**.

Gaon (plural, **Geonim**). The formal title of the heads of the leading rabbinic academies in Babylonia. The geonim were recognized by Jews the world over as the supreme rabbinic authority from the end of the sixth century to the middle of the eleventh century. Since the close of their era, neither Jewish law nor rabbinic tradition has recognized any supreme rabbinic authority, but the term "gaon" is still used as an honorific for a great rabbinic authority.

Gezel (with **gozel** being one who commits **gezel**). Most narrowly refers to "robbery." But used commonly to encompas a broader set of wrongs, including fraud, withholding payment from laborers, and other monetary and commercial matters. Applied to refer to wrongful competition in the sense of misappropriating a business opportunity or depriving another of his means of livelihood in a manner that violates the fundamental halakhic precept forbidding such **hasagat gvul**.

Halakha. Derived from the root for "walking" and thus connoting the *proper path*, it refers to all aspects of normative Jewish law, whether derived from the Torah or rabbinic in nature. It extends to both ritual and ethical behavior, encompassing both civil and criminal strictures.

Ḥaredi (plural, **Ḥaredim**). Literally referring to a person who "trembles" before God, it refers to what is frequently called "ultra-Orthodox," characterized by a rejection of secular culture and even of modernity itself. A converse phenomenon is **Modern Orthodoxy**, describing adherents who, like **ḥaredim**, view themselves as religiously committed and authentic, but who simultaneously find value in post-Enlightenment knowledge.

Hasagat gvul. "Trespass; Wrongful competition." Derived from the Torah's prohibition of moving a neighbor's landmarks (Deut. 19:14), it has been extended beyond its core meaning of a permanent trespass on land to apply generally to every wrongful encroachment on another's property. In the wrongful competition sense, it refers to wrongfully encroaching on another's business or means of earning a livelihood.

Ḥasidim and Mitnagdim. Starting in the eighteenth century, a movement developed in response to what its adherents viewed as the remote elitism of mainstream rabbinic culture. Called **Ḥasidism** (from a root meaning "pious"), it embraced mysticism and ecstatic practices that would be accessible to ordinary, uneducated Jews. The movement attracted many **Ḥasidim**, followers in Poland, throughout eastern Europe, and elsewhere. It also sparked a countermovement. Its self-styled opponents were the **Mitnagdim** (meaning "those in opposition"). In rough measure, **Mitnagdism** was centered in Lithuania's highly intellectual approach to Talmud study.

Haskalah. The Enlightenment movement and ideology that began within Jewish society in the 1770s. Those Jews who adopted its philosophy to govern their own lives were called **maskilim** (singular, **maskil**; adjective **maskilic**).

Haskama (plural, Haskamot). A rabbinic approbation consisting of a statement of imprimatur and praise for a particular book (and frequently for its pious author as well). **Haskamot** often included a reprinting ban, backed by the threat of **ḥerem** as well. Sometimes the word "haskama" is used to connote both the approbation and the ban, and sometimes just the approbation.

Ḥerem (plural, Ḥaramim and also Ḥaramot). A decree of ban or excommunication, typically the final stage of isolating a recalcitrant individual, consisting of near absolute isolation from social interaction and community religious ritual for an indefinite period of time. It follows the lesser, temporary punishments of **niddui** (ostracism) and **shamta** (anathema). The word **naḥash** (snake) serves as an acronym combining all three of those stages.

Ḥidushei Torah. Translated into English as "Torah novellae," this refers to new exegeses of foundational Jewish texts.

Ḥilul ha-Shem. The "desecration of God's name," meaning behavior that, even if not illegal, brings disgrace upon the entire Jewish community, and concomitantly, upon God.

Ḥoshen Mishpat. One of the four sections of the **Shulḥan Arukh**. It sets out the entire body of Jewish civil law insofar as applicable in the Diaspora.

The jealousy of scholars increases wisdom. An axiom derived from a passage in the Talmud (BT Baba Batra 21b), **kinat sofrim tarbeh ḥokhmah**, interpreted to mean that, in contrast to those in ordinary professions who might give up in the face of superior competition, competition among scholars and teachers of Jewish law moves them to intensify their study and teaching of **Torah**.

Kabbalah. Esoteric, theosophical teachings of uncertain origin that, following the advent of print, came to be the dominant form of Jewish mystical theology and, indeed, the dominant theology of most early modern Jewish communities.

Kinyan. Literally the means by which property is acquired by a symbolic act. But also used to refer to property itself.

Ktav dat. An edict or pronouncement of Jewish law.

Laredet le-omanut ḥavero. Literally: to encroach on another's craft or livelihood. A commonly used expression for wrongful competition in Jewish law.

Law of the sovereign is the law; see **Dina de-malkhuta dina**.

Ma'arufia. From the Arabic meaning literally "a constant friend," it refers to a permanent business associate. In rabbinic tradition, the concept typically refers to a Christian client and to the related rule or custom prohibiting one Jew from attempting to "steal" another's established commercial client.

Maḥzor. In the Ashkenazic sphere, the term used since the advent of print for the prayerbook used for the Jewish holidays, as opposed to the prayerbook for just the Sabbath and daily use.

Maskilim. See **Haskalah.**

Mikraot Gedolot (literally, "great scriptures"). A multi-volume edition of the Bible, printed with rabbinic commentaries.

Mishnah. A collection of rabbinic teachings redacted at the beginning of the third century. The term "a Mishnah" refers to one of those teachings.

Mishneh Torah. The twelfth-century code of Jewish law written by **Maimonides.**

Mitnagdim. See **Ḥasidim.**

Mitzvah (plural, **mitzvot).** A commandment, precept, or religious duty. There are traditionally 613 Biblical commandments, which are divided into 248 positive mandates and 365 prohibitions. The term "mitzvah" is also used to connote a meritorious act or good deed, such as disseminating books of Jewish learning.

Mizraḥi. Literary "of the East." The term in modern Hebrew for a Jew of Middle Eastern origin.

Modern Orthodoxy. See the entry on **Ḥaredi,** with which it is contrasted. See also **National-Religious.**

National-Religious (or **National Orthodox).** Jewish Israelis for whom both Zionism and the observance of Jewish law and tradition are central values. National Religious Jews tend to identify as **Modern Orthodox,** as opposed to **Ḥaredi,** although there are also **Ḥaredim** who share similar values.

Noaḥide laws. The seven commandments given to the descendants of Noah, in other words, the obligations that Jewish law places on all non-Jews.

Pentateuch. The first five books of the Bible: Genesis, Exodus, Leviticus, Numbers, and Deuteronomy.

Posek (plural, **poskim).** A rabbinic authority who issues rulings that interpret and apply **halakha.** Frequently rendered into English as a **decisor.** The leading decisor of the generation is called the **posek ha-dor.**

Responsa. In Hebrew, **She'elot u-Tshuvot** (literally "questions and answers"), sometimes abbreviated as **Shutim.** Written answers by particularly learned rabbinic scholars to written questions posed to them (or sometimes issued *sua sponte*).

Rishonim. Literally "the first ones," this term refers to the medieval sages whose interpretations were authoritative, prominent examples being **Maimonides** and **Naḥmanides.** They followed the **Geonim** (whose era closed around 1040) and were succeeded at the advent of the era of printing by the **Aḥaronim.**

Sephardic. See **Ashkenazic.**

She'elot u-Tshuvot. See **Responsa.**

Shulḥan Arukh. Meaning "set table," **Joseph Karo**'s comprehensive code (largely reflecting Sephardic customs and interpretations), setting out the law without sources, commentary, or alternative opinions. Though not the first codification of Jewish law, this work, completed in 1563 and first printed in 1565, represents the first one to be composed after the advent of the printing press. Moses Isserles's glosses, called the *Mappa* (meaning "tablecloth"), reflected Ashkenazic (particularly Polish) customs and contributed to the widespread adoption of the Shulḥan Arukh across the Jewish world.

Shut. See **Responsa.**

Talmud. See **Babylonian Talmud**.

Torah. Most narrowly, "Torah" refers to the Pentateuch. However, "Torah" is often used more broadly to refer to all of Jewish law. Accordingly, the study of "Torah" refers the study of any facet of Jewish law and religion.

Tosafists. Meaning "those who make additions," a school of medieval commentators on the Talmud from northern France and Germany.

Yoreh De'ah. One of the four sections of the **Shulḥan Arukh**. It deals primarily with dietary and ritual laws.

Yeshiva (plural, **yeshivot**). A rabbinic academy or, more broadly, a school of study of Jewish law and canonical texts.

Zkhuyot yotzrim. Modern Hebrew term for *copyright law*. The literal translation is "authors' rights," which is the term typically use for copyright law in civil law countries. The operative root verb here is **yotzer**, meaning "to create" and, in its participle form, referring to an "author."

Selected Individuals Who Contributed to the Jewish Law of Copyright (whether directly or through their enunciation of building blocks used to construct that law).

NOTE ON HEBREW ACRONYMS: As explained on page xi, some acronyms for famous rabbis will not seem like acronyms to non-Hebrew speakers.

Aderet, Shlomo ben. See **Rashba**.

Asher, Jacob ben. See **Rabbeinu Asher**.

Banet, Mordekhai (1753–1829). Served for 40 years, beginning in 1789, as chief rabbi of Moravia, head of the rabbinic court of Nikolsburg (now Mikulov), and head of Nikolsburg's large and prestigious yeshiva. His collection of responsa is known as *Parshat Mordekhai*.

Eiger, Akiva (1761–1837). Rabbi of Pozen (in Polish territory annexed by Prussia) and one of the most highly respected halakhic **decisors** of his generation; he was also the father-in-law of **Moses Sofer** after the latter remarried.

Eliezer ben Joel Ha-Levi (1160–1235). German scholar, known by his acronym Ravyah, who authored *Avi'asaf*, a commentary on the Talmud tractates Nashim and Nezikin.

Eliashiv, Yosef Shalom (1910–2012). Born in Lithuania and long-time resident of Jerusalem, leader of the Lithuanian-Ḥaredi community; regarded by many as the **posek ha-dor**.

Feinstein, Moshe (1895–1986). Born in Belarus and long-time resident of New York. Preeminent rabbinic **decisor** of the twentieth century, regarded in the United States (and sometimes beyond) as the **posek ha-dor**.

Gerondi, Nissim ben Reuven. See **Ran**.

Ḥatam Sofer. See **Moses Sofer**.

Ḥaver, Yitzḥak Eizik (1789–1843). Born in Belarus and died in Poland, he authored the essay *Concerning Reprinting Bans and Wrongful Competition in Book Publishing, as is Customary Today.*

Horowitz, Pinḥas (1730–1805). Chief Rabbi of Frankfurt am Main, succeeded in that role by his son **Tzvi Hirsch Horowitz** (1730–1817).

Isserles, Moses (1520? 1530?–1572). Known by his acronym as "Rema," he authored the Mappa to offer Ashkenazic glosses on the Sephardic compendium of laws contained in the **Shulḥan Arukh**. He became rabbi of Krakow at a young age, known for his Talmudic brilliance.

Judah, ben Gershom. See **Rabbeinu Gershom Me'or Ha-Golah**.

Karelitz, Nissim (born 1926). Born in Lithuania and long-time resident of Bnei Brak, among the leaders of the Lithuanian-Ḥaredi community and head of a Bnei Brak **Beit Din**.

Karo, Joseph (1488–1575). Sephardic Talmudic authority, codifier of rabbinic law, and Kabbalist. Author of the **Shulḥan Arukh**.

Luria, Solomon. See **Maharshal**.

Maharik (c. 1420–1480). The acronym for "Our teacher, Rabbi Yosef Colon" ben Solomon Trabotto. Italy's foremost Judaic scholar and Talmudist of the latter part of the fifteenth century. He ruled that even the greatest rabbi of the generation is not allowed to issue a regulation that results in a commercial benefit to one person and a loss to the other, except in exigent circumstances.

Maharshal (c. 1510–1573). The acronym for "Our teacher, Rabbi Shlomo ben Yeḥiel Luria" (Solomon Luria); of Polish origin, he served as a rabbi in Lithuania and Lublin. He stressed the need to return to Talmudic text in halakhic rulings.

Maimonides, Moses (1135–1204). Known as Rambam, an acronym for "Rabbi Moses ben Maimon," he was the most famous of the **rishonim.** A medical doctor, he fled his native Spain to settle in Egypt. Most famous as the author of the *Mishneh Torah*, he also authored many other books, including the philosophical work *Guide for the Perplexed* (in Arabic) written in an Aristotelian vein.

Meir ben Samuel (1060–1135). One of the founding **tosafists,** he married **Rashi**'s daughter and was the father of **Jacob ben Meir**.

Mordekhai ben Hillel (c. 1250–1298). Author of a digest of halakhic teachings of Ashkenazic sages (eponymously named *The Mordekhai*), which was included in the first printed edition of Talmud and served as one of the sources for the **Shulḥan Arukh.** His writings address the doctrine of **ma'arufia**.

Naḥmanides, Moses (1194–1270). Known as Ramban, an acronym for "Rabbi Moses ben Naḥman," he was a leading medieval scholar, and one of the great lights of Spanish (Sephardic) Jewry.

Nathanson, Joseph Saul (1808–1875). Rabbi of Lemberg, then the capital of Galicia, a crown land of the Habsburg Empire and a major center of Jewish printing in the nineteenth century. He was not only a prodigious **decisor** but is remembered also for the profusion of **haskamot** that he issued.

Perfet, Isaac ben Sheshet. See **Rivash**.

Rabbeinu Asher (c. 1269–1343). The name by which Jacob ben Asher is remembered. Born in Cologne, he fled to Spain at age 33. Author of the seminal code of Jewish law, the *Arba'a Turim*, which served as a foundational text for the **Shulḥan Arukh**.

Rabbeinu Gershom Me'or Ha-Golah (c. 960–1028? 1040?). "Our rabbi Gershom, the light of the exile," is the honorific given to Gershom ben Judah, who was a leading halakhic authority in the Ashkenazic community. He imposed a ban carving out exclusivity in certain retail markets in order to save Jewish store owners from the losses that would arise from mutual competition.

Rabbeinu Tam (1100–1171). The name by which Jacob ben Meir Tam is remembered. The most prominent of the **tosafists.** Born in Ramerupt, France, he was the son of **Meir ben Samuel** and grandson of **Rashi**.

Ran (1320–1376). The acronym for Rabbi Nissim ben Reuven Gerondi of Barcelona. He extended the ruling of **Rashba** by holding that one is *obligated* to follow the rulings of one's local rabbi.

Rashba (1235–1310). The acronym for Rabbi Shlomo ben Aderet of Barcelona, a prolific author of responsa. One of his rulings was that it is *permissible* to follow one's local rabbi even when his halakhic ruling contradicts the majority opinion elsewhere.

Rashi (1040–1105). The acronym for "Rabbi Solomon Yitzḥaki" of Troyes, France. The preeminent medieval commentator, his explications of the Torah and Talmud have been ubiquitous since the advent of print.

Rema. See **Moses Isserles.**

Rivash (1326–1408). The acronym for "Rabbi Issac ben Sheshet" Perfet of Spain, who later sought refuge in Algeria. He ruled that a rabbinic court has no authority to impose excommunication outside of the territory of its jurisdiction.

Rosh (1250 or 1259–1327). The acronym for "Rabbi Asher" ben Yeḥiel, a Talmudist who was born in Germany and died in Spain.

Schmelkes, Yitzḥak (1828–1906). Known after his writings as Beit Yitzḥak, he served as head of the rabbinic court of Przemyśl, in Austrian Galicia, during the late nineteenth century. Formerly a student of Joseph Saul Nathanson, he was a noted **posek** of his generation.

Schneersohn, Menaḥem Mendel (1789–1866). Known after his writings as Tzemaḥ Tzedek, he was the spiritual leader and third Rebbe of Ḥabad Ḥasidism. Born in Belarus, he died in Lubavitch, Russia.

Sofer, Moses (1762–1839), known as Ḥatam Sofer, which both means "seal of the scribe" and serves as an acronym for *Ḥiddushei Torat Moshe* ("Moses' Torah Novellae"). Rabbi of Pressburg, at that time the most important Jewish community in Hungary, he was a prodigious **decisor**, authoring numerous volumes of **responsa**.

Tam, Jacob ben Meir. See **Rabbeinu Tam**.

Trabotto, Joseph Colon ben Solomon. See **Maharik**.

Yeḥiel, Asher ben. See **Rosh**.

Yitzḥaki, Solomon. See **Rashi**.

Yosef, Ovadia (1918–2013). Born in Iraq, he served as Sephardic Chief Rabbi of Israel from 1973 to 1983. Besides other works, he published two collections of responsa, rendering him the most authoritative Sephardic **decisor** of his generation.

Zuenz, Aryeh Leib (1768–1833). Born in Poland but grew up in Prague, he is known in Jewish tradition by the honorific "Maharal Zuenz." His present-day disciples highlight that he promised, shortly before his death, to intercede in heaven on behalf of anyone who would reprint one of his many works; that same promise is engraved on his tombstone.

NAMES INDEX

Figures and illustrations are indicated by "f" following the page numbers.

SUBJECT INDEX

Figures and illustrations are indicated by "f" following the page numbers.